Constantine and the Captive Christians of Persia

TRANSFORMATION OF THE CLASSICAL HERITAGE

Peter Brown, General Editor

I. *Art and Ceremony in Late Antiquity,* by Sabine G. MacCormack

II. *Synesius of Cyrene: Philosopher-Bishop,* by Jay Alan Bregman

III. *Theodosian Empresses: Women and Imperial Dominion in Late Antiquity,* by Kenneth G. Holum

IV. *John Chrysostom and the Jews: Rhetoric and Reality in the Late Fourth Century,* by Robert L. Wilken

V. *Biography in Late Antiquity: The Quest for the Holy Man,* by Patricia Cox

VI. *Pachomius: The Making of a Community in Fourth-Century Egypt,* by Philip Rousseau

VII. *Change in Byzantine Culture in the Eleventh and Twelfth Centuries,* by A. P. Kazhdan and Ann Wharton Epstein

VIII. *Leadership and Community in Late Antique Gaul,* by Raymond Van Dam

IX. *Homer the Theologian: Neoplatonist Allegorical Reading and the Growth of the Epic Tradition,* by Robert Lamberton

X. *Procopius and the Sixth Century,* by Averil Cameron

XI. *Guardians of Language: The Grammarian and Society in Late Antiquity,* by Robert A. Kaster

XII. *Civic Coins and Civic Politics in the Roman East, A.D. 180–275,* by Kenneth Harl

XIII. *Holy Women of the Syrian Orient,* introduced and translated by Sebastian P. Brock and Susan Ashbrook Harvey

XIV. *Gregory the Great: Perfection in Imperfection,* by Carole Straw

XV. *"Apex Omnium": Religion in the "Res gestae" of Ammianus,* by R. L. Rike

XVI. *Dioscorus of Aphrodito: His Work and His World,* by Leslie S. B. MacCoull

XVII. *On Roman Time: The Codex-Calendar of 354 and the Rhythms of Urban Life in Late Antiquity,* by Michele Renee Salzman

XVIII. *Asceticism and Society in Crisis: John of Ephesus and "The Lives of the Eastern Saints,"* by Susan Ashbrook Harvey

XIX. *Barbarians and Politics at the Court of Arcadius,* by Alan Cameron and Jacqueline Long, with a contribution by Lee Sherry

XX. *Basil of Caesarea,* by Philip Rousseau

XXI. *In Praise of Later Roman Emperors: The Panegyrici Latini,* introduction, translation, and historical commentary by C. E. V. Nixon and Barbara Saylor Rodgers

XXII. *Ambrose of Milan: Church and Court in a Christian Capital,* by Neil B. McLynn

XXIII. *Public Disputation, Power, and Social Order in Late Antiquity,* by Richard Lim

XXIV. *The Making of a Heretic: Gender, Authority, and the Priscillianist Controversy,* by Virginia Burrus

XXV. *Symeon the Holy Fool: Leontius's "Life" and the Late Antique City,* by Derek Krueger

XXVI. *The Shadows of Poetry: Vergil in the Mind of Augustine,* by Sabine MacCormack

XXVII. *Paulinus of Nola: Life, Letters, and Poems,* by Dennis E. Trout

XXVIII. *The Barbarian Plain: Saint Sergius between Rome and Iran,* by Elizabeth Key Fowden

XXIX. *The Private Orations of Themistius,* translated, annotated, and introduced by Robert J. Penella

XXX. *The Memory of the Eyes: Pilgrims to Living Saints in Christian Late Antiquity,* by Georgia Frank

XXXI. *Greek Biography and Panegyric in Late Antiquity,* edited by Tomas Hägg and Philip Rousseau

XXXII. *Subtle Bodies: Representing Angels in Byzantium,* by Glenn Peers

XXXIII. *Wandering, Begging Monks: Spiritual Authority and the Promotion of Monasticism in Late Antiquity,* by Daniel Caner

XXXIV. *Failure of Empire: Valens and the Roman State in the Fourth Century A.D.,* by Noel Lenski

XXXV. *Merovingian Mortuary Archaeology and the Making of the Early Middle Ages,* by Bonnie Effros

XXXVI. *Quṣayr 'Amra: Art and the Umayyad Elite in Late Antique Syria,* by Garth Fowden

XXXVII. *Holy Bishops in Late Antiquity: The Nature of Christian Leadership in an Age of Transition,* by Claudia Rapp

XXXVIII. *Encountering the Sacred: The Debate on Christian Pilgrimage in Late Antiquity,* by Brouria Bitton-Ashkelony

XXXIX. *There Is No Crime for Those Who Have Christ: Religious Violence in the Christian Roman Empire,* by Michael Gaddis

XL. *The Legend of Mar Qardagh: Narrative and Christian Heroism in Late Antique Iraq,* by Joel Thomas Walker

XLI. *City and School in Late Antique Athens and Alexandria,* by Edward J. Watts

XLII. *Scenting Salvation: Ancient Christianity and the Olfactory Imagination,* by Susan Ashbrook Harvey

XLIII. *Man and the Word: The Orations of* Himerius, edited by Robert J. Penella

XLIV. *The Matter of the Gods,* by Clifford Ando

XLV. *The Two Eyes of the Earth: Art and Ritual of Kingship between Rome and Sasanian Iran,* by Matthew P. Canepa

XLVI. *Riot in Alexandria: Tradition and Group Dynamics in Late Antique Pagan and Christian Communities,* by Edward J. Watts

XLVII. *Peasant and Empire in Christian North Africa,* by Leslie Dossey

XLVIII. *Theodoret's People: Social Networks and Religious Conflict in Late Roman Syria,* by Adam M. Schor

XLIX. *Sons of Hellenism, Fathers of the Church: Emperor Julian, Gregory of Nazianzus, and the Vision of Rome,* by Susanna Elm

L. *Shenoute of Atripe and the Uses of Poverty: Rural Patronage, Religious Conflict, and Monasticism in Late Antique Egypt,* by Ariel G. López

LI. *Doctrine and Power: Theological Controversy and Christian Leadership in the Later Roman Empire*, by Carlos R. Galvão-Sobrinho

LII. *Crisis of Empire: Doctrine and Dissent at the End of Late Antiquity*, by Phil Booth

LIII. *The Final Pagan Generation*, by Edward J. Watts

LIV. *The Mirage of the Saracen: Christians and Nomads in the Sinai Peninsula in Late Antiquity*, by Walter D. Ward

LV. *Missionary Stories and the Formation of the Syriac Churches*, by Jeanne-Nicole Mellon Saint-Laurent

LVI. *A State of Mixture: Christians, Zoroastrians, and Iranian Political Culture in Late Antiquity*, by Richard E. Payne

LVII. *Constantine and the Captive Christians of Persia: Martyrdom and Religious Identity in Late Antiquity*, by Kyle Smith

Constantine and the Captive Christians of Persia

MARTYRDOM AND RELIGIOUS IDENTITY
IN LATE ANTIQUITY

Kyle Smith

UNIVERSITY OF CALIFORNIA PRESS

University of California Press, one of the most distinguished university presses in the United States, enriches lives around the world by advancing scholarship in the humanities, social sciences, and natural sciences. Its activities are supported by the UC Press Foundation and by philanthropic contributions from individuals and institutions. For more information, visit www.ucpress.edu.

University of California Press
Oakland, California

© 2016 by The Regents of the University of California

First Paperback Printing 2019

Library of Congress Cataloging-in-Publication Data

Smith, Kyle, author.

    Constantine and the captive Christians of Persia : martyrdom and religious identity in Late Antiquity / Kyle Smith.
      p. cm. — (Transformation of the classical heritage ; 57)
    Includes bibliographical references and index.
    ISBN 978-0-520-30839-8 (pbk.)

    1. Syriac Christians—Iraq—History—To 1500. 2. Syriac Christians Iran—History—To 1500. 3. Syriac Christians—History—To 1500—Sources. 4. Constantine I, Emperor of Rome, –337. 5. Iraq—History—To 634. 6. Iran—History—To 640. 7. Church history—Primitive and early church, ca. 30–600. I. Title. II. Series: Transformation of the classical heritage ; 57.

    DS59.S94S65 2016
    935′—.07—dc23
                                                                  2015029054

23 22 21 20 19
10 9 8 7 6 5 4 3 2 1

In keeping with a commitment to support environmentally responsible and sustainable printing practices, UC Press has printed this book on Natures Natural, a fiber that contains 30% post-consumer waste and meets the minimum requirements of ANSI/NISO Z39.48-1992 (R 1997) (*Permanence of Paper*).

For Liz

CONTENTS

Acknowledgments xiii
Abbreviations xvii

Introduction: Constantine and the Writing of
Fourth-Century History 1

PART I
THE ROMAN FRONTIER AND THE PERSIAN WAR

1 · Patronizing Persians: Constantine's Letter to Shapur II 17

2 · Constantine's Crusade: The Emperor's Last
Days and the Persian Campaign 45

3 · Rereading Nisibis: Narrating the Battle for
Roman Mesopotamia 65

PART II
ROMAN CAPTIVES AND PERSIAN ENVOYS

4 · On War and Persecution: Aphrahaṭ the Persian
Sage and the *Martyrdom* and *History of Blessed
Simeon bar Ṣabbaʿe* 99

5 · The Church of the East and the Territorialization
of Christianity 125

6 · Memories of Constantine in the *Acts of the
Persian Martyrs* 154

Appendix A. Constantine's Letter to Shapur: Eusebius's
Life of Constantine IV.8–14   181
Appendix B. *Martyrdom of the Captives of Beth Zabdai*   184
Appendix C. *Martyrdom of Abbot Barshebya, Ten Fellow
Brothers, and One Magus*   191
Bibliography   197
Index   217

ACKNOWLEDGMENTS

Constantine and the Captive Christians of Persia was a long time in the making. Technically, it began as my doctoral dissertation at Duke University, but the foundation for it was laid years earlier when I knew little about Constantine and even less about the *Acts of the Persian Martyrs*. As a master's student at the University of Notre Dame, I was more interested in the Egyptian Desert Fathers and the Greek monk Evagrius of Pontus than I was in the Roman eastern frontier or Syriac martyrdom literature. But Robin Darling Young convinced me that if I truly wanted to know anything about Evagrius, I would have to learn how to read the ancient translations that preserve much of his work in Syriac and Armenian. I tried to begin both languages at the Hebrew University of Jerusalem, where I studied for a year as a Fulbright Fellow, but did not get very far with either. It was much more fun to hike out to the ruins of Byzantine monasteries in the Judean Desert.

When I finally began studying Syriac in earnest, it was with Luk Van Rompay, one of my two wonderful advisers at Duke. He suggested that we read the *Martyrdom of Blessed Simeon bar Ṣabbaʿe* together as a translation exercise. The story of Simeon's trial and death in the city of Karka d-Ledan was my first real exposure to the *Acts of the Persian Martyrs*. It had a lasting impression. Once I realized that there were scores of virtually unstudied martyrdom narratives in Syriac, I abandoned Evagrius and began reading all I could about the history of Christianity in Roman Mesopotamia and Sasanian Persia.

Before I could write about late ancient history, however, I had to understand how to read it. And for that I have Liz Clark to thank. Over the course of several doctoral seminars at Duke and the monthly meetings of LASRG (the Late Ancient Studies Reading Group) at Liz's apartment, I learned how read ancient texts and critique scholarly sources. Liz spent more time than I deserved reading drafts of my work and giving me sound advice on how to organize and think about the material with which I was working, even though she herself was often unfamiliar with my sources. Liz continues to mentor me (and dozens of others) in the field of early Christianity, and I still learn something from her every time we speak. I will never be able to repay Liz for all that she has given me.

I owe debts to plenty of others too. When I was still an undergraduate at Notre Dame, it was Cornelius O'Boyle who first opened my eyes to scholarly conversations, while Andrew Ciferni, OPraem, subsequently introduced me to eastern Christianity. As a master's student in the Early Christian Studies program at Notre Dame, I was indelibly marked by conversations with Corey Barnes; Sidney Blanchet; Brian Daley, SJ; Kevin Garvey; Michael Hutson; Blake Leyerle; Jeanne-Nicole Mellon Saint-Laurent; Sam Thomas; and Robin Darling Young. When I lived at the École Biblique in Jerusalem, it was Jerome Murphy-O'Connor, OP, and Olivier-Thomas Venard, OP, who helped me immensely, while, beyond the walls of the École, Mike Ravvin became a trusted friend. Besides Liz and Luk, I am thankful for many other "Dukies" who offered support and, frequently, collaboration, including Aaron Butts, Susanna Drake, Emanuel Fiano, Christine Luckritz Marquis, Michael Penn, Jeremy Schott, Bart Scott, and Kristi Upson-Saia. I also thank the three readers on my dissertation committee—Kalman Bland, Zlatko Pleše, and especially James Rives—who freely gave me their time and insight. A Julian Price Dissertation Research Fellowship and a Dolores Zohrab Liebmann Fund Fellowship allowed me the unencumbered time I needed to research and write the first draft of this book, much of which was undertaken peripatetically during long walks around my neighborhood in Durham, North Carolina, with an infant strapped to my chest and a dog tied to my belt. During that same time, Adam Becker and Richard Payne became valuable intellectual partners. It is their work, more than that of anyone else, which continues to guide me the most.

At the University of Toronto, my academic home for the past four years, I have Amir Harrak to thank for his help with all things Syriac. And I have the chairs of my two departments—Shafique Virani and then Rebecca Wittmann in the Department of Historical Studies, and John Kloppenborg in the Department for the Study of Religion—to thank for granting me reduced service loads and teaching releases so I could focus on research. Rebecca, in the meantime, has become my closest friend at the U of T.

Another friend in Toronto, Christopher Wahl, usually takes photographs of people like Roger Federer and Neil Young. My thanks to Chris for deigning to take one of me.

More recently, I have Peter Brown to thank for meeting me for coffee while he was visiting Toronto for a lecture in November 2014. Hardly a week after our chat, I was thrilled to get an email from him encouraging me to send on my manuscript to Eric Schmidt, the classics and religion editor at University of California Press. Eric, along with Maeve Cornell and Cindy Fulton, transformed the rough manuscript into this book. I am especially grateful to Juliana Froggatt for her meticulous copyediting and to Adam Becker, Joel Walker, and an anonymous reader for their valuable comments. At a later stage, Simcha Gross and Yakir Paz each read the full manuscript and offered several helpful suggestions. Of course, all of these friends, colleagues, and editors bear no responsibility for the remaining shortcomings of this book.

Finally, I am tremendously thankful to my parents, Richard and Mary Gus Smith, to my wife, Maggie Fost, and to our children, Arlo and Frances, whose love and support are unconditional, even when my laptop is casting its glow much longer into the night than it should be.

Toronto, May 2015

ABBREVIATIONS

CLASSICAL AUTHORS AND TEXTS

Amm. Marc.	Ammianus Marcellinus, *Res Gestae*
Aph. *Dem.*	Aphrahaṭ, *Demonstrations*
Aur. Vict. *Caes.*	Aurelius Victor, *Caesars*
Cons. *Or.*	Constantine, *Oration to the Assembly of the Saints*
Eph. *CJ*	Ephrem the Syrian, *Hymns against Julian*
Eph. *CNis*	Ephrem the Syrian, *Hymns on Nisibis*
Eph. *Mem. Nic.*	Ephrem the Syrian, *Memre on Nicomedia*
Eunap. *VS*	Eunapius, *Lives of the Sophists*
Euseb. *HE*	Eusebius of Caesarea, *Church History*
Euseb. *VC*	Eusebius of Caesarea, *Life of Constantine*
Eutr. *Brev.*	Eutropius, *Summary of Roman History*
Fest. *Brev.*	Festus, *Summary of Roman History*
Jul. *Caes.*	Julian, *The Caesars*
Jul. *Ep. ad. Them.*	Julian, *Letter to Themistius the Philosopher*

Jul. *Or.*	Julian, *Orations*
Lactant. *De mort. pers.*	Lactantius, *On the Deaths of the Persecutors*
Lib. *Or.*	Libanius, *Orations*
Soc. *HE*	Socrates, *Church History*
Soz. *HE*	Sozomen, *Church History*
Theod. *HE*	Theodoret of Cyrrhus, *Church History*
Theoph. *Chron.*	Theophanes, *Chonography*
Zos. *HN*	Zosimus, *New History*

JOURNALS AND MULTIVOLUME PUBLICATIONS

AAE	*Arabian Archaeology and Epigraphy*
AAntHung	*Acta Antiqua Academiae Scientiarum Hungaricae*
AB	*Analecta Bollandiana*
AF	*Altorientalische Forschungen*
AJP	*American Journal of Philology*
AJSL	*American Journal of Semitic Languages and Literatures*
AJSR	*Association for Jewish Studies Review*
AMS	P. Bedjan, *Acta Martyrum et Sanctorum,* 7 vols. (Leipzig: Otto Harrassowitz, 1890–97)
BAI	*Bulletin of the Asia Institute*
BAR	British Archaeological Reports
Bizantinistica	*Bizantinistica: Rivista di Studi Bizantini e Slavi*
Britannia	*Britannia: A Journal of Romano-British and Kindred Studies*
BSOAS	*Bulletin of the School of Oriental and African Studies*

Byz	*Byzantion: Revue internationale des études byzantines*
ByzF	*Byzantinische Forschungen*
ByzZ	*Byzantinische Zeitschrift*
CCCOGD	*Corpus Christianorum Conciliorum Œcumenicorum Generaliumque Decreta*
CFHB	Corpus Fontium Historiae Byzantinae
CH	*Church History*
CP	*Classical Philology*
CQ	*Classical Quarterly*
CSCO	Corpus Scriptorum Christianorum Orientalium
CSEL	Corpus Scriptorum Ecclesiasticorum Latinorum
CSHB	Corpus Scriptorum Historiae Byzantinae
DOP	*Dumbarton Oaks Papers*
Florilegium	*Florilegium: Journal of the Canadian Society of Medievalists*
GCS	Griechischen Christlichen Schriftsteller
GRBS	*Greek, Roman, and Byzantine Studies*
Historia	*Historia: Zeitschrift für alte Geschichte*
HTR	*Harvard Theological Review*
HUCA	*Hebrew Union College Annual*
Hugoye	*Hugoye: Journal of Syriac Studies*
IJAIS	*Name-ye Iran-e Bastan: International Journal of Ancient Iranian Studies*
Iranistik	*Iranistik: Deutschsprachige Zeitschrift für iranistische Studien*

JA	Journal asiatique
JCSSS	Journal of the Canadian Society for Syriac Studies
JECS	Journal of Early Christian Studies
JEH	Journal of Ecclesiastical History
JESHO	Journal of the Economic and Social History of the Orient
JJS	Journal of Jewish Studies
JLA	Journal of Late Antiquity
JNES	Journal of Near Eastern Studies
JRAS	Journal of the Royal Asiatic Society of Great Britain and Ireland
JRS	Journal of Roman Studies
JSJ	Journal for the Study of Judaism
JTS	Journal of Theological Studies
Klio	Klio: Beiträge zur alten Geschichte
MedArch	Mediterranean Archaeology
Mus	Le Muséon: Revue d'études orientales
Numen	Numen: International Review for the History of Religions
OC	Oriens Christianus
OCA	Orientalia Christiana Analecta
OCP	Orientalia Christiana Periodica
OLA	Orientalia Lovaniensia Analecta
OrSyr	L'Orient syrien
PdO	Parole de l'Orient
Persica	Persica: Uitgave van het Genootschap Nederland-Iran
Phoenix	Phoenix: The Classical Association of Canada
PO	Patrologia Orientalis
PS	Patrologia Syriaca

RÉArm	*Revue des études arméniennes*
RecAug	*Recherches augustiniennes*
RHR	*Revue de l'histoire des religions*
SC	Sources chrétiennes
SP	*Studia Patristica*
ST	*Studia Theologica*
StIran	Cahiers de Studia Iranica
Traditio	*Traditio: Studies in Ancient and Medieval History, Thought and Religion*
VChr	*Vigiliae Christianae*
ZKG	*Zeitschrift für Kirchengeschichte*

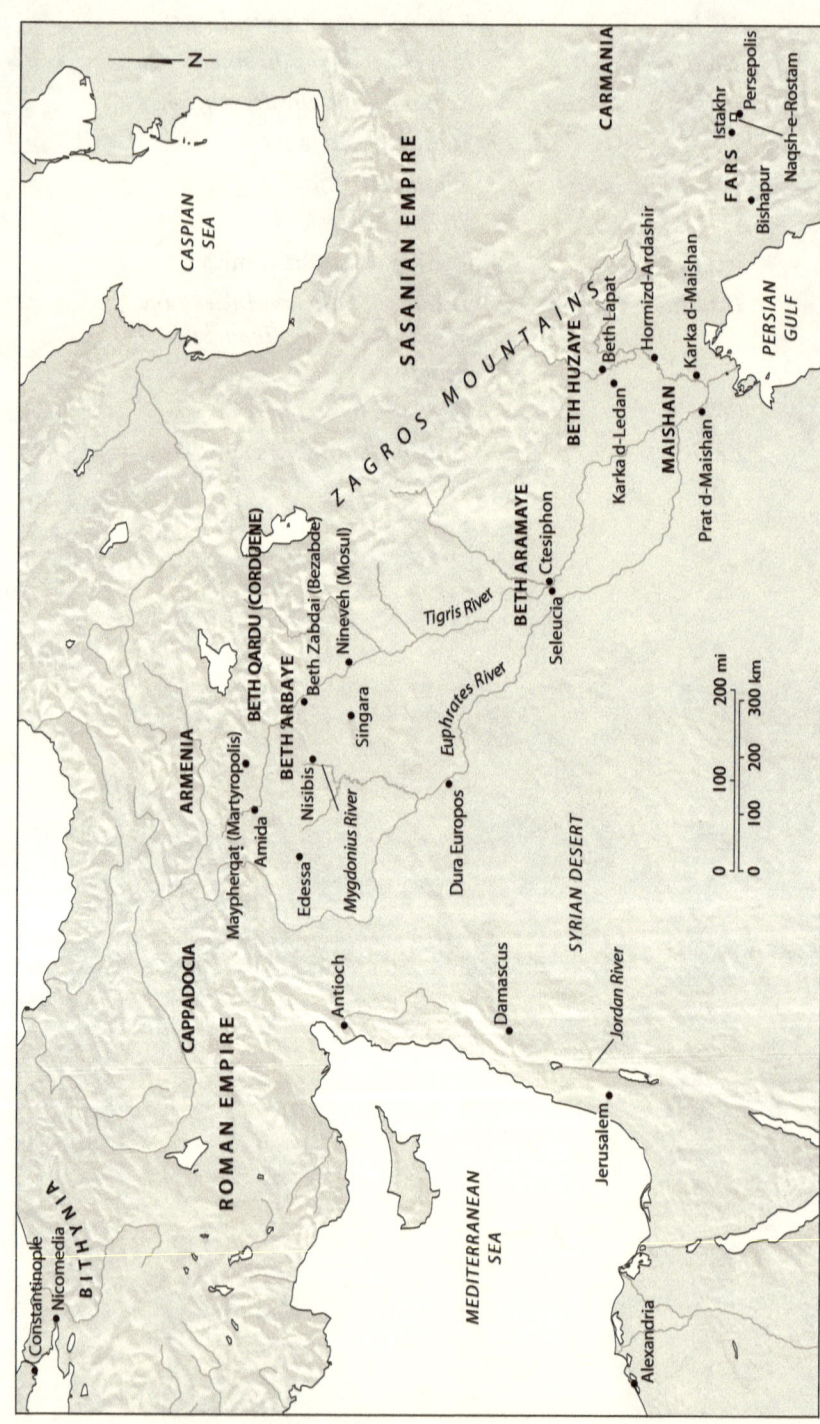

The eastern Roman Empire and Sasanian Persia

Introduction

CONSTANTINE AND THE WRITING OF
FOURTH-CENTURY HISTORY

NEAR THE END OF WINTER in 2008, the body of Monsignor Paulos Rahho, the Chaldean Catholic archbishop of Mosul in northern Iraq, was found on the outskirts of his city. As with many accounts of violence in twenty-first-century Iraq, the details of the archbishop's death are sketchy—even contradictory.

Once the security situation in Mosul began to improve, the archbishop apparently stopped paying the "protection money" that he had been delivering to a group of militants for some time.[1] A few months later, deprived of their easy racket, gunmen attacked Rahho's car as it left the Church of the Holy Spirit in Mosul. His driver and two bodyguards were killed. Some American media sources suggested that Rahho may have been mortally wounded in the attack. The *New York Times,* citing eyewitness testimony, said that the archbishop's car was indiscriminately "sprayed with bullets."[2] Quoting an Iraqi police chief, the *Los Angeles Times* reported that the archbishop was "shot when kidnapped and died of his injuries."[3]

Other reports suggested that Rahho survived the attack and was thrown alive into the trunk of a getaway car. The gunmen intended to hold him for ransom. Yet according to Louis Sako, the Chaldean Catholic archbishop of

---

1. A. E. Kramer, "For Iraqi Christians, Money Bought Survival," *New York Times,* June 26, 2008.
2. E. Goode, "Archbishop Kidnapped in Mosul Is Found Dead," *New York Times,* March 13, 2008.
3. N. Parker, "Iraqi Christians Mourn Archbishop," *Los Angeles Times,* March 15, 2008.

Kirkuk, Rahho was able to thwart their plans. From the trunk of his attackers' car, he used his mobile phone to call his church. Sako said that Rahho clearly had a sense of what was happening, who his kidnappers were, and what their demands were going to be, and that when he spoke with the church officials who answered the phone, he begged that no one pay any ransom for his release. Such payments, Rahho explained, would only encourage more violent acts.[4]

Two weeks later, an anonymous caller directed authorities to the site outside Mosul where Rahho's body had been buried. Preliminary reports said that when "relatives and authorities went to the location and found the body," it had "gunshot wounds."[5] Other reports, quoting representatives of Mosul's morgue, declared that Rahho had not been shot. Instead, they claimed that he had died from natural causes, presumably related to the heart problems for which he required daily medication.[6]

The basic outline of what happened to Rahho is not in dispute: the archbishop was attacked and, somehow, died as a result. But several key elements of the incident were contested. Was he shot, or did he die because he did not have his heart pills? Was he killed with his driver and bodyguards, or was he kidnapped alive and able to phone his church? Had he been paying the militants protection money for years, or, as others claimed, were all such payments "against his religion"?[7] In her study of memory and early Christian

---

4. A. O'Mahony, "Obituary: Archbishop Paulos Faraj Rahho, Brave Iraqi Christian Leader Determined to Stand with His Flock," *Guardian,* April 1, 2008.

5. "Source: U.S. Is Sent Severed Fingers of Iraq Kidnap Victims," CNN.com, March 13, 2008. The web page that provided this quotation seems to no longer exist.

6. According to Reuters, "police at the Mosul morgue said he appeared to have been dead a week and his body bore no bullet wounds." See J. al-Taie, "Iraqi Police, Mehdi Militia Clash despite Truce," Reuters.com, March 14, 2008.

7. Kramer, "For Iraqi Christians" claims that the archbishop had long been paying protection money: "As priests do everywhere, Archbishop Paulos Faraj Rahho, the leader of the Chaldean Catholics in this ancient city [Mosul], gathered alms at Sunday Mass. But for years the money, a crumpled pile of multicolored Iraqi dinars, went into an envelope and then into the hand of a man who had threatened to kill him and his entire congregation. 'What else could he do?' asked Ghazi Rahho, a cousin of the archbishop. 'He tried to protect the Christian people.'" Kramer cites Canon Andrew White, the Anglican vicar of Baghdad, who claimed that the financing behind the protection money paid by Monsignor Rahho (and other Christians) came largely from the charitable contributions of Christians in Europe and the United States: "'People deny it, people say it's too complex, and nobody in the international community does anything about it.'" On the other hand, Fr. Najeeb Mikhail said that it went against Rahho's religion "to pay money that would be used to finance violence." See P. Lamprecht, "Kidnappers Demand Huge Ransom for Iraqi Bishop," *Christianity Today,* March 3, 2008.

martyrdom, a book that concludes with a chapter on the Columbine High School shooting in 1999, Elizabeth Castelli explains that it is "one thing to reach the limits of the question of historicity when one is concerned with very distant events for which there are fragmentary and competing sources of information. It is quite another to be immersed in the moment itself—surrounded by newspapers, magazines, videotape, and eyewitness testimony—and still to have the question of 'the real' emerge almost immediately."[8]

There was at least one constant in the reports about Rahho's death: al-Qaeda was to blame. Once the archbishop's body had been recovered, the Iraqi prime minister, Nouri al-Maliki, immediately condemned al-Qaeda for committing what he called an act of religious violence.[9] The following day, the U.S. embassy in Baghdad distributed a press release suggesting the same thing.[10] The politicians' statements may have supported the idea held by some that Iraqi Christians are under the protection of the U.S. military and the "Christian" West. A Kurdish news site, citing an unnamed source "close to the family of the deceased archbishop," said that the gunmen who had abducted Rahho demanded that he organize an Iraqi Christian militia to fight against U.S. forces. If he did this, it would help prove that the Christians of Mosul were not traitors.[11]

One reporter for the Associated Press put the suspicions surrounding the Christians of Iraq in historical terms: "Since the US-led invasion in 2003, Iraqi Christians have been targeted by Islamic extremists who label them 'crusaders' loyal to US troops."[12] This sentence was frequently repeated. On the day that Rahho's body was found, it appeared in copy on the websites of numerous major television and print outlets, dozens of local papers affiliated with the AP wire service, and countless blogs.[13] The very same sentence appeared two weeks earlier too, in a report filed on the day that Rahho was

---

8. E. A. Castelli, *Martyrdom and Memory: Early Christian Culture Making* (New York: Columbia University Press, 2004), 173–74.

9. "Iraqi Archbishop Found Dead, al Qaeda Blamed," Reuters.com, March 13, 2008.

10. "U.S. Embassy Baghdad and the MNF-I [Multi-National Force—Iraq] Statement on the Murder of the Chaldean Catholic Archbishop, Paulo Faraj Rahho," March 14, 2008.

11. "Archbishop's Kidnappers Demand to Form Christian Militia," KurdishAspect.com, March 14, 2008.

12. S. N. Yacoub, "Abducted Archbishop Found Dead in Iraq," *Boston Globe*, March 14, 2008.

13. Internet search of June 12, 2009.

kidnapped.¹⁴ In fact, it appeared four months before Rahho was kidnapped, in a story about Prime Minister Maliki's vow to protect the Christians of Iraq.¹⁵ If the recycling of this sentence is any indication, then Rahho was an actor in the already written drama surrounding his kidnapping and death before it had even happened.

TAXES, PERSECUTION, AND "WESTERN" CHRISTIANITY

Far removed as it is from late antiquity, Rahho's story will nevertheless sound familiar to those who are acquainted with the history of Christianity in Persia—especially the martyrdom narratives that emerged in the aftermath of the supposed persecution of the Sasanian king Shapur II. In the fourth century, during the reigns of Shapur and the Roman emperor Constantine I, the first glimmers of this discourse binding Christianity to "the West" emerge. A few months before his death, Rahho himself alluded to the early beginnings of this narrative of Christianity-as-Western: "We, Christians of Mesopotamia," he said, "are used to religious persecution and pressures by those in power. After Constantine, persecution ended only for Western Christians, whereas in the East threats continued. Even today we continue to be a Church of martyrs."¹⁶ As Rahho implied, Constantine may have done more than put an end to persecution in the West. Many still believe that the emperor's conversion to Christianity inadvertently compounded the suffering of Christians in the East—those who lived beyond the bounds of the Christian Roman Empire.

Such ideas about West and East, and the role of Constantine as a hinge between the two, are ingrained in the collective memory of Assyrian Christians. During World War I, against the backdrop of the Assyrian genocide in the Ottoman Empire, Abraham Yohannan wrote a brief survey

---

14. "Chaldean Archbishop Kidnapped in Northern Iraq," FoxNews.com, February 29, 2008.

15. "Iraqi PM Pledges to Protect Christians," *Washington Post*, October 29, 2007. Note the slight difference, which I have indicated with italics: "Since the U.S.-led invasion in 2003, Iraqi Christians, *who are mostly Chaldeans,* have been targeted by Islamic extremists who label them 'crusaders' loyal to U.S. troops."

16. "Despite Being Left at the Mercy of Terrorists, Christians Continue to Hope, Says Bishop of Mosul," AsiaNews.it, November 26, 2007.

history of the Church of the East. He called it *The Death of a Nation, or The Ever Persecuted Nestorians or Assyrian Christians*.[17] Yohannan, a professor of Oriental languages at Columbia University, leaned heavily upon the earlier studies of William Wigram and Jérôme Labourt, both of which had quickly become classics. All three studies highlight the role of Constantine in the history of the Church in Persia.[18] Summarizing the martyrdom of Simeon bar Ṣabbaʿe, a fourth-century bishop of Seleucia-Ctesiphon on the Tigris, Yohannan describes the effects of Constantine's conversion this way:

> As long as the Roman Empire was pagan, the Persian Church was tolerated, but with the Christianization of the Emperor himself and his empire, things were changed. Christians in Persia were looked upon by the Zoroastrians as political suspects and as sympathizers with their co-religionists in Rome. The suspicion became their death warrant. Thus, when Shapur returned from the war with Rome, sore at his humiliating defeat, he turned furiously upon Christians, declaring: "At least we will make these Roman sympathizers pay." A *firman* was issued requiring the Christians to pay exorbitant taxes, as a contribution to the cost of a war in which they were taking no part, the Mar Shimun Bar Sabbāʿi, Catholicos, being ordered to collect the same. He refused to obey the order on the double ground that his people were poor, and that tax-collecting was no part of a Bishop's business. On this it was easy to raise the cry "he is a traitor and wishes to rebel"; a second *firman* was issued, ordering the arrest and death of the clergy and the general destruction of all the Christian churches. Finally another *firman* was given, commanding that all Christians should be imprisoned and executed. The persecution lasted forty years, during which period men of all ranks suffered martyrdom, among them officers of the King who had embraced Christianity.[19]

Yohannan's account of what happened during the episcopate of Simeon bar Ṣabbaʿe remains widely accepted. In a recent sourcebook canvassing Roman-Sasanian relations in late antiquity, Beate Dignas and Engelbert Winter insist that Constantine's conversion resulted in "dramatic religious changes." These changes helped escalate a mundane border dispute between

---

17. A. Yohannan, *The Death of a Nation, or The Ever Persecuted Nestorians or Assyrian Christians* (New York: Knickerbocker, 1916).

18. Yohannan acknowledges his debts to Wigram and Labourt in his preface; see *Death of a Nation*, vii. See also W. Wigram, *An Introduction to the History of the Assyrian Church, or The Church of the Sassanid Persian Empire, 100–640 A.D.* (London: Society for Promoting Christian Knowledge, 1910); and J. Labourt, *Le christianisme dans l'empire perse sous la dynastie sassanide (224–632)* (Paris: Librairie Victor Lecoffre, 1904).

19. Yohannan, *Death of a Nation*, 45–46.

the two powers into a religious war between "Christian Rome and the Zoroastrian Sasanian Empire."[20] According to Jacques Duchesne-Guillemin, "waging war against Rome and persecuting the Christians" were "two facets of one struggle" for the Persian kings.[21] And, in a frequently cited article in the *Journal of Roman Studies,* Timothy Barnes maintains that, in 337, "Constantine was preparing to invade Persia as the self-appointed liberator of the Christians of Persia... and the hopes which he excited [among them] caused the Persian king to regard his Christian subjects as potential traitors—and hence to embark on a policy of persecution."[22]

The consensus opinion is that Shapur II persecuted Christians in his empire while he was at war with Rome, and that he did so because he believed that those who worshiped the Christian god were necessarily partisans of Caesar.[23] As this book seeks to demonstrate, however, the first late ancient sources to advance such a view are Syriac martyrdom narratives, none of which can be securely dated to the fourth century and several of which may have been composed in the eastern *Roman* Empire. These sources include the

---

20. B. Dignas and E. Winter, *Rome and Persia in Late Antiquity: Neighbours and Rivals* (Cambridge: Cambridge University Press, 2007), 210.

21. J. Duchesne-Guillemin, "Zoroastrian Religion," in *The Cambridge History of Iran,* vol. 3, pt. 2, *The Seleucid, Parthian and Sasanian Periods,* ed. E. Yarshater (Cambridge: Cambridge University Press, 1983), 886.

22. T.D. Barnes, "Constantine and the Christians of Persia," *JRS* 75 (1985): 126.

23. A comprehensive list of studies that advance this view is difficult to compile. Some of the more notable studies, however, are Barnes, "Constantine and the Christians of Persia"; G.G. Blum, "Zur religionspolitischen Situation der persischen Kirche im 3. und 4. Jahrhundert," *ZKG* 91 (1980): 11–32; S.P. Brock, "Christians in the Sasanian Empire: A Case of Divided Loyalties," in *Religion and National Identity,* ed. S. Mews (Oxford: Oxford University Press, 1982), 1–19; M.-L. Chaumont, *La christianisation de l'empire iranien: Des origines aux grandes persécutions du IVᵉ siècle,* CSCO 499, Subsidia 80 (Leuven: Peeters, 1988); A. Christensen, *L'Iran sous les Sassanides,* 2nd ed. (Copenhagen: Ejnar Munksgaard, 1944); F. Decret, "Les conséquences sur le christianisme en Perse de l'affrontement des empires romain et sassanide: De Shâpûr Iᵉʳ à Yazdgard Iᵉʳ," *RecAug* 14 (1979): 91–152; W. Hage, "Die oströmische Staatskirche und die Christenheit des Perserreiches," *ZKG* 84 (1973): 173–87; Labourt, *Le christianisme;* V. Poggi, "Costantino e la chiesa di Persia," in *Costantino il Grande nell'età bizantina: Atti del Convegno internazionale di studio, Ravenna, 5–8 aprile 2001* (*Bizantinistica* V), ed. G. Bonamente and A. Carile (Spoleto: Fondazione Centro italiano di studi sull'alto medioevo, 2003), 61–95; J. Rist, "Die Verfolgung der Christen im spätantiken Sasanidenreich: Ursachen, Verlauf und Folgen," *OC* 80 (1996): 17–42; W. Schwaigert, "Das Christentum in Khuzistan im Rahmen der frühen Kirchengeschichte Persiens bis zur Synode von Seleukeia-Ktesiphon im Jahre 410," PhD diss. (Philipps-Universität Marburg, 1989); and J. Wiesehöfer, "'Geteilte Loyalitäten': Religiöse Minderheiten des 3. und 4. Jahrhunderts n. Chr. im Spannungsfeld zwischen Rom und dem sasanidischen Iran," *Klio* 75 (1993): 362–82.

martyrdom narratives of Simeon bar Ṣabbaʿe and several related texts from the Syriac *Acts of the Persian Martyrs*. The Greek, Arabic, and later Syriac histories that discuss the persecution of Christians under Shapur all derive their content, tone, or perspective on fourth-century history from these earlier Syriac martyrdom narratives.

It is certainly true that Constantine eventually played an important role in the history of Christianity in Persia, but the narrative about a Christian Roman emperor and a persecuting Persian king does not seem to have emerged until the early fifth century, during the reign of Theodosius II. What is clear is that the persecution of Christians in fourth-century Persia on the basis of their presumed allegiances to the Roman Empire is an ex post facto story. It is one driven by the victory of Christianity in the Roman Empire under Constantine, and one subsequently embellished by dozens of conflicting sources that were composed decades, even centuries, after the events they describe.

CONSTANTINE AND THE PERIODIZATION OF LATE ANTIQUITY

Even though most of the Syriac sources that this book discusses are not well known to scholars of late ancient Christianity, neither they nor the Christians of Persia were isolated from the Roman Empire. Imperial frontiers were shifting and porous, and linguistic boundaries were easily permeable. Greek Christian texts moved freely into Syriac, and Syriac sources were often known to Greek Christian writers.[24] Besides this fluidity of geographic and linguistic boundaries, there is a historiographical reciprocity that cannot be ignored. Neither the Roman nor the Persian Empire can be studied in isolation. If we reconceptualize the reign of Shapur II, that has powerful repercussions beyond the Sasanian Empire. If our account of Shapur changes, then how we talk about Constantine's last days and the war between Rome and Persia following the emperor's death must change too.

The inherence of this connection between Shapur and Constantine is not often observed. While it is hardly an overstatement to say that Constantine's conversion, and subsequent patronage of the Christian cult, was one of the

---

24. The interchange between Greek and Syriac goes beyond translation. There are hundreds of Greek loanwords in late ancient Syriac texts that were not translated from Greek. See, for example, A. M. Butts, "The Use of Syriac Derivational Suffixes with Greek Loanwords," *Orientalia* 83 (2014): 207–37.

most consequential events in the ancient world, even scholars whose primary interest is Constantine's reign rarely discuss the question of how his religious reforms may have altered Roman foreign policy toward Persia or directly affected the Christians living there. Studies of Constantine's conversion and religious reforms are much more likely to focus on the emperor's changes within the Roman Empire—not the effects of those changes elsewhere. If effects outside the empire are discussed, it is with reference to the emperor's campaigns in Germanic lands, not any new policies toward Persia.[25]

Without question, the social ascent of Christianity in the Roman Empire occasioned the forging of new loyalties, new allegiances, and a new social order. Constantine supported Christianity, and he opened the sluice gates of the imperial exchequer for Christian building projects. As Arnaldo Momigliano once quipped in a committedly Gibbonian tone, after Constantine "money which would have gone to the building of a theatre or of an aqueduct now went to the building of churches and monasteries."[26] There is some truth to this, but just how quickly such changes took place, and just how rapidly old Rome became in any real sense a "Christian" empire, is much more open to debate than Momigliano lets on. Recent scholarship has shown that the Christianization of the Roman Empire was a slower process than triumphalist narratives suggest.[27] But the pace of Rome's Christianization is not a topic on which I will dwell in this book. What I am interested in considering is how narratives about Constantine and the Christians of Persia might have functioned when they were written, both for those who wrote these texts and for those who received them.

By analyzing diverse Greek, Latin, and Syriac sources, I seek to show that there was not, and never has been, just one history of fourth-century

---

25. See, for example, the following major studies of Constantine and his reign: N. H. Baynes, *Constantine the Great and the Christian Church* (London: Milford, 1931); A. H. M. Jones, *Constantine and the Conversion of Europe* (London: English Universities Press, 1948); T. D. Barnes, *Constantine and Eusebius* (Cambridge, MA: Harvard University Press, 1981); H. A. Drake, *Constantine and the Bishops: The Politics of Intolerance* (Baltimore: Johns Hopkins University Press, 2000); C. M. Odahl, *Constantine and the Christian Empire* (London: Routledge, 2004); and R. Van Dam, *The Roman Revolution of Constantine* (Cambridge: Cambridge University Press, 2007).

26. A. Momigliano, "Christianity and the Decline of the Roman Empire," in *The Conflict between Paganism and Christianity in the Fourth Century,* ed. Momigliano (Oxford: Clarendon, 1963), 9.

27. See, for example, the intervention of K. Bowes, *Private Worship, Public Values and Religious Change in Late Antiquity* (Cambridge: Cambridge University Press, 2008).

Mesopotamia. What we have are multiple and fragmented histories with competing historiographical, hagiographical, and ideological agendas. As later historians appropriated these texts as source material, they became all the more fragmented and subverted. By reading our sources against one another, I argue that we need to rethink how we understand fourth-century history.

CONSTANTINE AND THE CHRISTIANS OF PERSIA

In order to reconsider the history of Christianity in the fourth century, the first part of this book examines Constantine and the conflict between Rome and Persia from the perspective of those in the Roman Empire. No one disputes that there was war between the Roman and Persian Empires immediately after Constantine's death in 337. It persisted until the emperor Julian's death deep in Mesopotamia in 363. What is in dispute is how and why it began. The first half of this book thus considers how various historians in the Roman Empire conceptualized and remembered this war.

As early as the mid-320s, Constantine's public patronage of and support for Christianity was growing steadily and was well known throughout his empire. According to Eusebius's *Life of Constantine,* the emperor trumpeted his Christian bona fides beyond the borders of the Roman Empire too, when he sent a curious letter to the Persian king.[28] In this letter (see appendix A for a full translation), Constantine bills himself as a representative of the Christian god and declares that the entirety of the Roman army under his command bears the sign of this god, the one responsible for his military successes. As a result of such rhetorical chest pounding, Constantine is believed to have endangered all the Christians of Persia. The Persian authorities soon looked upon them as traitors, rebels, and adherents of the god of Rome. They were an internal threat to the stability of the Persian Empire.

In chapter 1, I offer a different reading of Constantine's letter. I argue that the letter, which is probably authentic, was only a small part of a Eusebian construction of Constantine. Later Christian historians subsequently co-opted and stretched this construction. The reception history of Constantine's letter may thus tell us much more than the original epistle.

---

28. Euseb. *VC* IV.9–13. Eusebius claims to have translated Constantine's letter to Shapur from the emperor's Latin into Greek.

In the second chapter, I move from a discussion of Constantine's letter to the sources that narrate the last days of the emperor's life—particularly those concerned with his Persian campaign and its possible motivations.[29] Constantine's march toward the Mesopotamian battlefields where he planned to meet Shapur was ill fated. He died hardly a hundred kilometers from Constantinople and nowhere near the Roman eastern frontier. I argue that although the accounts of Constantine's campaign are odd, maybe even suspiciously so, there is little evidence that he saw himself as a savior of the Christians of Persia or that the plight of the Christians there spurred a military campaign. The war was over territory, not the Christians of Persia.

Within months of Constantine's death, Shapur's armies began attacking fortified cities throughout Mesopotamia, even laying siege to the important Roman stronghold of Nisibis. This siege, which was the first of three attempts on the city over the next dozen years, was a failure. In chapter 3, I consider how contemporary observers narrated the battle for the Roman East, including the city of Nisibis. I focus on two eyewitness testimonies in particular: the Latin military history of Ammianus Marcellinus and the Syriac hymns of the poet-theologian Ephrem the Syrian. Not surprisingly, Ammianus and Ephrem have very different views on the Christians of Roman Mesopotamia. They also present Shapur in different ways. For Ammianus, he is but another savage Persian foe, one who is envisaged in predictable ways following the Roman historiographical tradition that Ammianus had learned. For Ephrem, however, Shapur is something of a paradox: the Persian king did cause widespread death and destruction, but he also brought about the downfall of the emperor Julian, "the Apostate." For Ephrem, Julian, not Shapur, was the much more worrisome persecutor of Christians. The sixth-century Syriac *Julian Romance* confirms Ephrem's interpretation and goes so far as to claim that Shapur conspired to have Julian killed so that Jovian (a Christian soldier) could become the next emperor of Rome.

29. *VC* IV.56–57 explains that Constantine discussed the Persian campaign with a number of bishops who promised to fight alongside the emperor in prayer during his expedition. Timothy Barnes has perhaps most strongly emphasized the peculiarly religious nature of Constantine's final campaign, suggesting that he intended to liberate the Christians of Persia. See Barnes, "Constantine and the Christians of Persia." Roger Blockley does not go nearly so far as Barnes; he does suggest, however, that the introduction of Christianity into Roman and Persian relations complicated the allegiances of peoples in the Mesopotamian borderlands—a point that is certainly not without merit. See Blockley, "The Romano-Persian Peace Treaties of A.D. 299 and 363," *Florilegium* 6 (1984): 28–49.

While the first part of this book focuses on how Constantine and the Roman-Persian war were seen from within the Roman Empire, the second part considers how Syriac-speaking Christians of the Persian Empire remembered the fourth century. Although it was Christian historians in the Roman Empire who first equated *Romanitas* with *Christianitas*, Christians in Persia soon—but by no means immediately—took over this intellectual and theological paradigm.

In the mid-fourth century, an enigmatic Syriac author known as Aphrahaṭ, the "Persian Sage," wrote a series of twenty-three homiletic exhortations called the *Demonstrations*. The fifth, "On Wars," and the twenty-first, "On Persecution," are frequently read as contemporary, fourth-century witnesses proving that there was a persecution under Shapur and that the Christians of Persia eagerly hoped for Constantine's invasion. In chapter 4, I argue that Aphrahaṭ's work is an exercise in biblical exegesis and offers little, if any, evidence for a persecution.

Aphrahaṭ is an important source because of his chronological proximity to the events in question, but there are sources that much more clearly claim that Christians were persecuted—most notably the martyrdom narratives about the bishop of Seleucia-Ctesiphon Simeon bar Ṣabbaʿe. Two very different versions of Simeon's death exist: the *Martyrdom of Blessed Simeon bar Ṣabbaʿe*, which likely dates to the early fifth century, and the later, much longer, and much more rhetorically complex *History of Blessed Simeon bar Ṣabbaʿe*, which dates to the late fifth century.[30] While the general outlines of the texts are similar enough that they are often harmonized into a single story about Simeon, there are crucial differences between the two. The shorter and earlier version, the *Martyrdom of Simeon*, sees the Christians of Persia as an isolated people under threat in a strange land. The text—uniquely among late ancient Christian martyrdom narratives in any language—reads Simeon not in parallel with other Christian martyrs but as a recapitulation of Judah the Maccabee.[31] By contrast, the *History of Simeon* omits all references to the Maccabees, instead comparing the Christians of the East (the Sasanian Persian Empire) to the persecuted Christians of the West (the Roman Empire) prior to Constantine. Simeon's martyrdom narratives, and

30. On the dates of Simeon's martyr acts, see K. Smith, *The Martyrdom and History of Blessed Simeon bar Ṣabbaʿe* (Piscataway, NJ: Gorgias, 2014), xx–xxiv.

31. I do not discuss the comparison between Simeon and Judah at any length in chapter 4. Instead, see K. Smith, "Constantine and Judah the Maccabee: History and Memory in the Acts of the Persian Martyrs," *JCSSS* 12 (2012): 16–33.

their important differences, suggest that as the situation of Christian communities in Persia changed, so too did their hagiography and their understanding of their own history.

In chapter 5, I broaden the focus to consider other texts from among the Syriac *Acts of the Persian Martyrs*. Intriguingly, several fifth-century martyrdom narratives reconceptualize the Christians of Persia during Shapur's reign as "Roman captives." In fact, there is plenty of evidence that Shapur did capture many Romans during the course of his war. Like his predecessors, he deported his captives deep into Persia to help populate newly founded cities and to serve there as skilled laborers. This theme of Christians as Roman captives is present in the longer account of Simeon's death, the *History of Simeon*, and it figures prominently in the *Martyrdom of Pusai-Qarugbed* and the *Martyrdom of the Captives of Beth Zabdai*, which is translated in appendix B. This is all somewhat puzzling, though, because the early fifth century was a time of relative peace for Persian Christians. The Sasanian king Yazdgard I had even recently welcomed a bishop from Roman Armenia, Marutha of Maypherqaṭ, to the Persian court. According to Marutha's *Life*, he cured the king's chronic headaches and then co-convened the inaugural synod of the Church of the East, which was held with Yazdgard's blessing at Seleucia-Ctesiphon in 410. Following the synod, Marutha returned to his city, bringing with him the bones, and the stories, of earlier Persian Christian martyrs. It seems that just as Christianity was establishing itself more formally in Persia, Christians there were turning to the Roman Empire for practical pastoral guidance and for Roman martyrdom narratives and ecclesiastical histories. The latter came to serve as influential literary forms for Persian Christians, shaping how they wrote about their past.

In the sixth and final chapter, I address how our literary sources from late antiquity further established a religious binary—Christian Rome and Zoroastrian Persia. I examine images of Constantine (and, more vaguely, "Caesar") in several late ancient Syriac martyrdom narratives in order to consider how, when, and under what circumstances references to him are deployed. I am interested in showing how the authors of Syriac martyrdom narratives positioned the Christians of Persia vis-à-vis the Roman Empire and how the Constantine of the *Acts of the Persian Martyrs* is at once a multiple and an ephemeral character.

Constantine, other Christian emperors of Rome, and even the Christians of the Roman Empire are, it turns out, both less important and much more complexly (and contradictorily) presented in the *Acts of the Persian Martyrs* than has previously been acknowledged. By the sixth and seventh centuries, the memory of Constantine was firmly established. The emperor had become a powerful and zealous advocate of Christianity in Persia—much more so than the earlier sources suggest. In some texts, Constantine not only lives to face off against his Persian foes but even triumphs over them and becomes the reigning savior of the formerly captive Christians of Persia.

NOTE ON THE TRANSLITERATION SCHEME

Throughout this book, I use a simplified system to transliterate Syriac. The superscript mark ʿ renders the letter *ʿayn;* sublinear dots mark the emphatic letters *ḥeth* (*ḥ*), *ṭeth* (*ṭ*), and *ṣade* (*ṣ*); and *sh* (rather than *š*) denotes the letter *šin*. I omit macrons over long vowels and, when possible, use common Latinate equivalents—such as "Simeon" rather than "Šemʿon." All references to names, titles, and terms in Middle Persian are transliterated from the Syriac sources in which they appear. These spellings do not tend to reproduce proper Iranian orthography.

PART ONE

The Roman Frontier and the Persian War

ONE

Patronizing Persians

CONSTANTINE'S LETTER TO SHAPUR II

FROM THE OUTSET OF THE fourth and final book of his panegyrical *Life of Constantine* (*VC*), the Roman bishop and church historian Eusebius of Caesarea is keen to present the first Christian emperor as a patron and philanthropist of boundless generosity. Constantine, he tells us, insisted on "persistently providing repeated and continuous good works of every kind for all the inhabitants of every province alike."[1] So generous was the emperor that none who sought his favor was ever "disappointed in his expectations." While Constantine bestowed rank, honor, and other benefits of land and riches upon those closest to him, he also "showed general fatherly concern for all." According to Eusebius, the emperor granted formal titles to so many citizens that his bureaucrats had to invent new honorifics just so Constantine could "promote more persons."[2]

The emperor slashed taxes on landowners. He readjusted the financial contributions required from those who complained "that their estates were overburdened."[3] He even granted the losing party in the disputes he adjudicated money or land from his personal holdings. This was so that no one who had been in his presence should ever have reason to "depart disappointed and bitter."[4]

---

1. Euseb. *VC* IV.1. All citations of the *VC* are from the translation of A. Cameron and S. G. Hall, *Life of Constantine* (Oxford: Clarendon, 1999).
2. *VC* IV.1. Such generosity was not unique to Constantine. Simon Corcoran points out that his role "as giver of justice and distributor of benefits, whether largesse, offices or immunities," was "hardly new" and not different in kind from that of his predecessors. See Corcoran, "Emperor and Citizen in the Era of Constantine," in *Constantine the Great: York's Roman Emperor*, ed. E. Hartley, J. Hawkes, and M. Henig (York: Lund Humphries, 2006), 49.
3. *VC* IV.2–3.
4. *VC* IV.4.

Toward those who did not serve Rome, Constantine was less beneficent. His predecessors kept the incursions of the Goths and other barbarians at bay through tributes and annual payments, but such an extortionate system was unacceptable to Constantine.[5] Through brute force, or its threat, he compelled barbarian tribes to submit to Rome. As a result of the emperor's efforts to convert the barbarians "from a lawless animal existence to one of reason and law," Eusebius says that God granted Constantine "victories over all the nations."[6]

Constantine's victories over enemies abroad and challengers at home did not go unnoticed. His name soon became renowned throughout the world. According to Eusebius, his court had "constant diplomatic visitors who brought valuable gifts from their homelands."[7] Foreign emissaries streamed to pay homage to Constantine in such droves that outside the palace gates there formed a long line of distinctive-looking barbarians wearing exotic clothes, strange haircuts, and long beards. Those who waited in the line came from every corner of the world: some had red faces, some complexions "whiter than snow," while still others were "blacker than ebony or pitch."[8]

In the context of these diplomatic visits to the seat of Roman power, Eusebius explains that the Persian king "also saw fit to seek recognition by Constantine through an embassy" and therefore sent a representative bearing

---

5. *VC* IV.5. One sixth-century Syriac martyrdom narrative, the *History of the Holy Mar Ma'in*, discusses the tribute that the Persians paid to Constantine. On Roman payment and receipt of tribute, see the discussion about the *History of Mar Ma'in* in chapter 6.

6. *VC* IV.5–6. On Eusebius's use of the term *ethnē* (nations), see A. P. Johnson, *Ethnicity and Argumentation in Eusebius's "Praeparatio Evangelica"* (Oxford: Oxford University Press, 2006). For its broader use in early Christianity, see D. K. Buell, *Why This New Race: Ethnic Reasoning in Early Christianity* (New York: Columbia University Press, 2005).

7. *VC* IV.7.

8. *VC* IV.7. Eusebius was not the first to play upon this trope of the ingathering of all "nations" in homage to the one divinely appointed king. Bruce Lincoln gives a fascinating account of ancient Persian theologies of empire in his study of Achaemenid relief sculptures that depict long lines of variously clad supplicants coming to pay homage to the king. See Lincoln, "The Role of Religion in Achaemenian Imperialism," in *Religion and Power: Divine Kingship in the Ancient World and Beyond*, ed. N. Brisch (Chicago: University of Chicago Press, 2008), 221–41. For a more extended treatment of this theme, see Lincoln's *Religion, Empire, and Torture: The Case of Achaemenian Persia, with a Postscript on Abu Ghraib* (Chicago: University of Chicago Press, 2007). Discussing Darius, Lincoln describes the model empire as one wherein the king dominated all kinds of people, "who retained their ethnic identity but were politically and economically subordinated to him" (23).

"tokens of friendly compact."[9] What Eusebius says the Persian king received from Constantine in return for his friendly tokens is the focus of this chapter.

As with other emissaries, Constantine treated the Persian ambassador well and sent him home with a successfully negotiated peace treaty and gifts whose splendor far outshone those that the ambassador had brought with him.[10] Yet the gifts the emperor sent to the Persian king were just material displays of Rome's power and Constantine's greatness. Much more important was what accompanied them: a letter from Constantine.

Constantine's letter to Shapur, which is translated in appendix A, is an especially important, and exceptionally rare, source for Roman-Persian relations in the fourth century. Although letters between Roman emperors and their generals on the eastern frontier were surely written, none survive. And, as Fergus Millar points out, the only extant letters between a Roman emperor and a foreign king are those that have been reproduced in fourth-century literary sources. These include an exchange of two letters between Shapur and Constantine's son Constantius in 358, which Ammianus Marcellinus preserves in his *Res Gestae,* and Constantine's letter to Shapur, for which we possess no response. Although several late antique sources recycle Constantine's letter, it is found first and most fully in Eusebius's *Life of Constantine*.[11] In Millar's understandably cautious estimation, all three of these fourth-century letters "are of uncertain authenticity."[12]

When Constantine's letter to Shapur is accepted as authentic, it is typically viewed as *the* document underlying centuries of strife for the Christians of Persia. A cursory examination of its contents reveals why. In the section of the letter that Eusebius has preserved, the emperor spends most of his time

---

9. *VC* IV.8. Eusebius does not name the Persian king as "Shapur II" but refers to him simply as "the Persian emperor." While the date of Constantine's letter is uncertain, Shapur II would have been the only "Persian emperor" known to Eusebius during Constantine's sole rule. According to legend, Shapur, who was born in 309, was crowned in utero and reigned until his death in 379.

10. *VC* IV.8.

11. See Amm. Marc. XVII.5 and *VC* IV.9–13. All translations of the *Res Gestae* follow the Loeb edition of J. C. Rolfe, *Ammianus Marcellinus,* 3 vols. (London: Heinemann, 1935–40).

12. F. Millar, "Emperors, Frontiers and Foreign Relations, 31 B.C. to A.D. 378," *Britannia* 13 (1982): 2. Millar claims that Constantine's letter to Shapur is the first tangible symbol of how Christianity was believed to have changed Roman foreign relations.

telling Shapur about the power of the Christian god. Constantine speaks about persecutors of Christians in his letter too—oddly, however, not persecutors in fourth-century Persia but earlier persecutors in the Roman Empire. Constantine never refers to any of his predecessors or rivals by name, but it is unquestionably the Roman emperor Valerian who is the focus of his ire. Valerian reigned from 253 to 260, was well known as a persecutor of Christians, and, most notably insofar as his role in Constantine's letter is concerned, was taken captive by Shapur I (the Great) while campaigning against the Sasanians. Valerian died as Shapur's captive, and he holds the ignominious distinction of being the only Roman emperor ever taken as a prisoner of war.

In this chapter, I consider the content of Constantine's letter, its probable date and context, and the debates over its authenticity. I am especially concerned with two additional questions: first, whether the letter can (or should) be understood as a cause of persecution in Sasanian Persia, and second, how Constantine deploys Valerian's capture and death to write a new, Christian history of the Roman Empire. This chapter will not entirely resolve the first question. Constantine's letter to Shapur has a complex transmission history and, in any case, is a recurring theme in several chapters. For example, in chapter 2 I discuss how ecclesiastical historians writing long after the emperor's death reread and entirely recontextualized Constantine's letter, and in chapter 6 I look at how a Syriac martyrdom narrative from the sixth century constructed a new account of it.

I propose that the emperor's letter was written to communicate to the Persian king how Constantine was different from, and much stronger than, previous rulers of Rome. Its date is central to its interpretation. Contrary to what some sources suggest, there is no evidence (either internal or external) that the letter was written immediately before Constantine's death and the ensuing war between Rome and Persia, which began in 337. Rather, it seems to date to a period of peace between the two empires, with the most plausible time of composition being 324/25, after Constantine had become the sole ruler of the Roman Empire and when the many supplicants and ambassadors to him were arriving before the imperial gates. Altogether, the date, context, and content of the letter suggest that it should be read primarily as a reconfiguration of divine support for Roman kingship in the person of Constantine. The emperor's letter is undeniably unique, but it did not touch off a persecution or lead to a religious war.

CONSTANTINE AS THE PROTECTOR OF ALL CHRISTIANS IN ALL PLACES

Eusebius testifies that Constantine wrote the letter to Shapur himself, in Latin. Presumably, the copy entrusted to the Persian ambassador was not the autograph but a Greek translation. Greek was known among the literati of the Sasanian Empire, as several trilingual (Parthian, Middle Persian, Greek) inscriptions from the Sasanian period attest. And it was in Greek, not Latin, Eusebius says, that the letter was "in circulation among us" and has been transcribed in the *VC*, so as to be "more readily understood by the reader."[13]

Essentially, Constantine's letter is an announcement that the emperor of Rome had the support of the Christian god. By itself, such a proclamation of personal religiosity would have been odd, but the letter is more than just an imperial statement of Constantine's Christianity. The emperor goes much further. He regales the Persian king with lurid reminders of the consequences that had befallen those who persecuted Christians, and he suggests that if Shapur is wise, he will care for all the Christians living in the lands of the East. Intriguingly, such admonishments are made in rather symbolic fashion, using the emperor Valerian as the model to avoid.

According to Eusebius, Constantine learned from the Persian ambassador "that the churches of God were multiplying among the Persians and that many thousands of people were being gathered into the flocks of Christ."[14] As Eusebius tells it, Constantine knew nothing about the rapid growth and wide diffusion of Christianity in Persia, given that he says in his letter, as if in response to recent news, "how pleasing it is for me to hear that the most important parts of Persia too are richly adorned [with Christians]!"[15] In his

---

13. *VC* IV.8. This is not the only place in the *VC* where Eusebius claims that Constantine wrote something in Latin that was later translated into Greek. Shortly after his citation of the letter to Shapur, Eusebius comments, "Latin was the language in which the Emperor used to produce the texts of his speeches. They were translated into Greek by professional interpreters" (*VC* IV.32). In this same section, Eusebius explains that he has appended to the *VC* another of Constantine's translated works (the *Oration to the Assembly of the Saints*), "so that none may think our assertions about his speeches to be mere rhetoric." Much of the language in Constantine's letter to Shapur is similar to that of the *Oration*, a text that was, in fact, appended to the earliest manuscripts of the *VC*.

14. *VC* IV.8.

15. *VC* IV.13. There are several martyrdom narratives set earlier in Shapur's reign that predate the "Great Persecution" by as many as two decades, but all are late compositions,

introduction to the letter, Eusebius underscores just how happy Constantine was to learn that there were Christians in Persia and that the faith was flourishing there, explaining that the emperor "as one who had general responsibility for [Christians] everywhere ... took prudent measures on behalf of them all."[16] Constantine's concern for Christians knew no bounds. He took personal responsibility for all Christians in all places. Even those who were subjects of a foreign king.

The Contents of Constantine's Letter

Eusebius quotes Constantine's letter at length, but he cannot have preserved all of it. The letter reads as if he has begun quoting from it midstream. He fails to include any formal opening or greeting to the addressee, literary elements that must have been present under the most basic conventions of late ancient epistolary writing. The absence of a heading or a greeting, "such as we have with every other letter of Constantine in Eusebius's account," leads Averil Cameron and Stuart Hall to conclude, "This may suggest that Eusebius has this document from a secondary history or source."[17]

The first line of the letter that Eusebius quotes begins a long confessional section in which Constantine explains that he guards "the divine faith," participates "in the light of truth," and acknowledges "the most holy religion [*thrēskeia*]."[18] More forebodingly (at least in terms of how the letter has tra-

---

and there is no evidence that Constantine was aware of any specific Christian martyrs in Persia. The *History of Sultan Mahdukt* (*AMS* II, 1–39), for example, claims to tell the story of a Persian Christian nobleman who was persecuted in the ninth year of Shapur's reign (317/18), but the final redaction of the text dates to the late seventh century. The *History of Sultan Mahdukt* is more concerned to weave a narrative constructing an ancient, biblical past for the nobles it celebrates than to relate any historically credible details about Persia during Shapur's early reign. There is simply no credible evidence for ante-Nicene persecutions or martyrs in Persia, despite J.D. Strong's recent argument to the contrary, "Candida: An Ante-Nicene Martyr in Persia," *JECS* 23 (2015): 389–412.

16. *VC* IV.8.

17. Cameron and Hall, *Life of Constantine,* 314. See also B.H. Warmington, "The Sources of Some Constantinian Documents in Eusebius' *Ecclesiastical History* and *Life of Constantine,*" *SP* 18 (1986): 93–98. Warmington suggests from whom Eusebius may have acquired his copy of the letter: an imperial official called Marianus who is mentioned with high praise at *VC* IV.44.

18. *VC* IV.9. On the term *thrēskeia* and the problem of translating it as "religion," see B. Nongbri, *Before Religion: A History of a Modern Concept* (New Haven: Yale University Press, 2013), 34–38.

ditionally been read), Constantine tactfully but clearly proclaims that he has "the power of this God as ally." He declares that his army carries the sign of God on its shoulders and that, by means of his allegiance to the divine, he has "raised up the whole world step by step with sure hopes of salvation."[19]

Constantine portrays the victories that God has granted him as therapeutic and restorative, implying that his rise to sole rule over Roman lands has healed the world of its wounds, reviving it "like a patient after treatment" and freeing it from "the slavery of such great tyrants."[20] The "great tyrants" to whom he refers are not foreign kings, Goths or Persians, but his own predecessors and rivals—persecutors of Christians. Contrary to these haughtily tyrannical emperors, the God of the Christians "takes pleasure in works of kindness and gentleness." Yet this God is quick to shatter "all ostentatious power" and destroy the proud and the arrogant. Rome's pagan rulers were defeated, Constantine explains, because God "values highly righteous empire" and thus "strengthens it with his own resources, and guards the imperial mind with the calm of peace."[21] Addressing Shapur as "my brother," Constantine insists that he is justified and unmistaken "in confessing this one God the Author and Father of all." The Roman emperor makes a point of establishing a new era by directly contrasting himself with "many of those who have reigned here" (the Roman Empire), who, "seduced by insane errors," denied God and persecuted his followers.[22]

Up to this point, the letter seems to be mainly the self-aggrandizing bluster of a king who is thanking his divine patron while touting his own prowess on the battlefield. There is nothing particularly strange or novel about this, except perhaps for the considerable amount of time that Constantine spends on the topic. The emperor's rhetoric about the divine goes beyond the more perfunctory, but equally self-serving, recognition of the gods by Shapur himself, decades later, in his letter to Constantius of 358. According to Ammianus, Shapur identifies himself by citing his fraternal relationship to the heavens, beginning, "Shapur, King of Kings, partner with the Stars, brother of the Sun and Moon," but then formally greets Constantius and promptly turns to the business at hand.[23]

Constantine, by contrast, scrupulously details his relationship to the divine and explains how his alliance with his god distinguishes him from the

19. *VC* IV.9.
20. *VC* IV.9.
21. *VC* IV.10.
22. *VC* IV.11.
23. Amm. Marc. XVII.5.3.

earlier (impious) rulers of Rome. It takes quite some time for him to explain to Shapur why he is waxing on about his love for "the most holy religion" and the god who so majestically carried his armies to victory. In fact, all the preliminary sections that survive of Constantine's letter are a series of reminders of what happened to those who persecuted "the people devoted to God."[24] Only near the end of the letter does he utter the name "Christian" and thus reveal to Shapur the identity of the nameless god and the unspecified faith that he has been extolling at such length. After all this pomp and brass, Constantine finally concedes—at what Eusebius makes out to be the close of the letter—that his "whole concern" is "for them," adding, by way of explanation, "I mean of course the Christians."[25]

Assuming that Shapur received Constantine's letter, one cannot help but wonder what the Persian king would have made of it. The Persian ambassador, having spent some time in the Roman Empire, may have been key to helping his ruler understand the universalizing claims that the Roman emperor was making.[26] Constantine singles out a specific group of people in Persia for special consideration after proclaiming to Shapur that his own military successes are thanks to the god whom these people worship. At the same time that Constantine praises Shapur because Persia is "richly adorned" with Christians, he reminds him of what happens to those who persecute Christians. At the same time that he glorifies the goodness of the Christian god, he rails against the errors of non-Christians and the sickness of the cultic sacrifices of his predecessors, claiming that such perversions have "overthrown many of the nations and whole peoples."[27]

More than anything else, Constantine's letter is driven by the persistent sense that benefits accrue to those who support Christians (or at least refrain from persecuting them), while dreadful consequences await those who treat Christians poorly. Yet even given this, it is imperative to note that Constantine's letter is neither an indictment of Shapur nor a critique of the king's gods. Constantine never suggests that he suspects Shapur of persecut-

---

24. *VC* IV.12.

25. *VC* IV.13.

26. On this point see, for example, M. Canepa, *The Two Eyes of the Earth: Art and Ritual of Kingship between Rome and Sasanian Iran* (Berkeley: University of California Press, 2009).

27. *VC* IV.10. For a summary and analysis of the other Constantinian references in Eusebius that speak disdainfully of pagan sacrifices, see T.D. Barnes, "Constantine's Prohibition of Pagan Sacrifice," *AJP* 105 (1984): 69–72; and S. Bradbury, "Constantine and the Problem of Anti-Pagan Legislation in the Fourth Century," *CP* 89 (1994): 120–39.

ing the Christians in his realm. To the contrary, he specifically grants Shapur authority over the Christians of Persia. He is clear to indicate his pleasure in hearing that the choicest parts of Persia are overflowing with Christians, and he attempts to secure their continued safety through rhetorical persuasion and fraternal cajoling. The close of Constantine's letter even rings with a tone of congratulatory and communal well-wishing: "May the very best come to you therefore, and at the same time the best for them, since they also are yours." The emperor continues in this vein, saying, "These [Christians] therefore, since you are so great, I entrust to you, putting their very persons in your hands, because you too are renowned for piety. Love them in accordance with your own humanity. For you will give enormous satisfaction both to yourself and to us by keeping faith."[28]

Constantine's language at the end of his letter may sound condescending, but a patronal attitude toward Christians everywhere is precisely the one that he intends to adopt—or, at least, that Eusebius intends to fashion for him in the *VC*. From Constantine's point of view, Shapur should understand the Christians of Persia as a divine gift to his empire—a gift more splendid than any of those being delivered to him by his returning ambassador.

Eusebius and the Beginning of Imperial Christianity

While Eusebius may have had good reason to celebrate the emperor's overweening concern for Christians beyond the bounds of the Roman Empire, most scholars have, quite justifiably, read Constantine's letter with more trepidation. For in claiming to be so concerned about the Christians of Persia, Constantine effectively marks them as clients of Rome. Roger Blockley, for example, suggests that the obstreperous religiosity of Constantine's letter was "threatening" to the Persian king and must have "fuelled Persian suspicions by emphasising the universal mission of the Christian Church and [Constantine's] 'episcopal' responsibility for those without it."[29] Likewise, Timothy Barnes reads Constantine's letter to Shapur as sure evidence of an astonishing change in the Roman Empire's outlook on the rest of the known world. He argues that it demonstrates that Constantine's conversion and concomitant Christianization of the Roman Empire began "to affect foreign

---

28. *VC* IV.13.
29. R. C. Blockley, *East Roman Foreign Policy: Formation and Conduct from Diocletian to Anastasius* (Leeds: Francis Cairns, 1992), 11.

policy" as soon as Constantine became the sole ruler of the empire. Echoing what we hear in Constantine's letter, Barnes says that the emperor "regarded himself as a divinely ordained protector of Christians everywhere, with a duty to convert pagans to the truth, and this fundamental assumption about his mission in life inevitably shaped his policy toward Persia, where a large number of Christians lived under a Zoroastrian monarch."[30]

Among Syriac scholars who accept the authenticity of Constantine's letter, Sebastian Brock agrees that the emperor's vocal role as a patron of the Christians of Persia had negative repercussions for them. But he considers the problem to have been the historiographical legacy of Eusebius's portrayal of Constantine "as advocate for the Christian minority living under the Zoroastrian Sasanids," rather than Constantine's letter itself.[31] This is a subtle but crucial distinction. Throughout all of his works, the *VC* and the *Church History* included, Eusebius's overarching focus is, truly, on Christianity in the Roman Empire. This lopsided if predictable territorial emphasis, Brock argues, leaves "the reader with the impression that Christianity was essentially a phenomenon restricted to the Greco-Latin cultural world."[32] What Eusebius creates in his literary and historical works is thus, according to Brock, a "picture of the history of the Christian church as being inextricably interwoven with the history of the Roman empire," a combination of piety and power that has had enduring consequences for the Christians of Persia and "a pernicious influence on the writing of almost all subsequent ecclesiastical history down to our present day."[33]

---

30. T. D. Barnes, "Constantine and the Christians of Persia," *JRS* 75 (1985): 131. With respect to the treaties promulgated between Rome and the Goths and Sarmatians whom Eusebius mentions in *VC* IV.5–6, Barnes says that Constantine "insisted on including religious stipulations, which enabled him (and his panegyrist Eusebius) to claim that he had converted the northern barbarians."

31. S. P. Brock, "Christians in the Sasanian Empire: A Case of Divided Loyalties," in *Religion and National Identity*, ed. S. Mews (Oxford: Oxford University Press, 1982), 2.

32. S. P. Brock, "Eusebius and Syriac Christianity," in *Eusebius, Christianity, and Judaism*, ed. H. W. Attridge and G. Hata (Detroit: Wayne State University Press, 1992), 212.

33. Brock, "Christians in the Sasanian Empire," 2. Adam Becker extends Brock's assessment of Eusebius's "negative" effect on the history of Christianity in the East into a commentary on the general scholarly ignorance of Christianity (and Judaism) outside the Roman Empire. See Becker, "Beyond the Spatial and Temporal *Limes*: Questioning the 'Parting of the Ways' outside the Roman Empire," in *The Ways That Never Parted: Jews and Christians in Late Antiquity and the Early Middle Ages*, ed. Becker and A. Y. Reed (Minneapolis: Fortress, 2007), 373.

As Brock's frank assessment indicates, it is Eusebius, and a Eusebian-inspired approach to writing church history, that has had longer and deeper consequences for the Christians of Persia than any letter that Shapur may have received from Constantine. To be sure, many of Eusebius's works were translated into Syriac at a relatively early date. For example, his treatise *On Theophany* and his *Martyrs of Palestine* are both preserved in British Library Add. MS 12,150 (the oldest dated Christian literary manuscript in any language), which was copied in Edessa in 411. The *Church History* entered Syriac quite quickly too, possibly—some have argued—even before Eusebius's death.[34] As a result of his stature in the Roman Empire and his wide readership among Syriac-speaking Christians there and in the Persian Empire, Eusebius has had an undeniably outsized influence on Syriac historiography.[35]

Subsequent chapters consider this influence of Eusebian ecclesiastical history, especially Constantine's letter to Shapur as the *VC* presents it, but Brock's comments here help to make an important point: even a negative assessment of the authenticity of Constantine's letter does little to diminish its importance for the writing of fourth-century history. Every ecclesiastical history or martyrdom narrative that quotes from or otherwise uses Constantine's letter both postdates and draws from the *VC*. There is no other, independent source for the letter. What matters is not whether Shapur received this letter from Constantine but that Christians in the Roman and the Persian Empire alike believed that he did and thereby penned their histories of this period with Constantine and his letter in mind.

THE AUTHENTICITY OF CONSTANTINE'S LETTER

Questions about the long shadow of Eusebius notwithstanding, it is certainly true that the letter to Shapur is the obvious outlier among the dozen-plus Constantinian documents that the *VC* cites. Miriam Vivian, whose 1987

---

34. See W. Wright, *Catalogue of Syriac Manuscripts in the British Museum, Acquired since the Year 1838*, vol. 2 (London, 1871), 631–33; and the preface to Wright and N. McLean, *The Ecclesiastical History of Eusebius in Syriac* (Cambridge: Cambridge University Press, 1898).

35. Muriel Debié's studies of Syriac historiography demonstrate the extent to which Western traditions have influenced it. See Debié, "L'Héritage de la chronique d'Eusèbe dans l'historiographie syriaque," *JCSSS* 6 (2006): 18–26; and Debié, "L'Héritage de l'historiographie grecque," in *L'Historiographie syriaque*, Études syriaques 6, ed. Debié (Paris: Geuthner, 2009), 11–31.

dissertation examines the role of Constantine's letter on Roman-Persian relations, comments that it "has been viewed as so unique that many scholars have not known how to explain it." In fact, she continues, "it seemed so unthinkable that a document with such Christian witness should come out of the chancery of a Roman emperor that in the 1930's Henri Grégoire made it a crucial point in his arguments against the authenticity of the entire *VC*."[36] The overt religiosity of Constantine's letter led the Sasanian historian Karin Mosig-Walburg to doubt its authenticity too, although she concluded that Eusebius should probably be considered guilty of simple negligence in authenticating his sources rather than outright forgery of the letter.[37] For Mosig-Walburg, as for Grégoire and others, it is simply beyond the bounds of reason that a fourth-century emperor—even Constantine—could so let religion dictate his foreign policy.[38]

The Recipient and Date of the Letter

Perhaps partly on the basis of Grégoire's influential article, even the assumption that Shapur II was the letter's addressee has been questioned. It has been argued that although the letter may be authentic, Eusebius must have inadvertently misconstrued the identity of its recipient. Constantine was writing not to a pagan, Persian king but to a Christian vassal of the Roman Empire: the Armenian king Tiridates.[39] This argument has not been greeted with

---

36. See M. R. Vivian, "A Letter to Shapur: The Effect of Constantine's Conversion on Roman-Persian Relations," PhD diss. (University of California at Santa Barbara, 1987), 8, with reference to Grégoire's well-known article "Eusèbe n'est pas l'auteur de la *Vita Constantini* dans sa forme actuelle et Constantin ne s'est pas 'converti' en 312," *Byz* 13 (1938): 561–83. See also Vivian, "Eusebius and Constantine's Letter to Shapur: Its Place in the *Vita Constantini*," *SP* 29 (1997): 164–69.

37. K. Mosig-Walburg, *Römer und Perser: Vom 3. Jahrhundert bis zum Jahr 363 n. Chr.* (Gutenberg: Computus Druck Satz, 2009), 275. See also her "Christenverfolgung und Römerkrieg: Zu Ursachen, Ausmaß und Zielrichtung der Christenverfolgung unter Šāpūr II.," *Iranistik* 7 (2005): 5–84; and "Die Christenverfolgung Shāpūrs II. vor dem Hintergrund des persisch-römischen Krieges," in *Inkulturation des Christentums im Sasanidenreich*, ed. A. Mustafa and J. Tubach (Wiesbaden: Reichert Verlag, 2007), 171–86.

38. Mosig-Walburg, *Römer und Perser*, 282.

39. D. De Decker, "Sur le destinataire de la lettre au Roi des Perses (Eusèbe de Césarée, *Vit. Const.*, IV, 9–13) et la conversion de l'Arménie à la religion chrétienne," *Persica* 8 (1979): 99–116. Barnes, in discussing De Decker's work, notes that the tone of the letter—"polite, tactful, allusive, and indirect"—is such that it might lead one to conclude that Shapur was not the recipient. See Barnes, "Constantine and the Christians of Persia," 131. This implies that Barnes considers courteousness something that would have been out of place in a letter

much enthusiasm, but it is possible that Tiridates's conversion to Christianity may have played an exacerbating role in Roman-Persian relations.[40] In his *Church History*, Sozomen (writing in Constantinople around 440) precedes his assessment of Shapur's persecution by noting that certain regions of Persia were led to embrace Christianity in part through the influence of "Tiridates, the king of [the Armenian] people."[41] Georg Blum connects the dots to conclude that Constantine's conversion and subsequent heralding of the Christian god in his letter, coupled with the conversion of Tiridates and Armenia, must have led Shapur to feel as if "Christian states" were beginning to surround Persia.[42]

Even though the letter's intended recipient was not Tiridates but almost certainly Shapur, there is no question that it is the only document in the *VC* that was addressed beyond the bounds of the Roman Empire. Still, its date and the circumstances of its composition remain less than certain.[43] Because Eusebius suggests that it was written in response to an official emissary's visit to Constantine's court, it has been argued that the letter was probably composed in or around 324, when there is evidence for the presence of Persian officials in the Roman Empire—including Prince Hormizd, a defector from the Sasanian court. In fact, most of the Constantinian documents in the *VC*

---

to a Persian king. However, while direct, the letter that Constantius wrote to *fratri meo Sapori* at the height of the war between them is neither impolite nor tactless. See Amm. Marc. XVII.5.10–14.

40. Mosig-Walburg discusses the role of Armenia throughout her work on the confrontation between Rome and Persia in the fourth century, but see especially her account of Armenia during the time of Constantine in *Römer und Perser*, 240–66.

41. Soz. *HE* II.8.

42. G. G. Blum, "Zur religionspolitischen Situation der persischen Kirche im 3. und 4. Jahrhundert," *ZKG* 91 (1980): 26. References to religious states and church-state relations and even the secularized terms "religion" and "politics" are anachronistic for the fourth century. For the beginnings of such a critique among those who have addressed this period, see P. Gignoux, "Church-State Relations in the Sasanian Period," in *Monarchies and Socio-religious Traditions in the Ancient Near East (Papers Read at the 31st International Congress of Human Sciences in Asia and North Africa)*, ed. T. Mikasa (Wiesbaden: Otto Harrassowitz, 1984), 72–80; and, more recently and much more theoretically, A. H. Becker, "Political Theology and Religious Diversity in the Sasanian Empire," in *Jews, Christians and Zoroastrians: Religious Dynamics in a Sasanian Context*, ed. G. Herman (Piscataway, NJ: Gorgias, 2014), 7–25.

43. In 1988, Harold Drake pointedly remarked, "The Letter to Shapur still needs definitive treatment." See Drake, "What Eusebius Knew: The Genesis of the *Vita Constantini*," *CP* 83 (1988): 27n23. Perhaps such definitive treatment arrived with the publication of Vivian's dissertation.

were likely written during the first years of Constantine's sole rule over the Roman Empire, between 324 and 326. Timothy Barnes demonstrates that Eusebius had amassed copies of most of the documents he used in his work no later than 326.[44] Later dates for Constantine's letter, even as late as 337, the last year of the emperor's life, cannot be definitively ruled out, but they are much less likely than the mid-320s for several reasons. First, the letter reads very much like an announcement of Constantine's Christianity—a celebration of the Christian god for leading Constantine on to what seem to have been relatively recent victories—which would better suit a mid-320s than a late 330s context. And then there is the overly laudatory and fraternal tone of the letter, which is difficult to reconcile with a date closer to the end of Constantine's life, when the emperor seems to have been in the midst of planning a campaign against Shapur, as I discuss in the next chapter.[45]

A mid-320s date would seem to militate against the letter's having played a direct role in aggravating Shapur to turn against Christians. Fifteen years would have elapsed between his receipt of the letter and any subsequent oppression of the Christians of Persia, which began, as the martyr acts of Simeon bar Ṣabbaʿe suggest, no earlier than 339. Such an extended chronology of events makes it hard to read Constantine's letter as a document that galvanized any immediate concern over the Christians of Persia among the Sasanian nobility.

A Text or a Source?

While it is true that the letter to Shapur is unique among Constantinian documents in the *VC* and that it is unattested outside Eusebius and his continuators, these facts alone are insufficient to dismiss it as either inauthentic

---

44. T. D. Barnes, "Panegyric, History and Hagiography in Eusebius' *Life of Constantine*," in *The Making of Orthodoxy: Essays in Honour of Henry Chadwick*, ed. R. Williams (Cambridge: Cambridge University Press, 1989), 111.

45. For an overview of the possible dates of the letter's composition, see Drake, "What Eusebius Knew," 27; Barnes, "Constantine and the Christians of Persia," 131–32, with further explanation in Barnes, *Constantine and Eusebius* (Cambridge, MA: Harvard University Press, 1981), 258; D. Frendo, "Constantine's Letter to Shapur II: Its Authenticity, Occasion, and Attendant Circumstances," *BAI* 15 (2001): 60; and Vivian, "Letter to Shapur," 87–129, which considers the dates and circumstances of the letter's composition in direct conjunction with the supposed dates of Shapur's persecution.

or a Eusebian invention.[46] Thinking about how best to read the *VC* may be helpful in this regard. As Averil Cameron aptly puts it, the *VC* "has to be read as a *text* before it can be read as a *source*."[47] If understood as a source for episodes in the emperor's life, then it tends to be read as confirming or contradicting what the reader believes he or she already knows about Constantine. Approached in this way, the *VC* will be either accepted as trustworthy or dismissed as misinformed and spurious.[48] But if instead it is read as a text about Constantine rather than a source for his life, then questions about the authenticity of each Constantinian document that Eusebius cites are less urgent. The important point is that Constantine's letter to Shapur circulated in late antiquity as if it were authentic. And there are good reasons to believe that it actually was.

In 1950, T. C. Skeat's discovery of an early fourth-century papyrus (P. Lond. 878) helped confirm that the Constantinian documents that Eusebius cites—while they too must be read as texts—are likely authentic sources, from which Eusebius faithfully quotes. The London papyrus is important in this respect because it independently preserves part of Constantine's decree to the Eastern provincials in Palestine. Eusebius reproduces this decree in full in the *VC*, and his quotation is perfectly consistent with that in the papyrus.[49] The discovery of this papyrus "greatly reduced the likelihood that the documents [in the *VC*] as a group should be regarded as suspect."[50] Eusebius was

---

46. David Frendo comments, "The general trend [in Eusebian studies] has been toward acceptance of the Eusebian authorship of the *Vita Constantini* and of the authenticity of the greater part of the documents contained therein." See Frendo, "Constantine's Letter to Shapur," 58–60, which discusses arguments for and against the authenticity of Constantine's letter to Shapur at length. As Horst Schneider argues, however, the letter to Shapur is very much an anomaly among the documents in the *VC*, possessing a style and language that differ significantly from those of other imperial decrees. See B. Bleckmann and Schneider, *Eusebius von Caesarea, De Vita Constantini, Über das Leben Konstantins* (Turnhout: Brepols, 2007), 420n287.

47. My emphasis. See Cameron, "Eusebius' *Vita Constantini* and the Construction of Constantine," in *Portraits: Biographical Representations in the Greek and Latin Literature of the Roman Empire*, ed. M.J. Edwards and S. Swain (Oxford: Clarendon, 1997), 145.

48. A. Cameron, "Eusebius of Caesarea and the Rethinking of History," in *Tria Corda: Scritti in onore di Arnaldo Momigliano*, ed. E. Gabba (Como: New Press, 1983), 72.

49. For Eusebius's citation of the decree, see *VC* II.24–42. The portion preserved in P. Lond. 878 mirrors *VC* II.26.2–29.1. See A.H.M. Jones and T.C. Skeat, "Notes on the Genuineness of the Constantinian Documents in Eusebius' *Life of Constantine*," *JEH* 5 (1954): 196–200. See also S. Mitchell, "Maximinus and the Christians in A.D. 312: A New Latin Inscription," *JRS* 78 (1988): 105–24.

50. Cameron and Hall, *Life of Constantine*, 239.

writing a hagiography, that much is undeniable, but he does not seem to have invented the Constantinian sources at his disposal. Rather, as the papyrus evidence suggests, he quotes faithfully from the sources that he had before him and which he apparently believed were authentically Constantinian.

Put simply, we cannot be certain that Constantine wrote the letter to Shapur, but there is no more reason to doubt its authenticity than there is to doubt any of the other Constantinian documents that Eusebius cites. Indeed, Constantine's letter to the Eastern provincials in the mid-320s rehearses topics and themes that are very similar to those in the letter to Shapur.[51] Such similarities can only strengthen the arguments in favor of the authenticity of the letter to Shapur. Taking all of this into account, it is thus fair to assume that the letter was genuinely from Constantine's hand, that it was sent to Shapur sometime between 324 and 337 (with an earlier date being most likely), and that the Greek translation quoted by Eusebius is presumably not an injustice to the emperor's Latin. Shapur probably did receive a letter from Constantine, in which the Roman emperor declared his allegiance to the Christian god, critiqued past persecutors of Christians, and expressed his concern for Christians in Persia.

REASSESSING CONSTANTINE'S LETTER

Even given robust assumptions about the authenticity of Constantine's letter, it was hardly needed to alert Persians to the presence of Christians in their midst. The Persian ambassador himself is the one who supposedly informed Constantine that Christians were thriving in Persia. And besides ambassadors and other officials, plenty of merchants routinely passed from one realm to the other. The merchant-missionary, not a novel phenomenon in the mid-fourth century, was one of the many vehicles of Christianization in the Sasanian Empire.[52] No political or cultural border either would have hin-

---

51. *VC* II.48–60.

52. See the discussion of the Christianization of Persia in chapter 5. The comprehensive survey of Christian missionary activity in Persia by Christelle and Florence Jullien captures the variegated nature of Christianity in Iran in the third and early fourth centuries and references the many sources attesting to its diversity, spread, and means of growth. See Jullien and Jullien, *Apôtres des confins: Processus missionnaires chrétiens dans l'empire iranien,* Res Orientales XV (Bures-sur-Yvette: Groupe pour l'étude de la civilisation du Moyen-Orient, 2002), especially 43–117, on the literary accounts of Christian missionaries in Iran, and 153–87, on the consequences of earlier deportations of Roman citizens to the Iranian heartland.

dered the Persian awareness that changes were afoot under Constantine. The Sasanians were acutely attuned to power struggles in the Roman Empire, and information moved across an inevitably porous zone of contact.[53] As A. D. Lee points out, even though the absence of documentary evidence makes ascertaining both the existence and the means of transmission of strategic military intelligence difficult, "the very despatch of certain embassies implies that there was movement of information between the two empires." Lee further remarks that the Persian ambassador who arrived at Constantinople seeking to dissuade Constantine from marching to war in 337 is one obvious indication "that the Persians had somehow learned of Roman preparations."[54]

If Constantine's conversion to Christianity resulted in the immediate changes that are so often claimed for his reign by ancient and contemporary historians alike—such as the abolition of pagan sacrifices, an exceptional redistribution of wealth favoring Christians and Christian sites, and the promotion of Christianity above and beyond all other cults—then is it really plausible that the Persians would not have noticed such raucous and radical transformations? Indeed, the Persian ambassador to whom Constantine supposedly entrusted his letter to Shapur may have witnessed the burgeoning religious transformations of the Roman Empire firsthand. But if the religious changes within the Roman Empire were not nearly so overwhelming, in either their scope or their intensity, as some have claimed, then Constantine's announcement to Shapur about his own Christianity and his concern for all Christians may yet have been newsworthy.

In either case, the more important question here is whether Constantine's personal claim to an allegiance with the Christian god was sufficient to inexorably establish a link between that god and the Roman Empire such that the name "Christian" became immediately interchangeable with "Roman." Such

---

53. See J. F. Matthews, "Hostages, Philosophers, Pilgrims, and the Diffusion of Ideas in the Late Roman Mediterranean and Near East," in *Tradition and Innovation in Late Antiquity*, ed. F. M. Clover and R. S. Humphreys (Madison: University of Wisconsin Press, 1989), 29–49.

54. A. D. Lee, "Embassies as Evidence for the Movement of Military Intelligence between the Roman and Sasanian Empires," in *The Defence of the Roman and Byzantine East*, ed. P. Freeman and D. Kennedy (Oxford: BAR International Editions, 1986), 456. For more on the Roman-Persian negotiations (or, rather, Constantine's refusal thereof) in the months leading up to the war, see K. Mosig-Walburg, "Zur Westpolitik Shāpūrs II.," in *Iran, questions et connaissances: Actes du IVe congrès européen des études iraniennes, organisé par la Societas Iranologica Europaea, Paris, 6–10 septembre 1999*, vol. 1, *La période ancienne*, ed. P. Huyse (Leuven: Peeters, 2002), 329–47.

a link could not be instituted overnight, on the basis of a single letter. The connection between *Romanitas* and *Christianitas* took some time to establish, even in the Roman Empire. Although Constantine's letter was certainly a preliminary step in that direction, before the emperor could—with a few strokes of his pen—inaugurate the Byzantine-Christian future, he had to rewrite the Roman-pagan past.

Persecution and Divine Justice in the Letter to Shapur: The Example of Valerian

Christians, Constantine says, are the reason for his letter.[55] The emperor's concern for Christians far and wide is a theme that appears regularly in the *VC*. It might be most keenly encapsulated in this story that Eusebius tells: Constantine was present at an assembly of bishops who were gathered for dinner. He "let slip the remark that he was perhaps himself a bishop too, using some such words as these in our hearing: 'You are bishops of those within the Church, but I am perhaps a bishop appointed by God over those outside.'"[56]

In their commentary on this passage, Cameron and Hall call it "one of the most famous and puzzling statements in the *VC*."[57] To whom was Constantine referring when he called himself a bishop "over those outside"? Did he mean Christians outside Rome, those beyond the reach of the church of the empire? Or did he mean to anoint himself with a missionary role, as the shepherd who would lead non-Christians within the Roman Empire to the church?

While this passage—which Eusebius seems to regard as an intriguing but only anecdotal aside—may reinforce the view that the letter to Shapur is an expression of Constantine's sense of religious mission, the emperor's letter is not an oblique or surreptitious way of claiming the Christians of Persia as Roman subjects, or of girding Shapur for a war on their behalf. Constantine writes to Shapur seeking to ensure that the Persian king will *continue* to not

---

55. *VC* IV.13.
56. *VC* IV.24. See also W. Seston, "Constantine as a 'Bishop,'" *JRS* 37 (1947): 127–31.
57. Cameron and Hall, *Life of Constantine*, 320. It has also helped fuel the characterization of Constantine as a "caesaropapist." Claudia Rapp says that this passage, coupled with others that refer to Constantine as a "bishop," seems "to encapsulate the Byzantine vision of imperial authority in its relation to Christianity." See Rapp, "Imperial Ideology in the Making: Eusebius of Caesarea on Constantine as 'Bishop,'" *JTS* 49 (1998): 685.

persecute Christians. He remarks that he is commending the Christians of Persia to the protection of the Persian king, who is "renowned for piety [*eusebeia*]" and to whom he hopes "the very best" will come, "since they [the Christians] are also yours."⁵⁸ The letter warns Shapur, but in a way that is judiciously phrased as being helpful, not threatening. It is important to note too that according to Eusebius, Constantine accompanied it with peace guarantees and magnificent presents.⁵⁹

Constantine does focus largely on war and military victories in the opening sections of his letter, but the reasons behind such militarism have to be properly understood. The references to his victorious army should be read less as imperial saber rattling and more as a straightforward presentation of evidence that would have been readily intelligible to a leader, and reader, such as Shapur. Constantine offers tangible proof (his triumphs over adversaries) of the benefits that God accords to rulers who are benevolent toward Christians. He insists that Christians will be a boon to Shapur and to the Persian Empire, if only Shapur is wise enough to understand this: "For so you will keep the sovereign Lord of the Universe kind, merciful and benevolent."⁶⁰ In Constantine's estimation, those who failed to keep the Lord benevolent were not Persian kings but Roman emperors who persecuted Christians. Valerian in particular is singled out for special condemnation.

Even though the letter never names him (nor Shapur, for that matter), Valerian is the person on whom the whole message of Constantine's letter hinges.⁶¹ In transitioning from the sections that tout the power of the Christian god and attest to his patronage in ushering Constantine to victory, Constantine turns to critique "many of those who have reigned here"—non-Christian Roman emperors—who were "seduced by insane errors" and denied God. He strives to present the death and punishment of these persecuting emperors in providential terms, anticipating that Shapur will likewise account for their deaths as the result of divine vengeance. Constantine explains, "All mankind since has regarded their fate as superseding all other examples to warn those who strive for the same ends."⁶²

58. *VC* IV.13.
59. *VC* IV.8.
60. *VC* IV.13.
61. On the common rhetorical practice of keeping enemies unnamed in order to refer to them in a more allusive fashion, see R. MacMullen, "Roman Bureaucratese," *Traditio* 18 (1962): 364–78; Vivian ("Letter to Shapur," 66) brings up this point as well.
62. *VC* IV.11.

Referring to Valerian, Constantine tells Shapur that a Roman persecutor of Christians "was driven from these parts [the Roman Empire] by divine wrath as by a thunderbolt and was left in yours, where he caused the victory on your side to become very famous because of the shame he suffered."[63] Constantine could have chosen to single out other famous persecutors of Christians—Decius or Diocletian, perhaps—but Valerian's utility in a letter to a Persian king is obvious. Shapur II's great-grandfather Shapur I defeated Valerian's army in 260 and, as numerous sources attest, either killed the Roman emperor or led him off into a captivity from which he never returned.

Shapur the Great's victory over Valerian was, quite literally, a monumental defeat for the Romans. Several massive relief sculptures cut directly into the cliffs at Naqsh-e-Rostam, near the ancient Achaemenid capital of Persepolis, soon commemorated it.[64] These rock reliefs, as well as others near the city of Bishapur, depict a suppliant Valerian before a triumphant Shapur.[65] In a trilingual inscription (Parthian, Middle Persian, Greek) on the famous Ka'ba-ye Zartosht (Cube of Zoroaster), Shapur claims to have defeated Valerian and his army and deported the Roman emperor and scores of his officers to the Persian heartland.[66]

In turning to consider the fate of Valerian and his captivity in Persia, Constantine moves from extolling the power infused into Rome's armies by the Christian god to acknowledging that that same god once supported the Persians (apparently unbeknown to them) in their war against a Roman army that was led by an emperor who persecuted Christians. Constantine's intent

---

63. *VC* IV.11. Later commentators had no trouble understanding the identity of the person driven out by a thunderbolt. Sozomen, who summarizes Constantine's letter in a discussion of Shapur and the Christian martyrs of Persia, specifically names Valerian as the referent of Constantine's wrath. See Soz. *HE* II.15.4.

64. See G. Herrmann, D.N. Mackenzie, and R. Howell, *The Sasanian Reliefs at Naqsh-i Rustam: Naqsh-i Rustam 6, The Triumph of Shapur I,* Iranische Denkmaler 13 (Berlin: Dietrich Reimer Verlag, 1989); and Herrmann, "The Rock Reliefs of Sasanian Iran," in *Mesopotamia and Iran in the Parthian and Sasanian Periods: Rejection and Revival c. 238 BC–AD 642,* ed. J.E. Curtis (London: British Museum Press, 2000), 35–45.

65. On the visual depiction of Valerian's capture, see Canepa, *Two Eyes of the Earth,* 68. For a more comprehensive study of the use of such relief sculpture throughout Persia, see Canepa's "Topographies of Power: Theorizing the Visual, Spatial and Ritual Contexts of Rock Reliefs in Ancient Iran," in *Of Rocks and Water: Towards an Archaeology of Place,* ed. Ö. Harmanşah (Oxford: Oxbow Books, 2014), 55–92.

66. See M. Back, *Die sasanidischen Staatsinschriften,* Acta Iranica 18 (Leiden: Brill, 1978), ŠKZ, Mid. Pers. I.15, Parth. I.11, Gk. I.25; and E. Kettenhofen, *Die römisch-persischen Kriege des 3. Jahrhunderts. n. Chr. nach der Inschrift Šāhpuhrs I. an der Ka'be-ye Zartošt (ŠKZ)* (Wiesbaden: Reichert Verlag, 1982), 97–99.

is didactic. Rome was once an empire enslaved by tyrants, but with the elevation of a Christian emperor it has "enjoyed the general restoration of right" and "revived like a patient after treatment."[67] Constantine thereby contrasts his rise to power with the downfall of his non-Christian predecessors. Those who persecute "the people devoted to God" come to a bitter end, as Valerian's well-known fate attests.[68] And while the letter surely calls Valerian's paganism to task—Constantine calls his cult sacrifices "abominable blood and foul hateful odours"—this was not the main reason for his downfall.[69] Rather, it was Valerian's persecution of Christians.

This is an important point. For throughout his letter, Constantine demonstrates no interest in critiquing Shapur's gods or the cults of the Persians. He even remarks that Shapur is "renowned for piety."[70] The emperor is not proselytizing to non-Christian Persians but instead is intent on demonstrating to Shapur that rulers who persecute Christians enrage God, while those who protect them earn God's munificence.

That Valerian's death was a direct result of his oppression of Christians, not just his paganism, is a theme that other Christian sources from the Roman Empire echo. In his *Chronicle*, Jerome suggests a clear, causal connection between Valerian's persecution of Christians and his untimely death, indicating that the latter followed immediately from the former.[71] Likewise, Augustine's disciple Orosius places Valerian as the eighth in a long line of persecuting emperors beginning with Nero. He says that soon after Valerian began persecuting Christians, the Persians enslaved him.[72] Sozomen too claims that Valerian's reign was untroubled so long as he did not persecute Christians. But once the emperor began his oppression, the wrath of God delivered him to the Persians.[73] Following his death in Persia a century after Valerian's, the emperor Julian's demise was interpreted in an identical way.

67. *VC* IV.9.
68. *VC* IV.12.
69. *VC* IV.10.
70. *VC* IV.13.
71. On the year 258, Jerome comments that Valerian, after instigating a persecution against Christians, was immediately captured by Shapur, the king of the Persians. See R. Helm, *Eusebius Werke*, vol. 7, *Die Chronik des Hieronymus*, GCS 47 (Berlin: Akademie Verlag, 1956), 302.
72. Orosius, *Ad. Paganos* VII.22.3–4. For a translation, see R.J. Defarrari, *Paulus Orosius: The Seven Books of History against the Pagans* (Washington DC: Catholic University of America Press, 2001).
73. Soz. *HE* II.15.4.

Valerian and a New Roman History

Valerian surfaces in Christian texts written outside the Roman Empire too. The East Syrian *Chronicle of Seert,* a tenth-century ecclesiastical history in Christian Arabic, finds a providential purpose in the persecuting emperor. Although only a few sections of the formerly extensive *Chronicle* survive, what remains of it begins with Valerian's death. According to the *Chronicle,* there was a divine, double purpose to the emperor's demise. After the death of "the evil Valerian," the Christian priests he had exiled were allowed to return to their episcopal sees. More important, Shapur's many Roman captives, especially the citizens of Antioch, "multiplied in Persia," where they (anachronistically for the mid-third century) "built monasteries and churches." Valerian's death, at least according to East Syrian Christian legend, hastened the spread of Christianity in Persia, of which Shapur I was an unwitting tool by deporting the citizens of defeated Roman cities (Christians among them) en masse to Persia.[74]

From the perspective of the *Chronicle of Seert,* Christianity thus flourished in third-century Persia in ways that would have been impossible at the same time in the Roman Empire under rulers such as Valerian. As much as Constantine indicates an ignorance in his letter that Christians were prospering in Persia under Shapur II, he at least seems to have known that Christians had, in fact, fled the Roman Empire for other lands during times of persecution. In his letter to the provincials in Palestine, Constantine laments the persecutions of Diocletian and refers to "the boast of the barbarians who at that time welcomed refugees from among us, and kept them in humane custody, for they provided them not only with safety but with the opportunity to practise their religion in security. And now the Roman race bears this indelible stain, left on its name by the Christians who were driven at that time from the Roman world and took refuge with barbarians."[75]

One way to remove the "indelible stain" on the Roman race was by celebrating the gory but divine vengeance taken upon emperors such as Valerian. Thus Vincenzo Poggi refers to Constantine's letter as an exercise in "purificazione della memoria," a way of making amends for past oppression and

---

74. A. Scher, *Histoire nestorienne inédite (Chronique de Séert), première partie 1,* PO 4 (Paris: Firmin-Didot, 1908), 220–21. See also the further discussion of deportations and Christian captives in chapter 5.

75. *VC* II.53. See also Frendo, "Constantine's Letter to Shapur," 62.

perhaps of surreptitiously welcoming back those who had fled the Roman Empire or had been taken captive by the Persians.[76]

Like that between persecution and divine punishment, there seems to be a direct relationship between the stridency of an author's Christianity and the gruesomeness he attributes to Valerian's demise. The pagan historian Zosimus, for example, mentions only that Valerian shamed himself and the Roman Empire through the disgrace of his capture. Zosimus provides no details about the emperor's death.[77] On the other end of the spectrum is the Latin rhetorician Lactantius. His polemical *On the Deaths of the Persecutors* is a graphic litany of the deaths suffered by emperors who persecuted Christians, Valerian among them. This pamphlet reads, however, less as a celebration of the oppression of the oppressor (although it is that) and more as a new sort of historical tract, a definitive rewriting of Roman history along Christian lines, designed to show how God intervenes in history and severely punishes those who persecute Christians. More important, Lactantius's celebration of Valerian's death is key to further understanding Constantine's letter to Shapur.

Lactantius and Constantine on the Deaths of Persecutors

Lactantius reviles Valerian, saying that no Roman, not even Valerian's own son, bothered to avenge his dishonorable imprisonment.[78] But this was only the beginning of Valerian's humiliation. Lactantius claims that he was forced to serve as a human footstool, so that whenever Shapur wished to mount his horse, Valerian would have to kneel down on his hands and knees and bear the Persian king's weight upon his back. As Shapur mounted his horse, he

76. V. Poggi, "Costantino e la chiesa di Persia," in *Costantino il Grande nell'età bizantina: Atti del Convegno internazionale di studio, Ravenna, 5–8 aprile 2001* (*Bizantinistica* V), ed. G. Bonamente and A. Carile (Spoleto: Fondazione Centro italiano di studi sull'alto medioevo, 2003), 74.

77. Zos. *HN* I.36.2.

78. Lactant. *De mort. pers.* V.5. The *Chronicle of Seert*, by contrast, indicates that Valerian's son Gallienus sent Shapur magnificent presents. In return, Valerian's body was delivered to the Roman Empire. The *Chronicle* also specifies that Gallienus recalled those whom his father had exiled and repealed the edicts against the Christians. See Scher, *Histoire nestorienne inédite*, 223.

The ideas developed in this section were originally part of my formal response to "Religious Identity through the Prism of Spectacle in Early Christianity" by Elizabeth Castelli, both presented at the Center for Late Ancient Studies symposium "Constructing and Contesting Late Ancient Identities," Duke University, Durham, NC, February 20, 2009.

would smirk at the emperor-turned-footstool and remind him that *this* was the truth—Roman subjugation to Persian victors—not the imaginative false victories that the Romans painted on their walls.[79] Lactantius claims that after Valerian's death, his skin was peeled from his body, dyed red, and hung up "in the temple of the barbarian gods" as a warning to all future Roman ambassadors.[80]

Constantine, far from denying that Valerian's death was as shameful as the Persians would have it, in fact verifies, but then reclaims, his predecessor's notorious humiliation, to laud the power of the Christian god. He writes to Shapur in his letter, "It would appear that it has turned out advantageous that even in our own day the punishment of such persons has become notorious. I have myself observed the end of those next to me, who with vicious decrees had harassed the people devoted to God."[81] For Constantine, Valerian's shame is educative. His divine punishment was a spectacular warning, his skin a red flag flying for everyone in the future.

Just as the organizers of the bloody spectacles of the Roman arena sought to restage ancient myths, thereby renewing mythological reality by discursively and viscerally sustaining their narratives, Lactantius is attempting to stage (anew) a *truer* account of Roman history. In so doing, he presents not only a more pedagogically inclined spectacle of punishment but, at the same time, a correction of the historical record by showing how God raised up emperors such as Constantine to rescind the impious edicts of tyrants.[82] Lactantius seeks to display the power of God and to make clear that it is God who punishes the persecutors, judging the impious in order to "teach posterity" that he alone is God.[83]

Elizabeth Castelli argues that Lactantius's understanding of "divine punishment combines ... elements of Roman penal violence—retribution,

---

79. Lactant. *De mort. pers.* V.3.

80. Lactant. *De mort. pers.* V.6. On this episode, see E. Reiner, "The Reddling of Valerian," *CQ* 56 (2006): 325–29. For an overview of the varying accounts of Valerian's capture and death, see B. Isaac, "The Army in the Late Roman East: The Persian Wars and the Defence of the Byzantine Provinces," in *The Near East under Roman Rule: Selected Papers* (Leiden: Brill, 1998), 440–41. Isaac indicates that Lactantius was the first to add the grisly detail that Valerian was flayed. On the practice of hanging up human trophies in Persian temples, see also the Syriac *Martyrdom of Abbot Barshebya* (*AMS* II, 281–84), translated in appendix C.

81. *VC* IV.12.

82. Lactant. *De mort. pers.* I.3.

83. Lactant. *De mort. pers.* I.6.

humiliation, correction, prevention, and deterrence. But punishment is also educative... simultaneously a form of display and a form of teaching." And "the object of [such] correction," she points out, is ultimately "mistaken theological understanding." Correcting mistaken theology is, for Lactantius, part of his methodical renarration of Roman history. Valerian's mistaken theological understanding, manifested less in his paganism than in his persecution of the people of God, garnered many afterlives in Christian discourse. Yet, as Castelli emphasizes, there is no "anti-imperial character" to Lactantius's history. Lactantius distinguishes between "emperors" (such as Constantine) and "tyrants" (such as Valerian) but, she says, "never calls the notion of empire into question."[84]

Lactantius's rhetorical project pairs closely with Constantine's—both the emperor's letter to Shapur and his *Oration to the Assembly of the Saints*. In fact, as Harold Drake notes, "the enthusiastic identification of parallels" between Constantine's *Oration* and the works of "other writers such as Lactantius was beginning to sound like yet another search for alternative authors [of Constantine's *Oration*] until T. D. Barnes came to the sensible conclusion that words delivered by the emperor, no matter who wrote them, could safely be considered to be the emperor's own."[85]

In his *Oration to the Assembly of the Saints*, Constantine echoes Lactantius's portrayal of God's "righteous judgment" of Valerian while touting his own divinely inspired victories and rule over the Roman Empire as a Christian. According to Eusebius, Constantine's *Oration* was written in Latin and then translated into Greek—like the letter to Shapur. Eusebius also reminds us that a Greek version of Constantine's *Oration* was transmitted as an appendix to the *VC*.[86] In several manuscripts, the *Oration* is in fact appended to the *VC*. Constantine confirms Lactantius's reading of history in his *Oration*, and he reaffirms Shapur the Great's horse-mounting jibe

---

84. Castelli, "Religious Identity."

85. See H. A. Drake, *Constantine and the Bishops: The Politics of Intolerance* (Baltimore: Johns Hopkins University Press, 2000), 292, with reference to Barnes, *Constantine and Eusebius*, 74. See also Barnes, "Lactantius and Constantine," *JRS* 63 (1973): 29–46.

86. *VC* IV.32. Drake suggests that the history of Constantine's *Oration* "is a microcosm of classical scholarship in the modern age." The text moved from an early "period of hypercriticism (during which scholars freely dismissed whole passages for not conforming to what their science told them the emperor should have said)" to cautious admission "as a representative piece of fourth-century propaganda, though still held unlikely to be Constantine's own" and finally to recent times, when "scholars have been more willing to concede authenticity." See Drake, *Constantine and the Bishops*, 292.

at Valerian. If past defeat—even past defeat of the Roman Empire—is divine retribution, then present victory is thereby divinely sanctioned.[87] Constantine likens Valerian to Decius and condemns the emperor who died at the hands of the Persians, saying, "But you, Valerian, who showed the same murder-lust toward those who heeded God, you made the holy judgment manifest when you were caught and led as a prisoner in bonds with your very purple and all your royal pomp, and finally, flayed and pickled at the behest of Sapor the King of the Persians, you were set up as an eternal trophy of your own misfortune!"[88]

As Jeremy Schott indicates, Constantine evidently borrows from Lactantius in his *Oration* but diverges from him "by drawing connections between the persecutors and *biblical* tyrants."[89] Constantine refers to the destruction of the Assyrian Empire as a result of thunderbolts from heaven thanks to the impious rule of the tyrant Nebuchadnezzar, whose "whole line was wiped out" and whose power "passed to the Persians."[90] Just as one tyrant lost his kingdom to thunderbolts, "the thunderbolt and the fire from heaven" consumed the palace and bedchamber of the persecutor Diocletian—who thereafter lived his life in perpetual dread of the thunderbolt—in retribution for his persecution of Christians.[91] Constantine uses this idea of the thunderbolt, which comes up twice in the *Oration*, pairing a biblical tyrant with a persecutor of Christians, again in the letter to Shapur when he explains how Valerian "was driven from these parts by divine wrath as by a thunderbolt."[92]

Divine retribution results in the punishment of the tyrant or persecutor but also in the apotheosis of the divine drama and the restoration of proper

---

87. Jeremy Schott comments, "This portion of the *Oration* [XXIV.1–3] most certainly owes something to Lactantius' *On the Deaths of the Persecutors*. Lactantius and Constantine identify the same set of emperors (although Constantine omits the pre-Decian persecutors) and point to their ignominious destruction as evidence of God's retributive justice." See Schott, *Christianity, Empire, and the Making of Religion in Late Antiquity* (Philadelphia: University of Pennsylvania Press, 2008), 116. Schott affirms and expands on the work of Elizabeth Digeser, and both, as suggested, are attuned to the role of Lactantius in laying the rhetorical groundwork of Christian empire. See Digeser, *The Making of a Christian Empire: Lactantius and Rome* (Ithaca, NY: Cornell University Press, 2000).

88. Cons. Or. XXIV.1–3. All translations of the *Oration to the Assembly of the Saints* are from M. Edwards, *Constantine and Christendom* (Liverpool: Liverpool University Press, 2003).

89. Schott, *Christianity, Empire, and the Making of Religion*, 116. My emphasis.

90. Cons. Or. XVII.

91. Cons. Or. XXV.

92. VC IV.11.

order—the calm after the storm. In his letter to Shapur, Constantine refers to his victory over his enemies as "the general restoration of right," a restoration of peace in which all humanity can exalt, as the world revives "like a patient after treatment."[93] In his analysis of the *Oration*, Harold Drake notes that the "real subject" of the emperor's speech is a demonstration of God's providence, "the care that God exercises on behalf of those who worship him with true piety." Quoting the emperor's words, Drake points out that for both Eusebius and Constantine, God's providence consistently includes the Christian emperor's victories as much as the defeats of his opponents: "The world itself cries out and the pageant of stars shines brighter and more conspicuous, rejoicing (as I believe) in the *fitting judgment of unholy deeds*. The very times that succeed the wild and inhumane life are reckoned to rejoice because of their own good lot, and show *the goodwill of God* toward humankind."[94] But part of the result of Constantine's conversion and his linking of divine justice to his rise to power was the need to emphasize the providential aspect of his rule, along with his concern for Christians everywhere. Christians who had suffered under persecuting emperors needed reassurance of Constantine's fundamental difference from his predecessors. They needed an acknowledgment that he was *their* emperor.

This restoration of right order was what Constantine wished to announce to Shapur in his letter. In their literary works, Constantine, Eusebius, and Lactantius all put forth a new idea of a *Christian* Rome. While this was apparently not intended solely for consumption within the borders of the empire, it was not (at least initially) a way of injecting "religion" into foreign policy either. The logical leap from Constantine as a Christian—and, as his letter suggests, Constantine as a concerned father to Christians everywhere—to the idea of Rome as a fundamentally Christian empire with newfound subjects spread throughout Persia represents Eusebius's construction of Constantine. The emperor's letter was no precursor to any crusade, nor even a declaration of any fundamental change in the Roman Empire. It announced the restoration, not the institution, of order. As David Frendo reminds us, Constantine's letter was novel, as, "undoubtedly, new forces were at work, but one must not exaggerate their intensity or extent. What we are

---

93. *VC* IV.9.
94. Drake, *Constantine and the Bishops*, 296, with reference to Cons. *Or.* XXV (my emphasis).

witnessing are the first beginnings of a slow process of historical development and change."⁹⁵

Only in the fifth century, when tales about Christian martyrs in Persia began to reach the ears of Roman ecclesiastical historians, did Constantine's letter again come into play as a supposed factor in Shapur's persecution of Christians—and then, as I discuss in the next chapter, not as the cause but as the Roman emperor's response to the tremendous slaughter of Christians in Persia.

95. Frendo, "Constantine's Letter to Shapur," 65.

TWO

Constantine's Crusade

THE EMPEROR'S LAST DAYS AND
THE PERSIAN CAMPAIGN

IN CHAPTER 1, I ARGUED that Constantine's letter to Shapur II is an authentic imperial epistle that was probably written in 324/25. It is an undeniably novel sort of communication with a foreign king, but it bears clear literary and thematic resemblances to other Constantinian letters, to the Roman emperor's *Oration to the Assembly of the Saints,* and to the apologetic history *On the Deaths of the Persecutors* by Constantine's adviser Lactantius. Constantine's letter should be read as a reconceptualization of Roman history and a repudiation of his anti-Christian predecessors. Irrespective of how Shapur may have understood it, its tone, content, and context do not suggest that it was written near the end of the Roman emperor's life, nor that it was a prelude to a Roman military invasion of Persia on behalf of the Christians there. Nevertheless, the letter is often linked to Shapur's persecution of Christians in Persia and Constantine's ostensibly religious campaign on their behalf.

There is a very good reason for this: Constantine seems to have been preparing for war with Persia near the end of his life. Eusebius says that the emperor even discussed his plans with a group of bishops. But the war against Shapur was not for Constantine to wage. He died in May 337 at an imperial villa near the eastern shore of the Propontis (the Sea of Marmara), hundreds of miles from the Mesopotamian frontier. Almost immediately after Constantine's death the war began.[1] Hostilities persisted for the next quarter century, occupying the reigns of Constantine's son Constantius II and of Julian, who died in Mesopotamia in 363. The Christian soldier Jovian, elevated by the army as Julian's successor, was ultimately forced to cede a huge

---

1. See R. W. Burgess, "The Dates of the First Siege of Nisibis and the Death of James of Nisibis," *Byz* 69 (1999): 7–17.

swath of Roman Mesopotamia to Shapur in order to secure a peace and guarantee the safety of his beleaguered troops.

This war was hardly unprecedented. Persia was always a concern of Roman diplomacy, and the two empires frequently contested the important Mesopotamian borderlands. As a young man, Constantine fought under Diocletian and Galerius against the Persians. That time it was Shapur's grandfather Narseh who was on the losing end, in 299. The resulting treaty, which he had to negotiate while under duress, was never acceptable to the Persians.[2] In a letter to Constantius (from 358) that Ammianus Marcellinus quotes, Shapur explains his purpose in challenging the Romans as a "duty to recover Armenia with Mesopotamia, which double-dealing wrested from my grandfather."[3]

If Ammianus has faithfully represented Shapur's motivations, then Eusebius's comment about Constantine's defensive (not religious) preparations makes sense: "there were reports of disturbances among the eastern barbarians," he says, and Constantine was forced to take "military moves

---

2. For details of the peace treaty, see R. C. Blockley, "The Romano-Persian Peace Treaties of A.D. 299 and 363," *Florilegium* 6 (1984): 28–49.

3. Amm. Marc. XVII.5.6. All translations of the *Res Gestae* follow the Loeb edition of J. C. Rolfe, *Ammianus Marcellinus,* 3 vols. (London: Heinemann, 1935–40). Roman historians frequently interpret Persian territorial aims more grandly and with a classical context in mind, imagining Shapur's designs as akin to those of Darius or Xerxes and suggesting that the Persian king aimed to march all the way to Macedonia. See D. Frendo, "Sasanian Irredentism and the Foundation of Constantinople: Historical Truth and Historical Reality," *BAI* 6 (1992): 59–66. For thorough assessments of Shapur's motives, see M. R. Shayegan, "On the Rationale behind the Roman Wars of Šābuhr II the Great," *BAI* 18 (2004): 111–33; and K. Mosig-Walburg, *Römer und Perser: Vom 3. Jahrhundert bis zum Jahr 363 n. Chr.* (Gutenberg: Computus Druck Satz, 2009).

Citing Shapur's letter to Constantius, Alireza Shahbazi claims that the "memory of the Achaemenids" lingered in the Sasanian imagination until the time of Shapur II but "was lost with the rise of the 'State Religion' under Šāpūr II... [when] Zoroastrianism and Iranian sovereignty were threatened when Christianity became the official religion of the Roman empire." See A. S. Shahbazi, "Early Sasanians' Claim to Achaemenid Heritage," *IJAIS* 1 (2001): 69. Through the promotion of Zoroastrianism as the primary marker of Persian identity, Shahbazi argues, the memory of the Achaemenids was slowly lost and replaced by a particularly religious and Avestan memory of early Persian history. For a more moderate view, but one which also suggests that a Sasanian "national history" of the Achaemenid period changed as a result of later Zoroastrian rewriting, see J. Wiesehöfer, *Iraniens, grecs et romains,* StIran 32 (Leuven: Peeters, 2005), 129–49. Adam Becker's article challenging the idea of "state religion" in late antiquity is an important corrective to Shahbazi, Wiesehöfer, and others. See Becker, "Political Theology and Religious Diversity in the Sasanian Empire," in *Jews, Christians and Zoroastrians: Religious Dynamics in a Sasanian Context,* ed. G. Herman (Piscataway, NJ: Gorgias, 2014), 7–25.

against Persia."⁴ Other fourth-century commentators also saw Constantine's preparations as a necessary bulwark against a gathering Persian threat.⁵ Still, they were carried out with what might be called "religious" undertones.⁶ In chapter 56 of book IV of his *Life of Constantine*, Eusebius claims that the bishops at Constantine's court were eager to accompany the emperor on his campaign against the Sasanians: "Once the decision [to go to war] was made he set the military officers to work, and also discussed the campaign with the bishops at his court, planning that some of those needed for divine worship should be there with him. They said that they would only too gladly accompany him as he wished, and not shrink back, but would soldier with him and fight at his side with supplications to God. He was delighted with their promises and made arrangements for their journey..."⁷

But there ends the story. Given such a striking combination of martial and spiritual power, one would expect to hear more from Eusebius about Constantine's preparations for war and any further consultations he may have had with his bishops. Yet the ellipses concluding Eusebius's remarks signify an extended trailing off. In all the extant manuscripts of the *VC*, a substantial (half-page) lacuna follows this discussion between the emperor and his bishops, thereby obscuring what Eusebius might have said about what arrangements were made for the bishops or even what became of Constantine's campaign. Once the narrative resumes, in chapter 58 of book IV, it is in the middle of an altogether different topic—a description of a glorious shrine to the apostles in which Constantine hoped to be interred.

At least insofar as the manuscript evidence attests, Eusebius says nothing else about Constantine's preparations for war against the Persians. But chapter 57 of the *VC*, which is, in Garth Fowden's words, "a Renaissance scholar's attempt to plug" the half-page lacuna, does explain how Constantine arranged to have his bishops properly equipped for war.⁸ According to the

---

4. Euseb. *VC* IV.56.1. All citations of the *VC* are from the translation of A. Cameron and S. G. Hall, *Life of Constantine* (Oxford: Clarendon, 1999).

5. Robin Seager emphasizes that until Julian's death and Rome's defeat at Shapur's hands in 363, all commentators—not just Eusebius—perceived Constantine's posture toward Persia as defensive. See Seager, "Perceptions of Eastern Frontier Policy in Ammianus, Libanius, and Julian (337–363)," *CQ* 47 (1997): 253–68.

6. But cf. Mosig-Walburg, *Römer und Perser*, 267–82, which expresses skepticism that religious concerns may have motivated the war.

7. *VC* IV.56.2–3.

8. G. Fowden, "The Last Days of Constantine: Oppositional Versions and Their Influence," *JRS* 84 (1994): 147.

plug, which may be an expansion of Eusebian chapter headings, Constantine ordered that a tent be fashioned into a portable church so that he would have an appropriate place in which to "make supplications to God the Giver of victory together with the bishops" while he was on campaign.⁹

Constantine never had an opportunity to use his traveling church. The same plug that fills the lacuna with news about the tent church also explains how the emperor's campaign ended before it began: "Meanwhile the Persians, learning of the Emperor's preparations for war, and being much afraid of doing battle with him, asked him by an embassy to make peace. At this the most pacific Emperor received the Persian embassy, and gladly came to friendly terms with them."¹⁰ Neither Eusebius nor the later editor who informs us about the tent church and the Persian embassy discusses Constantine's campaign any further.

In his meticulous survey of the last days of Constantine's life, Fowden argues that we should be suspicious of this lacuna in the *VC*, to say nothing of Eusebius's apparent reluctance to discuss the emperor's Persian campaign. Fowden claims that the lacuna is clear evidence "that something is being hidden from us" by whoever is responsible for the break in the text. It is "beyond doubt," he says, that Constantine was unable or unwilling to resolve the conflict with Shapur peaceably before it began and that the Christian emperor died en route to war. Plenty of non-Christian historians, including "Libanius, Julian, [the author of] the *Origo Constantini,* Sextus Aurelius Victor, Eutropius, and Festus," Fowden writes, "all state or suggest that Constantine died on campaign"—an "unfortunate and embarrassing" truth that, in his view, Eusebius and all subsequent Christian commentators preferred to cover up or avoid altogether.¹¹ Many who have written about

---

9. *VC* IV.57.

10. *VC* IV.57. On the Persian embassy at this time, see A. D. Lee, "Embassies as Evidence for the Movement of Military Intelligence between the Roman and Sasanian Empires," in *The Defence of the Roman and Byzantine East,* ed. P. Freeman and D. Kennedy (Oxford: BAR International Editions, 1986), 456; and K. Mosig-Walburg, "Zur Westpolitik Shāpūrs II.," in *Iran, questions et connaissances: Actes du IVᵉ congrès européen des études iraniennes, organisé par la Societas Iranologica Europaea, Paris, 6–10 septembre 1999,* vol. 1, *La période ancienne,* ed. P. Huyse (Leuven: Peeters, 2002), 329–47.

11. G. Fowden, "Last Days of Constantine," 148. In their commentary on the *VC,* Averil Cameron and Stuart Hall insist that there is "no reason to suspect deliberate tampering with the text or to suppose that Eusebius himself is hiding something." See Cameron and Hall, *Life of Constantine,* 336. On the other hand, Richard Burgess agrees with Fowden, pointing to "Eusebius' omission of Constantine's Persian campaign and his reworking of the narrative to cover the omission" as evidence of a cover-up. Burgess concludes that in addition to his

Constantine and the Christians of Persia share Fowden's perspective. Vincenzo Poggi, for instance, says that the lacuna is an intentional omission and that whoever was responsible for it evidently thought it very important to hide Constantine's failed attempt to help the Christians of Persia.[12]

In this chapter, I reconsider Constantine's planned campaign against Persia and the connections that have been drawn among the emperor's war plans, his letter to Shapur, and the persecution of Christians in the Sasanian Empire. I argue that the war fought after Constantine's death had nothing to do with Christians, even though it was later narrated in ways that suggest it did. Constantine was preparing to engage Shapur in 337, but what was at stake were the security and territorial integrity of the Roman eastern frontier, not the lives of Christians beyond the border. Yet because Constantine's final days were directed toward the East, they were inevitably reread against the backdrop of his letter to Shapur and the Syriac martyrdom narratives that later emerged from both Sasanian Persia and Roman Mesopotamia. The second half of the book addresses the Syriac martyrdom literature about Constantine and the Christians of the West. In this chapter I focus on how Roman ecclesiastical historians reread the emperor's last days based on Eusebius's account of his life. Of particular interest, of course, is the letter to Shapur in the *VC* and Eusebius's construction of Constantine as a second Moses—an emperor who commissioned a wilderness tabernacle (a traveling tent church) for his bishops and hoped to be baptized in the Jordan.[13]

THE PERSIAN WAR AND ITS AFTERMATH

Although hostilities between Rome and Persia began in 337, Shapur did not establish a true foothold in Roman Mesopotamia for another two decades. Once it became apparent to Constantius that defeating Shapur would require his full attention, he requested reinforcements from among Julian's army in

---

"failed Persian expedition," Constantine's baptism at the hands of Eusebius of Nicomedia was cause for concern among later Christians. See Burgess, "ΑΧΥΡΩΝ or ΠΡΟΑΣΤΕΙΟΝ: The Location and Circumstances of Constantine's Death," *JTS* 50 (1999): 156, 161.

12. See V. Poggi, "Costantino e la chiesa di Persia," in *Costantino il Grande nell'età bizantina: Atti del Convegno internazionale di studio, Ravenna, 5–8 aprile 2001* (*Bizantinistica* V), ed. G. Bonamente and A. Carile (Spoleto: Fondazione Centro italiano di studi sull'alto medioevo, 2003), 68.

13. *VC* IV.58, 62.

the West. Neither the preoccupied western army nor Julian had any intention of trekking all the way from Gaul to Persia. Julian's rebellious troops proclaimed him emperor in 360, and, by the summer of the following year, he and Constantius were on the verge of civil war. After Constantius fell ill and died that November, Julian found himself alone atop the Roman Empire.[14]

A year and a half later, in the spring of 363, Julian set out on an ill-fated mission to end Shapur's harassment of Roman Mesopotamia once and for all. Desire to win the support of Constantius's former troops in the East and to acquire the prestige of victory over a respectable foe may have had more than a little to do with Julian's decision to march on Persia.[15] The emperor and a huge contingent of troops left Antioch with the grand aim of capturing Ctesiphon, the Persian capital on the Tigris in central Mesopotamia. Needless to say, the Christians of Persia were nowhere on the mind of Julian, the "Apostate."

Just two months after departing from Antioch, Julian's army had already won a major battle within sight of Ctesiphon's walls. The Romans seemed poised to take the city and with it a strategic hold on all of central Mesopotamia. But the victory was short lived. Julian and his generals were unable to consolidate their gains against the heavily fortified Ctesiphon, and the Persian army, drawing upon reinforcements, was still strong enough to force the Romans into retreat. Falling back to the western side of the limes was an unworkable proposition, since the Roman army was on the eastern side of the Tigris and had no easy means of fording the river. Before Julian could lead his army north into safer territory, he was wounded by a spear and died.[16] The trapped and demoralized Roman army elected Jovian, a Christian, to succeed

---

14. See R.C. Blockley, "Constantius II and Persia," in *Studies in Latin Literature and Roman History* V (*Latomus: Revue d'études latines* 206), ed. C. Deroux (Brussels: Latomus, 1989), 465–90.

15. Ammianus, whose history lauds Julian at the expense of other emperors, is especially negative toward Constantius. For a summary of the views of Ammianus and other ancient historians vis-à-vis Constantius, see H.C. Teitler, "Ammianus and Constantius: Image and Reality," in *Cognitio Gestorum: The Historiographic Art of Ammianus Marcellinus*, ed. J. den Boeft, D. den Hengst, and Teitler (Amsterdam: Royal Netherlands Academy of Arts and Sciences, 1992), 117–22.

16. Amm. Marc. XXV.3.6 indicates that Julian was hit in the liver with a spear. While Ammianus blames no one in particular, Libanius (*Or.* XVIII.274.5) claims that Christians in the Roman army were probably responsible. This is not an idea from which Christian historians shied away. Sozomen (*HE* VI.1–2) quotes Libanius and confirms that a Christian probably did kill Julian.

Julian and to negotiate the terms of a humiliating surrender. He ceded five provinces and more than a dozen fortified cities, including the great city of Nisibis, to the Persians.[17]

Christian historians of the period forgave Jovian's territorial concessions as lamentable yet unavoidable, given the precarious situation of the Roman army.[18] They sought to pin ultimate responsibility for the defeat on the anti-Christian Julian. As Fowden explains, however, non-Christian historians tended to see things differently. They shifted their perspective to the long view following Julian's death. Looking back over the course of the war to Constantine's initial false start against Persia in 337, non-Christian historians declared that he was to blame—he was the warmonger who had initiated the improvident and unnecessary campaign in the first place. As Fowden puts it, what "had seemed a justifiable response to Sasanian aggression, came to be represented, in the light of the dismal subsequent history of Romano-Iranian relations, as frivolous and culpable aggression."[19] The struggle over how to represent Constantine and write the history of the fourth century had begun.

The Letter to Shapur and the Persian War

For non-Christian historians such as Ammianus, the fourth-century conflict between Rome and Persia was (and always had been) territorial in nature—a border dispute. But even the relatively temperate Ammianus suggests that Constantius, Julian, and finally Jovian were left to clean up a mess that Constantine had started. Still, Ammianus gives little credence to the idea that Constantine's war was predicated on religious ideals. In fact, he cites avarice as Constantine's primary motivation, claiming that "it was not Julian, but Constantine, who kindled the Parthian fires, when he confided too greedily in the lies of Metrodorus."[20]

---

17. On the loss of Nisibis, see J. Teixidor, "Conséquences politiques et culturelles de la victoire sassanide à Nisibe," in *Les relations internationales: Actes du Colloque de Strasbourg,* ed. E. Frézouls and A. Jacquemin (Paris: De Boccard, 1995), 499–510; and R. Turcan, "L'Abandon de Nisibe et l'opinion publique (363 ap. J.-C.)," in *Mélanges d'archéologie et d'histoire offerts à André Piganiol,* ed. R. Chevallier (Paris: Service d'édition et de vente des publications de l'Education nationale, 1966), 875–90.

18. At the end of "L'Abandon de Nisibe," Turcan provides an overview of all the late ancient commentators' perspectives on the "abandonment" of Nisibis. The general sentiment is that it was necessary, albeit regrettable.

19. G. Fowden, "Last Days of Constantine," 150.

20. Amm. Marc. XXV.4.23.

The "lies of Metrodorus" is an apocryphal tale preserved in just two places: the eleventh-century history of George Cedrenus and this glancing mention by Ammianus. Unfortunately, the section of the *Res Gestae* that relates the story of Metrodorus in full is lost, but Cedrenus explains that Metrodorus was a philosopher (apparently of Persian origin) who had traveled between the Roman Empire and India. After a long stay in the East, he returned to the West, bringing with him many precious jewels. Some of these were gifts for Constantine from the king of India, while Metrodorus had duplicitously acquired others for himself. When Constantine saw the jewels, their fineness and beauty amazed him. Metrodorus explained that the hoard had once been much larger but that the Persians had confiscated many jewels along the way. Confiding in these "lies," Constantine wrote to Shapur and demanded the return of the stolen jewels. Shapur scoffed at the emperor's letter, and, so the story goes, Constantine began preparing for war.[21]

While scholars have dismissed Constantine's anger over stolen jewels as a farfetched motive for war, they have seen the emperor's Christian faith as a much more plausible explanation. Jan Willem Drijvers, for instance, remarks how strange it is that Ammianus cites the lies of Metrodorus as a spur for war but then fails to mention Shapur's persecution of Christians.[22] According to Timothy Barnes, Constantine's letter to Shapur is what tipped the already precarious balance between Rome and Persia. The emperor's letter, he says, fundamentally altered the nature of the conflict and "injected a religious dimension into a normal frontier dispute."[23] Shapur was not bothered by the

---

21. Cedrenus mentions Shapur's persecution, claiming that eighteen thousand Christians were killed in the "twenty-first year" of Constantine's reign (326/27), but he cites the jewel heist as the primary reason for the war. See I. Bekker, *Synopsis Historiarum* I.516–17, CSHB (Bonn, 1838); and B. H. Warmington, "Ammianus Marcellinus and the Lies of Metrodorus," *CQ* 31 (1981): 464–68.

22. See J. W. Drijvers, "Ammianus Marcellinus' Image of Sasanian Society," in *Ērān ud Anērān: Studien zu den Beziehungen zwischen dem Sasanidenreich und der Mittelmeerwelt—Beiträge des Internationalen Colloquiums in Eutin, 8–9 Juni 2000*, ed. J. Wiesehöfer and P. Huyse (Stuttgart: Franz Steiner Verlag, 2006), 48.

23. T. D. Barnes, "Constantine and the Christians of Persia," *JRS* 75 (1985): 136. Earlier in this article, Barnes claims that Constantine intended "to conduct his Persian expedition as a religious crusade" (132). For the same characterization of Constantine's final campaign, see Barnes, *Constantine and Eusebius* (Cambridge, MA: Harvard University Press, 1981), 259. While scholars of Sasanian Iran might avoid the term *crusade,* they tend to agree that Constantine instigated the war. See, for example, J. Wiesehöfer, "'Geteilte Loyalitäten': Religiöse Minderheiten des 3. und 4. Jahrhunderts n. Chr. im Spannungsfeld zwischen Rom und dem sasanidischen Iran," *Klio* 75 (1993): 377.

Christians in his empire until Constantine made Christianity a sticking point and until there were open hostilities with Rome.[24]

In this reading of fourth-century history, not only was there a persecution of Christians in Persia, but Constantine was unwittingly responsible for it: he wrote the letter to Shapur; he undertook military measures against the Sasanians; he led Shapur to be wary of a Christian fifth column in his empire. One would therefore expect to find in Christian histories of this period some connection between Constantine's letter and his Persian campaign. But there is no such connection. Of the two fifth-century Roman ecclesiastical historians who discuss Constantine's letter and the persecution of Christians in Persia, neither refers to the Roman emperor's campaign and both mangle the chronology.

The Letter to Shapur According to Sozomen and Theodoret

The church historian Sozomen was born in Gaza several decades after Constantine's death, around 400. His Christian family was wealthy, and he trained as a lawyer. When Sozomen was in his early forties, around 443, he was living in Constantinople, possibly working at the court of Theodosius II. It was then that he wrote his extensive *Church History*. Although Sozomen uses many sources, he relies particularly heavily on the *Church History* of Socrates, which had only just been finished when Sozomen started his work. For the first two books of his *History*, which discuss the reign of Constantine, Sozomen also draws heavily on Eusebius—notably the *VC*. Sozomen's work is of special interest among the many Roman ecclesiastical histories from late antiquity because it provides an extensive account of Shapur's persecution of

---

24. See the classic study of Christianity in Persia by J. Labourt, *Le christianisme dans l'empire perse sous la dynastie sassanide (224–632)* (Paris: Librairie Victor Lecoffre, 1904), 56. Sebastian Brock also notes the connection between war and persecution, saying, "Significantly, persecution was most likely to take place in the Persian Empire during times of hostility between the two empires, and this was particularly the case in the mid fourth century, when it continued on and off during the last 35 years of the long reign of Shapur II (309–79)." See Brock, *The History of the Holy Mar Ma'in with a Guide to the Persian Martyr Acts*, Persian Martyr Acts in Syriac: Text and Translation, fasc. 1. (Piscataway, NJ: Gorgias, 2009), vii. There are a few martyr acts from the time of Shapur set prior to Simeon's death and the commencement of the "Great Persecution." One of these, the *Martyrdom of Zebina and His Companions*, dates to the eighteenth year of Shapur's reign (327). According to this narrative, the martyrs were persecuted not for political reasons or because of their purported allegiance to Rome but simply for refusing to worship "fire, the sun, and water." See *AMS* II, 39–51.

Christians.²⁵ Near the end of his narrative about Christianity in Persia, Sozomen calculates that Shapur must have killed at least sixteen thousand Christians in his realm. According to Sozomen, in some places the bodies were piled so high that those who sought to keep track of the martyrs were overwhelmed. Just registering the names of the dead was unmanageable. Most never had the stories of their heroic deeds written down.²⁶

Some stories, however, were preserved. And Sozomen summarizes several of them, beginning with the trial and death of Simeon bar Ṣabbaʿe, the bishop of Seleucia-Ctesiphon on the Tigris.²⁷ Sozomen's account suggests that he, or his source, had access to not just oral narratives but also written accounts of the martyrs—possibly already in Greek translation—and demonstrates broad knowledge of this literature.²⁸ Hewing closely to the story set forth in the Syriac *Martyrdom of Blessed Simeon bar Ṣabbaʿe* (as opposed to the later *History of Simeon,* which Sozomen did not know), he says that the Persians persecuted Christians because the Jews and the magi in Persia had accused Simeon of betraying secrets to the "Caesar of the Romans."²⁹ According to Simeon's acts, the bishop was killed in 339/40, two or three years after Constantine's death.³⁰ But Sozomen inverts the order of events. Whether through guile or ignorance (probably ignorance), in his retelling of the story Constantine was alive when Christians were being persecuted, and the emperor wrote his letter to Shapur with the hope of dissuading the Sasanian king from killing even more Christians. Still, Sozomen draws no connection between Shapur's persecution and Constantine's letter or any planned campaign against Persia. After recounting the trials of Simeon and several other martyrs, he simply says that Constantine was angry to hear about the suffering of Christians in Persia and hoped to assist them. According to Sozomen, around the time when Constantine first heard about

25. Soz. *HE* II.9–14.
26. Soz. *HE* II.14.5.
27. Most of Sozomen's reflections on the martyrs of Persia (*HE* II.9–12) stem from Simeon's acts and narratives about martyrs from Beth Huzaye. See K. Smith, *The Martyrdom and History of Blessed Simeon bar Ṣabbaʿe,* Persian Martyr Acts in Syriac: Text and Translation, fasc. 3. (Piscataway, NJ: Gorgias, 2014), xxiv–xli.
28. See Brock, *History of the Holy Mar Maʿin,* 91, for a list of Syriac martyrdom narratives in Greek translation. For some of the texts themselves, see H. Delehaye, *Les versions grecques des actes des martyrs persans sous Sapor II,* PO 2.4 (Paris: Firmin-Didot, 1907).
29. Soz. *HE* II.9.1–2.
30. Others have dated Simeon's death to 344. See Smith, *Martyrdom and History,* xx–xxii.

the persecution, some ambassadors from Persia arrived at his court. After he "granted their requests," he wrote a letter to Shapur on behalf of the persecuted Christians living in Persia.[31]

The letter to Shapur in Sozomen is clearly a synopsis of the one that Eusebius preserves in the *VC*. Sozomen's quotations are garbled and only roughly in accord with Eusebius's version. The gruff textual note in the Nicene Fathers' edition of Sozomen's *HE* bears repeating: "As usual, Soz. quotes briefly, and with no regard to the language and little to the thought."[32] Still, Sozomen's summary conveys the general sense of Constantine's letter and successfully encapsulates its main points. But it has most certainly only a tepid approximation of the original letter's rhetorical force. Sozomen's Constantine—in contradistinction to Eusebius's self-assured and confident leader—is deferential and submissive. Rather than magnify his accomplishments effected through the power of the Christian god, Sozomen's Constantine pleads with the Persian king to recognize that Christianity is a pure and peaceful religion.[33] Sozomen's Constantine is perplexed over how best to address the persecution or effectively win the safety of Persian Christians. Rather than take immediate measures on hearing of the tragic events in the East, according to Sozomen, he waited for a favorable opportunity—namely, the departure of the visiting ambassadors—to write a letter to Shapur in which he could request an end to the violence.[34]

Sozomen may have been trying to preserve Constantine's legacy by covering up the emperor's preparations for a campaign against Shapur, but his account does little to advance the emperor's image. In his telling, plenty of Christian blood was shed while Constantine stood idly by. From Eusebius to Sozomen, Constantine transforms from a victor over the enemies of the people of God into a rather impotent king whose too little, too late response to overwhelming violence against Christians is merely a letter of protest. Sozomen fails to confirm that Constantine's letter was even successful in ending the persecution. Before explaining (in his next chapter) how Constantine's baptizer, Eusebius of Nicomedia, was restored to his see after a temporary exile for Arianism, Sozomen simply remarks that Constantine,

---

31. Soz. *HE* II.15.1.

32. P. Schaff and H. Wace, *A Select Library of Nicene and Post-Nicene Fathers of the Christian Church*, vol. 2 (New York: Christian Literature, 1890), 268n1.

33. Soz. *HE* II.15.3. Sozomen's version of the letter does include the fate of Valerian as an example of what happens to those who persecute Christians.

34. Soz. *HE* II.15.2.

by writing to Shapur, sought to express his concern for Christians of every place, both Roman and foreign.[35] He says nothing else about the persecution and nothing at all about any planned campaign against the Persians.

Theodoret of Cyrrhus, the only other fifth-century Roman ecclesiastical historian to engage the plight of Christians in Persia at any length, reads the letter to Shapur in the same framework that Sozomen outlines. Although Theodoret quotes the entirety of the emperor's letter as the *VC* preserves it—and should thus appreciate its fraternal tone and the emperor's pleasure to hear about the spread of Christianity in Persia—he too misunderstands its chronological context. He says that Constantine wrote to Shapur after hearing that Christians were being persecuted in Persia.[36] Putting aside this similarity, Theodoret's narrative is very different from Sozomen's report. This is not surprising. Although Theodoret's *Church History* was completed after Sozomen's (around 450), he relies on Sozomen very little, basing his stridently anti-Arian history mainly on the works of Eusebius and Rufinus. Whereas Sozomen knows a number of Syriac martyrdom narratives set in the 330s and provides many details about Christians in Persia, Theodoret hardly mentions them. He gives neither an approximation of the scale of the violence nor a single martyr's name. According to Theodoret, Constantine wrote to Shapur out of a desire to protect the Christians of Persia once he learned that they were being persecuted and that the Persian king was concocting further plans to destroy them.[37]

Like Sozomen, Theodoret concludes by emphasizing that Constantine was so solicitous about Christians that he watched over those who were the subjects of other kings.[38] Yet he too fails to indicate whether Constantine's letter had the desired effect of ending the persecution. Theodoret, more than Sozomen, stresses that Constantine overcame all foreign adversaries, through either war or diplomacy, and that trophies of the emperor's victories were erected everywhere.[39] He thus implies that Shapur submitted to Constantine but never says so explicitly.

If Constantine was planning a crusade on behalf of the Christians of Persia, then neither Sozomen nor Theodoret seems to have gotten the message. In their reading, his letter did not ignite Shapur's persecution; rather, it

---

35. Soz. *HE* II.15.5.
36. Theod. *HE* I.23–24.
37. Theod. *HE* I.23.
38. Soz. *HE* II.15.5; Theod. *HE* I.24.
39. Theod. *HE* I.24.

was an attempt to douse the existing flames. Instead of covering up the beginnings of a failed war, Sozomen and Theodoret present an idealized account of Constantine based on the histories they had received: he was a patron and protector of Christians. If they confused the details, mangled their sources, or misunderstood what happened when and to whom, this can be taken as the consequence of messy and piecemeal historiographical work—not a calculated attempt at a cover-up.

THE ROAD TO ANTIOCH: CONSTANTINE'S BAPTISM AND TENT CHURCH

What is most notable about the histories of Sozomen and Theodoret is that although neither mentions that Constantine planned to go to war on behalf of the Christians of Persia, both read the emperor's letter to Shapur as evidence of his sincere interest in the Christians' well-being—even if, as the historians' chronologically inverted readings attest, the letter was addressed to a king who had already proved to be a persecutor of Christians. They believed that Constantine was the patron he said he was, but they did not extend the emperor's patronage to planned military action against Persia. In fact, not one of Eusebius's continuators mentions the Persian campaign at the end of Constantine's life.[40] As Eusebius tells it, after the Persian issue was peaceably resolved, Constantine went to his villa near Nicomedia—for health reasons, not as a stopover on his way to Mesopotamia.

Constantine's Baptism

Eusebius suggests that at some point after Easter in 337, when the dispute with the Persians had supposedly been resolved, the emperor took ill and so went to the hot baths in Constantinople. He soon realized that he was dying and thus decided to retire from the hustle and bustle of the capital to the more pleasant air of Nicomedia, which had been his interim capital and main residence from 324 to 330. At Nicomedia, Constantine gathered his bishops

---

40. See G. Fowden, "Last Days of Constantine," 152: "Rufinus (d. 410) says nothing of the Iranian campaign in his account of Constantine's death [*HE* X.12]; neither do Philostorgius (d. *c.* 439) [*HE* II.16], Socrates (d. after 439) [*HE* I.39], Sozomen (d. after 450) [*HE* II.34.21], or Theodoret (d. *c.* 466) [*HE* I.32]."

and received baptism.[41] In his speech before his baptism, Constantine acknowledged that although he "once intended to receive [baptism] at the streams of the river Jordan," God, "who knows what is good for us," did not allow this to come to pass.[42]

In Eusebius's discussion of Constantine's baptism, there is no mention of military preparations nor any hint that Constantine had been on his way to Persia. There may thus be a rather simple explanation for why not one of the church historians writing after Eusebius mentions Constantine's "Persian" campaign: if they took his account of Constantine's last days at face value, then there would have been no need to cover up the emperor's campaign, because, insofar as they could gather from Eusebius, there was no campaign.

Still, even though Eusebius does not say it, there is reason to believe that Constantine was in the process of staging a campaign against Persia when he was in Nicomedia, as so many non-Christian historians seem to believe. Nicomedia was on the road to Antioch, the city where Constantius was in residence and from which any assault on Persia would necessarily begin.[43] Further, Eusebius acknowledges that Constantine had convened his war council in preparation for "military moves against Persia,"[44] but then the notorious lacuna follows and neither Persia nor any war is mentioned again. So does Eusebius's account of the Persian campaign contradict those of non-Christian historians? Did he and his heirs intentionally hide Constantine's preparations for war? And did any of this have anything to do with the Christians of Persia?

A confrontation between the Romans and the Persians had, by all accounts, been brewing for some time, and whether or not a Persian embassy visited the Roman Empire to stave off the conflict, Constantine died—even according to Eusebius's chronology of events—within weeks of his initial

---

41. See *VC* IV.61–64; Cameron and Hall, *Life of Constantine*, 339–41; and B. Bleckmann and H. Schneider, *Eusebius von Caesarea, De Vita Constantini, Über das Leben Konstantins* (Turnhout: Brepols, 2007), 90–91. That the Arian bishop Eusebius of Nicomedia presided over Constantine's baptism was perhaps the most embarrassing aspect of the emperor's last days for some commentators writing several centuries later. Theophanes, a ninth-century Byzantine chronicler, claims it is a lie and that the bishop Sylvester baptized Constantine in Rome. See Theoph. *Chron.*, AM 5828. The translation and commentary in C. Mango and R. Scott, *The Chronicle of Theophanes Confessor: Byzantine and Near Eastern History, AD 284–813* (Oxford: Clarendon, 1997), are invaluable for making sense of this historian.

42. *VC* IV.62.2.

43. See Burgess, "ΑΧΥΡΩΝ or ΠΡΟΑΣΤΕΙΟΝ," 159–60, which notes that Nicomedia "was the standard launching point for a journey across Asia to Antioch."

44. *VC* IV.56.1.

preparations for war. As a result, claiming that the emperor had died while on campaign or at least while beginning preparations for war would have been a legitimate way of narrating his last major political act. The epitome of the Latin historian Festus, for example, notes that Constantine "prepared an expedition against the Persians toward the end of his life," but Festus also seems to indicate that the war never happened. Sounding much like Eusebius, he explains that on hearing that Constantine was marching toward Persia, "the court at Babylonia went into such a panic that a suppliant legation of Persians went to him with all haste, promising to do what he commanded."[45]

Because of the nature of the sort of history they were writing, to say nothing of their personal views about the importance of the emperor's Christianity, Festus, Libanius, and other pagan historians had no interest in continuing their narratives about the end of Constantine's life until its last day. The emperor's baptism and his supposed speech to the bishops gathered at Nicomedia were of no concern to them. In fact, in contrast to Eusebius, some non-Christian historians mention that the sighting of a comet foretold the emperor's death[46]—an astrological sign that Eusebius omitted for reasons opposite why non-Christian historians omitted any discussion of the emperor's baptism. Eusebius was writing a fundamentally different sort of history than that of Festus or Libanius. He wanted to leave his readers with an account of Constantine's piety and formal submission to the fold of Christ. He can thus hardly be faulted for focusing on the emperor's baptism—not astrological omens or negotiations with Persian envoys—as the most memorable episode at the close of Constantine's life.[47]

Constantine as a Second Moses: The Tent Church

Although we learn little from Eusebius about Constantine's preparations for war, there is, as I have noted, some information about them in the material that plugged the lacuna—namely, a reference to Constantine's tent church.[48]

---

45. Fest. *Brev.* 26.6–13. Translation by M. H. Dodgeon, in Dodgeon and S. N. C. Lieu, eds., *The Roman Eastern Frontier and the Persian Wars, AD 226–363: A Documentary History* (London: Routledge, 1991), 159.

46. See Aur. Vict. *Caes.* 41.16; Eutr. *Brev.* X.8.2.

47. See Bleckmann and Schneider, *Eusebius von Caesarea*, 91.

48. The plug may be an expansion of a Eusebian chapter heading that mentions the tent church. See G. Fowden, "Last Days of Constantine," 147n4–7; see also the commentary of Cameron and Hall, *Life of Constantine*, 335–37.

The statement about it follows naturally from the emperor's discussion with his bishops. They had agreed "that some of those needed for divine worship" should accompany Constantine to Persia, and it is fitting to explain where and how that worship might have taken place.[49]

This is not, however, the only time that Eusebius talks about Constantine's "tent," so the reference to it in the lacuna plug should not be read as a sign that the Persian campaign was unique or uniquely religious in nature. When Eusebius mentions the tent elsewhere in the *VC,* he takes care to connect it with Moses's tabernacle. This parallel would have been familiar to readers of his *Church History* too. In that text, Eusebius presents the emperor's victory at the Milvian Bridge as a recurrence of Moses's victory over the Egyptians. Just as the parted Red Sea closed up and swallowed Pharaoh's army after Moses had led his people across its bed, a bridge of conjoined boats collapsed under Maxentius and his infantry, who sank "like lead in much water" (Exodus 15:10) and drowned as punishment for rejecting the divine power that accompanied Constantine.[50]

Eusebius returns to the parallel between Constantine and Moses, between the Milvian Bridge and the Red Sea, in book I of the *VC.*[51] Indeed, his comparisons of Constantine and Moses are much more pervasive in the *VC* than in the *HE*. Yet they are not peppered throughout his panegyric. Rather, they cluster almost entirely in book I and the first parts of book II. They virtually disappear by book IV, in which Eusebius discusses Constantine's letter to Shapur and last days.[52] In book II, narrating Constantine's war with Licinius, Eusebius mentions that he "pitched his tent outside the camp a long way off, and there he observed a chaste and pure rule of life, offering up his prayers to God, just like that ancient prophet of God, who, so the divine oracles assure us, pitched the tent outside the encampment."[53] No such refer-

---

49. *VC* IV.56.2–3.

50. Euseb. *HE* IX.9.3–8. See also M.J. Hollerich, "The Comparison of Moses and Constantine in Eusebius of Caesarea's *Life of Constantine,*" *SP* 19 (1989): 80–85; Hollerich, "Religion and Politics in the Writings of Eusebius: Reassessing the First 'Court Theologian,'" *CH* 59 (1990): 309–25; and the more recent R. Van Dam, *Remembering Constantine at the Milvian Bridge* (Cambridge: Cambridge University Press, 2014).

51. *VC* I.38.

52. The idea of Constantine as Moses is hard to shake. Claudia Rapp accounts for the dearth of references to Moses in books III and IV of the *VC* by claiming that Eusebius did not have an opportunity to fully develop the parallel there. See Rapp, "Imperial Ideology in the Making: Eusebius of Caesarea on Constantine as 'Bishop,'" *JTS* 49 (1998): 695.

53. *VC* II.12.1.

ence is found in book IV. In other words, Eusebius does not present Constantine as a Moses figure for the Christians of Persia, although he does present him as such for the Christians of the Roman Empire.

Moreover, there is no evidence that later ecclesiastical historians took the references to a tent church to mean that Constantine saw himself as a second Moses, for the Christians of Persia. Socrates, one of the few Christian historians of this period to mention Constantine's Persian campaign, repeats the explanation that a peace agreement prevented the war. After discussing the construction of the tent church and, notably, comparing it to Moses's tabernacle, he concludes his version of the story by saying, "The war was not carried out at that time," because the Persians feared Constantine. Socrates never mentions either Constantine's letter to Shapur or any persecution of Christians in Persia.[54]

In Sozomen's presentation, Constantine's tent was something that the pious emperor carried with him on all his campaigns. It was not a marker that distinguished a particularly "religious" campaign from a nonreligious one—such a distinction would not even make sense in a late antique context.[55] According to Sozomen, the tent was more of a precaution. It could be unfurled when the emperor found himself in some deserted place beyond easy reach of a church. Moreover, Sozomen does not associate the tent with Constantine's last days or even a campaign against the Persians—in fact, he does not mention the Persians at all when he discusses it, nor does he connect it with any particular war. It was, quite simply, just part of the standard field kit for a campaigning Christian king who liked to keep his devotions. All Constantine's victories were thanks to God.[56] But what is remarkable about

---

54. Soc. *HE* I.18.12. Garth Fowden suggests that Socrates may have gleaned his information not from the *VC* but from an intermediary source—namely, the late fourth-century *Church History* of Gelasius of Caesarea. See G. Fowden, "Last Days of Constantine," 147. He bases this argument on the fact that the late fifth-century church historian Gelasius of Cyzicus (not Caesarea) relates a similar story and seems to draw on the same source as Socrates—the *History* of Gelasius of Caesarea. Gelasius of Cyzicus, like Socrates, mentions Constantine's campaign and goes on to claim that the emperor decided against an invasion of Persia out of concern over possible repercussions for the Christians living there (*HE* III.10.26–27).

55. Soz. *HE* I.8.10–11.

56. "When Constantine concluded a treaty with the Goths in 332, and again when he concluded a treaty with the Sarmatians in 334, he insisted on including religious stipulations, which enabled him (and his panegyrist Eusebius) to claim that he had converted the northern barbarians." See Barnes, "Constantine and the Christians of Persia," 131, with reference to *VC* IV.5–6.

that? "Close association with divinity," as Hal Drake rightly notes, "was an important part of a late Roman ruler's claim to legitimacy"[57]—*any* late Roman ruler's claim to legitimacy, Christian or pagan.

Did Constantine Think of Himself as Moses?

While it may not be possible to know whether it was Constantine or Eusebius who initiated the idea of Constantine as bishop (Constantine refers to himself as a bishop to "those outside" at *VC* IV.24), the evidence for the idea of Constantine as Moses lies squarely (and solely) at the feet of Eusebius. In contrast to Eusebius, Constantine never compares himself to Moses, although he does, like Eusebius, compare the tyrants who preceded him on the throne to biblical persecutors.[58] In fact, in his *Oration to the Assembly of the Saints,* Constantine brings up Moses, who defeated Pharaoh through prayer alone, and Daniel, who gave godly counsel to Nebuchadnezzar.[59] In neither instance, however, does he construct himself as Moses. Rather, he seeks to demonstrate (as in his letter to Shapur) the terrible end to which the tyrants who ignore prophecy and persecute the people of God will come. He does not number himself among the prophets.

Without question, the comparison of Constantine to Moses was Eusebius's narrative innovation. It was a historiographical creation necessary for constructing a new sort of emperor who, nevertheless, had deep roots in the past. The *VC* is Eusebius's vision of Constantine the Christian emperor, not Constantine's self-conception, and, as Drake argues, "historians must remain alive to a difference in priorities between the two."[60] Clearly, there was a burgeoning appreciation of the interrelationship and interpenetration of

---

57. H. A. Drake, *Constantine and the Bishops: The Politics of Intolerance* (Baltimore: Johns Hopkins University Press, 2000), 296.

58. Cons. *Or.* XXVII.

59. Cons. *Or.* XVI, XVII.

60. As Drake memorably suggests, although "Eusebius and Constantine spoke a common language ... it may have been just enough of a common language for them to completely misunderstand one another." See Drake, "What Eusebius Knew: The Genesis of the *Vita Constantini*," *CP* 83 (1988): 37–38. See also Drake, *Constantine and the Bishops,* especially chapter 10, in which he discusses how Eusebius created a portrait of the emperor that extended beyond Constantine's own use of Christianity to mostly politicizing ends. Although his reading of Eusebius is ultimately quite different from Drake's, J.-M. Sansterre emphasizes that Eusebius's vision of Constantine's role exceeded that of the emperor himself. See Sansterre, "Eusèbe de Césarée et la naissance de la théorie 'césaropapiste,'" *Byz* 42 (1972): 131–95, 532–94.

church and empire in the person of Constantine during the latter years of his reign—an idea expressed most notably in Eusebius's later works, such as the *VC*—but the reality of this nascent idea was not manifest by the end of Constantine's life, nor even immediately thereafter. Eusebius, as Averil Cameron puts it, was writing about a novel sort of emperor and had to find a fresh way of presenting him: "In writing the *Life*, Eusebius was not composing a scientific history, he was writing as a believer, with the avowed aim of revealing to the world Constantine's actions and the march of Christian providence."[61]

By the end of Constantine's reign there existed neither any pronounced, widespread sensibility that Christianity was coextensive with the Roman Empire nor any widespread supposition that Constantine was a second Moses who was sent to deliver all Christians everywhere from oppressive tyranny. A reimagining of his legacy as analogous to that of Moses did eventually take root among later Christian authors, but in its time, the *VC* was a unique presentation of Constantine. It was an original discourse and the lone panegyric of an altogether new species: the Christian king. Claudia Rapp acknowledges this when she writes that Moses as "a model for those who hold political and spiritual authority ... became particularly prominent among the Christian authors, and especially the hagiographers, of the fourth and fifth centuries"—only after Constantine's death.[62]

In short, the Roman-Persian war following Constantine's death had nothing to do with the Christians of Persia. He may have taken defensive measures against a young Persian king who was intent on vindicating his grandfather, but there is no evidence that Constantine thought of himself as a second Moses or that he was planning an intervention on behalf of the Christians in Persia. Nor, for that matter, is there any evidence that any of the fourth- and

---

61. A. Cameron, "Eusebius of Caesarea and the Rethinking of History," in *Tria Corda: Scritti in onore di Arnaldo Momigliano*, ed. E. Gabba (Como: New Press, 1983), 86.

62. Rapp, "Imperial Ideology in the Making," 691. See also Rapp, "Comparison, Paradigm and the Case of Moses in Panegyric and Hagiography," in *The Propaganda of Power: The Role of Panegyric in Late Antiquity*, ed. M. Whitby (Leiden: Brill, 1998), 277–98. For the rarity of Moses as a model in the fourth century, see Rapp, "Imperial Ideology," 693n44, which explains that "F. Heim, 'Les figures du prince ideal au IVe siecle: du type au modele', in *Figures de l'Ancien Testament chez les Pères*, Cahiers de Biblia Patristica, 2 (Strasbourg[: Centre d'analyse et de documentation patristiques], 1989), [277–301,] has demonstrated that the interpretation of Christian emperorship was significantly 'toned down' between the time of Constantine and the end of the fourth century."

fifth-century historians who discussed his reign believed that he saw himself as a liberator of Christians in Persia. Patron, protector, and letter writer? Yes, absolutely. Liberator? No—not yet, anyway. There was no controversy or cover-up: Constantine was not going to war for Christians when he died.

THREE

Rereading Nisibis

NARRATING THE BATTLE FOR
ROMAN MESOPOTAMIA

ACCORDING TO ONE LATE FIFTH-CENTURY martyrdom narrative, the *History of Blessed Simeon bar Ṣabbaʿe*, Constantine's death touched off a momentous chain of events. King Shapur II took advantage of the power vacuum left by the passing of the great Roman emperor and began to wage war "against [Constantine's] sons who were still young."[1] The narrator of the *History of Simeon* does not provide much information about how or where Shapur challenged Constantine's sons. He says only that the Persian king "continually raided the land of the Romans."[2] Shapur's raids on the Roman eastern frontier were not entirely successful, but his efforts are well

---

1. *History of Blessed Simeon bar Ṣabbaʿe* 4. All translations of the *Martyrdom* and *History of Simeon* are from K. Smith, *The Martyrdom and History of Blessed Simeon bar Ṣabbaʿe*, Persian Martyr Acts in Syriac: Text and Translation, fasc. 3. (Piscataway, NJ: Gorgias, 2014). On the upheaval following Constantine's death and the theory that he had planned "an unassailable college of Christian emperors" to succeed him and pursue his policies, see R. W. Burgess, "The Summer of Blood: The 'Great Massacre' of 337 and the Promotion of the Sons of Constantine," *DOP* 62 (2008): 5–51; quote on 9. Michael Whitby points out that history has been unfair to Constantius II, in that "most Christian writers regarded him as heretical [i.e., Arian], while the major contemporary secular author, Ammianus Marcellinus, misrepresented him because of his clash with the pagan Julian." See Whitby, *Rome at War: AD 293–696* (Oxford: Osprey, 2002), 37. For more on Constantius's poor treatment at the hands of ancient historians, see R. C. Blockley, "Constantius II and Persia," in *Studies in Latin Literature and Roman History* V (*Latomus: Revue d'études latines* 206), ed. C. Deroux (Brussels: Latomus, 1989), 465–90; and H. C. Teitler, "Ammianus and Constantius: Image and Reality," in *Cognitio Gestorum: The Historiographic Art of Ammianus Marcellinus*, ed. J. den Boeft, D. den Hengst, and Teitler (Amsterdam: Royal Netherlands Academy of Arts and Sciences, 1992), 117–22.

2. *History of Simeon* 4. There is no mention of a war between Rome and Persia in the *Martyrdom of Simeon*, the earlier account of the bishop's death.

attested in other late ancient sources in Latin, Greek, and Syriac.³ Especially well remembered is how he tried and failed to take the Roman stronghold of Nisibis three times between 337 and 350.⁴ Although the narrator of the *History of Simeon* does not specify that Shapur's defeats at Nisibis in particular drove him to persecute Christians in Persia, he does suggest that "the land of the Romans" was Christian land and that because of his losses there, Shapur was "increasingly incensed with hatred for the servants of God who [dwelt] in the land of his jurisdiction."⁵

THE FALL OF NISIBIS AND THE WRITING OF IMPERIAL HISTORY

At the time of Constantine's death, Nisibis was the defensive linchpin of Roman Mesopotamia. It was already an old settlement, and as it changed hands over the centuries, it was constructed and reconstructed many times on the site it occupied—one ideally suited for a fortress.⁶ The city was the

---

3. For an overview of the ancient commentaries on this fourth-century Roman-Persian war, see the chronologically organized compendium of sources compiled and edited by M. H. Dodgeon and S. N. C. Lieu, *The Roman Eastern Frontier and the Persian Wars, AD 226–363: A Documentary History* (London: Routledge, 1991). Particularly helpful is C. S. Lightfoot, "Facts and Fiction: The Third Siege of Nisibis (A.D. 350)," *Historia* 37 (1988): 105–25.

4. The first siege happened in either 337 or 338. Ancient authors (e.g., Jerome in his *Chronicle*) generally suggest that it occurred in 338, whereas Timothy Barnes and Richard Burgess argue for 337—in part on the presumption that Constantine was on his way to deal with Shapur when he died at Nicomedia in the spring of 337, but mainly because they reckon the death year of Jacob of Nisibis to have been 337. Jacob was the Christian bishop of Nisibis who died during this siege and whose prayers were credited with saving the city from the Persian army. See R. W. Burgess, "The Dates of the First Siege of Nisibis and the Death of James of Nisibis," *Byz* 69 (1999): 7–17; and T. D. Barnes, "Constantine and the Christians of Persia," *JRS* 75 (1985): 133, with reference to P. Peeters, "La légende de Saint Jacques de Nisibe," *AB* 38 (1920): 285–373.

5. *History of Simeon* 4.

6. No diachronic study of Nisibis exists—at least nothing along the lines of J. B. Segal, *Edessa: The Blessed City* (Oxford: Clarendon, 1970). That said, there is a study of the ecclesiastical history of the city that focuses mainly on its monasteries, J.-M. Fiey, *Nisibe, métropole syriaque orientale et ses suffragants des origines à nos jours*, CSCO 388 (Leuven: Peeters, 1977). Beyond this work, there are good overviews and studies of particular periods in the city's history. For an account that focuses on Nisibis during the Hellenistic and Parthian periods, see N. Pigulevskaja, *Les villes de l'état iranien aux époques parthe et sassanide: Contribution à l'histoire sociale de la basse antiquité* (Paris: Mouton, 1963), 49–59. Pigulevskaja points out (50–51) that the city dates to Assyrian times and that Alexander the Great used it in

mustering point for Ursicinus, the *magister militum per Orientem* under whom Ammianus Marcellinus served, and it guarded the main east-west highway traversing the northern Mesopotamian marchlands between the Syrian desert to the south and the Armenian mountains to the north.[7] Its location meant that Nisibis was commercially as well as strategically important. As an easily accessible border town, it was an imperially designated site of trade between Rome and Persia. Fine luxury goods from the East, heavily taxed on their arrival, often passed through Nisibis on their westerly journey to other parts of the Roman Empire.[8] If only on the basis of its location, the intermingling brought about by trade, and the presence of several Roman legions, there is good reason to believe that Nisibis was more ethnically, culturally, and religiously diverse than one might suspect of a town so far from the sea, on a minor river in northern Mesopotamia.[9]

While Roman Nisibis was an important stronghold and center of trade in the days of Constantine and Constantius, it was equally if not more important to later memory after it was lost to the Persians following Julian's defeat in 363. While in exile, the city's most renowned Christian resident, Ephrem the Syrian, wrote the *Hymns on Nisibis* and *Hymns against Julian*, some of which lament the loss of the city while detailing its heroic defense.[10] But its loss was

---

his conquest of the East. More recent is a study of the city when Ephrem the Syrian was living there, in the fourth century; see P. S. Russell, "Nisibis as the Background to the Life of Ephrem the Syrian," *Hugoye* 8 (2005): 179–235. For the monastic "school movement" in Sasanian Nisibis during the sixth and seventh centuries, see A. H. Becker, *Fear of God and the Beginning of Wisdom: The School of Nisibis and Christian Scholastic Culture in Late Antique Mesopotamia* (Philadelphia: University of Pennsylvania Press, 2006).

7. See Amm. Marc. XXIV.9.1–2; Lightfoot, "Facts and Fiction," 107; and J. F. Matthews, "Ammianus and the Eastern Frontier in the Fourth Century: A Participant's View," in *The Defence of the Roman and Byzantine East*, ed. P. Freeman and D. Kennedy (Oxford: BAR International Editions, 1986), 549–64.

8. H. Elton, *Frontiers of the Roman Empire* (Bloomington: Indiana University Press, 1996), 88.

9. On this point see most notably F. Millar, "Ethnic Identity in the Roman Near East, AD 325–450: Language, Religion and Culture," *MedArch* 11 (1998): 159–76. Millar questions just how Roman many in the Roman Near East would have considered themselves. He reasonably concludes, based on the sheer diversity of the area, that we are on unstable ground in attempting to speak of "Syrian" (or even Syriac Christian) ethnolinguistic religious identity in this time and place. See also N. J. Andrade, *Syrian Identity in the Greco-Roman World* (Cambridge: Cambridge University Press, 2013).

10. See the edition and German translation of E. Beck, *Des heiligen Ephraem des Syrers Carmina Nisibena*, CSCO 218–19, 240–41, Scriptores Syri 92–93, 102–3 (Leuven: Peeters, 1961–63). Only a few of these hymns record details of the three sieges and defense of Nisibis,

painful, and painfully important, all around—not just to the city's Christian inhabitants, such as Ephrem, but also to the ego and identity of Rome's pagan historians. When it was finally given over to Shapur without a fight—as a result of the terms of the treaty with Jovian—Ammianus decried the decision as "betraying Nisibis." He chastised Jovian's abandonment of the city as "unworthy of an Empire," particularly since Nisibis had, for so many years, been the primary bulwark against Persian occupation of the Roman East.[11] Ammianus dolefully describes the evacuation of Nisibis, noting that the citizens of the once proud city were cast to the wind without any imperial support in moving their families or belongings to other cities west of the newly redrawn border.[12]

In addition to the eyewitness accounts of Ephrem and Ammianus, we have epic tales by other late ancient authors who wrote about Shapur's great sieges of Nisibis, complete with supernatural visions, stampeding elephants, divinely inspired gnats, and even a naval battle fought beneath the city's walls on a flooded plain created when Shapur dammed the river Mygdonius. As Paul Russell comments in his survey of the city's history during Ephrem's residence, there is an obvious conclusion to be drawn from the Persian king's lavish expenditure of blood and treasure: "So great a value was placed on possession of Nisibis by Shapur that he was willing to waste armies and move rivers to acquire it."[13] In successfully repelling Shapur's forces three times, Nisibis duly earned its epithet: the Shield of Empire.

Although the narratives of the fourth-century struggle for northern Mesopotamia—and in particular, the city of Nisibis—make for compelling reading, what I am primarily interested in addressing in this chapter is how the various accounts of the defense, loss, and evacuation of Nisibis were written (and later developed) to serve quite different historiographical ends.

Much of our knowledge of Roman Nisibis in the fourth century comes from two sources that I have already mentioned: the Latin military history

---

and even then the focus is primarily on the third siege, in 350; see Eph. *CNis* I–III, XI–XIII, with details in Lightfoot, "Facts and Fiction," 111.

11. Amm. Marc. XXV.9.8. See also Lightfoot, "Facts and Fiction," 106; the survey of various late ancient authors' views of the "abandonment" of Nisibis in R. Turcan, "L'Abandon de Nisibe et l'opinion publique (363 ap. J.-C.)," in *Mélanges d'archéologie et d'histoire offerts à André Piganiol*, ed. R. Chevallier (Paris: Service d'edition et de vente des publications de l'Education nationale, 1966), 875–90; and S. Belcher, "Ammianus Marcellinus and the Nisibene Handover of A.D. 363," in *War and Warfare in Late Antiquity*, vol. 2, ed. A. Sarantis and N. Christie (Leiden: Brill, 2013), 631–52.

12. Amm. Marc. XXV.9.5–6.

13. Russell, "Nisibis as the Background," 217.

of Ammianus Marcellinus, and the Syriac *madrashe* (teaching hymns) of Ephrem the Syrian. Other noteworthy sources include the emperor Julian's *Orations* in praise of his cousin Constantius, and the fifth-century *Church History* of Theodoret of Cyrrhus. Ammianus says relatively little about Mesopotamian Christians in the context of the Roman-Persian war, and Julian never mentions them, but for Ephrem and Theodoret it was the god of the Christians who spared Nisibis from Shapur's armies. Surprisingly, though, neither Ephrem nor Theodoret says anything about the Christians of Persia when discussing Nisibis.[14] For Ephrem, it was Julian (not Shapur) who was the threat to Christians. He celebrates Julian's downfall at Shapur's hands as a providential boon to Christians in the Roman Empire.

A relatively obscure text known as the Syriac *Julian Romance* expresses a similar sentiment. Like Ephrem's *Hymns on Nisibis* and *Hymns against Julian*, the *Julian Romance* was written in Roman Edessa, but in the early sixth century, not the late fourth, when Ephrem was writing. Following Ephrem, the *Romance* reads Shapur's victory over Julian as a benefit to Christians in the Roman Empire. Unlike Ephrem, however, this later text is also concerned with the Christians of Persia. Still, the narratives of both clearly reflect the Roman ecumene in which they were composed. Syriac sources originating in the Sasanian Persian Empire, such as the *History of Simeon*, tell a different story. Julian, if he is even mentioned, is not a major concern.[15] I address the distinctiveness of these Persian Christian sources in

---

14. Theodoret discusses the persecution of Christians in the 420s, during the reigns of Yazdgard I and Bahram V, but he says nothing about the persecution under Shapur II. On the importance of this later episode of "persecution" in his *HE*, see the discussion in chapter 5 and Geoffrey Herman's reevaluation "The Last Years of Yazdgird I and the Christians," in *Jews, Christians and Zoroastrians: Religious Dynamics in a Sasanian Context*, ed. Herman (Piscataway, NJ: Gorgias, 2014), 67–90.

15. The *History of Simeon* discusses Julian, but only as part of its anti-Jewish polemic, which mentions how he attempted to rebuild the Jerusalem Temple: "After twenty-four years, once the sons of victorious Constantine, Constans and Constantius, had died, Julian reigned over the Romans. From the outset of his reign he sacrificed to idols. And, in order to provoke Christians and falsify the words of Christ—who prophesied about the destruction of Jerusalem and said, 'There will not be left on it a stone upon a stone that is not overturned' [Matthew 24:2; Mark 13:2; Luke 21:6]—for this reason, (Julian) commanded the Jews in all of his empire to go up and rebuild Jerusalem and the Temple and to offer sacrifices as the law commands. Indeed, many went up and began to dig the foundations of Jerusalem. While these things were happening, a charlatan came to the land of the Persians and proclaimed to all the Jews and said, 'It is the time of the return that was predetermined by the prophets! [Daniel 9:25; Isaiah 27:13] I have been commanded by God to proclaim the return to you so

the second half of the book, but in this chapter I focus on how Christians and pagans in the Roman Empire wrote their own (usually very different) histories about the conflict with Shapur. These cannot be read in isolation but must be considered against, and in light of, one another. The loss of Nisibis and five provinces in Roman Mesopotamia was a pivotal moment for all Roman historians. And quite remarkably, what both Christian and non-Christian historians in the Roman Empire have in common—at least until the fifth century—is an apparent ignorance of any persecution of Christians in Persia. Such an argument from silence does not, in and of itself, demonstrate that there was no persecution, but it does suggest that we must pay renewed attention to how, when, and for what purposes these histories of the fourth century were written.

THE NISIBIS OF FANTASY: JULIAN'S *ORATIONS* IN PRAISE OF CONSTANTIUS

Classicizing Roman historians drew upon their predecessors in the historiographical arts and the historical-literary genre to understand and explain the

---

that you would go up (to Jerusalem)!' The charlatan also went to Maḥoza in Beth Aramaye and led astray masses of Jews. They set forth and went out from Maḥoza in the hope of the return, and they went three *parasangs* from the city. When word of their departure reached King Shapur he sent out a force and destroyed many thousands of them." See *History of Simeon* 14–15; bracketed biblical citations are in the original translation.

Maḥoza, a suburb of Seleucia-Ctesiphon, had a large Jewish population. If its Jews were apprehended three parasangs (about fifteen kilometers) from the city, that could have been in Maiozamalcha, which, according to Ammianus, was a low-walled town that its "Jewish inhabitants" had abandoned prior to the arrival of Julian's soldiers, who burned it. See Amm. Marc. XXIV.4.1. On Julian's attempt to rebuild the Temple, see D. B. Levenson, "The Ancient and Medieval Sources for the Emperor Julian's Attempt to Rebuild the Jerusalem Temple," *JSJ* 35 (2004): 409–60; Simeon's acts are addressed at 426. Levenson suggests that the author of the *History of Simeon* may have relied on Theodoret's *HE* (ca. 450) for his account of the rebuilding of the Temple and furthermore that there is probably "some connection" between this episode in the *History of Simeon* and that in the Syriac *Julian Romance*. On the rebuilding of the Temple according to Ammianus Marcellinus, see J. W. Drijvers, "Ammianus Marcellinus 23.1.2–3: The Rebuilding of the Temple in Jerusalem," in *Cognitio Gestorum: The Historiographic Art of Ammianus Marcellinus*, ed. J. den Boeft, D. den Hengst, and H. C. Teitler (Amsterdam: Royal Netherlands Academy of Arts and Sciences, 1992), 19–26. Finally, for a new—and more skeptical—consideration of the persecution of Jews in the Sasanian Empire, see R. Kalmin, *Jewish Babylonia between Persia and Roman Palestine* (Oxford: Oxford University Press, 2006), 121–46.

events of their own time. Before he went to Roman Mesopotamia, Julian wrote a classicizing history of the region—one that, ironically, celebrates the military exploits of his Christian cousin Constantius. The first two of Julian's famed *Orations* are the "Panegyric in Honor of Emperor Constantius" and the closely related "Heroic Deeds of Constantius."[16] Both are ornately structured rhetorical exercises that painstakingly follow all the rules for a panegyric in praise of an emperor. And both seem to have been written during a protracted period of conflict between Julian and Constantius in the mid-350s. According to Robert Browning, Julian may have composed *Oration* II "in an attempt to bridge the growing gap between his cousin and himself." It is, Browning continues, "a cold, technically competent piece of work" that makes "a series of comparisons between Constantius and various Homeric heroes, in which Constantius naturally always comes off best."[17]

Julian was not present at Nisibis, or anywhere else in Roman Mesopotamia, during Shapur's three sieges of the city, but much of *Oration* II recounts its third siege (in 350) in great detail. Since the Romans are the heroes of the tale in the guise of the "Greeks," the Sasanians are presented as the Persians of old, the sons of Darius and Xerxes. Though Julian refers to Shapur as "the king of the Parthians," he depicts him as "imitating Xerxes."[18] Just as the ancient Persian king watched the battle of Salamis from on high, so too did Shapur observe the siege of Nisibis from a hillside vantage.[19] Julian describes Shapur's army as a transparently inauthentic replica of true Persians. In a strange chronological twist, he presents the Sasanians as the usurpers of Seleucid lands. By wearing retro, Achaemenid battle dress, the Sasanians "try to evade the truth and to make it appear that they have not revolted from Macedon, but are merely resuming the empire that was theirs of old."[20] As Christopher Lightfoot comments, "It is not surprising that the historical

---

16. All translations of the *Orations* follow W. C. Wright, *The Works of the Emperor Julian*, vol. 1 (London: William Heinemann, 1913).

17. See R. Browning, *The Emperor Julian* (Berkeley: University of California Press, 1976), 97.

18. Jul. *Or.* II.62c, 63b.

19. Alain Chauvot notes that both Philip the Arab and Julian insisted on the cognomen Parthicus rather than Persicus, thereby highlighting a constructed image (not ignorance) of Persia which resulted in the purposeful negation of Sasanian political realities. See Chauvot, "Parthes et Perses dans les sources du IVe siècle," in *Institutions, société et vie politique dans l'empire romain au IVe siècle ap. J.-C.*, ed. M. Christol, S. Demougin, and Y. Duval (Rome: École française de Rome / Palais Farnèse, 1992), 115–25.

20. Jul. *Or.* II.63b.

facts get distorted by Julian as he strives to exploit every possible device in the well-developed and highly literary genre of panegyric.... The intention is clearly to flatter Constantius by implying that the repulse of Sapor's army at Nisibis was as great an exploit as the defeat of Xerxes in 480 BC."[21]

Putting aside this flattery, it is important to note that the *Orations*' presentation of both Constantius and the defense of Nisibis is fully classical. Neither Julian nor Ammianus harbored warm feelings for the Christian cult, but both—even though they knew that Roman Mesopotamia was populated with Christians—are noticeably silent about the relevance of Constantius's Christianity to his defense of the Roman East. Neither claims that there were any Christian or other religious underpinnings to the war with the Persians, and Julian certainly says nothing about the Christian bishops whose prayers Ephrem credits with saving Nisibis.

One could conjecture that the silence of Ammianus and Julian on these points represents an attempt to refute a prevailing Christian interpretation of the war by hiding it under the veneer of a classical, pagan past. But it seems much simpler to conclude that neither had reason to see this war as fundamentally different in kind from previous Roman engagements with barbarians on the eastern frontier. At least in terms of how they conceived of and wrote about it, Christianity was largely, if not wholly, irrelevant.

Later on, following Constantius's death and Julian's elevation to sole Augustus, Julian conceptualized his Persian campaign in thoroughly classical yet strikingly zealous terms. In a letter to the eulogist Themistius, he boasts that he is the heir to Alexander and Marcus Aurelius.[22] In the emperor's satirical work *The Caesars*, which he composed in Antioch while preparing for the Persian campaign, Constantine is made to play the pious fool, while the caricatures of Alexander and Marcus Aurelius are designed as representations of Julian himself. Polymnia Athanassiadi-Fowden notes that he was "increasingly mesmerized by an Alexandrian vision of Persian conquest."[23] Indeed, he portrays Alexander as someone who was on a quasi-religious mission, someone who, in Glen Bowersock's words, "subdued the Persians in the name of Hellenism."[24] Libanius comments that Julian anticipated bringing Roman

21. Lightfoot, "Facts and Fiction," 123.

22. Jul. *Ep. ad Them.*

23. P. Athanassiadi-Fowden, *Julian and Hellenism: An Intellectual Biography* (Oxford: Clarendon, 1981), 224.

24. G. W. Bowersock, *Julian the Apostate* (Cambridge, MA: Harvard University Press, 1978), 15.

governance to Persia, but much more than that too: he believed the Persians would become Romans in everything from language, dress, and hairstyle to law, cult, and fondness for sophistry.²⁵

THE PERSIAN WAR IN THE *RES GESTAE* OF AMMIANUS MARCELLINUS

Whatever veiled "crusading" impulses may have undergirded Constantine's interest in Persia or later supported Julian's from a very different foundation, such motivations were not present when Constantius assumed full control of the Roman East. Shapur's letter to Constantius and Constantius's response present the conflict as solely territorial. According Ammianus, Shapur's aims were well known to the Roman emperor.²⁶ Although the empire of the ancient Achaemenids reached as far west as the "river Strymon and the boundaries of Macedonia," and although, moreover, he believed he was entitled to demand the return of all these lands since his rule surpassed those of the "kings of old" in its grandeur, Shapur humbly announced himself content with recovering only Armenia and Mesopotamia. These were territories that the Romans, he said, had stolen from his grandfather Narseh.²⁷

Constantius's lofty rhetorical response to the Persian king ignores Shapur's claim that he should be able to demand the return of all the lands of Darius and Xerxes. As Ammianus records it, Constantius emphasizes that although the Romans do indeed seek peace with the Persians, it would be ridiculous for them to give up Armenia and Mesopotamia. Further, he warns Shapur, if the Persians persist in their militant course of action there will be a battle, in which Rome will surely not be bested.²⁸ According to Ammianus, when Constantius's letter received no response, the Roman emperor sent several

25. See Athanassiadi-Fowden, *Julian and Hellenism*, 192, with reference to Lib. *Or*. XVIII.282.
26. Amm. Marc. XVII.5.4.
27. Amm. Marc. XVII.5.5–6. See also M.R. Shayegan, "On the Rationale behind the Roman Wars of Šābuhr II the Great," *BAI* 18 (2004): 111, with reference to K. Mosig-Walburg, "Zur Westpolitik Shāpūrs II.," in *Iran, questions et connaissances: Actes du IVᵉ congrès européen des études iraniennes, organisé par la Societas Iranologica Europaea, Paris, 6–10 septembre 1999*, vol. 1, *La période ancienne*, ed. P. Huyse (Leuven: Peeters, 2002), 329–47.
28. Amm. Marc. XVII.5.10–14.

ambassadors to Shapur, among them the philosopher Eustathius, a sophist whom Ammianus describes as a "master persuader."[29]

Constantius's decision to send a philosopher—not a Christian bishop—to speak with Shapur was not lost on Eunapius, a vigorous opponent of Christianity and the author of the famous *Lives of the Sophists*. He explains that Eustathius was so skilled in the arts of persuasion that Constantius, although "held fast by the books of the Christians," sent for the renowned philosopher in order to manage the Persian threat.[30] In detailing the philosopher's pacific disposition and eloquence, Eunapius remarks that Eustathius—alone among the Roman ambassadors at the Persian court—gained the trust of Shapur, with whom he was even invited to dine. He so dazzled the previously barbarous Shapur that the Persian king came close to renouncing his crown and putting on the philosopher's cloak, the *tribonian* of the sort worn by Eustathius. But the magi prevented this and accused Eustathius of using sorcery against their king.[31]

The general contours of this account of the near conversion of a Persian king to a life of philosophy thanks to the gentility and wisdom of a Roman ambassador recur several decades later in the story of Marutha, the Christian bishop of Maypherqaṭ in Roman Armenia who was sent to Seleucia-Ctesiphon to help formally establish the Church of the East in the early fifth century.[32] According to Marutha's *Life*, the Roman bishop cured the Sasanian king Yazdgard I of his chronic headaches and nearly converted him to Christianity. Yazdgard was held back from converting, however, by the magi, who claimed that Marutha (just like Eustathius before him) was a sweet-talking sorcerer.[33]

29. Amm. Marc. XVII.5.15.
30. Eunap. *VS* VI.5.2.
31. Eunap. *VS* VI.5.7–9.
32. Marutha's *Life* is preserved in both Greek and (more completely) Armenian. For a translation of the Armenian version and an overview of the sources that deal with Marutha, see R. Marcus, "The Armenian *Life* of Marutha of Maipherkat," *HTR* 25 (1932): 47–71. For an analysis of the role of Marutha and other clerical ambassadors in the establishment of the Church of the East, see L. Sako, *Le rôle de la hiérarchie syriaque orientale dans les rapports diplomatiques entre la Perse et Byzance aux Ve–VIIe siècles* (Paris: Lille–Atelier national de reproduction des thèses, 1986). Marutha and other Roman Christian envoys are the focus of chapter 5.
33. On the interaction between Yazdgard and Marutha, see S. J. McDonough, "A Second Constantine? The Sasanian King Yazdgard in Christian History and Historiography," *JLA* 1 (2008): 127–41.

As the detailed historical account of Ammianus and the anti-Christian, philosophical hagiography of Eunapius imply, however, many in the late fourth century were still narrating Rome as *Rome*—classical, pagan Rome. A Christian king may have been on the throne when Ammianus was serving in the war and again when he was memorializing it in his *Res Gestae,* but in narrating the exchange of letters between Constantius and Shapur, he gives no hint that either ruler thought of the conflict as being waged over the Christians of Persia.[34]

When, later in the *Res Gestae,* Ammianus engages in a long excursus on Persian culture and customs (his "Persian digression"), he provides an ethnography of the Achaemenids that makes little reference to and demonstrates little understanding of contemporary Sasanian society.[35] As Jan Willem Drijvers points out, this tells us vastly more about the persistence of earlier Greco-Roman literary tropes and methods of historiographical representation than about fourth-century Sasanian Persia.[36] Importantly, though, Ammianus's digression shows that Shapur's forays into Roman lands were still being conceived of in the Roman historiographical imagination as part

---

34. As any reader of his *Res Gestae* knows, Ammianus mentions Christians and Christianity, but not in the context of the means and ends of the imperial struggle that he is narrating. See, for example, E.D. Hunt, "Christians and Christianity in Ammianus Marcellinus," *CQ* 35 (1985): 186–200. Hunt acknowledges that Ammianus is exceptional among late ancient pagan historians in even mentioning Constantius's Christianity. Other Latin historians (such as Aurelius Victor, Eutropius, and Festus) "managed to write about Christian emperors without so much as a word about their Christianity" (186). Hunt nevertheless argues persuasively against those who would put "the pagan/Christian issue at the heart of the historian's purpose ... [as] part and parcel of the last pagan reaction at Rome in the late fourth century" (188). For a broader consideration of this point, see E.J. Watts, *The Final Pagan Generation* (Berkeley: University of California Press, 2015).

35. Amm. Marc. XXXIII.6.

36. J.W. Drijvers, "Ammianus Marcellinus' Image of Sasanian Society," in *Ērān ud Anērān: Studien zu den Beziehungen zwischen dem Sasanidenreich und der Mittelmeerwelt—Beiträge des Internationalen Colloquiums in Eutin, 8–9 Juni 2000,* ed. J. Wiesehöfer and P. Huyse (Stuttgart: Franz Steiner Verlag, 2006), 45–69. On Roman historians' preoccupation with the "Orient," and on late ancient (Roman pagan and Christian) visual depictions of Persians and magi, see R.M. Schneider, "Orientalism in Late Antiquity: The Oriental in Imperialism and Christian Imagery," in *Ērān ud Anērān,* 241–78. For the Roman image of Persia in the Parthian period, which undoubtedly fed how Rome conceptualized the Sasanians, see C. Lerouge, *L'Image des Parthes dans le monde gréco-romain: Du début du Ier siècle av. J.-C. jusqu'à la fin du Haut-Empire romain* (Wiesbaden: Franz Steiner Verlag, 2007).

of a Persian longing to reestablish the glory of the ancient Achaemenid Empire.[37]

After relating Constantius's death, Ammianus rehearses the emperor's virtues and vices (mainly vices) and pointedly acknowledges his Christianity. The historian refers to it as a "plain and simple religion" that Constantius foolishly made complex by engaging in abstruse questions of doctrine.[38] Nevertheless, he does not raise his criticism of the dead emperor's religious proclivities in the context of the defense of the Roman East, even if, in his estimation, Constantius handled foreign wars rather badly.[39] As Ammianus sees it, Constantius's Christianity did not directly factor into his motives or account for his incompetence in defending Roman Mesopotamia against Shapur.[40]

Christianity and the Roman East in the Res Gestae

The differences in the narrative approaches of Julian, Ammianus, Ephrem, and the later Christian historians who derive their account of the sieges of Nisibis from Ephrem are striking. Ammianus is concerned with conveying the history of the Roman army, and he does so with more than a modicum of deference to the historiographical tradition in which he was trained. Similarly, tales of the defense of the East afforded Julian an opportunity to

---

37. See D. Frendo, "Sasanian Irredentism and the Foundation of Constantinople: Historical Truth and Historical Reality," *BAI* 6 (1992): 59–66; and the discussion of Shapur's letter and the "notion of Achaemenid reminiscences" in Shayegan, "On the Rationale," 113–15, with reference to Ammianus's recycling of Cassius Dio and Herodian's remarks on the ancient boundaries of Persia. Philip Huyse argues that Roman historians (such as Ammianus and those on whom he relied) invented the idea that the Sasanians had an interest in attempting to reclaim Achaemenid territories. See Huyse, "La revendication de territoires achéménides par les Sassanides: Une réalité historique?," in *Iran, questions et connaissances: Actes du IVe congrès européen des études iraniennes, organisé par la Societas Iranologica Europaea, Paris, 6–10 septembre 1999*, vol. 1, *La période ancienne*, ed. Huyse (Leuven: Peeters, 2002), 297–311.

38. Amm. Marc. XXI.16.18. See also V. Neri, "Ammianus' Definition of Christianity as *absoluta et simplex religio*," in *Cognitio Gestorum: The Historiographic Art of Ammianus Marcellinus*, ed. J. den Boeft, D. den Hengst, and H.C. Teitler (Amsterdam: Royal Netherlands Academy of Arts and Sciences, 1992), 59–65. Neri suggests that here Ammianus may be referring to Constantius's Arianism by way of currying favor with the Theodosian audience for his *Res Gestae*. A more likely explanation (which Neri also proposes) is that he is simply criticizing Constantius's overinvolvement in frivolous and inconsequential religious affairs, which distracted him from more pressing issues of imperial governance.

39. Amm. Marc. XXI.16.15.

40. See Hunt, "Christians and Christianity," 187.

laud his cousin Constantius and to indulge in the welcome intellectual diversion of writing a fantastical narrative set piece.

For Ephrem and his heirs, however, the whole conflict took on an eschatological tone, with Christians pitted against those who would lead them away from God. Indeed, God summoned the opponents of Nisibis to the city, Ephrem says, as punishment for its sins. Yet paradoxically, some of those opponents were also the force behind the recommitment of the city's citizens to Christ: "He afflicted us by the breaches, that He might punish our crimes," Ephrem writes. "He raised the mounds that thereby, He might humble our boasting. He made a breach for the seas that thereby, He might wash away our pollution. He shut us in that we might gather together in His Temple."[41] For Ephrem, as for most Christian historians of the period, all is to be interpreted against the backdrop of providence. By contrast, when Ammianus writes about the citizens of Nisibis, he hardly mentions their Christianity.[42] That said, there are two noteworthy instances when Ammianus reveals that Shapur dealt directly with Christians on the Roman frontier.

The Mesopotamian Fortresses of Reman and Busan

The first instance occurs in Ammianus's discussion of the surrender of two Roman fortresses, Reman and Busan.[43] According to him, Shapur had learned that these were repositories of much of the wealth of the people who lived in the area and that the wife of Craugasius of Nisibis, a distinguished and influential citizen, happened to be in residence in one of them. After sacking both fortresses, Shapur sought out and captured Craugasius's wife, believing that through her he could pressure Craugasius into betraying Nisibis.[44] Ammianus does not say that Craugasius's wife was a Christian,

---

41. Eph. *CNis* II.9, translated by J. T. Stopford in Dodgeon and Lieu, *Roman Eastern Frontier*, 194.

42. See Hunt, "Christians and Christianity," 188.

43. Amm. Marc. XVIII.10.1–4.

44. Amm. Marc. XVIII.10.3. According to Ammianus, Craugasius did desert to the Persian side to be with his wife (XIX.9.3–8). In fact, he became an adviser to Shapur, who regarded him as the most useful Roman deserter second only to Antoninus. Antoninus was a rich merchant who became the accountant and bodyguard of the governor of Mesopotamia and then ran into debt with his creditors. To save his skin and his station, he learned all he could about the movements of supplies, soldiers, and money along the Roman eastern frontier. He then fled across the border with that information (and his family), offering it to Shapur in exchange for asylum. See Amm. Marc. XVIII.5.1–3.

but he does say that when Shapur was interrogating her, he learned that some other women among those present at the fortresses of Reman and Busan were ritually consecrated "Christian virgins." Just as Shapur sought to persuade Craugasius that it was in his interest to turn traitor, he surmised that being kind to these Christian virgins—by keeping them unharmed and allowing them to practice their faith unhindered—would be good way of guilefully demonstrating that he was a kind and genteel ruler.[45]

One wishes that Ammianus said more about the Christian virgins of Reman and Busan. While some have read this passage as evidence that he knew that Shapur was a persecutor of Christians, such an interpretation is entirely speculative.[46] In mentioning the king's good behavior toward Christian virgins—specifically in the story about Craugasius's wife—Ammianus does not suggest that it was just Christians who thought Shapur was cruel. Rather, he says that the king acted kind in this way so that all the inhabitants of Roman Mesopotamia, so many of whom had endured his raids and the dangers of war for years, might lay aside their fears and be persuaded to support the Persian side. Ammianus seems to imply that Shapur—in demonstrating that neither he nor his soldiers would harm either the pagan wives of well-connected citizens or the city's Christian virgins—believed that he had found a way of winning over the populace of the region, through a cunning combination of blackmail, false humility, and calculated magnanimity.

Bezabde on the Tigris

As much as we can speculate about the Christian virgins of Reman and Busan whom Ammianus mentions in passing, there is another instance of Shapur's direct dealings with Christians, which is of much more than passing interest. Ammianus provides an account of the siege and loss of a fortified city called Bezabde, which was on a bend of the Tigris roughly one hundred kilometers east of Nisibis.[47] According to him, Shapur marched there in 359,

---

45. Amm. Marc. XVIII.10.4.
46. Hunt ("Christians and Christianity," 189n19) suggests this passage indicates that Ammianus "is obviously aware of the reputation of Sapor II as a persecutor of Christians." In fact, there is no evidence of this in the *Res Gestae*.
47. Amm. Marc. XX.7.1-16. See also the discussion of Bezabde (or Beth Zabdai) in chapter 5 and the related Syriac martyrdom narrative, the *Martyrdom of the Captives of Beth Zabdai*, which is translated in appendix B.

purposefully bypassing the road to the well-defended city of Nisibis, after he took Singara, a Roman garrison town in the Sinjar Mountains farther to the south.[48] Ammianus explains that Singara, which had been defended by the First Flavian and First Parthian legions, as well as many native citizens, had fallen to the Persians because it was insufficiently provisioned with troops. In fact, much of the Roman army in the area was stationed at Nisibis.[49]

Bezabde's defenses were stronger than those of Singara: three legions rather than two defended it, and the castra had the services of a large contingent of local bowmen.[50] When Shapur arrived before the walls of the fortress, he hoped to persuade the citizens with "sweet promises," an approach he had tried at Singara and with the captured women of Reman and Busan.[51] But his promises fell on deaf ears, so his armies laid siege to the city. On the first attack, "the king himself, with a troop of horsemen gleaming in full armor," taunted the Romans by galloping back and forth at "the very edge of the trenches."[52] For two days "great heaps of the dead" piled up on both sides.[53] And then, on the dawn of the third day, something remarkable happened.

Ammianus says that "the chief priest of the sect of the Christians" went beyond the walls and was granted a brief audience with the Persian king. During the meeting, the bishop of Bezabde pointed to the terrible losses that each side had incurred and urged Shapur to return home in peace. Shapur flew into a rage over the bishop's impudence and "swore that he would not leave the place until the fortress had been destroyed."[54] When hostilities resumed, it did not take long for the Persian siege engines to finish their work. The Romans valiantly resisted, but it was not long before all the inhabitants of Bezabde were either captured or killed. As for the unnamed bishop, Ammianus says that he "incurred the shadow of a suspicion, unfounded in my opinion, though circulated confidently by many, of having told Shapur in a secret conference what parts of the wall to attack, as being slight within and weak. And in the end there seemed to be ground for this, since after his visit the enemy's engines deliberately battered those places which were tottering

48. Amm. Marc. XX.7.1.
49. Amm. Marc. XX.6.8–9.
50. Amm. Marc. XX.7.1.
51. Amm. Marc. XX.7.1; see also XX.6.3, XVIII.10.4.
52. Amm. Marc. XX.7.2.
53. Amm. Marc. XX.7.6.
54. Amm. Marc. XX.7.7–8.

and insecure from decay . . . as if those who directed them were acquainted with conditions within."⁵⁵

This is an astonishing passage. Some scholars, John Matthews and Roger Blockley among them, claim that Ammianus is an impartial observer of Christianity. In fact, Blockley cites this passage as evidence of Ammianus's "disinterested objectivity" in religious matters, since he goes out of his way to defend the Christian bishop by calling the allegations against him "unfounded in my opinion."⁵⁶ Others read this passage in precisely the opposite way, pointing to it as proof of Ammianus's anti-Christian bias. According to Timothy Barnes, it shows how Ammianus shrewdly uses rumor and innuendo (a skill he learned from Tacitus) to suggest disreputable conduct while absolving himself of responsibility for the dubious information he conveys.⁵⁷

Pushing further, John Weisweiler suggests that Ammianus may have been aware of how Christians, such as Ephrem the Syrian, sought to lionize the bishops of Mesopotamia and proclaim them the "wartime leaders of their cities." Although Ammianus says relatively little about Christianity in his work, "the accusations of treason against the bishop of Bezabde" are important, Weisweiler says, because they "disrupted this link between Christian religious devotion and the maintenance of empire by reversing the narratives of the heroic rescue of Roman cities by their Christian clergy. In Ammianus' version, a bishop undermined rather than secured the defence of the empire."⁵⁸

It is not likely that Ammianus knew Ephrem's work in particular, but if Weisweiler is correct in his tantalizing suggestion that Ammianus—writing well after the war's end—was at least aware of generally circulating Christian narratives about the defense of the Roman East, then it is to Ephrem and his heirs that we must turn in order to get a better sense of how Christians in

---

55. Amm. Marc. XX.7.9.

56. R. C. Blockley, *Ammianus Marcellinus: A Study of His Historiography and Political Thought* (Brussels: Collection Latomus, 1975), 132. See also J. F. Matthews, *The Roman Empire of Ammianus* (Baltimore: Johns Hopkins University Press, 1989), 445–51.

57. T. D. Barnes, *Ammianus Marcellinus and the Representation of Historical Reality* (Ithaca, NY: Cornell University Press, 1998), 87–88; similarly, see G. A. J. Kelly, *Ammianus Marcellinus: The Allusive Historian* (Cambridge: Cambridge University Press, 2008), 3–4.

58. J. Weisweiler, "Christianity in War: Ammianus on Power and Religion in Constantius' Persian War," in *The Power of Religion in Late Antiquity*, ed. A. Cain and N. Lenski (Burlington, VT: Ashgate, 2009), 390, 391.

Mesopotamia understood the war with the Persians and of how Ammianus may have sought to subtly counter their claims.

CHRISTIAN HISTORY AND NISIBIS DIVINE

Unlike non-Christian authors such as Ammianus and Julian, Christian historians were explicit in claiming that Roman Mesopotamia was divinely defended. They credited the prayers of Jacob, the bishop of Nisibis, with preventing the Persians from breaching the city's walls during Shapur's first siege. While many authors (both Christian and pagan) wrote about the third siege of Nisibis, in 350, information about the first siege (in 337 or 338) has been preserved mainly in Christian hagiography and ecclesiastical history.[59] The tales of Christian and non-Christian authors often have much in common, in that they comment on the same events. Of course, the explanations for these events are quite different, and therein lies their interest.

The Church History *of Theodoret of Cyrrhus*

Theodoret's mid-fifth-century account of the miraculous defense of Nisibis presumably derives from the original, Syriac *Life* of Ephrem the Syrian.[60] Ephrem's *Life* is a hagiographical portrait of the renowned theologian that preserves several stories used by Theodoret, including the flood of Nisibis, Shapur's vision of Constantius on the city's walls, and two miracles wrought by Jacob, the city's bishop.[61] Its account of the defense of Nisibis differs from

---

59. As Lightfoot notes ("Facts and Fiction," 111), "The second siege has left even less trace in the historical record; the only certain fact known about it is its date, 346. By contrast, the third siege has almost an overabundance of material." On the first siege of the city, the legends about Jacob of Nisibis, and the use of his hagiography in the establishment of Nisibis as a divinely defended Christian city, see Peeters, "La légende de Saint Jacques"; P. Kruger, "Jacob von Nisibis in syrischer und armenischer Überlieferung," *Mus* 81 (1968): 161–79; J.-M. Fiey, "Les évêques de Nisibe au temps de Saint Éphrem," *PdO* 4 (1973): 123–35; and D. Bundy, "Jacob of Nisibis as a Model for the Episcopacy," *Mus* 104 (1991): 235–49.

60. M. Marôth, "Le siège de Nisibe en 350 après J.-Ch. d'après des sources syriennes," *AAntHung* 27 (1979): 239–45.

61. By way of demonstrating the extremely complex interplay among the various sources for Ephrem and Nisibis, it is important to note that there is also a sixth-century Syriac *Life* of Ephrem, which, according to Sebastian Brock, descends from Syriac translations of Greek translations of Syriac stories about Ephrem that Sozomen transmits. Theodoret may therefore have gleaned his information about the siege of Nisibis from either Sozomen or a

Theodoret's version, however, in that the former champions Ephrem as a co-hero and credits his prayers (along with Jacob's) with securing the city's salvation.[62] Ephrem's *Life* seems to be based on his own eyewitness account of the sieges of Nisibis.

Theodoret correctly believes that at the time of the war between Shapur and Constantius, the Roman army defending Nisibis was not predominantly Christian. In fact, the Roman soldiers were mainly pagans from the western hinterlands of the empire.[63] Theodoret is thus keen to point out that it was not the skill or discipline of these legions that defeated Shapur and his armies but rather the god that was worshipped by the pious among the city's Roman citizens.[64]

According to Theodoret, the city's successful defense was all the more miraculous in that Shapur's tactics to win it included incredible feats of engineering and formidable amounts of manpower. The Persians, he says, constructed a series of massive earthen levees to dam the city's water source, the river Mygdonius. Their intent was not to deprive the Nisibenes of water but to collect enough of it so that when they broke the dam, the resulting torrent could be directed straight at the walls of the city. This farfetched plan proved brilliantly successful. According to Theodoret, once Shapur ordered his men to break the dam and unleash the water, it obliterated the fortifications on the sides of the city into, and out of, which it flowed. On seeing that his laborious scheme had, in a single cascade, demolished the city's meticulously constructed walls, Shapur rested his army for the remainder of the day. Nisibis was exposed and indefensible. So the Persian king, in no rush to complete his conquest, decided that he would allow the sodden earth to dry overnight in order to ease his army's crossing the following morning.[65]

---

shared Greek source rather than directly from the earlier Syriac *Life*. This may explain why he sometimes conflates elements of the first and third sieges. See Soz. *HE* III.16; S. Brock, "St. Ephrem in the Eyes of Later Syriac Liturgical Tradition," *Hugoye* 2 (1999): 5–25. According to Sidney Griffith, the sixth-century Syriac *Life* of Ephrem paints a portrait of an anachronistic "Ephrem Byzantinus" as opposed to an earlier, and more authentic (if such a term can be used), "Ephrem Syrus." See Griffith, "Images of Ephraem: The Syrian Holy Man and His Church," *Traditio* 45 (1989): 7–33. See also J.P. Amar, "Byzantine Ascetic Monachism and Greek Bias in the *Vita* Tradition of Ephrem the Syrian," *OCP* 58 (1992): 123–56.

62. For Ephrem's defense of Nisibis in the *Life,* see *Historia Ephraemi* in T.J. Lamy, *Sancti Ephraem Syri: Hymni et Sermones,* vol. 2 (Mechelen, 1886), cols. 15–19.

63. See Lightfoot, "Facts and Fiction," 112; for Theodoret's two accounts of the war, see *HE* II.30.1–14 and *Religious History* I.11–12.

64. Theod. *HE* II.30.1.

65. Theod. *HE* II.30.6–7.

Theodoret is not the only late ancient historian to discuss the Persians' use of the river Mygdonius. In Julian's telling, Shapur, "the King of the Parthians," encircled Nisibis with levees, "then he let the Mygdonius flow into these, and transformed all the space about the city into a lake, and completely hemmed it in as though it were an island, so that only the ramparts stood out and showed a little above the water. Then he besieged it by bringing up ships with siege-engines on board."[66] This account bears some resemblance to Theodoret's, in that both discuss the use of levees and the river, but the emperor's story of a shipborne assault on Nisibis via an artificial lake is much more similar to a tale in Heliodorus of Emesa's novel *Aethiopica*. According to Heliodorus, the Nile was once channeled into a ring of embankments around the Egyptian city of Syene. Some have argued that this scene in the *Aethiopica* must be a fictionalized version of real events at Nisibis, as Julian reported them. Others have declared the opposite, saying that Julian must have absorbed elements of the assuredly fictional *Aethiopica* in order to narrate his fanciful account of Shapur's efforts.[67] In either case, Julian, just like the Christian Theodoret, discusses how Shapur used the Mygdonius as part of his siege tactics, and both men give the river a prominent narrative role.[68]

In Theodoret's version, which does not mention a naval battle, when the sun rose the day after the flood, and the morning's first light fell on Nisibis, Shapur and his army were dumbfounded to see that the huge breaches in the city walls had been filled during the night—miraculously repaired thanks to the prayers of Jacob, the bishop of Nisibis.[69] As he gazed in wonder on the rebuilt walls, Shapur saw Constantius adding insult to injury by parading atop the battlements wearing the imperial diadem. Since the Roman emperor was supposed to have been in Antioch at the time, Shapur berated his

---

66. Jul. *Or.* II.62c.
67. In addition to Jul. *Or.* II.62c, see I.28b on the waters around Nisibis; cf. Heliodorus, *Aethiopica* IX.3–11. For a brief discussion of the similarities between the two accounts, see Lightfoot, "Facts and Fiction," 117–19.
68. See Jul. *Or.* I.30a. See also Lightfoot, "Facts and Fiction," 119. Lightfoot reasonably concludes that some of Julian's material "accurately reflects the events at Nisibis." However, he also notes that the emperor "added to this material certain aspects that can only be regarded as pure invention, and Heliodorus remains the most plausible source for the episode involving the embankment, the lake and the ships."
69. Theod. *HE* II.30.8. There is some confusion here. Jacob was the bishop of Nisibis during the first siege, in 337/38, and he died at that time, but Theodoret's account of the flood refers to the third siege of the city, in 350.

advisers for failing to inform him that Constantius was in Mesopotamia. They insisted that Constantius really was in Antioch, and Shapur realized that he was seeing an apparition, which, according to Theodoret, led him to exclaim, "God is fighting for the Romans."[70]

In the Christian memory of Nisibis, Shapur's realization became all the more clear when Jacob summoned swarming clouds of gnats and mosquitoes.[71] The thousands of insects that he called forth filled the trunks of the fearsome Persian elephants and the noses and ears of the Persians' horses, sending the battle-clad animals into a frenzied stampede and summarily ending the siege with the Persian army fleeing in disarray, overrun by its own terrified beasts of war.[72] Just like the story about Shapur's use of levees and the river Mygdonius, this story about gnats and mosquitoes also makes an appearance in the non-Christian historical tradition. Ammianus explains that in light of the debacle that the Persians suffered at Nisibis (namely, the mosquito-caused stampede of their own elephants and cavalry), the Sasanian elephant drivers who pursued the Romans as they retreated from Mesopotamia after Julian's death all wore knives bound to their right hands, so that they could quickly sever the spinal column of any beast that became uncontrollable.[73]

The Raising of the Persian Standard and the Fall of Julian

Despite the heroic defense of Nisibis as commemorated by Julian, Ammianus, Ephrem, and Theodoret, the city was given to the Persians in 363. The way in which its stinging loss has been remembered may be more important than how its defense was memorialized. Ammianus explains that after Julian's death and the army's elevation of Jovian to the purple, the new emperor gave Shapur "five provinces on the far side of the Tigris ... with fifteen fortresses, besides Nisibis, Singara and Castra Maurorum, a very important stronghold."[74] Only with difficulty, Ammianus says, did Jovian succeed "in bringing it about that Nisibis and Singara should pass into control of the Persians without their inhabitants, and that the Romans in the fortresses that were to be taken from

---

70. Theod. *HE* II.30.9–10.
71. Theod. *HE* II.30.12.
72. Theod. *HE* II.30.13–14.
73. Amm. Marc. XXV.1.15.
74. Amm. Marc. XXV.7.9.

us should be allowed to return to our protection."⁷⁵ Singara had already been taken a few years earlier, in 359/60, with many of its inhabitants captured and deported to Persia.⁷⁶ As Nisibis did not suffer such a fate, it seems to have received special treatment. In his *New History*, written in the early sixth century, Zosimus claims that its citizens alone were exempt from being handed over along with the territory.⁷⁷ This may have been by Shapur's design. Julian, obviously writing well before the handover of Nisibis, apparently believed that he desperately wanted to win the city and colonize it with Persian families.⁷⁸ The tenth-century Persian historian al-Ṭabari concurs, noting that twelve thousand Persians from good families were sent to Nisibis after the Roman population left. It was, he claims, necessary that the city be depopulated of its Roman inhabitants, because Shapur was of a "different religion" from them.⁷⁹

By allowing for the relocation of the citizens of Nisibis, Shapur unwittingly contributed to the literary coming to terms with the city's loss as Ephrem narrates it. Ephrem composed both the *Hymns on Nisibis* and the *Hymns against Julian* during his ten-year exile in Edessa—sometime between his departure from Nisibis in 363 and his death in Edessa, while ministering to plague victims, in 373. Although those who are interested in Julian and what happened to Roman Mesopotamia in the aftermath of the emperor's death often cite the *Hymns against Julian*, few have considered how Ephrem narrates and conceptualizes Shapur's role in them. What he says about the Persian king is not just surprising but runs totally contrary to the idea of

---

75. Amm. Marc. XXV.7.11.
76. Amm. Marc. XX.6.1–9.
77. Zos. *HN* III.34.1. According to Zosimus, the inhabitants of Nisibis were sent to Amida. The chapter headings in Ammianus's *Res Gestae*, which Adrien de Valois supplied in the seventeenth century, also suggest that the evacuees went to Amida (modern-day Diyarbakır), but Ammianus does not specify this in his text. See G. Kelly, "Adrien de Valois and the Chapter Headings in Ammianus Marcellinus," *CP* 104 (2009): 233–42; and Kelly, "Ammianus and the Difference between Chapter Headings and Text," *Ausonius* (blog), April 29, 2011, http://ausonius.blogspot.co.uk/2011/04/ammianus-and-difference-between-chapter.html.
78. Jul. *Or* I.27a–b.
79. On the reign of Shapur II as narrated by Ṭabari, see C. E. Bosworth, *The History of al-Ṭabari*, vol. 5, *The Sāsānids, the Byzantines, the Lakmids, and Yemen* (Albany: State University of New York Press, 1999), 50–66; discussion of Nisibis at 62–63. One Syriac martyrdom narrative, the early seventh-century *History of Saba Pirgushnasp*, speaks of a Christian convert and martyr who was the son of a Zoroastrian family that was sent to Nisibis after Shapur acquired it. See *AMS* IV, 222–49.

Shapur as a persecutor of Christians. For Ephrem, Julian was the threat to Christians—not Shapur. Ephrem's silence about any oppression of Christians in Persia suggests that the king's reputation as a persecutor may not have been known in Nisibis (or Edessa) even more than twenty-five years after the purported start of his Great Persecution, in 339/40.[80]

Ephrem's reminiscences are theological hymns that might also be thought of as historical poetry.[81] He clearly refers to the flooded Mygdonius, to the fallen walls of the city, and to the formidable Persian elephants. He points to its three bishops (Jacob, Babu, and Vologeses) as the true defenders of Nisibis: "The first siege was defended by the first glorious priest; the second siege was defended by the second merciful priest; and the prayers of the last one repaired our ruptured [walls] secretly."[82] Ephrem insists that mere "sackcloth" defeated the warriors of Persia, who were clad in full battle regalia: "The seas invaded and were conquered by sackcloth; hills were raised and they humbled them. Elephants arrived and were defeated by sackcloth, ashes and prayer."[83] In the second of his *Hymns against Julian,* Ephrem again says that the "sackcloth of the blessed one preserved the city that was head of the region of Mesopotamia, and it was magnified."[84]

Yet inasmuch as sackcloth and prayer may have held back the Persians, the same hymn decries the extent to which Nisibis had abandoned God during Julian's reign. A bishop had preserved the city during each of the three sieges, but it was ultimately lost because its citizens reverted to paganism:

---

80. This is not to suggest that Shapur did not have a reputation among late ancient Roman historians as a vicious and brutal king. Ammianus claims that he was known to be a cruel and terrifying ruler. This accusation is not made uniquely because of how Shapur dealt with Christians, however, but rather reflects the "barbarization" of Rome's enemies that is the standard practice in Ammianus's history. See Amm. Marc. XVIII.10.4; and the analysis in J. W. Drijvers, "Ammianus Marcellinus' Image."

81. Parts of several of them refer to the third siege of Nisibis: Eph. *CNis* I.3, I.8, II.9, II.17–19, III.6, XI.15–17, XIII.4–6, XIII.17–18. Ephrem's *Mem. Nic.* (XV.97–120, 145–70) refers to the leadership of Bishop Vologeses of Nisibis during the third siege, and his *CJ* deals with this battle for Nisibis and the aftermath of its loss.

82. Eph. *CNis* XIII.17.

83. Eph. *Mem. Nic.* XV.110–18, translated by S. Vince in Dodgeon and Lieu, *Roman Eastern Frontier,* 196.

84. Eph. *CJ* II.25. All translations of the *Hymns against Julian* follow K. E. McVey, *Ephrem the Syrian: Hymns* (Mahwah, NJ: Paulist, 1989).

> For thirty years the truth encompassed it [Nisibis].
> In the summer in which an idol was set up in the city [when Julian came to power],
> compassion fled from it and anger overran it.
> For empty sacrifices emptied its fullness.
> The [pagan] altar that was built rooted out and expelled
> that altar whose sackcloth had delivered us.[85]

The pagan "altar" that Ephrem mentions here seems to have been more than just a solitary place of sacrifice set up by Julian's decree. As his subsequent remarks attest, the formerly Christian Nisibenes widely embraced paganism. Still, even though these citizens had wandered from Christ, Shapur, according to Ephrem, was wise enough to see that it was Christ who had protected the city. Ephrem explains that when the Persian king finally entered Nisibis in triumph, he first paid homage to Christian churches, while bypassing or destroying the city's pagan shrines, including the site of the Zoroastrian fire cult:

> The Magus who entered our place regarded it as holy, to our disgrace.
> He neglected his fire temple but honored the sanctuary.
> He cast down the [pagan] altars built by our laxity;
> he destroyed the enclosures to our shame.
> For he knew that from one temple alone emerged
> the mercy that had saved us from him three times.[86]

As this remarkable passage indicates, although the *Acts of the Persian Martyrs* presents Shapur as the destroyer of churches and the arch-persecutor of Christians, according to Ephrem he was, to the shame of the Nisibenes, the protector of churches and the one who honored the altar of the god that had held back the Persian siege engines. Here God uses Shapur to reveal the fickleness of the Nisibenes. Ephrem says that God delivered the city to the Persian king to show the weak-willed Christians of Nisibis that even an idolater's understanding exceeded theirs:

> Whereas the [Roman] king became a [pagan] priest and dishonored our churches,
> the Magian king honored the sanctuary.
> His honoring our sanctuary has doubled our consolation.
> [God] saddened and gladdened us but did not exile us.

85. Eph. *CJ* II.20–21.
86. Eph. *CJ* II.22.

He reproved that errant one [Julian] by means of his erring counterpart [Shapur];
since the priest [Julian] oppressed, He rewarded the Magus.[87]

In his third *Hymn against Julian,* Ephrem further explains God's motives during the years that Nisibis endured war with the Persians. He understands that if he is going to claim that God sent Shapur to bring down the pagan Roman emperor, he must first explain why God defended Nisibis during Constantius's reign but failed to help him defeat the Persians. Ephrem's tortuous explanation is that victory had to be forestalled so that Julian could come to the throne, invade Persia, and then be killed:

He prevented the cross that came down from gaining victory,
not because the victorious [Jesus/cross] was unable to gain victory,
but so that a pit might be dug for the evildoer [Julian]
who came down with his conjurers to the east.
But since he came down and was struck [by a javelin], the discerning saw
that the battle in which he would be put to shame had been lying in wait for him.
Know that because of this the time was long and delayed
so that the pure one [Constantine/Constantius?] might complete the years of his kingship
and the accursed one [Julian] might also complete the measure of his paganism.[88]

For Constantine and Lactantius, it was the elder Shapur, Shapur I, who was the tool of providence, to bring down Valerian. For Ephrem, it was Shapur II who was the tool, to bring down Julian. In this interpretation of history, God did not forsake his flock when he allowed the Persians to triumph over the Romans; rather, he used the Persians to depose persecuting Roman emperors. The power divinely granted to Shapur to unseat Julian took on a striking visuality when the Roman emperor's corpse arrived in Nisibis. The body was en route to Tarsus and, as Ephrem and Ammianus both explain, passed through Nisibis as the city was being handed over to Shapur.[89] Ammianus says that with Jovian's permission, Bineses, a Persian noble,

---

87. Eph. *CJ* II.27.
88. Eph. *CJ* II.7–8.
89. Eph. *CJ* III.1–7; Amm. Marc. XXV.9. Ammianus says that Julian had told his general Procopius that he wanted to be interred in Tarsus (XXV.9.12), the city where he had planned on wintering had his retreat from Mesopotamia been successful (XXIII.2.5). On the conveyance and burial of Julian's corpse, see M. Dimaio, "The Transfer of the Remains of the Emperor Julian from Tarsus to Constantinople," *Byz* 48 (1978): 43–50.

entered Nisibis and raised the Persian flag over the citadel. The Romans, in keeping with the terms of the treaty, were to evacuate immediately.[90]

Respectfully, Ammianus does not dwell on the arrival or departure of Julian's corpse during the flag raising, but Ephrem exclaims in wonder how "by chance the corpse of that accursed one, / crossing over toward the rampart met me near the city!"[91] He delights in the simultaneity of "the standard of the captor [being] set up on the tower" and "the corpse of the persecutor [being] laid in a coffin," asking rhetorically, "Who indeed set a time for meeting / when corpse and standard-bearer both at one moment were present?"[92] As Sidney Griffith explains, in Ephrem's "paradoxical view, the image of Nisibis, with her symbolic Persian flag standing out in the breeze, came to stand as a symbol for the defeat of the very paganism which, by the poet's own account, had been the ultimate cause of the city's surrender to the Persians."[93] The Persian flag over Nisibis represented not only the defeat of paganism in the Roman Empire but also the concomitant interpretation of Shapur as a useful adversary. The Persian king was an errant magus, but Ephrem does not describe him as a persecutor—that was Julian's role.

Shapur, Jovian, and the Christians of Persia in the Julian Romance

The Syriac *Julian Romance*, a polemical work written in early sixth-century Roman Edessa, considers anew Julian as the true persecutor of Christians.[94]

---

90. Amm. Marc. XXV.9.1.
91. Eph. *CJ* III.1.
92. Eph. *CJ* III.2–3.
93. S. H. Griffith, "Ephraem the Syrian's Hymns 'Against Julian': Meditations on History and Imperial Power," *VChr* 41 (1987): 249.
94. Although H. J. W. Drijvers suggests a late fourth-century date that seems impossibly early given the text's scope and way of handling Shapur II, his conclusions about it are otherwise reasonable: "The so-called Romance of Julian was written at Edessa, in the School of the Persians, where Ephraem and other exiles from Nisibis had a great influence. Ephraem's typological view of history and the rôle of the Christian emperor laid the foundations for the elaborate form they took in this Romance. It was originally written in Syriac, made use of Syriac sources like the Abgar legend and its legendary local offspring, and came into existence probably shortly after Shapur II's death, when persecution of Christians in the Sassanian empire had stopped for a time." See Drijvers, "The Syriac Romance of Julian: Its Function, Place of Origin and Original Language," in *VI Symposium Syriacum 1992*, OCA 247, ed. R. Lavenant (Rome: Pontificio Istituto Orientale, 1994), 213–14.

For a summary and full bibliography of the competing narratives of the text's origins, see A. M. Butts, "Julian Romance," in *Gorgias Encyclopedic Dictionary of the Syriac Heritage*, ed.

A novelistic account of his reign, the text draws on Ephrem's *Hymns* and advances a narratively sophisticated account of Shapur's role in bringing down the pagan king of Rome. Unlike Ephrem's *Hymns,* however, it acknowledges, but then moderates, Shapur's role as a persecutor of Christians.[95]

The *Romance* begins by portraying Julian, eagerly assisted by the Jews, as the persecutor of Christians in the Roman Empire. Constantine, the narrator reminds his readers, had ended the persecution of Christians before he wrote a letter to Shapur and threatened to invade Persia. But Julian also wrote to Shapur, and then went to war against him, because the Sasanian king had stopped killing Christians.[96] In the first two parts of the text, which are narratively distinct from the third, Julian's adversary is not Shapur but Eusebius of Rome. As Han J. W. Drijvers points out, Eusebius of Rome "undoubtedly finds his legendary origin in Eusebius of Nicomedia, who baptized Constantine on his death-bed and was in charge of Julian's education."[97]

S. P. Brock, A. M. Butts, G. A. Kiraz, and L. Van Rompay (Piscataway, NJ: Gorgias, 2011), 208–9. The text is problematic in that the main manuscript witness (BL Add. 15,641) is acephalous and contains parts written in the sixth century along with other folios written centuries later. A transcription of the manuscript is available; see J. G. E. Hoffmann, *Iulianos der Abtruennige* (Leiden: Brill, 1880). Paul Bedjan published parts of the Syriac text in *AMS* VI, 218–97. The only published English translation (which is also the only complete translation in any language) is often inaccurate: H. Gollancz, *Julian the Apostate* (London: Oxford University Press, 1928).

95. Jan Willem Drijvers has published a number of articles on the *Julian Romance,* most of which include a good deal of summary and evaluation of the text. One of these deals with Jewish-Christian polemics in the text; another addresses the pagan-Christian polemics in the first two parts of the *Romance,* which are set in Rome; a third compares the material about Jovian in the *Romance* to his treatment by Ammianus; and a fourth looks at how the text presents the Christian Jovian as a new Constantine. See Drijvers, "The Syriac Julian Romance: Aspects of the Jewish-Christian Controversy in Late Antiquity," in *All Those Nations . . . Cultural Encounters within and with the Near East,* ed. H.L.J. Vanstiphout (Groningen: Styx, 1999), 31–42; Drijvers, "Julian the Apostate and the City of Rome: Pagan-Christian Polemics in the Syriac *Julian Romance,*" in *Syriac Polemics: Studies in Honour of Gerrit Jan Reinink,* Orientalia Lovaniensia Analecta 170, ed. W.J. van Bekkum, Drijvers, and A.C. Klugkist (Leuven: Peeters, 2007), 1–20; Drijvers, "Ammianus, Jovian, and the Syriac *Julian Romance,*" *JLA* 4 (2011): 280–97; and Drijvers, "The Emperor Jovian as New Constantine in the Syriac *Julian Romance,*" *SP* 45 (2010): 229–33. Daniel Schwartz situates the *Romance* among non-Chalcedonians in sixth-century Edessa and reads it as a response to Justinian's overtures against them. See Schwartz, "Religious Violence and Eschatology in the *Syriac Julian Romance,*" *JECS* 19 (2011): 565–87.

96. Gollancz, *Julian the Apostate,* 111.

97. H.J.W. Drijvers, "Syriac Romance of Julian," 208. Amm. Marc. XXII.9.4 indicates that Julian was "brought up" by Eusebius and was distantly related to him. After Constantine's death, Eusebius became the bishop of Constantinople, "New Rome."

The first two parts of the *Romance* are a litany of pagan affronts against Christians and Christianity—attacks that Julian encouraged. But Eusebius (of Rome) prophesies that God's justice will prevail and that Julian will die "in the country of the Chaldeans."[98] Of much greater interest than Julian's anticipated death, however, is the intrigue prior to it: The *Romance* explains that Jovian, Shapur, and Shapur's general and chief mobed (priest), who is called Arimhar, sent a series of furtive letters to one another while Julian was still alive. This unlikely trio hoped to forge a peace agreement between Rome and Persia, the terms of which would include the overthrow of Julian and the return of a Christian (Jovian) to the Roman throne.

It quickly becomes clear that the *Romance* is a novelistic attempt at explaining away all the theologically difficult questions that must have arisen for Christians during Julian's reign and its aftermath: Why did Jovian (and other Christians) serve in Julian's army? Why did Jovian hide his Christianity from Julian? Why was Julian initially so successful against the Persians, before losing so mightily? Why did Nisibis have to be surrendered to the Persians? What was Shapur's role in Jovian's rise to the throne? In answering these questions and many others, the *Romance* minimizes the importance of the fall of Nisibis in two ways: first, by interpreting Julian's death as providentially decreed, and second, by explaining the elevation of Jovian, with the help of Shapur and Arimhar, as the means by which Christians in both the Roman and the Persian Empires could be freed from persecution.

According to the *Romance,* even though Jovian knew that Shapur had persecuted Christians, he was willing to work with him, and with his mobed Arimhar, in order to depose Julian. One of the main narrative devices is the furtiveness of Jovian's plotting against Julian. Jovian has to appear loyal to the emperor, so the *Romance* goes to great lengths to explain how he secretly contrived to topple Julian, save the Christian people, and make peace with Persia. His first step is to cultivate a friendship with Arimhar. They exchange many letters, and Jovian eventually persuades the Zoroastrian priest to convert to Christianity. Once the mobed has become a Christian, Jovian proposes that he assassinate Shapur to prove that his conversion was made in earnest.[99] As

---

98. H. J. W. Drijvers, "Syriac Romance of Julian," 208, with reference to Gollancz, *Julian the Apostate*, 10.

99. Gollancz, *Julian the Apostate*, 167. Later, Jovian again attempts to persuade Arimhar to kill Shapur, but in the convoluted sequence of events that follows, Jovian ends up helping Shapur—on Arimhar's advice—so that the king will owe him a debt of gratitude (192–93). For the love between Jovian and Arimhar, see 113.

Drijvers notes, this is "a very ingenious narrative plot: two pagan kings assisted by two crypto-Christian subordinates."[100]

On one occasion, an officer loyal to Julian apprehends a messenger bearing a letter from Arimhar to Jovian. It seems as if Jovian's double-dealing is about to be revealed, but, in a plot twist worthy of a spy novel, the letter turns out to be a fake. Arimhar had anticipated that it would be intercepted, and so he composed it accordingly. Rather than reveal Jovian's treachery, the letter suggests that Arimhar had betrayed Shapur and that he and Jovian had been diligently collaborating behind the scenes toward Julian's victory.[101]

Jovian is equally savvy in his dealings with the Persians. He colludes with Shapur in the event that Arimhar cannot (or will not) assassinate the Persian king. With Jovian's full knowledge, Shapur sends a letter to the Roman camp after Julian dies. In it, he touts Jovian as the most qualified person to rule over the Romans. Far from reading this as evidence of Jovian's treachery, the Roman soldiers take it as a divine message: Julian's death and Shapur's endorsement of Jovian, they exclaim, must be the will of the god of the Christians.[102] After Jovian reveals that he was secretly Christian all along, the soldiers acknowledge that they too had hidden their faith out of fear of Julian.[103]

Following the common theme in the *Romance* that nothing is ever as it seems, the text ends by presenting Shapur in a whole new light: as a peacemaker. According to the *Romance,* once Jovian became emperor, he did not negotiate a peace treaty with Shapur. Instead, he writes a bellicose letter to the Persian king, declaring that God would lead the Persians to sue the Romans for peace—this apparently to avoid the embarrassing reality that the Romans had no choice but to ask for Shapur's mercy. Shapur, however, discards Jovian's letter and fabricates a new one from the emperor, which he then reads aloud to the assembled Persian nobles. The invented letter presents Jovian as supplicating for peace and referring to himself as the servant of the

---

100. H. J. W. Drijvers, "Syriac Romance of Julian," 208–9.

101. For this episode, which includes an account of those spying on Jovian being kind to the Christians of Edessa and not persecuting them as Julian wished, see Gollancz, *Julian the Apostate,* 167–71. Elsewhere (151), Jovian is described as fasting in sackcloth and ashes for the Christians of Edessa while he is resident in Nisibis. According to the *Romance* (161–63), the Jews of Nisibis complained to Julian that Jovian would not persecute the city's Christians.

102. Gollancz, *Julian the Apostate,* 207.

103. Gollancz, *Julian the Apostate,* 211–12.

Persians. Shapur knows that this is the only way the Sasanian nobles will relent in their continued push for war and territorial conquest.[104]

Of course, the key to peace is Nisibis. In other late ancient sources, Jovian's cession of the city is a regrettable but necessary way for the Christian emperor to win the safety of the Roman army trapped in Mesopotamia. In the *Romance*, however, Shapur and Jovian converse as father and son: the Persian king does not demand Nisibis as a condition of peace but rather asks for it as recompense for the destruction that Persia had endured thanks to Julian. In return, he offers his "son" Jovian anything he likes. Jovian's sole request is that while Nisibis remains under Sasanian control, no Christian in Persia be persecuted.[105] Roman Nisibis, in other words, becomes the price paid by the West to save fellow Christians in the East. Of course, Shapur readily agrees to Jovian's request and issues an edict declaring a penalty of death for anyone who harms or steals from a Christian. At the royal treasury's expense, he then rebuilds all the churches in Persia that he had destroyed.[106]

---

104. Gollancz, *Julian the Apostate*, 218–20. Following this scene, Shapur sends a letter to Jovian demanding the emperor's blood as a sacrifice for peace (223). Jovian, having seen in a vision that Julian's sacrifice would end the war (192), seems to understand the ruse and thus consents to come before Shapur. Once in the presence of the Persian king and his nobles, he is at the same time so fearless and so deferential that the nobles insist that Shapur refrain from killing him. Shapur and Jovian then embrace, and Shapur declares that Jovian's act of submission is sufficient to erase the debt of sacrifice owed by the Romans to the Persians (224–25).

105. According to the *Romance* (Gollancz, *Julian the Apostate*, 237), the citizens of Nisibis had already departed for Edessa by the time that Jovian and Shapur reached the city. See J. Teixidor, "Conséquences politiques et culturelles de la victoire sassanide à Nisibe," in *Les relations internationales: Actes du Colloque de Strasbourg*, ed. E. Frézouls and A. Jacquemin (Paris: De Boccard, 1995), 504.

This notion of a limited occupation of Nisibis (one hundred years, according to the *Romance*) is, in H.J.W. Drijvers's view, unique to Syriac histories and historians with an Edessene background. See Drijvers, "Syriac Romance of Julian," 213. Similarly, the idea that Jovian's cession of Nisibis ended the persecution of Christians in Persia also seems to be unique to later Syriac histories and chronicles. See Teixidor, "Conséquences politiques," 503. On this point, the late seventh-century *Resh Melle* of John bar Penkaye appears to draw heavily from earlier sources, such as the *Romance* and Ephrem's *Hymns against Julian*. Like the *Romance*, John portrays Jovian as the deliverer of Christians in both the East and the West and suggests that he gave Nisibis to Shapur by way of ending the persecution of Christians in Persia. Like Ephrem's *Hymns*, John acknowledges that Shapur honored the Christian altars of Nisibis whereas Julian persecuted Christians and destroyed Christian churches. See John bar Penkaye, *Resh Melle* XIV, in A. Mingana, *Sources syriaques*, vol. 1 (Leipzig: Otto Harrassowitz, 1907), pt. 2, 115–31; and H. Kaufhold, "Anmerkungen zur Textüberlieferung der *Chronik* des Johannes bar Penkaye," *OC* 87 (2003): 65–79.

106. For the polite conversation about Nisibis between Jovian and Shapur and for the edict outlining the protections accorded to Christians, see Gollancz, *Julian the Apostate*, 233–37.

CONCLUSIONS

Through the interwoven histories presented in this chapter, I have tried to show how the defense and loss of Nisibis were often narrated in very similar yet radically different ways to serve competing historiographical ends. Christian and non-Christian authors in the Roman Empire do not tell two wholly different stories. In fact, they use the same narrative elements—rivers and levees, gnats and elephants, corpses and flags—to recount their histories. Yet Julian was writing a panegyric; Ephrem, Christian historical poetry; Ammianus, a Roman military history; and Theodoret, an ecclesiastical history. While it makes a good story to say that Nisibis was a Christian city and that its Christian defenders must have spurred Shapur into turning against the Christians of his empire, it is just that—a good story and a good bit of hagiography about the bishops of Nisibis. There are plenty of late ancient narratives that cloud the idea of a stalwartly Christian Nisibis in the mid-fourth century, not the least of which is Ephrem's ex post facto account of how the city's paganism led to its loss. He is, moreover, the one person among all those who comment on the loss of Nisibis whom we would most expect to malign Shapur as a persecutor of Christians, yet he says nothing about the martyrs of Persia or about Shapur as their oppressor. That this great Christian poet—who was religiously, linguistically, geographically, and culturally closer than any other fourth- or fifth-century Roman writer to the Christians of Persia—fails to present Shapur as a persecutor is strong evidence that Roman Christians had no knowledge of any persecution of Christians in Persia even long after the violence was supposed to have begun.

By the early sixth century, with the composition of the Syriac *Julian Romance* in Roman Edessa, a very different story was in circulation. The narrator, who relied on the Greek novel tradition and many of the historical sources that had long been known about the Roman-Persian war, had also heard about a persecution of Christians in Persia. There is an insistence throughout the *Romance,* though, that Rome had long been a Christian empire and that Julian's army was Christian too, albeit afraid to say so. Indeed, the clarity of *Christian* Rome, temporarily under the sway of a pagan king and set against another pagan ruler in Shapur, comes across quite strongly in the *Romance*. Despite what seems to have been a Roman emperor's humbling submission to a Persian king, it insists that Jovian and Shapur reached a mutual peace, with the Romans freely turning over Nisibis as an apology for Julian's rampage. But the people of that city, Christians all, were not part of the deal. They were able to depart to the West to escape the rule of a pagan king, with Jovian—a second Constantine—staying behind to negotiate the safety of the Roman Empire's fellow Christians in the Persian East.

PART TWO

Roman Captives and Persian Envoys

FOUR

On War and Persecution

APHRAHAṬ THE PERSIAN SAGE AND
THE *MARTYRDOM* AND *HISTORY OF BLESSED
SIMEON BAR ṢABBAʿE*

MORE THAN SIXTY NARRATIVES ABOUT Christian martyrs in Persia have survived. For the most part, these are preserved in Syriac, although some exist in other languages or in both Syriac and some other ancient version. The non-Syriac narratives are found mainly in Greek and Armenian, but there are also a few in Sogdian, a central Asian language whose various writing systems derive from Aramaic.[1] While the *Acts of the Persian Martyrs* attest to persecutions in the mid- and late Sasanian eras and again in the early Islamic period, fully two-thirds of the narratives are set in the fourth century, during the reign of Shapur II. Some, including several that must have been written near the end of the Sasanian period or after the rise of Islam, provide a unique perspective on the historiographical legacy of the fourth-century war between Rome and Persia. Unfortunately, only a few are accessible in the languages of modern scholarship. Most of the *Acts of the Persian Martyrs* remain understudied or completely unexamined, with some notable exceptions.[2] Recent interest in the history of Sasanian Persia and the Syriac

---

1. A small number of texts grouped with the *Acts of the Persian Martyrs* are in Georgian, Latin, Arabic, or Coptic. Additionally, there are modern translations from Syriac into Latin and Arabic. For a full overview of the *Acts,* with references to critical editions, secondary sources, and translations, see the "Guide to the Persian Martyr Acts" in S. P. Brock, *The History of the Holy Mar Maʿin with a Guide to the Persian Martyr Acts,* Persian Martyr Acts in Syriac: Text and Translation, fasc. 1 (Piscataway, NJ: Gorgias, 2009), 77–84.

2. In addition to the studies and translations listed in Brock's guide, see the other books in the Persian Martyr Acts in Syriac: Text and Translation series, A. C. McCollum, *The Story of Mar Pinḥas,* fasc. 2 (Piscataway, NJ: Gorgias, 2013); K. Smith, *The Martyrdom and History of Blessed Simeon bar Ṣabbaʿe,* fasc. 3 (Piscataway, NJ: Gorgias, 2014); and Brock, *The Martyrs of Mount Berʾain,* with an introduction by P. C. Dilley, fasc. 4 (Piscataway, NJ: Gorgias, 2014).

martyrological literature that was written there is, however, poised to transform our understanding of these texts and their utility for the writing of late ancient history.³

While it is of course true that hagiographical literature alone cannot paint a historiographically nuanced picture of Sasanian history, Syriac martyrdom narratives remain among our best and most extensive sources for the period. In fact, many were written as histories. This is not to say that they are thus any more historically "accurate" than hagiographies, but rather that in their frequent attention to broader civic, political, and social concerns, they tend to go beyond the celebration of a single individual. Unlike Greek and even West Syrian writers, East Syrian writers do not tend to draw any distinction between what sort of material should be included in a "history" and what should instead be reserved for a "hagiography." As Joel Walker points out, although East Syrian historians "inherited both the chronicle and church history genres from Syriac translations of Eusebius," the development of these genres among Christians in Persia "quickly became intertwined with hagiography."⁴ This is evident in virtually every East Syriac text from late antique Persia, reflecting the pronounced tendency among East Syrian writers to use biographies as their historiographical models.⁵ With rare exceptions, one cannot, Muriel Debié demonstrates, find any "regular Syriac equivalent to the Greek *bios*, designating saints' *Lives*, nor to *martyrion* for the martyr acts," but instead "all Syriac hagiographical texts are indiscriminately entitled *taš'itâ*, 'story', or *šarbâ*, 'account', 'tale', whatever the literary genre to which they belong."⁶

While the *Acts of the Persian Martyrs* are thus indeed historiographically rich, we are unable to compare the "tales" and "stories" that they preserve to

---

3. The collection of essays in *Jews, Christians and Zoroastrians: Religious Dynamics in a Sasanian Context*, ed. G. Herman (Piscataway, NJ: Gorgias, 2014), is a good recent example of the wide-ranging and interdisciplinary approaches to Sasanian studies that are now being published.

4. J.T. Walker, "A Saint and His Biographer in Late Antique Iraq: The *History of St. George of Izla* (†614) by Babai the Great," in *Writing 'True Stories': Historians and Hagiographers in the Late Antique and Medieval Near East*, ed. A. Papaconstantinou (Turnhout: Brepols, 2010), 40.

5. The literary archetypes for East Syrian historians "are not," Muriel Debié explains, "the expected Western Christian ones of ecclesiastical histories and chronicles but *biographical* histories." See Debié, "Writing History as 'Histoires': The Biographical Dimension of East Syriac Historiography," in *Writing 'True Stories,'* 58. My emphasis.

6. Debié, "Writing History as 'Histoires,'" 43.

histories written by non-Christian Sasanian elites. Juxtaposing the dissimilar accounts of Ammianus Marcellinus and Ephrem the Syrian opens up fourth-century Roman history in intriguing ways, but the only evidence that may attest to how non-Christian Persians in late antiquity conceptualized the fourth century is what can be gleaned (or hypothesized) from relatively sparse inscriptional, numismatic, and sigillographic evidence. As I discussed in earlier chapters, Ammianus purports to preserve an exchange of letters between Shapur and Constantius, but it is only a Latin summary of what the Persian king wrote and is of uncertain accuracy and authenticity. Even the much later Zoroastrian texts that we do have—texts that postdate the Sasanian era—are "strangely silent on Byzantine matters," as Bo Utas points out. "Although *hrôm*, i.e. both the original and the Eastern Rome, now and then appears [in Middle Persian (Pahlavi) literature], it is generally a mere cliché, a label for sundry barbarian countries of the West, just like *chîn* represents the East in general, not just the Chinese Empire."[7] This dearth of Sasanian histories has led to a strange state of affairs, wherein historians of late antique Persia often turn to Syriac Christian martyrdom narratives as their primary literary sources for the history of the Sasanian Empire.

In the late 1970s, Philippe Gignoux ranked the literary sources for the study of Sasanian history. He listed texts written in (and in the languages of) the Sasanian Empire first, post-Sasanian texts composed in the languages of the empire second, and texts written in non-Sasanian languages third.[8] Many Syriac martyrdom narratives thus occupy the top spot in Gignoux's system, but they too are often subdivided, following Paul Devos's estimation of their "valeur historique." Devos's tripartite ranking descends from what he considers the generally reliable "Passions historiques" through the more heroic "Passions épiques" to the mostly fanciful "Passions romantiques."[9] How Sasanian history can and should be written is still a vexing question, and the use of what are essentially hagiographical texts as historical sources

---

7. B. Utas, "Byzantium Seen from Sasanian Iran," in *Aspects of Late Antiquity and Early Byzantium,* ed. L. Rydén and J. O. Rosenqvist (Uppsala: Swedish Research Institute in Istanbul, 1993), 25.

8. P. Gignoux, "Problèmes de distinction et de priorité des sources," in *Prolegomena to the Sources on the History of Pre-Islamic Central Asia,* ed. J. Harmatta (Budapest: Akadémiai Kiadó, 1979), 137–41.

9. P. Devos, "Les martyrs persans à travers leurs acts syriaques," in *Atti del Convegno sul tema: La Persia e il mondo greco-romano* (Rome: Accademia Nazionale dei Lincei, 1966), 213–25.

has led to even more debate in recent years. Although many Sasanian historians remain focused on traditionally positivist concerns about dates, events, and questions of historicity, some have criticized those who have made or used such rankings of the relative historical value of our sources or who have accepted the historical accounts presented in some Syriac martyrdom narratives while dismissing those of others.[10] Still others have fruitfully taken up investigations that center more on interpreting Sasanian material culture than on parsing Christian literary texts.[11]

This chapter continues the reframing of the scholarly discussion about Syriac martyrdom narratives by examining two sources that are typically the first to be used in writing the history of fourth-century Persia. Each chronicles the death of Simeon bar Ṣabbaʿe, the bishop of Seleucia-Ctesiphon who, according to his acts, was "the first one to excel in the land of the East as a blessed martyr of God."[12] Although his name is probably unfamiliar to most modern historians of Christian antiquity, Simeon's martyr acts are key to understanding the hagiography and historiography of the early post-Constantinian period in Persia.

These acts, which are two of the longest texts among the *Acts of the Persian Martyrs*, have a lot to say about the circumstances that spurred Shapur's violence against the Christians of Persia. It is important not to confuse these two versions of Simeon's death, each of which the scholarly literature refers to by several names. The shorter and earlier one, the *Martyrdom (Sahduta) of Blessed Simeon bar Ṣabbaʿe*, is known as the "Short Version," the *Martyrium*, the *recensio antiquior* (following the text's early twentieth-century editor, Michael Kmoskó), or "Simeon A" (following the philological study of Gernot Wiessner in the late 1960s). It was probably composed at the very end of the fourth century or the beginning of the fifth century. The much longer and later version of Simeon's death, the *History (Tashʿita) of Blessed Simeon bar Ṣabbaʿe*, which seems to date to the late fifth century, is alternately known as the "Long Version," the *Narratio*, the *recensio recentior* (Kmoskó), or "Simeon

---

10. The debate is outlined in M.R. Shayegan, "Approaches to the Study of Sasanian History," in *Paitimāna: Essays in Iranian, Indo-European, and Indian Studies in Honor of Hans-Peter Schmidt*, ed. S. Adhami (Costa Mesa, CA: Mazda, 2003), 363–84.

11. Most impressively, M. Canepa, *The Two Eyes of the Earth: Art and Ritual of Kingship between Rome and Sasanian Iran* (Berkeley: University of California Press, 2009).

12. *History of Blessed Simeon bar Ṣabbaʿe* 1. All translations of the *Martyrdom* and *History of Simeon* are from Smith, *Martyrdom and History*.

B" (Wiessner).[13] As a result of their close relationship and similar narrative arcs, the *Martyrdom* and *History of Simeon* (as I refer to them) have frequently, but erroneously, been elided into a single hagiographical history about the fourth century. Yet they must be kept apart and interpreted as quite independent literary constructions, as each presents a strikingly different conception of the fourth century and the history of Christianity in Persia.

Richard Burgess, in his evaluation of Simeon's acts, is quick to acknowledge the differences between the two narratives. In fact, he sees the earlier *Martyrdom* as a historically valuable source but considers the *History* "practically worthless" for the historian, dismissing it as of interest only "to the student of hagiography."[14] Such thinking has to be discarded. The historical value of Syriac martyrdom narratives lies not in how they might be used as historical documents but in how they demonstrate the ways in which Persian Christians claimed and wrote about their past. The differing narrative aims and interpretations of Christian community in the *Martyrdom* and the *History of Simeon* provide evidence of remarkable changes in how the past was understood. By comparing these sources, we are able to see how, for at least two Syriac authors, the relationship between "religion" and "empire" changed dramatically over the course of the fifth century. The differences between the *Martyrdom* and the *History* demonstrate other conceptual shifts as well—in the realms of episcopal authority, Christian-Jewish relations, and the place of the Christians of Persia within a broader Christian history of suffering, persecution, and martyrdom.

THE *DEMONSTRATIONS* OF APHRAHAṬ, THE PERSIAN SAGE

Before I can discuss the *Martyrdom* and *History of Simeon* any further, it is important to consider one earlier Syriac source, a series of twenty-three

---

13. M. Kmoskó, *S. Simeon Bar Ṣabbaʿe: Martyrium et Narratio*, PS 1.2 (Paris: Firmin-Didot, 1907), cols. 715–960; G. Wiessner, *Untersuchungen zur syrischen Literaturgeschichte I: Zur Märtyrerüberlieferung aus der Christenverfolgung Schapurs II.* (Göttingen: Vandenhoeck und Ruprecht, 1967). On the date of Simeon's death and the composition of his acts, see Smith, *Martyrdom and History*, xx–xxix.

14. R. W. Burgess, "The Dates of the Martyrdom of Simeon Bar Ṣabbāʿē and the 'Great Massacre,'" *AB* 117 (1999): 29.

argumentative homilies known as the *Demonstrations* of Aphrahaṭ, the "Persian Sage."[15] The *Demonstrations* predate the *Martyrdom of Simeon* by several decades and the *History of Simeon* by more than a century. They are among the few pieces of Syriac Christian literature that can be dated to the first half of the fourth century.[16] Unfortunately, it is difficult to place where they were written with much accuracy. Little is known about who Aphrahaṭ was or where he lived, other than that it was probably somewhere in Sasanian Persia. It seems that late ancient commentators did not know much about him either. There are few manuscript witnesses to the *Demonstrations,* and one fifth-century Armenian scholiast incorrectly identified them as the work of Jacob the bishop of Nisibis.[17] Whoever he was, Aphrahaṭ was clearly skilled in the art of biblical interpretation. Presumably he was also an authority of some standing in his church, as his homilies seem to have been prompted by an interlocutor's concerns about theology, community, and church order.

Of special interest are *Demonstration* V, "On Wars," and XXI, "On Persecution." Both are typically read as historical testimonies verifying that Shapur persecuted the Christians of Persia, who were unified with the Roman Caesar in their opposition to Shapur's non-Christian regime.[18] But there are reasons to be wary of reading Aphrahaṭ in such a robust way. We

---

15. My thanks to James Walters of Princeton University, who is currently completing his dissertation on the *Demonstrations,* for helping me think through some of my considerations about Aphrahaṭ.

16. For discussions of the dates of the various homilies—long one of their main points of scholarly interest and debate—including their historical context and their relevance to the *Acts of the Persian Martyrs,* see most notably M. J. Higgins, "Aphraates' Dates for Persian Persecution," *ByzZ* 44 (1951): 265–71; T. D. Barnes, "Constantine and the Christians of Persia," *JRS* 75 (1985): 126–28; and Burgess, "Dates of the Martyrdom," 9–17.

17. Aphrahaṭ's baptismal name was apparently Jacob, hence the misidentification. For a discussion of his identity and the ancient reasons for and modern reasons against thinking that he should be identified with Jacob of Nisibis, see the introduction to the French translation of the *Demonstrations* by M.-J. Pierre, *Aphraate le Sage persan: Les Exposés I–X,* SC 349 (Paris: Éditions du Cerf, 1988), 33–41. J. Parisot published a Syriac edition of Aphrahaṭ's work (with a Latin translation) as *Aphraatis Sapientis Persae Demonstrationes I–XXII,* PS I.1 (Paris: Firmin-Didot, 1894) and *Aphraatis Sapientis Persae Demonstrationes XXIII* (with a glossary and an index), PS I.2 (Paris: Firmin-Didot, 1907), 1–489. For an English translation of all twenty-three *Demonstrations,* see A. Lehto, *The Demonstrations of Aphrahat, the Persian Sage,* Gorgias Eastern Christian Studies 27 (Piscataway, NJ: Gorgias, 2010). Unless otherwise noted, I have used Lehto's translation.

18. See Barnes, "Constantine and the Christians of Persia"; and C. E. Morrison, "The Reception of the Book of Daniel in Aphrahaṭ's Fifth Demonstration, 'On Wars,'" *Hugoye* 7 (2004): 55–82.

know little about him, and rarely does he provide much information about what drove him to write each of his *Demonstrations*. More often than not, his discourses are tediously long winded on biblical interpretation and the elucidation of prophecy but frustratingly terse and elliptical about historical events. As the name of his collected homilies suggests (the Syriac noun *taḥwyata* means "examples" or "demonstrations"), Aphrahaṭ tends to make his point by providing his readers with one biblical example after another on a given topic.

There are plenty of biblical examples in "On Persecution"—which is believed to have been inspired by Shapur's violence against Simeon bar Ṣabbaʿe and the one hundred clerics who were martyred with him—but few historical details. Aphrahaṭ never mentions Shapur or Simeon in *Demonstration* XXI, nor does he name or discuss the trial of any other Christian martyr in the Sasanian Empire. Oddly, he says more about an earlier persecution in the Roman Empire than about any ongoing persecution in the Persian Empire, and even then not much information is provided. He says only that there was "for our brothers in the West in the days of Diocletian a great oppression and persecution upon the entire Church of God throughout its whole realm. Churches were torn down and uprooted, and many confessors and martyrs confessed."[19]

From its outset, *Demonstration* XXI is an intellectual exercise in biblical exegesis that reads less as a response to an ongoing persecution and more as Aphrahaṭ's learned rebuttal in a theological debate. He explains that he has heard how the Jews scoff at Christians and categorize their (unnamed) trials as proof that God has rejected them: "I heard a reproach that greatly distressed me," Aphrahaṭ begins. "The unclean say, 'This people that has been gathered from the peoples has no God.' And the wicked say, 'If they have a God, why does he not seek vengeance for his people?' The gloom thickens around me even more whenever the Jews reproach us and magnify themselves over our people."[20] As a result of passages such as this, Aphrahaṭ's work has been taken as an attempt to refute Jewish criticism of Christianity and, as Naomi Koltun-Fromm puts it, to forestall Persian Christians from "returning to their native Judaism in the face of martyrdom."[21]

---

19. Aph. *Dem.* XXI.23; my translation.
20. Aph. *Dem.* XXI.1.
21. N. Koltun-Fromm, *Hermeneutics of Holiness: Ancient Jewish and Christian Notions of Sexuality and Religious Community* (Oxford: Oxford University Press, 2010), 23.

Although Aphrahaṭ provides no evidence for us to conclude that Christians in Persia had once been Jews or were becoming Jews again to escape persecution, it is true that the primary agenda of *Demonstration* XXI is to combat Jewish criticism of Christianity. To do so, Aphrahaṭ employs the written testimony of the prophets and the lived example of the persecuted righteous ones to concoct a series of ripostes against the Jews, using their own biblical exempla as evidence. He calls as witnesses Jacob, Moses, Joshua, Jephthah, David, Elijah, Elisha, Hezekiah, Josiah, Daniel, Hananiah, and Mordecai, who were persecuted just "as Jesus was persecuted."[22] If Aphrahaṭ intended a litany of persecuted Jews as balm for oppressed Christians in the Sasanian Empire, then such a purpose becomes evident in only the most general way in one of the last lines of his homily. He refers to a persecution "in our days" that occurred "because of our sins."[23] Nothing else is said. No martyr is named; no further details are provided. In fact, the belief that the persecution "in our days" must have been Shapur's comes not from this homily—the one supposedly about Shapur's persecution—but from a brief aside at the end of Aphrahaṭ's twenty-third and final *Demonstration,* "On the Grape Cluster." The closing lines of this *Demonstration* date the text by referring to its composition in "the thirty-sixth year of Shapur, king of Persia, who has stirred up the persecution, and in the fifth year after the churches had been uprooted, and in the year in which there was a great ravaging of martyrs in the land of the East."[24]

We cannot rule out that this closing line was appended by a later copyist and not written by Aphrahaṭ, but it does indicate that the Christians of Persia did not consider Shapur's reign a pleasant one. Nevertheless, it is imperative to understand that this one comment at the end of Aphrahaṭ's work is the only explicit reference to Shapur's persecution in all twenty-three of his *Demonstrations*. Nowhere in the *Demonstrations* does Aphrahaṭ comment on even the most basic question of why Shapur is angry with Christians. He does not cite the Roman emperor as a cause, and he discusses neither the execution of Simeon bar Ṣabbaʿe nor the supposed decimation of priests and bishops in Persia. All we have is this lone reference to Shapur's "great ravaging

---

22. Aph. *Dem.* XXI.9–23. On Aphrahaṭ and Judaism, see J. Neusner, *Aphrahat and Judaism: The Christian-Jewish Argument in Fourth-Century Iran* (Leiden: Brill, 1971); and N. Koltun-Fromm, "A Jewish-Christian Conversation in Fourth-Century Persian Mesopotamia," *JJS* 47 (1996): 45–63.

23. Aph. *Dem.* XXI.23.

24. Aph. *Dem.* XXIII.69.

of martyrs," which appears at the end of a long series of homilies in a manuscript that was written centuries after the events in question.

Historical details are similarly lacking in *Demonstration* V. This homily has traditionally been dated to several years before "On Persecution," and it may have been written in the late 330s. Aphrahaṭ begins by speaking rather cryptically about some sort of impending turmoil, only gradually revealing that he is referring to a brewing conflict between Rome and Persia.[25] He seems uncomfortable openly advancing his thoughts about the looming war: "Because the time is evil," he writes, "listen in secret to what I am writing you."[26] Aphrahaṭ then puts forth an interpretation of the Book of Daniel that foretells Rome's triumph over Persia. Some have suggested that he does more than that. In his reading of the text, Jacob Neusner claims that Aphrahaṭ soothed his readers in the "Church of Iran" with the hopeful promise that Shapur would soon be vanquished. This leads Neusner to conclude that the Christians of Persia must have "regarded Shapur's wars as those of Satan, and the victory of Byzantium as the triumph of Christ."[27] While Aphrahaṭ can only be referring to Constantine and Shapur (even though the text names neither), and while he does find in Daniel a prophetic message of the imminent triumph of the Roman Empire, more has to be said. For Aphrahaṭ does not begin with contemporary events and then turn to the Bible for passages to support his views. He does just the opposite. He begins with the Bible and seeks to find how biblical prophecies might be becoming manifest in his day. The distinction is subtle but consequential.

When Aphrahaṭ's biblical starting place is acknowledged, one can see that the common interpretation of his hope in "On Wars" is in error. He does not turn to Daniel to express his desire for a Roman victory, full stop. In fact, there is no evidence in "On Wars" that he believes the Roman Empire and its Christian king will "liberate" the Christians of Persia. Aphrahaṭ is not so shortsighted. His views about the coming war, filtered as they are through the lens of biblical prophecy, are entirely apocalyptic. He sees in Daniel and in the growing tension between the two empires possible evidence of the coming eschaton. As David Lane argues, when Aphrahaṭ says that Rome will

---

25. On this gradualness, see Morrison, "Reception of the Book of Daniel," 7, 15.
26. Aph. *Dem.* V.2.
27. J. Neusner, "Babylonian Jewry and Shapur II's Persecution of Christianity from 339 to 379 A.D.," *HUCA* 43 (1975): 79. See also Morrison, "Reception of the Book of Daniel"; and F. Decret, "Les conséquences sur le christianisme en Perse de l'affrontement des empires romain et sassanide: De Shâpûr Ier à Yazdgard Ier," *RecAug* 14 (1979): 134.

triumph over Persia, he is merely reiterating a "commonplace among Jews of the Babylonian diaspora." He operates in what might be called a midrashic exegetical frame of mind and approaches eschatological ideas in this way.[28]

For Aphrahaṭ, as for other late antique interpreters of Daniel (both Jewish and Christian), Rome is an ephemeral kingdom. A Roman victory over Persia would be merely a stepping-stone toward a grander providential hope. The Roman Empire per se is not a liberator but only an expedient, a tool, that from the Christian perspective advances the aims of the true Liberator. Rome is, after all, the fourth beast in Daniel. At root, it is thus part of the great procession of empires, along with Babylonia, Persia, and Greece. As "On Wars" reveals, Aphrahaṭ was clearly aware that a Christian emperor was leading the Roman Empire. Indeed, he acknowledges that the "banner" of Jesus "is everywhere in that land" and even says that Rome's armies "are clothed with his [Jesus's] armour and will not be defeated in war."[29] As Sebastian Brock points out, however, Aphrahaṭ speaks in terms not of "the Romans" versus "the Persians" but of the "people of God" versus those "outside." Even an empire that is led by a Christian and flies the banner of Jesus is not an empire that, qua empire, is equivalent to the "people of God."[30] For Aphrahaṭ, it is not "Rome" but "the descendants of Esau" that "will not be conquered"—until the kingdom of God conquers them.[31] Even the descendants of Esau are not abiding liberators but temporary placeholders.[32]

In his article assessing the circumstances of Constantine's letter to Shapur, David Frendo comments that the *Demonstrations* are completely out of place in any discussion of Roman military policy. Aphrahaṭ's "veiled prophetic

---

28. D. Lane, "Of Wars and Rumours of Peace: Apocalyptic Material in Aphrahaṭ and Šubḥalmaran," in *New Heaven and New Earth: Prophecy and the Millennium—Essays in Honour of Anthony Gelston*, ed. P.J. Harland and C.T.R. Hayward (Leiden: Brill, 1999), 240. On Aphrahaṭ's "Judaizing" tendencies and exegetical approach and style, see M.-J. Pierre, "Thèmes de la controverse d'Aphraate avec les tendances judaïsantes de son église," in *Chrétiens en terre d'Iran II, Controverses des chrétiens dans l'Iran sassanide*, StIran 36, ed. C. Jullien (Leuven: Peeters, 2008), 115–28.

29. Aph. *Dem.* V.24.

30. S.P. Brock, "Christians in the Sasanian Empire: A Case of Divided Loyalties," in *Religion and National Identity*, ed. S. Mews (Oxford: Oxford University Press, 1982), 12–14.

31. Aph. *Dem.* V.24.

32. This exegesis of Daniel evokes the interpretive tradition of the Christ-Augustus synchrony—the supposed correlation between Jesus's birth and the beginning of the Roman principate under Caesar Augustus—which is found in a number of early Christian writers, including Eusebius. See J.M. Schott, *Christianity, Empire, and the Making of Religion in Late Antiquity* (Philadelphia: University of Pennsylvania Press, 2008), 154.

musings (if that is what they are) might tell us something about the plight of the Christians of Persia," he says, but "they can tell us nothing about Constantine's policy towards Iran."[33] This is certainly correct, but I would press the conclusion further: attempting to glean any evidence from Aphrahaṭ "about the plight of the Christians of Persia" is nearly as difficult as using his work as evidence for Roman military policy. Unquestionably, Aphrahaṭ's *Demonstrations* tell us a remarkable amount about how one Persian Christian used and interpreted the Bible in the mid-fourth century, but they provide little to go on about Shapur, Constantine, or the war between Rome and Persia. Fortunately, Aphrahaṭ is not our only source.

THE *MARTYRDOM* AND *HISTORY OF BLESSED SIMEON BAR ṢABBAʿE*

According to the *Martyrdom* and *History of Blessed Simeon bar Ṣabbaʿe*, the executioners of Shapur II beheaded Simeon, "the Son of Dyers," in 339.[34] Simeon was the bishop of Seleucia-Ctesiphon on the Tigris, the winter capital of the Sasanian Empire. He was arrested there and then deported to the king's summer palace at Karka d-Ledan, in the foothills of the Zagros Mountains, where he was tried and executed. Simeon was among the first to be killed in the "Great Persecution," as Shapur's forty-year oppression of Christians came to be known in Syriac martyrological literature, and his acts present him as Shapur's most prominent victim.

Although their details differ, the two Syriac versions of Simeon's death (the shorter and earlier *Martyrdom of Simeon* and the longer and later *History of Simeon*) agree that the bishop of Seleucia-Ctesiphon was the leader of the Christians of Persia and that he was arrested for refusing to collect taxes from his flock. If it was tax avoidance that led to his arrest, then it was brazenness before the king that hastened the bishop's execution. Simeon openly mocked the king's gods, keenly aware of the likely consequences of his actions. His

---

33. D. Frendo, "Constantine's Letter to Shapur II: Its Authenticity, Occasion, and Attendant Circumstances," *BAI* 15 (2001): 69n73.

34. According to the *Martyrdom of Simeon* 7 and *History of Simeon* 4, Simeon's arrest, trial, and execution took place in the thirty-first year of Shapur. As Shapur's reign began in 309, the date of Simeon's death would thus be 339/40. But for various reasons, including the brief aside about the date of Shapur's persecution in Aph. *Dem.* XXIII, his death has been dated to 344. See the discussion (with references) in Smith, *Martyrdom and History*, xx–xxiv.

responses to Shapur's interrogations, which the *Martyrdom* and *History of Simeon* recall in rather different ways, are illuminating. In both texts, Shapur quickly puts aside the issue of taxes and focuses instead on persuading Simeon to join him in worshiping the sun.[35] It is no surprise that Simeon rejects the king's entreaties and rails against Shapur's sun god. In the *Martyrdom of Simeon*, he disparages the sun as an ignorant creature unworthy of the veneration that is more rightly due to its creator.[36] In the *History of Simeon*, by contrast, there is a more protracted debate between Simeon and Shapur, in which the bishop offers the king a nuanced theological explanation of why he will not worship fire, the sun, or the moon.[37] The level of the king's discourse is more elevated too. The Shapur of the *History* has enough knowledge of Christianity to ask the bishop difficult theological questions that compel him to address and correct the king's misunderstandings and, in the process, to explain how "Christians" differ from "Marcionites."[38]

In his meticulous philological study of Simeon's acts and several related Syriac martyrdom narratives from Sasanian Persia, Gernot Wiessner argues that the *Martyrdom* and *History of Simeon* should be classed as siblings. Both texts, he argues, are indebted to the same sources, and therefore, however much the particular tendencies of one might differ from those of the other, they ultimately spring from the same font.[39] Wiessner uses the stemmatic method to posit a common "ABx" source for both "A" (the *Martyrdom of Simeon*) and "B" (the *History of Simeon*), a *vorlage* that in turn goes back to a hypothetical *Steuerquelle* (tax source) and a hypothetical *Judenquelle* (Jewish source). The *Steuerquelle* and *Judenquelle* represent, for Wiessner, the two main reasons why the Christians of Persia were persecuted: they refused to pay their taxes, and the Jews who had Shapur's ear accused them of being traitors.

In my study of the two versions of Simeon's death, I argue that their differences are better explained by reading the *History* as a substantially revised and expanded version of the *Martyrdom*.[40] The *History* is not the *Martyrdom*'s sibling, as Wiessner would have it, but its child. In analyzing how the *History* changes and expands on the *Martyrdom*, one senses that the

---

35. *Martyrdom of Simeon* 17; *History of Simeon* 41.
36. *Martyrdom of Simeon* 10, 31.
37. *History of Simeon* 43, 45, 77.
38. *History of Simeon* 44. See also the discussion of this episode in chapter 5.
39. Wiessner, *Untersuchungen zur syrischen Literaturgeschichte*.
40. See the introduction to Smith, *Martyrdom and History*.

two must have been written in very different social, political, and religious contexts.[41] And by comparing these versions of Simeon's martyrdom, we gain many insights into the changing approaches to the writing of fourth-century history among the Christians of Persia.

The Causes of Shapur's Persecution in the Martyrdom *and* History of Simeon

One of the most obvious differences between the two texts is how each accounts for the cause of Shapur's oppression. The introductory sections of the later text, the *History of Simeon,* invoke "blessed Constantine" several times. The *History* refers to Shapur's suspicions about the Christians of Persia and to Constantine's role in keeping them unharmed, saying that as soon as "blessed Constantine began to rule until his death, a span of thirty-three years that he reigned over the Romans, there were no martyrs to be found in the land of the West. But immediately upon the death of the triumphant Constantine, Shapur, the king of the Persians, began to harass the Christian people, to afflict and persecute the priests and the *qyama,* and to destroy the churches in all of his realm."[42] Alluding to the Persian king's advances on the Roman eastern frontier, the narrator of the *History of Simeon* says, "After the death of blessed Constantine, king of the Romans, Shapur took the opportunity to contend against (Constantine's) sons who were still young. He continually raided the land of the Romans, and, for this reason, he became increasingly incensed with hatred for the servants of God who (dwelled) in the land of his jurisdiction."[43]

According to the narrator, Shapur registered a connection between Christians across imperial boundaries and as a result saw those in his realm

---

41. Michael Penn's excellent study of changes in Syriac manuscripts as reactions to the rise of Islam shows—albeit at a more limited, line-by-line level—how different social, political, and religious contexts affected the transmission of these texts. See Penn, "Monks, Manuscripts, and Muslims: Syriac Textual Changes in Reaction to the Rise of Islam," *Hugoye* 12 (2009): 235–57.

42. *History of Simeon* 2. The *qyama,* often known as either the *bnay* or *bnat qyama,* (the "sons" or "daughters of the covenant"), was a quasi-monastic ascetic group. The *qyama* has a long history in Syriac literature. See S. H. Griffith, "Asceticism in the Church of Syria: The Hermeneutics of Early Syrian Monasticism," in *Asceticism,* ed. V. L. Wimbush and R. Valantasis (New York: Oxford University Press), 220–45.

43. *History of Simeon* 4.

as a threat—a Roman fifth column resident in Persia.[44] On returning from "the land of the Romans," presumably following his first failed siege of Nisibis, he composed an unusual edict. The narrator says that the king "wanted, and schemed for, an occasion to persecute the faithful. And he found excuses to subject all Christians in the land of the Persians to a double tax and tribute." Shapur demanded that the authorities in the province of Beth Aramaye arrest and hold Simeon until the bishop agreed to collect a "double poll tax [*ksep resha*] and double tribute [*maddata*]" from all the Christians in Persia.[45] Apparently, Christians were the only residents of Persia subject to these double taxes, which were, in effect, tariffs on their faith.[46] During Simeon's trial, he declares to the king, "Behold, for our faith we should not be compelled to pay a tax, but rather to give a defense of our faith and our teaching. Be sure that for the truth of our teaching we are prepared to give not only our property but also our lives."[47]

As the *History* attests, Simeon's refusal to collect the double tax confirmed for the king that the bishop and his flock were rebels. From the narrator's point of view, the double tax was thus as much a way for Shapur to punish Persian Christians for their presumed allegiance to Christians in the West as

---

44. This idea of the Persian Christians as a "fifth column" is repeated often. See, for example, Barnes, "Constantine and the Christians of Persia," 136, which is sympathetic to Shapur's view of the Christians in his realm as a potential threat, given Constantine's strident Christianity. The noted scholar of pre-Islamic Persia Josef Wiesehöfer also points to the change in Roman foreign policy after Constantine's conversion and the Persians' unease about it. See Wiesehöfer, "'Geteilte Loyalitäten': Religiöse Minderheiten des 3. und 4. Jahrhunderts n. Chr. im Spannungsfeld zwischen Rom und dem sasanidischen Iran," *Klio* 75 (1993): 377–78.

45. *History of Simeon* 4. According to the text, Shapur demanded the tax "from all the people of the *naṣraye* who are in our land." The term *naṣraye*, which is not used in the *Martyrdom of Simeon* but is frequently employed in the *History*, seems to have carried religious, ethnic, and geographic connotations, all at the same time. In different scholarly interpretations, the term ranges from a slur based on a geographical epithet for followers of Jesus, the "Nazarene," through a word for Jewish-Christians, to merely a way of differentiating Syriac-speaking Christians from their Greek-speaking counterparts in the Persian Empire. On the use of the term *naṣraye*, see the discussion in chapter 5.

46. For an interpretation of the double tax as a way of testing the loyalties of Christians while serving as a mechanism by which to keep them under strict imperial control, see Koltun-Fromm, "Jewish-Christian Conversation," 45. For the idea that the tax on Christians and the violence against them was not a persecution but only an emergency measure during the Persians' war with Rome, see K. Mosig-Walburg, "Christenverfolgung und Römerkrieg: Zu Ursachen, Ausmaß und Zielrichtung der Christenverfolgung unter Šāpūr II.," *Iranistik* 7 (2005): 5–84.

47. *History of Simeon* 38.

it was an impromptu fiscal measure designed to raise capital to help defray the cost of the ongoing war against those same Western Christians. Once Shapur hears that Simeon has refused to obey his edict and collect the taxes he has demanded, he announces, "Simeon wants to assemble his disciples and people in rebellion against my kingdom! He wants to make them into servants of Caesar, who shares their devotion. That is why he does not obey my commands."[48] As Shapur sees it, the Christians of Persia "dwell in our land and yet they are of one mind with Caesar, our enemy, and we fight but they enjoy quiet."[49]

A markedly different narrative emerges in the *Martyrdom of Simeon*. While this text emphasizes that the oppression of Christians began via the imposition of taxes, it never claims that preexisting taxes were doubled. Nor does it explain what kinds of taxes were imposed, whether a land tax, a poll tax, some sort of new tax on Christians, or just general extortion via the tax collectors' inappropriate use of their office. We are left to surmise, thanks to the evidence provided in the *History of Simeon*, that zealous tax collectors were taxing Christians at the direction of the king's edict. But if this evidence is kept aside, it at once becomes obvious that the *Martyrdom of Simeon* is telling another story entirely. The *Martyrdom* does not mention Shapur's anger toward Christians or even that the king has addressed the Christians

---

48. *History of Simeon* 11. A more literal translation is "He wants to make them into servants of Caesar, who is a son of their fear." The use of "son" (*bar*) in this case implies cooperation or corporate action, as another translation, "who is one of their co-fearers," suggests. "Their fear [*deḥlta*]" is a way of saying something akin to "religion," although that translation is problematic in a late antique context. The use of *fear* to describe a particular sect comes up again in *History of Simeon* 22, where Simeon lists the "fears" (in this case the heresies) that his followers should avoid. On the use of the term *deḥlta* in the *Acts of the Persian Martyrs*, see A. H. Becker, "Martyrdom, Religious Difference, and 'Fear' as a Category of Piety in the Sasanian Empire: The Case of the *Martyrdom of Gregory* and the *Martyrdom of Yazdpaneh*," *JLA* 2 (2009): 300–336.

49. *History of Simeon* 4. Literally, they are "sons of the thinking of Caesar." Shapur's implication that Christians do not fight in the army of the king seems to be contradicted at the end of the *History of Simeon*, where the narrator refers to an episode when "some from among the faithful who inhabited other regions, *and who happened to be there in the army of the king*, asked for relics from the bodies of the holy ones" (*History of Simeon* 98; my emphasis). This request is another indication of the late date of the *History*. The *Martyrdom of Simeon* never mentions relics, and martyrs' cults were not established in Persia until the fifth century, with the formal establishment of the Church of the East. See R. E. Payne, "The Emergence of Martyrs' Shrines in Late Antique Iran: Conflict, Consensus and Communal Institutions," in *An Age of Saints? Power, Conflict and Dissent in Early Medieval Christianity*, ed. P. Sarris, M. Dal Santo, and P. Booth (Leiden: Brill, 2011), 89–113.

directly, until Shapur receives a letter from Simeon overtly challenging the authority of the king's men to tax Christians.

With his congregation already wearied by tax collectors, Simeon writes to Shapur, "Jesus is the king of kings, and we will not put the yoke of your subjugation upon our shoulders."[50] The *Martyrdom of Simeon*, through Simeon's statements to the king, espouses a radical economic theology: it rejects the payment of taxes altogether, as a matter of staying true to the gospel of Christ. Were Christians to bow to the authority of a king by paying taxes—any taxes—they would be betraying their god. Jesus, according to the *Martyrdom of Simeon*, freed Christians from taxes. Rather than focus on a connection between Constantine and the Christians of the West, it presents Simeon as the leader of a people apart, comparing him at length to the famous Jewish warrior Judah the Maccabee.[51] The Christians of Persia, according to the *Martyrdom*, are a holy and poor people who are set against any accommodation with king or empire: "Far be it from us now liberated people," Simeon writes to the king,

> to work once more in the service of a man. Our Lord is lord of your lordship, therefore, we will not assume upon our head the lordship of our fellow men. Our God is the creator of your gods, and we do not worship his creatures such as you. He commanded us, 'do not acquire gold or silver for your purses' [Matthew 10:9], thus, we have no gold to give you, nor money to bring to you for taxes. His apostle warned us, 'you were ransomed with a heavy price, so do not become servants of men' [1 Corinthians 7:23]."[52]

From the perspective of the narrator of the *Martyrdom of Simeon*, a demand that Christians pay taxes is no different from a demand that they bow before a pagan god. When the discussion shifts in the *Martyrdom of Simeon* from the payment of taxes, it is merely to another, less tangible means of paying homage to the king and his realm: Shapur's insistence that Simeon bow to the sun. From Shapur's point of view, this is a gift: he is offering to write off the taxes due from Christians and even to protect them from the magi who seek their lives, so long as Simeon makes a token display of allegiance to the king and his gods. But from the Christian point of view, at least

---

50. *Martyrdom of Simeon* 10. The epithet for Jesus here is an intentional subversion of the common title for the king of Persia, "the king of kings" (*shahanshah*).

51. See *Martyrdom of Simeon* 1–8; and K. Smith, "Constantine and Judah the Maccabee: History and Memory in the *Acts of the Persian Martyrs*," *JCSSS* 12 (2012): 16–33.

52. *Martyrdom of Simeon* 10.

insofar as the *Martyrdom of Simeon* narrates it, Shapur has upped the ante and required an even more egregious act of apostasy than the payment of taxes, from which Christians have been divinely delivered. The *Martyrdom of Simeon* thus proposes a theological argument about taxation and authority that is completely different from the *History of Simeon*'s much more modest claim that Christians pay taxes and respect the king's authority but will not (and cannot) be strong-armed into paying a double tax levied exclusively on them.

Worldly and Spiritual Authority: The Role of the Bishop in Simeon's Acts

The *Martyrdom of Simeon*'s near-full rejection of the king and his authority is substantially tempered in the *History of Simeon*. The *History* is, moreover, quite clear that Simeon was once good friends with the Persian king and that he would have continued this friendship so as long as it did not entail worshiping the sun. In response to Shapur's threats in the *History*, he says, "And that which you said to me—'Lest the king's friendship toward you turn into enmity because of your disobedience, and lest he spill your blood upon the earth'—I will speak the truth before your authority: I would be glad if the king continued to love me, if only he would allow me to love my God."[53] Simeon explains that contrary to the accusations of the Jews and the magi, Christians "bow to the King of Kings" and even "pray for the king to whose kingdom God has subjected us."[54]

Whereas the Simeon of the *Martyrdom* cites passages that he interprets as enjoining the nonpayment of taxes, the Simeon of the *History* explains that Christians are subject to governing authorities by the command of scripture. Christians, Simeon says in the *History*, are subject to those who govern to such an extent that if they were to spurn the authorities, they would risk spurning God:

> Truly, our scriptures command this of us: 'let every person be subject to the governing authorities, for there is no authority except from God, and whoever defies the authorities will receive judgment' [Romans 13:1–2]. We, too, are commanded to pray for kings and nobles. Indeed, one of our teachers said to us: 'before all things, offer prayers for kings and princes' [1 Timothy

---

53. *History of Simeon* 10.
54. *History of Simeon* 5.

2:1–2]. Therefore, when our scriptures command this of us, how are we able to be enemies and adversaries of the King of Kings without also becoming the opponent of God, who commands these things of us through our teachers?[55]

Far from prohibiting the payment of taxes, the scriptures, Simeon says, "have taught us to submit, and they have also shown us the measure of submission. Indeed, concerning this matter, our scriptures have taught us the following: 'Render to every man as is due to him—taxes to whom taxes (are due), and tribute to whom tribute (is due)' [Rom 13:7]. But they do not command us to pay a double tax, so why are we now to pay twice the tax or tribute?"[56] Given the accusation that Christians are partisans of Caesar's god, it is not surprising that, in defending Christian submission to taxes and worldly authority, Simeon chooses to cite Paul before Shapur rather than quote Jesus's admonition to "render unto Caesar" (Mark 12:13-17).

Beyond emphasizing that Christians are required to pay a fair rate of tax but should be exempt from excessive taxes, the *History of Simeon* introduces a practical, procedural matter: Simeon refuses to collect the double tax from Christians not only because it is unjustified and because Christians are not wealthy enough to pay it but also because a bishop simply does not have authority over such mundane matters as tax collection. In the *History of Simeon*, the question is thus not whether Christians should pay taxes (yes, they should, just not double taxes) but whether bishops are able to collect the empire's legitimately imposed taxes from other Christians. The *History*'s answer to the latter question is an emphatic no: bishops cannot collect taxes, because this task is reserved for those who hold worldly authority. That of bishops is limited to the spiritual arena. As Adam Becker notes, "There is a persistent emphasis on the existence of two distinct jurisdictions, *šulṭānē*: one, that of the Catholicos Simeon, pertains to people's souls and the invisible world, and the other, the shah's, is *ʿālmānāyā*, 'worldly,' and concerns visible creation."[57] Several times in the *History*, Simeon refers to Shapur as "your authority." But with reference to his fellow bishops, Simeon declares to the magi, "We do not accept the payment of taxes because our authority is not worldly such that we can exert force upon our brothers. Rather our authority is from God, who teaches us humility in all our books."[58]

55. *History of Simeon* 5.
56. *History of Simeon* 7.
57. Becker, "Martyrdom, Religious Difference, and 'Fear,'" 319.
58. *History of Simeon* 38.

This separation of religion from empire, a characterization of Christianity and episcopal authority as spiritual but not worldly, is a novel argument that completely conflicts with the understanding of Simeon's power as the *Martyrdom of Simeon* presents it. Yet this separation is necessary to explain why Simeon is so opposed to collecting taxes when, as the *History* has also made clear, Christians are loyal Persian citizens whose own scriptures decree that they obey the king. This is a wholly different rendering of events from how the *Martyrdom of Simeon* describes them. The *History of Simeon* transforms the discussion from one about taxation as oppression into one about double taxation as oppression and, moreover, a spiritual leader's inability to operate in a role that should be delegated to those who hold worldly authority.

Did the Sasanian Empire Tax "Religious Groups"?

Although there is no extant non-Christian Sasanian source, either literary or inscriptional, that attests to the "double poll tax" and "double tribute" recounted in the *History of Simeon,* the prevailing scholarly view is that taxes were imposed on the Christians of Persia either as punishment (because they worshiped the same god as the Romans who had vanquished Shapur) or possibly as a test of loyalty.[59] As the *Martyrdom* and *History of Simeon* both reveal, the argument over taxes in a fourth-century Persian context is less of a discussion and more of a monologue: we hear the Christian side of the story and the Christian interpretation of Shapur's response but only silence from the Persian authorities and other non-Christian sources. We possess no imperial documents that suggest the Persian Empire regarded Christians in particular as a threat. There is no edict preserved in Middle Persian that levies a double tax on Christians. There are no rescripts that authorize the destruction of Christian churches. Thus, if Simeon's acts are the only evidence we have for the levying of taxes specifically on Christians in fourth-century Persia, then we must ask whether it is reasonable to accept their testimony and believe that "religious groups" there could have been singled out for taxation in that period.

As David Goodblatt demonstrates in an important article in the *Journal of the Economic and Social History of the Orient,* there is hardly any evidence about taxes and their assessment in Sasanian Persia prior to the tax reforms

---

59. Naomi Koltun-Fromm speaks of Shapur's tax as "revenge" and a "ploy" to determine the allegiances of Persian Christians. See Koltun-Fromm, "Jewish-Christian Conversation," 45.

of King Khusro I Anoshirvan in the mid-sixth century.⁶⁰ And as Zeev Rubin argues, even Khusro's attempts at imposing a uniform and regular taxation system (two hundred years after Simeon's death) proved futile because he tried "to superimpose the framework of a centralized state with a salaried civil bureaucracy and an army, financed by an efficient and easily manageable taxation apparatus, on a realm that was too weak to carry the burden of such reforms."⁶¹

Still, it is generally assumed, Goodblatt explains, that the head of the exiled Jewish community in Babylonia "was responsible for the collection of taxes from the Jews" in Sasanian Persia. In his book on the exilarch in the Sasanian era, Geoffrey Herman repeats this, noting that "it used to be widely believed that the Exilarchs were involved in the collection of taxes for the Persian authorities."⁶² Yet as both Goodblatt and Herman point out, there is no evidence for this in the Babylonian Talmud. This incorrect idea is based entirely on two false (and circular) assumptions: first, as the *History of Simeon* demonstrates, that the bishop-catholicos of Seleucia-Ctesiphon was called on to collect taxes from the Christians of Persia, and second, that Simeon's acts must accurately represent the taxation regime in Sasanian Persia, which demanded that taxes be collected from each religious community.⁶³ In other words, the supposition that the *History of Simeon* correctly reflects fourth-century Sasanian tax policy is put forth as the evidence—the only evidence—for believing that the exilarch collected taxes from Jews and, moreover, that this must have been the standard practice for the heads of all the religious communities in late antique Persia.

Given the paucity of evidence for fourth-century forms and methods of taxation and the apparent difficulty of regularly collecting taxes even two centuries after Simeon's death, it is highly doubtful that Christians, or other religious groups, were singled out for special taxes. The idea of taxing a par-

---

60. D. M. Goodblatt, "The Poll Tax in Sasanian Babylonia: The Talmudic Evidence," *JESHO* 22 (1979): 249–50. For a broader, albeit rather dated, study of taxation in Sasanian antiquity, see F. Altheim and R. Stiehl, *Ein asiatischer Staat: Feudalismus unter den Sasaniden und ihren Nachbarn* (Wiesbaden: Limes-Verlag, 1954).

61. Z. Rubin, "The Reforms of Khusro Anushirwan," in *The Byzantine and Early Islamic Near East*, vol. 3, *States, Resources and Armies*, ed. A. Cameron (Princeton, NJ: Darwin, 1995), 251.

62. Goodblatt, "Poll Tax in Sasanian Babylonia," 250; G. Herman, *A Prince without a Kingdom: The Exilarch in the Sasanian Era* (Tübingen: Mohr Siebeck, 2012), 176.

63. Goodblatt, "Poll Tax in Sasanian Babylonia," 249–50; Herman, *Prince without a Kingdom*, 177–78.

ticular people or religious group, especially as the *Martyrdom* and *History of Simeon* narrate it, reinforces the idea of that group, though: it makes it seem as if Christians are quite separate, quite clearly identifiable as a people and quite obviously set apart as a religious group. And in putting forth the bishop of Seleucia-Ctesiphon as the head of all Christians in Persia, even if he cannot collect taxes from them, this also substantially underscores, and helps create, his authority.

In the centuries following the Islamic Conquest, Christians, as a protected non-Muslim minority, or *dhimmi*, living under Muslim rule, were compelled to pay a discriminatory "protection tax," or *jizya*, in lieu of military service.[64] And because there are no fourth-century Sasanian sources with which to adjudicate the claims of Simeon's martyr acts, it has often been implied, if not outright declared, that the circumstances the *History of Simeon* describes—Christians enjoying the fruit of Persian lands while not participating in the empire's defense—must be similar to the later situation under Islamic rule. With respect to studies of the ecclesiastical-legal systems that developed in late fifth-century Persia, Richard Payne notes that a number of scholars "have gone so far as to suggest that separate Christian and Zoroastrian communal judges and laws foreshadowed, or were even the genetic forerunners of, the Ottoman millet system."[65] While it is certainly true that what we might call religious allegiances more concretely determined one's sociopolitical identity in later centuries, it is difficult to see how such a sophisticated social typology could have been applied in a mid-fourth-century Sasanian context.

Nevertheless, the assumption that religious groups were clear-cut and self-evident in late antique Persia informs the third part of Michael Morony's exhaustive study *Iraq after the Muslim Conquest*, in which he examines the "religious communities" of pre- and post-conquest Iraq. What one finds,

---

64. One of the classic studies of the jizya is D. C. Dennett, *Conversion and the Poll Tax in Early Islam* (Cambridge, MA: Harvard University Press, 1950), although in light of more recent studies (e.g., that of Chase Robinson discussed below) its claims must be reconsidered.

65. R.E. Payne, *A State of Mixture: Christians, Zoroastrians, and Iranian Political Culture in Late Antiquity* (Berkeley: University of California Press, 2015), 14, with reference to T. Daryaee, "Ethnic and Territorial Boundaries in Late Antique and Early Medieval Persia (Third to Tenth Century)," in *Borders, Barriers, and Ethnogenesis: Frontiers in Late Antiquity and the Middle Ages*, ed. F. Curta (Turnhout: Brepols, 2005), 123–73; R.N. Frye, "Minorities in the History of the Near East," in *A Green Leaf: Papers in Honour of Professor Jes P. Asmussen*, Acta Iranica 12, ed. W. Sundermann, J. Duchesne-Guillemin, and F. Vahman (Leiden: Brill, 1988), 461–71; and Brock, "Christians in the Sasanian Empire," 12.

according to him, are effectively self-contained and autonomous religious groups. As a result of such clear boundaries, Sasanian bureaucrats could easily identify specific groups for particularized rates of taxation. Again, though, the only evidence is that provided in the *History of Simeon*. Morony writes that the idea of considering "the poll tax as a levy on non-Magians appears underway by at least the fourth century when Shāpūr II, in order to offset the expense of his wars and arguing that the Christians in his empire were living in peace even though their faith differed from the established one, required the bishop of Ctesiphon (Mada'in) Shem'ōn bar Sābbā'ē, to collect a double poll tax (Syr. *k°saf reshā*) and land tax (Syr. *m°dātā*) from Christians." In Morony's interpretation, "the religious dimension of the poll tax" only increased throughout the Sasanian period and then "merged easily with the tribal Arab definition of *jizya* as the personal ransom paid by a person defeated and captured in battle, and with the Qur'ānic use of *jizya* as the collective tribute paid to Muslims following political submission by those non-Muslims with a revealed scripture."[66]

As Chase Robinson has convincingly argued, however, "sophisticated ideas," such as specific taxes regularly levied on members of religious communities, "usually take some time to become sophisticated."[67] At least in northern Mesopotamia, which is the focus of his study, a more systematic approach to taxation is unlikely to have existed prior to the end of the seventh century. Only in the late eighth century, in the Syriac *Chronicle of Zuqnin*, Robinson argues, do we first hear of "the introduction of an entirely unprecedented tax regime—the levy of the *gizya*—rather than simply an increase in the rate of a pre-existing tax."[68] As a result of analyses such as this, the idea of a religious group being singled out for taxation in fourth-century Persia appears all the more flimsy. It seems that much more recent phenomena—such as the jizya and the dhimmi communities under Islamic law—have colored our reading of late ancient texts and the context that they describe.

---

66. M. Morony, *Iraq after the Muslim Conquest* (Princeton, NJ: Princeton University Press, 1984; repr., Piscataway, NJ: Gorgias, 2005), 109. Elsewhere, Morony explains how the Sasanian Empire came to be a segmented society of clearly distinguishable religious groups, each with its own legal and social institutions. "Ethnic identities," he claims, sometimes survived "because they coincided with religious communities which gave them institutional form." See Morony, "Religious Communities in Late Sasanian and Early Muslim Iraq," *JESHO* 17 (1974): 113–35.

67. C. Robinson, *Empire and Elites after the Muslim Conquest: The Transformation of Northern Mesopotamia* (Cambridge: Cambridge University Press, 2000), 33.

68. Robinson, *Empire and Elites*, 45–46.

Roman Analogues: Edicts Enforced against Christians

Recent reconsiderations of persecutions in the Roman Empire offer additional support for a more skeptical reading of the taxation regime imposed on Christians in the *Martyrdom* and *History of Simeon*. In some of the Roman Christian martyrdom narratives set during Decius's reign, in the mid-third century, the Roman emperor is bent on singling out Christians for persecution. Evidence discovered in non-Christian sources has muddied the waters, however—indeed, the evidence for any prolonged persecution specifically and aggressively directed at Christians in the mid-third century is becoming more and more piecemeal, forcing us to distinguish between "persecutions" actively organized and carried out against Christians (of which there were few) and Christian sentiments about Roman decrees that may have negatively affected some Christians. This kind of distinction is also useful for rereading Syriac martyrdom narratives from Sasanian Persia.

In the Roman Empire, Decius, rather than seeking out Christians for punishment, seems to have issued a general edict in 249 that, according to James Rives, commanded *"all the inhabitants of the Empire* [to] sacrifice to the gods, taste the sacrificial meat, and swear that they had always sacrificed. It further arranged for a formal procedure to ensure universal compliance."[69] As Rives argues, this was an "unprecedented" and innovative "edict that did not simply enjoin the general observance of a particular occasion, but instead required a particular cult act of all the inhabitants of the Empire and established a mechanism to ensure its performance on an individual basis."[70] The decree was revolutionary, he notes, as a primary instance of a move away from the traditional localism inherent in even widespread religious cults toward a universalizing, empire-wide conception of cultic responsibilities that displaced "the city from its central position in religious life."[71]

What motivated Decius to issue such a far-reaching decree, which required everyone in the empire (except perhaps Jews) to offer sacrifice, is not clear.[72]

---

69. J. B. Rives, "The Decree of Decius and the Religion of Empire," *JRS* 89 (1999): 137. My emphasis.

70. Rives, "Decree of Decius," 148.

71. Rives, "Decree of Decius," 152. Rives concludes his article by suggesting that it was Decius's decree, "whether or not Decius himself was clearly aware of it, that first addressed the problem of defining the religion of the Empire" (154).

72. Rives speculates that Decius probably "followed the long established principle of making allowances for the ancestral traditions of the Jews" and exempted them from the law. Rives, "Decree of Decius," 138n16.

It does seem to be the case, however, that the edict was not directed solely at Christians, irrespective of how Christian martyrological and historical sources later interpreted the so-called Decian persecution. Other religious groups were affected too, although one would hardly know it if we did not possess testimonies besides those of Eusebius and Lactantius, both of whom understood Decius's decree as a direct attack on the Church. Rives, bypassing Christian martyrological and historiographical witnesses, points instead to the discovery of several dozen Egyptian papyrus certificates that, he argues, can be used to reevaluate the Christian historiographical tradition about Decius's decree: "Although it had always been assumed that Decius' measure affected Christians alone," he writes, "there was little to suggest that the people who appeared in the papyri were Christians; one of them, Aurelia Ammounis, describes herself as 'priestess of the god Petesouchos.'"[73]

It is possible, as Rives acknowledges, that Decius intended his edict "primarily as an anti-Christian measure," but there is ultimately "no compelling reason" (according to Rives) to continue to see it as specifically directed against Christians.[74] Indeed, the papyrus certificates seem proof enough of this. The time and effort involved in verifying the sacrifice of a non-Christian, such as a priestess of the god Petesouchos, would have been a remarkable waste of imperial resources if the edict was intended primarily as an anti-Christian effort. Nevertheless, it clearly had a negative effect on Christians. They were put into a position of either disobeying an imperial order or, as they saw it, apostatizing. It is no wonder that Christian sources contemporary with the promulgation of Decius's edict "consistently describe the situation as a persecution," even if, in hindsight, this description is unwarranted.[75] We cannot presume to know the emperor's motivations, but as Rives indicates, "neither the decree itself nor the consequent persecution of Christians left any trace in the non-Christian historical tradition."[76]

The same can be said about fourth-century Persia: outside the Christian tradition—namely, Simeon's acts and other, closely related Syriac texts—there is simply no evidence for Christian-specific taxes or a wide-ranging persecution of Christians. Christians may have believed that they were being singled out, but there is little evidence beyond the martyrdom narratives to suggest that this was the case.

73. Rives, "Decree of Decius," 140.
74. Rives, "Decree of Decius," 141–42.
75. Rives, "Decree of Decius," 141.
76. Rives, "Decree of Decius," 151.

CONCLUSIONS

Aphrahaṭ's *Demonstrations* and the *Martyrdom* and *History of Blessed Simeon bar Ṣabbaʿe* are among our best Syriac sources for the history of Christianity in fourth-century Persia. None of these three, however, is particularly useful for writing an event history of the period. In any rich sense, such a historical narrative may lie beyond our capabilities: Ephrem, as I discussed in chapter 3, has nothing to say about Christians in the Persian Empire; Aphrahaṭ's *Demonstrations* are primarily exercises in biblical interpretation; and the *Martyrdom* and *History of Simeon* present two very different accounts of the past while appearing to tell similar stories about taxes, persecution, and martyrdom.

The *Martyrdom* and *History of Simeon* were clearly written in different "presents." On the one hand, we have a story of a Christian community that saw itself as wholly set apart from and immeasurably oppressed by the Sasanian authorities. This community—as I have discussed elsewhere—found more in common with the Maccabees than with its fellow Christians in the West.[77] Much later, probably in the late fifth century, someone else—the author of the *History of Simeon*—wrote about a Christian community that was struggling with how best to understand the place of Christians in a Sasanian context. This community recognized its co-religionists in the West but at the same time was trying to determine what it meant to be Christian outside the Roman Empire. For the author of the *History of Simeon*, unlike the author of the *Martyrdom*, a practical path was the only way forward: paying reasonable taxes, praying for the health of Shapur's kingdom, and corralling the leader of the Christians by presenting him not as a rebel or firebrand but as a simple spiritual father whose authority was limited to the realm of incorporeal things.

One of the major ways that the Christians of the *History of Simeon* differ from those of the *Martyrdom of Simeon* is in their memory of the war between Rome and Persia. The *Martyrdom* says nothing about it—the only reference beyond Persia is the muttered accusation that "Caesar" would look kindly on a letter from Simeon. But the *History* reads the war between Shapur and Constantine's sons as the motivating force behind both the double tax that was levied on Christians and the persecution that ensued when they refused to pay it. As I discuss in the next chapter, the Christians of the

---

77. Smith, "Constantine and Judah the Maccabee."

History of Simeon did not see themselves as just the unfortunate victims of a religiopolitical dispute. They remembered the Roman-Persian war in another way too. According to the *History,* many of the Christians in Persia, including some of those killed with Simeon, were captives—Roman Christians who had been taken in war and were now forced to call Persia their home.

FIVE

The Church of the East and the Territorialization of Christianity

IN CHAPTER 4, I BRIEFLY discussed how the *History of Simeon bar Ṣabbaʿe* (in contrast to the *Martyrdom of Simeon*) draws a number of comparisons between the Christians of the East and the Christians of the West. Yet even in remembering the martyrs "in the land of the West," it remains tentative in its embrace of the Roman Empire.[1] The *History of Simeon* honors "blessed Constantine" as an "angel of peace" but keeps the Roman emperor at arm's length.[2] Contrary to Sozomen's *Church History* and other sources from the Roman Empire (such as those that chapter 6 discusses), the *History of Simeon* does not depict Constantine as a patron or protector of the Christians of Persia. But it does see the emperor as a bridge. For the author of the *History of Simeon,* there is a clear association between, on the one hand, Constantine's rise to power and the end of persecution in the West and, on the other, Constantine's death and the beginning of persecution in the East.[3]

In reading the life of the first Christian Roman emperor as the hinge between two persecutions, the *History of Simeon* conveys a broad sense of Christian unity. If all Christians, in the East as well as the West, have a shared experience of persecution, then their oppression can be interpreted as divinely superintended. As the narrator of the *History of Simeon* puts it, "God—the venerated one who orchestrates all in his wisdom—allowed there to be a persecution in the

---

1. For references to the "land of the West," see the *History of Simeon* 2, 62, 97. All citations of the *History* and *Martyrdom of Simeon* refer to the section numbers in K. Smith, *The Martyrdom and History of Blessed Simeon bar Ṣabbaʿe, Persian Martyr Acts in Syriac: Text and Translation,* fasc. 3 (Piscataway, NJ: Gorgias, 2014).
2. *History of Simeon* 2–4.
3. *History of Simeon* 2.

land of the Romans for three hundred years." This tested the mettle of the faithful. Eventually "he sent them an angel of peace, King Constantine, and he allowed them to live in comfort." There was a brief period (an auspicious "thirty-three years") of tranquillity from Constantine's rise to power until the emperor's death. During this time, neither the "subjects of the Christian king" nor the "servants of the pagan king [Shapur II]" suffered persecution. But then, "while the memory of the first persecution [in the Roman Empire] had not been forgotten, but was still in the mind of those who had seen it, so that one generation would not pass away and another come and the memory of the persecution be erased," God allowed the magi to subjugate the Christians of Persia.[4]

The *History of Simeon*'s interpretation of Shapur's persecution does several things: it provides a rational, theological explanation for violence suffered by Christians; it joins East with West to write a larger history of Christian suffering; and it elevates the new martyrs in the East to a status on par with the older, and more acclaimed, martyrs of the West.[5] There is another layer of complexity, though: not all the Christians who were martyred in the East were from the East—some were from the West.

Several texts among the *Acts of the Persian Martyrs* tell stories about Romans who were taken as prisoners of war, deported to the Sasanian Empire, and then killed because they refused to exchange the "religion of Caesar" (*deḥlta d-qesar*) for the "religion of Shapur" (*deḥlta d-shabur*).[6] The

---

4. *History of Simeon* 3.
5. There is strong evidence that Greek Christian martyrdom narratives from the Roman Empire circulated in Syriac translation before the texts that became the collected *Acts of the Persian Martyrs* were composed. Eusebius's *On the Martyrs of Palestine* is preserved in British Library Syriac Add. MS 12,150, the oldest dated Christian literary manuscript in any language, which was copied in Edessa in November 411. Some have surmised that Eusebius's *Church History* was translated into Syriac even more quickly—possibly before his death in 339. See W. Wright, *Catalogue of Syriac Manuscripts in the British Museum, Acquired since the year 1838* (London, 1870–72), vol. 2, 631–33; and the preface to Wright and N. McLean, *The Ecclesiastical History of Eusebius in Syriac* (Cambridge: Cambridge University Press, 1898).
6. As I discuss in chapter 4, note 48, the Syriac *deḥlta* means "fear." The *Acts of the Persian Martyrs* uses it to refer to different sects. See *History of Simeon* 11, 22; *Martyrdom of the Captives of Beth Zabdai* (translated in appendix B); and, for a study of the term with references to later martyrdom narratives, A. H. Becker, "Martyrdom, Religious Difference, and 'Fear' as a Category of Piety in the Sasanian Empire: The Case of the *Martyrdom of Gregory* and the *Martyrdom of Yazdpaneh*," *JLA* 2 (2009): 300–336. While I am opting to translate *deḥlta* as "religion," I recognize the potential problem of thereby implying that "religion" (in the post-Lockean sense of the term) is a category native to late antique Syriac Christianity. See the useful critique of B. Nongbri, *Before Religion: A History of a Modern Concept* (New Haven: Yale University Press, 2013).

Martyrdom of the Captives of Beth Zabdai, which is set in the waning years of the Roman-Persian war near the end of Constantius's reign, is a key example.[7] According to this text (see appendix B for a full translation), the Persians captured thousands of men and women, apparently only some of them Christian, after Shapur's army besieged and stormed the Roman fortress of Beth Zabdai (or, as Ammianus Marcellinus calls it, Bezabde) on the upper Tigris. These Romans were offered fertile land, and their lives, in the Zagros Mountains of Beth Huzaye, but on one condition: they had to "renounce the god whom Caesar worships" and join Shapur in worshiping the sun and moon.[8]

While the captives and martyrs of Beth Zabdai are depicted as recent deportees from Roman Mesopotamia, another text narrates the martyrdom of a man called Pusai, who was a *bar shebya,* "son of the captivity," in Persia. Pusai, whom the ends of both the *Martyrdom* and the *History of Simeon* also mention, was a master embroiderer. Apparently, his faith did not prevent him from holding a place of social prestige as an artisan in the city of Karka d-Ledan in Beth Huzaye. Many Christians in Sasanian Persia may have been skilled workers and artisans. Simeon's parents were in the textile business. The bishop's surname, "bar Ṣabbaʿe," means "son of [cloth] dyers." And quite "rightly is he called by this name," comments the narrator of the *Martyrdom,* "because his parents dyed silk with foreign blood as clothing for the impious kingdom, but he dyed the garments of his soul with his own blood as a vestment for the holy kingdom."[9] Until Pusai renounced the title and proclaimed himself a Christian, he held his own trade-based epithet. He was called Pusai-Qarugbed, or Pusai "the Head of the Craftsmen," an honor that Shapur himself granted.[10]

These three texts—the *History of Simeon,* the *Martyrdom of the Captives,* and the *Martyrdom of Pusai*—all demonstrate a pronounced trend in the discourse of late fifth- and early sixth-century Syriac martyrdom narratives: the conceptualization of Persian Christians as Roman captives. This idea is evident again in the brief *Martyrdom of Abbot Barshebya* ("Son of the

---

7. See *AMS* II, 316–24. Soz. *HE* II.13 mentions the martyrs of Beth Zabdai ("Zabdaeus") but does not seem to know much about them.

8. *AMS* II, 318.

9. *Martyrdom of Simeon* 7. The *History of Simeon* does not comment on his name.

10. See *Martyrdom of Simeon* 44–48; *History of Simeon* 1, 96. For Pusai's acts, see *AMS* II, 208–32. Soz. *HE* II.11 briefly refers to Pusai, distilling the information about him from the *Martyrdom of Simeon.*

captivity"), which is translated in appendix C. In this chapter, I discuss how these Syriac martyrdom narratives talk about Christians as Roman captives, and then I offer some explanations for why they might do so. I suggest that the Sasanian practice of taking hundreds if not thousands of prisoners of war—a tactic that both preceded and followed its use during the reign of Shapur II—is only part of the reason why these Syriac martyrdom narratives speak so frequently about "Roman captives." Just as important are the history of the spread of Christianity in Persia; the two founding synods of the Church of the East, in 410 and 420; and the brief war between Rome and Persia that followed the Sasanian king Yazdgard I's death in 420.

Many Syriac martyrdom narratives that are set during Shapur's reign, including all of those that this chapter discusses, were written in the aftermath of the first two synods of the Church of the East. These were held in Seleucia-Ctesiphon during the reign of Yazdgard I, whom the introduction to the canons of the first synod praises as the antithesis of Shapur II. Yazdgard is called the "victorious King of Kings" who "rolled back the black cloud of persecution" and ordered the rebuilding of the churches that Shapur had destroyed.[11] He was remembered, for all intents and purposes, as a second Constantine for the Christians of Persia.[12] Yet neither the Synod of Isaac (in 410) nor the Synod of Yahbalaha (in 420) was convened solely by Persian Christians and their newfound patron on the Sasanian throne. Rather, each was co-convened by a Roman bishop whom Theodosius II had sent as an envoy to Yazdgard and to the Church in Persia. These Roman bishops, first Marutha of Maypherqaṭ and then Acacius of Amida, helped fashion an alliance between the Christians of the East and the Christians of the West.[13] As a result of these councils and the Roman-Persian war soon after Yazdgard's

---

11. J. B. Chabot, *Synodicon orientale, ou recueil de synods nestoriens* (Paris: Imprimerie nationale, 1902), 18.

12. See the survey of the sources in S. J. McDonough, "A Second Constantine? The Sasanian King Yazdgard in Christian History and Historiography," *JLA* 1 (2008): 127–41.

13. Another council, the Synod of Dadishoʿ, was supposedly held in 424 at some distance from the capital. The records of this synod, which produced no canons and had a limited attendance, preserve the speeches of several bishops. It was held in an attempt to convince the deposed catholicos Dadishoʿ to reclaim his place as archbishop of Seleucia-Ctesiphon. Because the bishops at this synod supposedly eliminated Roman oversight of the Persian Church, it is often referred to as the "declaration of independence" of the Church of the East. But it is hard to believe that the proceedings do not suffer from substantial, sixth-century interpolations. See my forthcoming introduction, translation, and analysis, K. Smith, "The Synod of Mar Dādīšoʿ—424 CE," in *CCCOGD*, vol. V, ed. A. Melloni and F. Lauritzen (Turnhout: Brepols).

death, *Christianitas* was increasingly seen as coterminous with *Romanitas*. To be Christian in the fifth century was to be Roman. And to be Christian in fifth-century Persia was, in the Christian martyrological imagination, to be a Roman captive or the son or daughter of an earlier Roman captivity.

SEEDS OF CHRISTIANITY IN PERSIA: MERCHANTS, MISSIONARIES, AND CAPTIVES

As Richard Payne notes, although the origins and spread of Christianity in Persia have interested many scholars, neither the textual nor the archaeological sources that survive "permit the writing of a detailed, regionally and chronologically nuanced history of the expansion of Christianity in Iran."[14] While Payne is correct that we know relatively little about how Christianity spread and developed in the Sasanian Empire (especially east of Mesopotamia, in Beth Huzaye and on the Iranian Plateau), it is generally acknowledged that before the time of Constantine and Shapur many Christians had gone to Mesopotamia and even onward to Persia quite willingly. Often they came as merchants or missionaries, sometimes as both. Amir Harrak has traced the spread of Christianity throughout Mesopotamia via the major trade routes, and similarly, Christelle and Florence Jullien have demonstrated the interpenetration of the worlds of the merchant and the missionary. The Julliens point to the common refrain about missionizing "under the habit of a merchant" in the Syriac *Doctrina Addai*, which tells the legendary story of Thaddeus (Addai), who was one of the seventy apostles.[15] The Eastern Christian churches too have long maintained that Thomas the Apostle evangelized Persia before making his way to India.

---

14. R.E. Payne, "Christianity and Iranian Society in Late Antiquity, ca. 500–700 C.E." (PhD diss., Princeton: Princeton University, 2010), 33–34.

15. See A. Harrak, "Trade Routes and the Christianization of the Near East," *JCSSS* 2 (2002): 46–61; and C. Jullien and F. Jullien, "Porteurs de salut: Apôtre et marchand dans l'empire iranien," *PdO* 26 (2001): 127–43. For more general accounts of the Christianization of Persia, see M.-L. Chaumont, *La christianisation de l'empire iranien: Des origines aux grandes persécutions du IVe siècle*, CSCO 499, Subsidia 80 (Leuven: Peeters, 1988); and, with a direct focus on "apostolic" testimonies, Jullien and Jullien, *Apôtres des confins: Processus missionnaires chrétiens dans l'empire iranien*, Res Orientales XV (Bures-sur-Yvette: Groupe pour l'étude de la civilisation du Moyen-Orient, 2002). For a study of the various hagiographical traditions about Christian missionaries in the East, see J.-N.M. Saint-Laurent, *Missionary Stories and the Formation of the Syriac Churches* (Berkeley: University of California Press, 2015).

Beyond the travels of merchants and missionaries—a slow and sporadic means of seeding Christianity beyond the bounds of the Roman Empire—there seems to have been a more direct method of religious transplantation: deportation. During the early Sasanian period—namely, in the third century—when Christianity was just beginning to establish a significant number of adherents throughout the eastern Roman Empire, there were several large deportations of Romans to Persia.[16] By examining these forcible transfers of populations, we might, as Michael Morony aptly puts it, be able to write the history of labor in late antiquity. The Sasanians, he and others have argued, had a labor shortage. The population of their massive, continental empire was not large enough, mobile enough, or concentrated enough to sustain the building and development projects of the ruling elite.[17] They desperately needed hydraulic engineers, metalworkers, stonemasons, textile artisans, and other skilled laborers.[18] So they borrowed them from the Romans on permanent loan.

The city of Bishapur in Fars—which, according to an inscription at the site, Shapur I founded in 266—was probably built by captured Roman soldiers. This is not merely the stuff of legend. Valerian and many of his soldiers were captured only a few years before Bishapur was constructed, and the plan

---

16. See E. Kettenhofen, "Deportations," in *Encyclopedia Iranica* VII.3, ed. E. Yarshater (Costa Mesa, CA: Mazda, 1994), 297–312, which addresses the Achaemenid, Parthian, Sasanian, and Islamic periods of Persian history. The classic study of the deportations of the third and fourth centuries remains S. N. C. Lieu, "Captives, Refugees and Exiles: A Study of Cross-Frontier Civilian Movements and Contacts between Rome and Persia from Valerian to Jovian," in *The Defence of the Roman and Byzantine East*, vol. 2, ed. P. Freeman and D. Kennedy (Oxford: BAR International Editions, 1986), 475–505.

17. See M. Morony, "Population Transfers between Sasanian Iran and the Byzantine Empire," in *La Persia e Bisanzio: Atti del Convegno internazionale (Roma, 14–18 Ottobre 2002)*, ed. G. Gnoli and A. Panaino (Rome: Accademia Nazionale dei Lincei, 2004), 161–62. For an overview of the differences between the Roman Empire (which, among other things, had the advantages in trade, travel, and communication that the Mediterranean Sea accorded) and the Sasanian Empire (a continental realm that, although served by the Persian Gulf, was bisected by difficult-to-navigate mountain terrain), see J. Howard-Johnston, "The Two Great Powers in Late Antiquity: A Comparison," in *The Byzantine and Early Islamic Near East*, vol. 3, *States, Resources and Armies*, ed. A. Cameron (Princeton, NJ: Darwin, 1995), 157–226. It was, according to Parvaneh Pourshariati, precisely this sort of internal weakness, in addition to dynastic decentralization, that led to the Sasanian Empire's quick collapse at the hands of invading Arab forces in the seventh century. See Pourshariati, *Decline and Fall of the Sasanian Empire: The Sasanian-Parthian Confederacy and the Arab Conquest of Iran* (London: I. B. Tauris, 2008).

18. See S. N. C. Lieu, "Captives, Refugees and Exiles."

of the city and its many mosaics demonstrate ample Roman influences.[19] In his expansive study of deportations by Sasanians and other movements of peoples between Rome and Persia in the third and fourth centuries, Samuel Lieu refers to the Bishapur mosaics as effectively Antiochene in scope and aesthetic ambition, although moderated for Iranian tastes.[20] According to Matthew Canepa, the Sasanians appropriated Roman styles as a way of publicly broadcasting that they had captured, and now possessed, Roman art, architecture, and design.[21]

While we can assume that only a small fraction of Valerian's soldiers were Christian, much later East Syrian accounts, such as the *Chronicle of Seert* (a tenth-century Christian Arabic history), consider Shapur I's sack of Antioch and the deportations that ensued to have been absolutely essential for transferring Christians into Persian lands.[22] There are, however, at least two reasons to be skeptical of what the *Chronicle of Seert* tells us: first, we cannot be at all sure how many people the elder Shapur deported from the Roman Empire, and second, even if we could estimate the number of these captives, there is little evidence to suggest that Christians represented any significant percentage of the population in either Antioch or the other eastern Roman cities whose inhabitants the Persians carried off. Relying on sociological estimates of Christian population growth in late antiquity, Morony argues that most of those whom Shapur I deported to Persia were likely "pagan or Jewish, with a few Christians among them."[23]

---

19. See R. Ghirshman, *Bīchāpour II: Les mosaïques sassanides* (Paris: Geuthner, 1956); and J. Balty, "Mosaïques romaines, mosaïques sassanides: Jeux d'influences réciproques," in *Ērān ud Anērān: Studien zu den Beziehungen zwischen dem Sasanidenreich und der Mittelmeerwelt—Beiträge des Internationalen Colloquiums in Eutin, 8–9 Juni 2000*, ed. J. Wiesehöfer and P. Huyse (Stuttgart: Franz Steiner Verlag, 2006), 29–44.

20. S. N. C. Lieu, "Captives, Refugees and Exiles," 478–79.

21. M. Canepa, *The Two Eyes of the Earth: Art and Ritual of Kingship between Rome and Sasanian Iran* (Berkeley: University of California Press, 2009), 53–78.

22. See A. Scher, *Histoire nestorienne inédite (Chronique de Séert), première partie 1*, PO 4 (Paris: Firmin-Didot, 1908), 220–21. See now also P. Wood, *The Chronicle of Seert: Christian Historical Imagination in Late Antique Iraq* (Oxford: Oxford University Press, 2013), especially 90–91.

23. Morony, "Population Transfers," 167–69. Plenty of attempts have been made to estimate the population of Christians in different periods of late antiquity. See, for example, R. Stark, *The Rise of Christianity: A Sociologist Reconsiders History* (Princeton, NJ: Princeton University Press, 1996). For the estimate that Morony uses, see K. Hopkins, "Christian Number and Its Implications," *JECS* 6 (1988): 185–226.

Greek, Syriac, and Non-Iranian: Naming the Christians of Persia

Despite the relatively small size of their communities, Christians did inhabit third-century Persia, and the Sasanian authorities seem to have been aware of them. Some of the most interesting evidence for this can be found in the well-known inscription of Shapur I's mobed Kirdir. Although we have to be exceedingly careful not to read too much into this inscription (or worse, read it as suggesting the existence of secularized categories of "religion" and "politics" in third-century Iran), part of it is typically understood as promoting "Zoroastrianism" over and against other cults in Persia, including those of the *naṣraye* and *krestyane*.[24] The precise meaning of *naṣraye* and *krestyane* is still debated, but they are usually translated as "Nazarenes" and "Christians," respectively.

The word *naṣraye* carries obvious geographic implications, suggesting the cult of a non-Iranian, Roman people. It is not found in the *Martyrdom of Simeon,* but the later *History of Simeon* employs it in spades, as does the late fifth- or early sixth-century *Martyrdom of Pusai*. Oddly, however, in neither text is *naṣraye* an auto-designation of Christians. Rather, it is used solely by the persecutors of Christians and, as such, seems to have been intended as a slur.[25] In the *History of Simeon,* when Shapur writes to the authorities in Beth Aramaye, he uses the "royal we" and says,

> As soon as you see this command of ours, gods, in this official letter of charge that was sent to you from us, arrest Simeon, the head of the *naṣraye,* and do not release him until he signs a document and takes it upon himself to collect and give (to us) a double poll tax and double tribute from all the people of the *naṣraye* who are in our land, we gods, and who inhabit the land of our author-

---

24. See P. Gignoux, *Les quatre inscriptions du mage Kirdīr* (Leuven: Peeters, 1991); P. Huyse, "Kerdir and the First Sasanians," in *Proceedings of the Third European Conference of Iranian Studies,* vol. 1, ed. N. Sims-Williams (Wiesbaden: Otto Harrassowtiz, 1998), 109–20; and M. Sprengling, "Kartir, Founder of Sasanian Zoroastrianism," *AJSL* 57 (1940): 197–228, which remains important despite its anachronistic use of the concept of religion.

25. On the term *naṣraye,* including how it is imbricated in ethnic discourse and still used as an auto-designation of the Christians of India (the Syrian Malabar Nasrani), see F. de Blois, "*Naṣrānī* (Ναζωραῖος) and *ḥanīf* (ἐθνικός): Studies on the Religious Vocabulary of Christianity and of Islam," *BSOAS* 65 (2002): 1–30. According to Louis Sako, the Chaldean Catholic patriarch of Baghdad, in the summer of 2014, after ISIS militants took the city of Mosul, some Christian homes were marked in red paint with the Arabic letter *nūn,* for *Nasrani.* See Sako, "ISIS in Mosul Marks Christian Homes, Patriarch Issues Urgent Appeal," *AINA News,* July 19, 2014, http://aina.org/news/20140719115241.htm.

ity. For to us, gods, there are tribulations and wars, while to them is rest and luxury. They dwell in our land and yet they are of one mind with Caesar, our enemy, and we fight but they enjoy quiet.[26]

What "Christians" should be called and who can properly be called one are extremely important to the Simeon of the *History*. Although he never responds to Shapur's use of the term *naṣraye*, he does become flustered when the king misunderstands the complexities of Christian theology. One exchange between them may serve as an instructive example. At one point, when Simeon is in the midst of justifying his faith and explaining to the king why he will not worship created things such as the sun and moon, he claims that the sun grew dark as a rebuke to the Jews at the hour of Jesus's crucifixion. The king accuses Simeon of lying, saying, "Until now I had heard something (different) about this. Namely, they say that the Jews crucified the *god* of the Christians." Simeon is aghast. According to his understanding of Christian theology, *Jesus* was crucified, died, and rose again—not God. He counters the idea that God could have been crucified by saying, "Far be it from Christians [*krestyane*] to say this, my lord King! Those who say this are Marcionites [*marqyone*], they who falsely call themselves by the name 'Christian.'"[27]

That Marcionites falsely called themselves "Christian," and further, that Zoroastrians remained confused about who was and who was not a "Christian" are reflected in the Syriac *Life* of Mar Aba—a Zoroastrian convert to Christianity. Daniel Boyarin uses one episode in this text to highlight the fuzziness of religious boundaries even as late as the sixth century, when it was written. When the not-yet-converted Aba encounters a follower of Jesus crossing the Tigris, the man tells him that he is a Jew, a Christian, and a worshiper of the Messiah. Aba demands to know how it is possible to be all three of these things at once. The man explains, "I am a Jew secretly [cf. Romans 2:29]; I worship the living God, and I believe in his son Jesus Christ and in the Holy Spirit. And I run away from idol worship and all filth. I am a Christian truly, not like the Marcionites, who defraud and call themselves Christians. For 'Christian' [*krestyana*] is a Greek word. And the translation

---

26. *History of Simeon* 4. Shapur uses the *pluralis majestatis* to refer to himself as "gods" several times in the *History of Simeon*. This device is never used in the *Martyrdom of Simeon*. On the Sasanian idea of divine kingship, see A. Panaino, "Astral Characters of Kingship in the Sasanian and Byzantine Worlds," in *La Persia e Bisanzio*, 555–94.

27. *History of Simeon* 44; my emphasis.

of 'Christian' in Syriac is *mshiḥaya* [worshiper of the Messiah]. And [therefore] with respect to that which you have asked me: 'Do you worship the Messiah?,' I worship him truly."[28]

The confusion over the meaning of all these terms for "Christian" has led some to conclude that *naṣraye* and *krestyane* might not suggest any theological differences but could instead refer to a divide between a native, Syriac-speaking community of *naṣraye/mshiḥaye* and a more recently arrived, predominantly Greek-speaking community of deported *krestyane*.[29] According to Sebastian Brock, once the Sasanian authorities appropriated *naṣraye* as a term of opprobrium, Christians in Persia eschewed it in favor of the more novel Greek term *krestyane* and renewed use of the Syriac *mshiḥaye*.[30]

More recently, some have proposed that the use of *naṣraye* and *krestyane* does not demonstrate an ethnolinguistic divide among the Christians of Persia so much as show the historical memory of such a division after political factors had subsumed it. For Christelle Jullien, traces of the memory of Roman Christian captives are apparent throughout Syriac chronicles and martyrdom narratives.[31] She and her sister Florence Jullien argue that the term *naṣraye* might even have been used for Iranian subjects who had become "non-Iranian" by virtue of their conversion to Christianity. Because the Greek-speaking Christians deported to Persia were already "Roman" and non-Iranian, even the Syriac-speaking Christians already resident there, the Julliens propose, would have come to see themselves as Roman (or been

---

28. D. Boyarin, *Dying for God: Martyrdom and the Making of Christianity and Judaism* (Palo Alto: Stanford University Press, 1999), 23 (slightly amended). For the Syriac text of the *Life,* see P. Bedjan, *Histoire de Mar-Jabalaha, de trois autres patriarches, d'un prêtre et de deux laïques, nestoriens* (Leipzig: Otto Harrassowitz, 1895); repr., *The History of Mar Jab-Alaha and Rabban Sauma* (Piscataway, NJ: Gorgias, 2007). For an alternate reading of this episode, see A. H. Becker, "The Comparative Study of 'Scholasticism' in Late Antique Mesopotamia: Rabbis and East Syrians," *AJSR* 34 (2010): 91–113.

29. See M.-L. Chaumont, "L'Inscription de Kartir à la 'Ka'bah de Zoroastre' (texte, traduction, commentaire)," *JA* 248 (1960): 358; and Chaumont, *La christianisation de l'empire iranien,* 117, which suggests that the two terms may imply a bilingual and bi-ethnic community of Christians.

30. S. Brock, "Some Aspects of Greek Words in Syriac," in *Synkretismus im syrisch-persischen Kulturgebiet: Bericht über ein Symposion in Reinhausen bei Göttingen in der Zeit vom 4. bis 8. Oktober 1971,* ed. A. Dietrich (Göttingen: Vandenhoeck und Ruprecht, 1975), 80–108.

31. C. Jullien, "La minorité chrétienne 'grecque' en terre d'Iran à l'époque sassanide," in *Chrétiens en terre d'Iran I, Implantation et acculturation,* StIran 33, ed. R. Gyselen (Leuven: Peeters, 2006), 105–42.

defined as such by others) because their faith necessarily excluded them from being Iranian.[32]

The Martyrdom of the Captives of Beth Zabdai

A century after the deportations of Shapur I, it was not just "Greek" Christians who were arriving in Persia from the Roman Empire. Christians now represented a more significant percentage than before of the population throughout the eastern Roman lands, including, of course, the Syriac-speaking Christian communities in the cities of Roman Mesopotamia. Beth Zabdai, a Roman fort perched on the southern bank of the Tigris about a hundred kilometers east of Nisibis, was one such city.

In the summer of 360, Shapur II captured Beth Zabdai and deported many of its inhabitants to the mountains of Beth Huzaye in southwestern Iran. This city, known to Ammianus Marcellinus as Bezabde, was not the only stronghold in Roman Mesopotamia to suffer at the hands of the Persians. Although Constantius reinforced the walls of Amida in 359, Ammianus describes how it was unable to withstand a seventy-three-day siege by Shapur.[33] Farther to the south, the Persians overran the fortress of Singara in the Sinjar Mountains. Ammianus is quick to point out, however, that "very few" of its defenders were killed. Most of them, he says, "were taken alive at Shapur's order and deported to the remotest parts of Persia."[34] Apparently, some of the captives from Singara remained with Shapur and his army when they arrived before the walls of Bezabde.

As I discussed in chapter 3, Ammianus provides many details about the siege of Bezabde. One of his most notable anecdotes reports a strange encounter between Shapur and the unnamed "chief priest of the sect of the

---

32. C. Jullien and F. Jullien, "Aux frontières de l'iranité: '*Nāṣrāyē*' et '*krīstyonē*' des inscriptions du mobad Kirdīr: Enquête littéraire et historique," *Numen* 49 (2002): 325. Muriel Debié addresses the term *naṣraye* in considering what it meant to "be" and to "convert" to Christianity in Sasanian Persia. See Debié, "Devenir chrétien dans l'Iran sassanide: La conversion à la lumière des récits hagiographiques," in *Le problème de la christianisation du monde antique,* ed. H. Inglebert, S. Destephen, and B. Dumézil (Nanterre: Picard, 2010), 332. For a broader discussion of what it meant to be "Iranian" or "non-Iranian," see now R. E. Payne, *A State of Mixture: Christians, Zoroastrians, and Iranian Political Culture in Late Antiquity* (Berkeley: University of California Press, 2015).

33. Book XIX of Ammianus's *Res Gestae* is entirely devoted to the siege of Amida.

34. Amm. Marc. XX.7.1. All translations of the *Res Gestae* follow J. C. Rolfe, *Ammianus Marcellinus,* 3 vols. (London: Heinemann, 1935–40).

Christians." Presumably a bishop, this "chief priest" attempted to persuade the Persian king to end the siege and return home in peace. According to Ammianus, after the king dismissed the bishop and the fighting resumed, the Persian siege engines "deliberately battered" (and very soon destroyed) the weakest parts of Bezabde's walls, leading some to speculate that the leader of the Christians must have betrayed the city.[35]

Ammianus does not say anything else about the bishop of Bezabde, nor does he speculate about what might have happened to the captives of the city, but the Syriac *Martyrdom of the Captives of Beth Zabdai* most certainly does. Unlike many other martyrdom narratives, which are often untethered from identifiable historical events, the *Martyrdom of the Captives* clearly relates to the narrative of Ammianus. It picks up right where he leaves off. The text begins, "In the fifty-third year of Shapur [362/63], the king of the Persians went up against the borders and the fortifications of the Romans. He besieged the fort [*qaṣṭra*] of Beth Zabdai and captured it. He demolished its walls and delivered many warriors to the blade of the sword. He captured about nine thousand people, men and women, including the bishop Heliodorus and the elderly priests Dawsa and Maryahb who were with him."[36]

Ammianus does not tell us the name of the bishop of Bezabde, yet here, in a later Syriac martyrdom narrative, we are told that he had a Greek name—one that means "gift of the sun." Heliodorus is not the goat of the text (no one accuses him of treachery), but neither does he die a martyr's death. The very next paragraph says that before the nine thousand captives arrived at their destination in Beth Huzaye, Heliodorus fell ill and died at "a certain way station called Dasqarta," where he was buried with honor. The narrator tells us just one more thing about Heliodorus: before he yielded to his illness, he laid hands on Dawsa—one of the two "elderly priests" with him—and ordained him as bishop.[37]

During the final trek from Dasqarta into Beth Huzaye, the new bishop, Dawsa, sequestered a small group of Christians from among the captives and then divided them into choirs. He led them in the singing of psalms as they walked. The magi overheard the Christians and accused them of slandering the gods of the Persians. On the order of Shapur, the chief mobed took three

---

35. Amm. Marc. XX.7.7–9. See also J. Weisweiler, "Christianity in War: Ammianus on Power and Religion in Constantius' Persian War," in *The Power of Religion in Late Antiquity*, ed. A. Cain and N. Lenski (Burlington, VT: Ashgate, 2009), 383–96.

36. *AMS* II, 316. See the full translation in appendix B.

37. *AMS* II, 317.

hundred Persian soldiers and led the same number of Christians (just a fraction of the original nine thousand captives) to a village on the mountain of Masabdan. There he said to them,

> You should know that because you dishonor the king every day and have reviled the gods of the Persians, the king has commanded that all of you are to be slain at this place. But now, if you listen to our advice, you will live and be saved. Therefore, do the will of the king and worship the sun and the moon. Abandon the religion of Caesar and embrace the religion of Shapur, the king of kings, because you are his servants and he has authority over you. If you are obedient in this, I have been granted authority by him to let you remain in these villages, which are rich and fertile, and in this land, which, as you can see with your eyes, is planted with vines and olive trees and palms.[38]

True to the martyr's form, Dawsa emerges victorious from this trial and rejects the mobed's temptation as a "secret treachery." He then implores the Persian soldiers to hurry up and unite the blood of his people ("the martyrs of the West") with "the blood of the martyrs of the East" that had already stained the Persians' swords.[39] The Christians of the West, the text suggests, will be not only remembered in the East but martyred there too. The unification of Christians from the West and the East comes full circle as blood is mixed with blood and captive Roman Christians declare, in the land of the shah, that they will not desist from worshiping the god of Caesar.

Seeing that Dawsa and those with him are not moved in the face of death, the soldiers lead the Christians forward in successive groups of fifty and behead them on the spot. Not all of the three hundred captives are killed. Twenty-five men and women, the narrator says, could not overcome their yearning to settle there on that fertile land, and so they "succumbed in the shame of themselves and worshiped the sun."[40] Two hundred and seventy-five faithful Christians were beheaded on the mountain of Masabdan. But one of them, a deacon called 'Abdisho' ("the servant of Jesus"), remained alive in the pile of decapitated corpses because the executioner's sword "did not strike on its edge." He became known as the one "who was killed by the sword and lived."[41] The narrative continues, now with the badly injured 'Abdisho' as the hero: "After sunset he got up and went into the village. He

---

38. *AMS* II, 319.
39. *AMS* II, 320.
40. *AMS* II, 321.
41. *AMS* II, 322.

met a poor man, who brought him into his house and washed and bandaged his wounds. When it was day, 'Abdisho' led this man and his two sons with him, and they walked to the place of those who had been killed. He showed them the bodies of Dawsa, Maryahb, and the other elderly priests. [The man and his sons] climbed a little farther up the mountain, found a small cave, and laid [the martyrs' bodies] in it, and sealed it with large stones. Then they went back down to 'Abdisho' and found him kneeling in prayer and crying at the place of those who had been killed."[42] Once he recovers from his injuries, 'Abdisho' stays in the village to instruct people in the faith. Shapur was not keeping him there. Rather, it was "the bones of the righteous ones," which were buried in the mountain, that prevented him from leaving. He stays, the text implies, because the land had been purified by the blood of the martyrs and because their entombed relics had transformed the Iranian mountain into a Christian holy site.[43]

Once the mayor of the village finds out that a Roman captive is walking around teaching Christianity to the villagers, he has him killed. The same poor man who had buried the other martyrs now buries 'Abdisho'. He piles a mound of stones over the deacon's corpse and calls it the Tomb of 'Abdisho'. Soon terrible things begin to happen in the village. Demons kill the mayor's sons, his wife starves to death, and he himself dies of disease and is eaten by his own dogs. Then the whole village is punished when God sends a plague of rats upon their water canal: "The rats dug and filled in the water canal with soil. And when the inhabitants of the village gathered together and removed the soil, the rats dug and filled it in again. This happened repeatedly. And since the village suffered from thirst and its plants withered, it became a desert for twenty-two years and was as a curse in the whole land."[44]

Eventually, one of the sons of the anonymous poor man who had buried the martyrs and piled stones over 'Abdisho' returns to his father's abandoned village. He prays at the martyrs' tombs and promises to return each year to offer a memorial. A few years later he decides to build a house in the village and thus digs out its buried water canal. This time the rats leave it alone. King Shapur is dead, the magi and the apostate Christians are gone, and the village has been baptized with living water that arrives through the labor of a Christian who honors the witness of the martyrs. The village soon becomes

---

42. *AMS* II, 321–22.
43. *AMS* II, 322.
44. *AMS* II, 323–24.

renowned for the healing miracles that occur during its annual memorial of the martyrs, and because of this, "a certain abbot [*resh dayra*] was inspired with beautiful zeal for God. He built a martyrium [*beit sahde*] there on that place, took those bones from the cave, and put them in the building he had built. And lo, unto this day gatherings are being held there."[45]

The text's concluding paragraph tells us nothing about the siege of Bezabde and no more about the fourth-century conflict between Rome and Persia, but it does tell us that the siege and subsequent deportation became the touchstone for the historiographical imagination of the Christians of Persia. By the early fifth century, two or three generations after the martyrdom of the captives of Beth Zabdai, Christianity could be practiced openly in the Sasanian Empire. A martyrs' cult could flourish on a mountain in Iran. An abbot could build a lasting martyrium and perhaps even commission the requisite martyrdom narrative to promote both the site and the authority of the now Christian elites of the village.[46] The fifth-century Christians of Masabdan were not prisoners of war, nor did they claim to descend from Christian captives and martyrs. But they still used the past—specifically, the persistent memory of what had happened in war—to think of themselves as the heirs of Christian captives from Roman Mesopotamia.

Roman Captives in the History of Blessed Simeon bar Ṣabbaʿe

References to Roman captives are much less overt in the *History of Simeon* than in the *Martyrdom of the Captives of Beth Zabdai*. This is not surprising: the *History* purports to detail the beginning of this war between Persia and Rome—not the sieges, deportations, and calamitous treaty that ended it more than two decades later. Nevertheless, there are plenty of references to "captives" in the *History of Simeon,* which clearly reveal the later context in which this martyrdom narrative was written. Some of the most notable are near the end of the text.

When Simeon and those with him are being led to their execution on the "outskirts of the city of Karka d-Ledan," the narrator mentions that thousands of onlookers came to see the "marvelous spectacle." This included "unbeliev-

---

45. *AMS* II, 324.
46. See R. E. Payne, "The Emergence of Martyrs' Shrines in Late Antique Iraq: Conflict, Consensus and Communal Institutions," in *An Age of Saints? Power, Conflict and Dissent in Early Medieval Christianity,* ed. P. Sarris, M. Dal Santo, and P. Booth (Leiden: Brill, 2011), 89–113.

ers" as well as many Christians, whom the narrator calls *bnay shebya*, "sons of the captivity."[47] Once the martyrs met their end, "Roman captives who lived in Karka d-Ledan" retrieved their bodies under the cover of night and took them away to be buried with honor.[48] How the Christian Roman captives of Karka d-Ledan escaped martyrdom is a question that the narrator is poised to answer: the city, he explains, had only just been built at the time of Simeon's death, and Shapur spared its Christian inhabitants because they were recently "taken captive and resettled from different regions."[49] The narrator seems to suggest, however, that this was less an act of mercy than a prudent way of keeping a semblance of peace in a new city freshly populated with exiles.

The "sons of the captivity" who inhabited cities outside Karka d-Ledan were not so lucky. At the beginning of the *History of Simeon*, the narrator introduces some of the martyrs, listing Simeon and the others whom the earlier *Martyrdom of Simeon* also mentions—namely, Gushtazad, a Christian convert and eunuch who was the tutor of the king; Pusai-Qarugbed, the head of the craftsmen; Pusai's daughter; and the "ninety-seven priests and deacons" who were killed with Simeon. But then the narrator of the *History* adds five bishops from other major episcopal sees in Persia, none of whom the *Martyrdom of Simeon* mentions: "Gadyahb and Subyana, the bishops of Beth Lapaṭ; Yoḥannan, the bishop of Hormizd-Ardashir; Bolidaʿ, the bishop of Prat d-Maishan; [and] Yoḥannan, the bishop of Karka d-Maishan."[50]

By including these five among the martyrs, the *History of Simeon* expands the geographical range of Shapur's persecution, making it a regional, rather

---

47. *History of Simeon* 85.

48. Zoroastrians left corpses exposed, believing that burying them would defile the earth. This practice is implied in the *Martyrdom of the Captives* and is a frequent sore point in the *Acts of the Persian Martyrs*. See G. Herman, "'Bury My Coffin Deep!' Zoroastrian Exhumation in Jewish and Christian Sources," in *Tiferet Leyisrael: Jubilee Volume in Honor of Israel Francus*, ed. J. Roth, M. Schmelzer, and Y. Francus (New York: Jewish Theological Seminary of America, 2010), 31–59.

49. *History of Simeon* 98.

50. *History of Simeon* 1. On the two bishops of Beth Lapaṭ and the idea that there were two Christian communities in Persia (one Syriac, the other Greek), see S. Gerö, "The See of Peter in Babylon: Western Influences on the Ecclesiology of Early Persian Christianity," in *East of Byzantium: Syria and Armenia in the Formative Period*, ed. N. G. Garsoïan, T. F. Mathews, and R. W. Thomson (Washington DC: Dumbarton Oaks, 1982), 45–51; and C. Jullien, "La minorité chrétienne 'grecque.'" According to the *Martyrdom of Miles*, the bishop of Susa (Miles) was consecrated by Gadyahb of Beth Lapaṭ, who was the city's "Syriac" bishop (see Gerö, 50n9, 50n21). BL Add. MS 12150, the Edessene manuscript from 411, lists all five of these bishops as martyrs. Sozomen (*HE* II.13) refers to three of them in his list of bishops who were killed with ʿAqebshma—not Simeon.

than just a localized, phenomenon. The text thereby raises the prestige of Christian bishoprics other than those of Seleucia-Ctesiphon and Karka d-Ledan. At the same time, by mentioning other bishops and other cities the narrator underscores the preeminence of Simeon and the primacy of the episcopal see of Seleucia-Ctesiphon, the home of the "the archbishop and catholicos of the Church of the East."[51] The title *catholicos* is never bestowed on Simeon in the *Martyrdom of Simeon*, but in the *History of Simeon* its use suggests that he belongs to all the Christians of Persia.[52] He is not the martyr-bishop of Seleucia-Ctesiphon but the martyr-catholicos of the Church.

The references to Simeon as the "catholicos of the Church of the East," coupled with the inclusion of bishops from the ecclesiastical provinces of Beth Huzaye and Maishan, demonstrate that the *History of Simeon* could not have been composed prior to the fifth-century synods that formally established the Church of the East and delineated the hierarchy of its episcopal sees.[53] According to the twelfth canon of the Synod of Isaac (410), the archbishop-catholicos of Seleucia-Ctesiphon holds the place of primacy in the Church.[54] The twenty-first canon ranks the order of the metropolitan sees following Seleucia-Ctesiphon.[55] Notably, the *History of Simeon* follows this synodal list in ordering the bishops whom it names—the two bishops of Beth Lapaṭ, the bishop of Hormizd-Ardashir, the bishop of Prat d-Maishan, and the bishop of Karka d-Maishan.[56]

---

51. *History of Simeon* 1. On the term *catholicos* and Western influences on the ecclesiology of the Church of the East, see Gerö, "See of Peter"; and L. Abramowski, "Der Bischof von Seleukia-Ktesiphon als Katholikos und Patriarch der Kirche des Ostens," in *Syrien im 1.-7. Jahrhundert nach Christus: Akten der 1. Tübinger Tagung zum Christlichen Orient (15.-16. Juni 2007)*, ed. D. Bumazhnov and H. R. Seeliger (Tübingen: Mohr Siebeck, 2011), 1–55.

52. Simeon is called the "catholicos" of the Church of the East at *History of Simeon* 1, 25, 29, 63, 92, 98–99.

53. According to Stephen Gerö, ecclesiastical titles such as *catholicos* are anachronistic even for the canons of the early fifth-century synods in which they appear. See Gerö, "See of Peter." For an earlier article arguing that the "Petrine" language in the *Synodicon orientale* reflects the influence of Patriarch Timothy I in the late eighth and early ninth century, see W. F. Macomber, "The Authority of the Catholicos Patriarch of Seleucia-Ctesiphon," in *I Patriarcati orientali nel primo millennio*, OCA 181, ed. I. Žužek (Rome: Pontificium Institutum Studiorum Orientalium, 1968), 179–200.

54. J.-B. Chabot, *Synodicon orientale, ou recueil de synodes nestoriens* (Paris: Imprimerie nationale, 1902), 26.

55. Chabot, *Synodicon orientale*, 32–35.

56. After the catholicos, the Synod of Isaac confers the next place of honor on the metropolitan of Beth Lapaṭ in the province of Beth Huzaye. He is to oversee the bishop of

Missing from the *History of Simeon*'s list of bishops who were killed with Simeon is the metropolitan of Nisibis in the province of Beth ʿArbaye, whom the canon ranks third, after the metropolitan of Beth Lapaṭ (who oversees the bishop of Hormizd-Ardashir) but before the metropolitan of Prat d-Maishan. This omission is not surprising. After all, Nisibis was still in Roman, not Persian, territory when Simeon's death is supposed to have occurred. To include its metropolitan here would be anachronistic. Yet later on, when the *History of Simeon* mentions a second time the five bishops who were killed with Simeon, the narrator includes Christians from the region of Nisibis with them. He says that many "captives from Arabia" (the northern Mesopotamian province of Beth ʿArbaye, not the Arabian Peninsula) and prisoners from "Singara, Beth Zabdai, Arzun, Qardu, Armenia, and various other places" were taken to Karka d-Ledan for execution.[57] Notably, when Ammianus laments the Roman territorial losses after Julian's death in 363, he lists the very same cities and regions around Nisibis: Singara, Zabdicena (the province of Bezabde / Beth Zabdai), Arzanena (Arzun), Corduena (Qardu), and other regions of lower Armenia such as Moxoëna.[58]

This parallel between Ammianus and the *History of Simeon* should be taken not as proof that Christians were being singled out for persecution but rather as an indication of the extent to which the *History of Simeon,* the *Martyrdom of the Captives,* and other texts among the *Acts of the Persian Martyrs* reflect an acute awareness of the fourth-century confrontation between Rome and Persia and how by the fifth century the authors of these texts had begun situating themselves within that broader history as Roman captives.

Hormizd-Ardashir and the bishop of Karka d-Ledan. The metropolitan of Nisibis is third in line, and behind him is the metropolitan of Prat d-Maishan, who oversees the bishop of Karka d-Maishan. See Chabot, *Synodicon orientale,* 33.

57. *History of Simeon* 25.

58. Amm. Marc. XXV.7.9–10. On the utility of the *Acts of the Persian Martyrs* for determining the geographic history of the Sasanian Empire, see C. Jullien, "Contributions des *Actes des martyrs perses* à la géographie historique et à l'administration de l'empire sassanide I," in *Contributions à l'histoire et la géographie historique de l'empire sassanide,* Res Orientales 16, ed. R. Gyselen (Bures-sur-Yvette: Groupe pour l'étude de la civilisation du Moyen-Orient, 2004), 141–69; and C. Jullien, "Contributions des *Actes des martyrs perses* à la géographie historique et à l'administration de l'empire sassanide II," in *Des Indo-Grecs aux Sassanides: Données pour l'histoire et la géographie historique,* Res Orientales 17, ed. Gyselen (Bures-sur-Yvette: Groupe pour l'étude de la civilisation du Moyen-Orient, 2007), 81–102.

The Martyrdom of Pusai-Qarugbed, the Son of a Roman Captive

Near the end of the *History of Simeon,* after the ninety-seven priests and deacons have been beheaded and only Simeon and two priests from Seleucia-Ctesiphon with him remain alive, we read the story of "an important man named Pusai—who held the honor of being ranked as the head of the craftsmen, which was called *qarugbed,* which in those days was an honor given to him from the king." The narrator explains that one of the two priests with Simeon, a man called Ḥananya, had been stripped of his clothes and then bound for execution: "His body trembled," the narrator says, "but his mind did not." Pusai stood nearby, "attending to the spectacle of the sacrifice of the holy ones. When he saw the old man whose body was shaking, he said to him, 'Do not fear, Ḥananya, do not fear! Close your eyes just for a wink and, lo, you will see the light of Christ!'"[59]

The head mobed hears Pusai's shout of encouragement and has him "chained until his words could be relayed to the king." After Ḥananya is killed, the narrator explains, Pusai too is "crowned in Christ, his hope."[60] The *Martyrdom of Simeon* says as much as well, but this earlier text (in a rare instance of saying more on a topic than the *History of Simeon*) also includes an account of Pusai's trial before Shapur. According to the *Martyrdom of Simeon,* after the craftsman's outburst he was seized, brought before the king, and accused of aiding a condemned prisoner. Dismayed by Pusai's rash deed, Shapur says to him, "Did I not give honor to you and send you to do your work? Why do you scorn me and remain to watch these worthless ones while they are dying?"[61] Pusai responds by renouncing the honor that Shapur has bestowed on him, characterizing it as "full of grief." He says that instead of embracing the king's honor, he prefers to confess the death given to the martyrs, because it is "full of joy."[62] He proclaims to the king, "I am a Christian, and I hope in their God. For this reason, I have come to love their killing and I repudiate your honor!"[63] The use of the perfect tense ("I have come to

---

59. *History of Simeon* 96.
60. *History of Simeon* 96.
61. *Martyrdom of Simeon* 44.
62. *Martyrdom of Simeon* 45.
63. *Martyrdom of Simeon* 64. On the importance of Pusai's declaration "I am a Christian" in the historical context of earlier Greek and Latin martyrdom narratives, see J. Lieu, *Neither Jew nor Greek? Constructing Early Christianity* (London: T&T Clark, 2002), 211–32.

love") suggests a process. In other words, Pusai has come to a love of martyrdom by witnessing it before his eyes. This phenomenon is not uncommon in Syriac martyrdom literature. In the *Martyrdom of Abbot Barshebya,* which is translated in appendix C, a passing magus witnesses eleven Christians calmly enduring torture and death and is inspired to confess Christ and join the abbot and his monks in their martyrdom.[64]

While Simeon's acts tell us a fair amount about Pusai, a narrative about the craftsman, the *Martyrdom of Pusai-Qarugbed,* has also been preserved. This text, which may date to as late as the sixth century in the form in which we have it, is connected to the *History of Simeon* as part of a cycle of Syriac texts that Gernot Wiessner has dubbed the "B-Zyklus."[65] The *Martyrdom of Pusai* continues the idea found in Simeon's acts that Shapur had bestowed great honor on Pusai, making him the head craftsman. It further emphasizes that Pusai was the son of a Roman captive—a detail that Simeon's acts leave out. Apparently, his father had been deported from Roman territory to the city of Bishapur in Fars. An expert weaver and embroiderer of gold filigree, Pusai married a Persian woman, who converted to Christianity under her husband's tutelage and then raised their children as Christians.

According to the *Martyrdom of Pusai,* when Shapur decided to build Karka d-Ledan, he collected captives from a variety of places, "about thirty families" from each, and then resettled them in his new civic foundation. Pusai's family was among those taken from Bishapur and resettled in Karka d-Ledan. This was a calculated decision by the king. He understood that intermarriage would occur, that families from one place would fuse with the families from other places, and that children would be born who had connections to both families. As family bonds became entangled, it would be all the more difficult for the captives to want to return to the lands from which they had been taken. The narrator of the *Martyrdom of Pusai* clearly under-

---

64. *AMS* II, 281–84.

65. On the difficulty of dating the *Martyrdom of Pusai,* see G. Wiessner, "Zum Problem der zeitlichen und örtlichen Festlegung der erhaltenen syro-persischen Märtyrerakten: Das Pusai-Martyrium," in *Paul de Lagarde und die syrische Kirchengeschichte* (Göttingen: Lagarde Haus, 1968), 231–51. For the "B-Zyklus," see Wiessner, *Untersuchungen zur syrischen Literaturgeschichte I: Zur Märtyrerüberlieferung aus der Christenverfolgung Schapurs II.* (Göttingen: Vandenhoeck und Ruprecht, 1967), 94–105. The "B-Zyklus" includes several martyrdom narratives that might be called spin-offs of the *History of Simeon.* In addition to Pusai, the *History* briefly mentions that Pusai's daughter was martyred. It does not give her name, but she is called "Martha" in her own acts, which also refer to her father and Simeon. See *Martyrdom of Martha,* in *AMS* II, 233–41.

stands the social and economic purpose behind Shapur's resettlement scheme, but he interprets it in a positive light, saying that God used Shapur's plan for the good so that Christian captives mixing with pagans could convert the latter to the true faith and thereby further the Christianization of Persia.[66]

KING YAZDGARD I: FROM PERSECUTION TO PATRONAGE . . . TO PERSECUTION?

Oddly, inasmuch as the martyrdom narratives from the fifth and sixth centuries stress the idea of Persian Christians as Roman captives, no such connection is made by Sozomen, the one fifth-century Greek ecclesiastical historian to discuss the Christian martyrs during Shapur's reign at length. Even though he explains that 250 clerics were captured and brought to Persia "from a place called Zabdaeus," he does not specify that these were *Roman* Christians.[67] Perhaps he was unaware that the Zabdaeans were Roman, or perhaps this is an intentional omission. Sozomen's story, even when it is about the Christians of Persia, is primarily about Constantine and the church in the Roman Empire—not the Christians of Persia. For him, it is Constantine who writes to Shapur to end the persecution and it is Constantine who is the humble Christian bishop to those outside the Roman Church.[68] If Sozomen were to mention that the captives "from a place called Zabdaeus" were taken in 360, near the end of the reign of Constantine's son Constantius, then his chronology would fall apart. How could Constantine have written to Shapur to end the persecution if the crux of what Sozomen describes took place decades after the emperor's death?[69]

Sozomen was not the only one who wished to see Constantine's hand at work in the protection of Persian Christians. Later Arabic chroniclers also discuss a standoff between Constantine and Shapur over the Christians of Persia, but they manage to insert someone else into the story as well: the

---

66. *AMS* II, 209. On Pusai's family bonds, see J. T. Walker, *The Legend of Mar Qardagh: Narrative and Christian Heroism in Late Antique Iraq* (Berkeley: University of California Press, 2006), 222–23.

67. Soz. *HE* II.13.

68. Soz. *HE* II.15.

69. See P. Devos, "Sozomène et les actes syriaques de S. Syméon bar Ṣabbā'ē," *AB* 84 (1966): 443–56.

bishop Marutha of Maypherqaṭ. According to the twelfth-century historian Ibn al-Azraq, Marutha, whose abilities as a physician were legendary, was brought to the Persian capital to heal Shapur's daughter. Following his successful cure of the girl, he negotiated a peace treaty between Shapur and Constantine.[70] Although later ecclesiastical historians omitted Marutha from the historical record or, like Ibn al-Azraq, included him but incorrectly retrojected his work into an earlier era, he is duly famous as an envoy to Persia.[71] Apparently at the invitation of King Yazdgard I, Theodosius II sent Marutha to co-convene the first official council of the Church of the East, in 410. This synod, held at Seleucia-Ctesiphon, came to be known as the Synod of Isaac, in honor of the bishop of the capital city at that time.

For his role as a patron of the two councils that formally established the Church of the East, some Christians saw Yazdgard as a liberator—even a Persian Constantine.[72] In Scott McDonough's analysis, Yazdgard's accommodation of Christians in Persia was a deliberate political move: by claiming the right to summon the synod, to enforce communal discipline, to designate the head of the Persian Church (in Yazdgard's capital of Seleucia-Ctesiphon), and to have Persian Christians pray for the king's reign, he could wield substantial control over the Christians of Persia even as they brought in bishops from the Roman Empire to help organize their ecclesiastical structures and regulate the developing theological orthodoxy of their Church.[73]

---

70. See J.-M. Fiey, "Maruta de Martyropolis d'après Ibn al-Azraq (†1181)," *AB* 94 (1976): 35–45; C. Robinson, "Ibn al-Azraq, His *Ta'rīkh Mayyāfāriqīn*, and Early Islam," *JRAS* 6 (1996): 7–27; and H. Munt, "Ibn al-Azraq, Saint Marūthā, and the Foundation of Mayyāfāriqīn (Martyropolis)," in *Writing 'True Stories': Historians and Hagiographers in the Late Antique and Medieval Near East,* ed. A. Papaconstantinou (Turnhout: Brepols, 2010), 149–74.

71. On the theme of bishops serving in a dual capacity as both political and ecclesiastical envoys, see N. G. Garsoïan, "Le rôle de l'hiérarchie chrétienne dans les rapports diplomatiques entre Byzance et les Sassanides," *RÉArm* 10 (1973): 119–38; L. Sako, *Le rôle de la hiérarchie syriaque orientale dans les rapports diplomatiques entre la Perse et Byzance aux Ve–VIIe siècles* (Paris: Lille–Atelier national de reproduction des thèses, 1986); and S. J. McDonough, "Bishops or Bureaucrats? Christian Clergy and the State in the Middle Sasanian Period," in *Current Research in Sasanian Archaeology, Art and History: Proceedings of a Conference held at Durham University, November 3rd and 4th, 2001,* ed. D. Kennet and P. Luft (Oxford: BAR International Series, 2008), 87–92.

72. See McDonough, "A Second Constantine?"

73. See McDonough, "Bishops or Bureaucrats?"; and McDonough, "Power by Negotiation: Institutional Reform in the Fifth Century Sasanian Empire" (PhD diss., University of California at Los Angeles, 2005).

Marutha's role as an envoy and co-convener of the Synod of Isaac was overshadowed by his role in helping to transmit to Western audiences the stories of those who had been martyred under Shapur II. It is possible that Sozomen relied on Marutha's Greek translations, or summaries, of some Syriac martyrdom narratives. In addition to translating the stories about the martyrs of Persia to the West, Marutha is credited with translating their bones. Yazdgard supposedly granted him the remains of many Christian martyrs, and the bishop brought them back to Maypherqaṭ, where he enshrined the relics in his cathedral and renamed the city Martyropolis in their honor.[74] So connected was Marutha to the bones and stories of the Persian martyrs that later Arabic chroniclers even (erroneously) attributed the authorship of the *Acts of the Persian Martyrs* to him.[75]

While things seemed hopeful for the Christians of the East in the early years of the fifth century, their situation was more precarious by the end of Yazdgard's reign. Whereas later Persian historians (such as al-Ṭabari) suggest that a run-of-the-mill dynastic crisis following Yazdgard's death spurred the war between Rome and Persia that began in 420/21, Roman tradition portrays it as fundamentally about religious freedom.[76] Although the Synod of Yahbalaha, in 420, was also co-convened by a bishop from the Roman Empire and the introduction to its canons also begins in praise of Yazdgard, several Syriac martyrdom narratives that discuss the shah's last years accuse

---

74. See R. Marcus, "The Armenian *Life* of Marutha of Maipherkat," *HTR* 25 (1932): 47–71. Marutha's Armenian *Life* is based on a lost Syriac account. For the Greek *Life*, see J. Noret, "La vie grecque ancienne de S. Maruta de Mayferqat," *AB* 91 (1973): 77–103. Other Greek sources for Marutha include Sozomen's brief mention of the bishop (in a discussion of an ecclesiastical gathering in the Roman Empire that was unrelated to his mission to Persia) and a much longer account by Socrates that is based on Marutha's *Life*. See Soz. *HE* VIII.16; and Soc. *HE* VII.8. For the medieval Arabic traditions about Martyropolis (Mayyāfāriqīn), which became a center of pilgrimage on the frontier zone, a "lieu d'osmose" (38) for rivals of various allegiances, see J.-M. Fiey, "Martyropolis syriaque," *Mus* 89 (1976): 5–38; and Munt, "Ibn al-Azraq." For the symbolic nature of Martyropolis as a site between the Roman and Persian Empires, see E.K. Fowden, *The Barbarian Plain: Saint Sergius between Rome and Iran* (Berkeley: University of California Press, 1999), 45–100.

75. In the fourteenth century, ʿAbdishoʿ bar Brikha catalogued several works written by Marutha, among them a "book concerning martyrs." See J.S. Assemani, *Bibliotheca Orientalis Clementino-Vaticana*, vol. 3 (Rome, 1725), 74. Although Wiessner has definitively shown that Marutha did not author any of the *Acts*, it was once commonly accepted that he had. See Wiessner, *Untersuchungen zur syrischen Literaturgeschichte*, 11; and L. Ter-Petrossian, "L'Attribution du receuil des passions perses à Maroutha de Maypherqat," *AB* 97 (1979): 129–30.

76. For the Syriac material, see O.J. Schrier, "Syriac Evidence for the Roman-Persian War of 421–422," *GRBS* 33 (1992): 75–86.

him of renewing a persecution of Christians.[77] The *Martyrdom of Jacob the Notary* and the *Martyrdom of Peroz*, for instance, spend quite some time discussing Yazdgard's transformation from a kind patron of Christians to, near the end of his life, their fearsome persecutor.[78]

Yazdgard was clearly a polarizing figure. While the Christians of Persia may have loved him (at least initially), the Zoroastrian elite despised him as a "sinner."[79] According to Lucas Van Rompay, the king's patronage of Christian bishops and the newfound freedom of Persian Christians to openly practice their faith may have "constituted a real threat to the Persian religion and to the feudal Sassanian society."[80] Indeed, this is what several Syriac martyrdom narratives set during (or shortly after) Yazdgard's reign suggest. This "threat" was, however, not in the appeal of the Christian faith or in the possibility that Christians would convert scores of Sasanian elites—although that became a prominent theme in the martyrdom narratives associated with the mid-fifth-century reign of Yazdgard II. Rather, the threat from Christians was their open disdain for the magian fire cult. Some, according to our sources, even destroyed fire temples in furious acts of anti-pagan zeal. The *Martyrdom of Narsai the Ascetic* tells one such story. According to this text, Narsai, a convert from Zoroastrianism, discovered that a church with a questionable deed of ownership had been desecrated and converted into a fire temple. Incensed, he destroyed the temple and extinguished the sacred fire that it had held. Because of his actions, he was arrested and told that he had to not only rebuild the fire temple but also relight the sacred fire after gathering flames from hundreds of different sources. Not surprisingly, he refused to do this and was killed.[81]

The *Martyrdom of 'Abda*, a narrative detailing the trial of the bishop of Hormizd-Ardashir and his companions, tells a similar story. This text also provides an example of how Christians, empowered by the protection they

---

77. For the narrator's praise of Yazdgard in the Synod of Yahbalaha, see Chabot, *Synodicon orientale*, 37.

78. For the *Martyrdom of Jacob the Notary*, see *AMS* IV, 189–200; for the *Martyrdom of Peroz*, who was killed in the first year of Bahram V's reign, see *AMS* IV, 253–62.

79. See, for example, A.S. Shahbazi, "The Horse that Killed Yazdagerd 'the Sinner,'" in *Paitimāna: Essays in Iranian, Indo-European, and Indian Studies in Honor of Hans-Peter Schmidt*, ed. S. Adhami (Costa Mesa, CA: Mazda, 2003), 355–62.

80. L. Van Rompay, "Impetuous Martyrs? The Situation of the Persian Christians in the Last Years of Yazdgard I (419–420)," in *Martyrium in Multidisciplinary Perspective: Memorial Louis Reekmans*, ed. M. Lamberigts and P. Van Deun (Leuven: Peeters, 1995), 372.

81. See *AMS* IV, 170–80.

believed they had under Yazdgard, turned on the non-Christians of Persia. As in Simeon's acts and others set during the time of Shapur II, in the *Martyrdom of 'Abda* the magi accuse the *naṣraye* of despising the gods and kingdom of Yazdgard. Upset by this betrayal, the king orders that the accused, including 'Abda, be brought before him for questioning. The trial and eventual martyrdom of 'Abda are lost in Syriac, but fortunately Theodoret of Cyrrhus preserves a Greek summary of 'Abda's acts, and he recounts how the martyr-to-be, a lover of the true faith, destroyed a fire temple.[82] According to Theodoret, Yazdgard ordered 'Abda to rebuild the temple, but just like Narsai, 'Abda refused to participate in the construction of a pagan cult site. In retelling the story of 'Abda, Theodoret inserts his own (much less zealous) perspective, declaring that the bishop's deeds were foolhardy. He gives the counterexample of Paul, who did not destroy altars to false gods while he was in Athens but instead convinced the Athenians that Jesus was the Messiah by appealing to their logic and reason. Theodoret's censure of 'Abda is mild, though, and the ecclesiastical historian concedes that once the fire temple had been destroyed, 'Abda was justified in refusing to rebuild it, as that would have meant honoring the fire cult and committing the sin of idolatry.

According to Theodoret, the bold actions of some, such as 'Abda, sparked renewed violence against Christians—this time under a king who, just a decade earlier, had "rolled back the black cloud of persecution."[83] Many Christians, fearing the worst, fled to the Roman Empire, which they saw as a safe haven. According to Socrates, the ensuing hostilities between Rome and Persia were the direct result of Theodosius's refusal to return to Persia these Christians who had sought refuge in the West.[84] Socrates differs from Theodoret, however, in claiming that it was Bahram V (Yazdgard's son and successor), not Yazdgard, who renewed the persecution of Christians. In either case, there is plenty of evidence that the war was, at the time, used as an ideological tool in the West to promote Roman-Christian identity.[85]

82. See *AMS* IV, 250–53; and Theod. *HE* V.39.
83. Chabot, *Synodicon orientale*, 18.
84. See Soc. *HE* VII.18; and the description of the sources in G. Greatrex, "The Two Fifth-Century Wars between Rome and Persia," *Florilegium* 12 (1993): 1–14.
85. Zeev Rubin argues that Roman missionaries were partly responsible for the war because of their efforts to entice Persia's Saracen allies, via "Christian missionary propaganda," into switching their allegiance to the Roman Empire. See Rubin, "Diplomacy and War in the Relations between Byzantium and the Sassanids in the Fifth Century AD," in *The Defence of the Roman and Byzantine East,* ed. P. Freeman and D. Kennedy (Oxford: BAR International Editions, 1986), 677–95.

In the analysis of Kenneth Holum, on the basis of both textual and numismatic evidence, the Christian ideological background for the war was constructed to strengthen the "dynastic pretensions" of Pulcheria, Theodosius's overly pious (and overly power hungry) sister.[86] But how much stock can we put in the Roman account of Yazdgard's final years—especially this idea that a war between the two powers was waged over a few Christian refugees?

Most scholars have accepted Theodoret's version as more historically likely than that of Socrates because, as Geoffrey Herman points out, Theodoret relies on primary sources—namely, fifth-century Syriac martyrdom narratives (especially the *Martyrdom of 'Abda*) that blame Yazdgard (not Bahram, as Socrates does) for terrorizing the Christians of Persia with the specter of a new persecution.[87] Yet, Herman argues, there are quite a number of problems with virtually all of them. For instance, the texts are chronologically further from the supposed persecution than many have assumed. The notion that Yazdgard persecuted Christians does not seem to have arisen until at least twenty years after the king's death—around the time when Theodoret was writing his *Church History*. Additionally, their description of Zoroastrian rites is often wildly inaccurate; they use dozens of loanwords derived from Greek, not the Middle Persian loanwords that are more typical of East Syriac texts; and they refer to both Christians and Zoroastrians with peculiarly Roman titles. As Herman puts it, "[The martyr] Tataq is a *domesticus,* Jacob is a *notarius* whilst the chief Zoroastrian persecutor Mihrshapur is a *hyparchos.* [Jérôme] Labourt hit the nail on the head when he commented, without, it would seem, a hint of irony: 'il semble que la cour de Iazdgerd et de Bahrām ait été organisée à la romaine.'"[88]

---

86. K. Holum, "Pulcheria's Crusade A.D. 421–22 and the Ideology of Imperial Victory," *GRBS* 18 (1977): 153–72; quote on 172. Holum argues that the "Long-Cross Solidi," which were not struck in the Roman Empire until 420, are the first clear instance of Christian imperial ideology in Roman coinage. Jill Harries explains that Theodosius sought to present himself as a "pious king" who, like Constantine, was keen to protect Christians. See Harries, "'Pius Princeps': Theodosius II and Fifth-Century Constantinople," in *New Constantines: The Rhythm of Imperial Renewal in Byzantium, 4th–13th Centuries,* ed. P. Magdalino (London: Variorum, 1994), 35–44.

87. See G. Herman, "The Last Years of Yazdgird I and the Christians," in *Jews, Christians and Zoroastrians: Religious Dynamics in a Sasanian Context,* ed. Herman (Piscataway, NJ: Gorgias, 2014), 67–90.

88. Herman, "Last Years of Yazdgird," 87, with reference to J. Labourt, *Le christianisme dans l'empire perse sous la dynastie sassanide (224–632)* (Paris: Librairie Victor Lecoffre, 1904), 113n4.

Ultimately, Herman concludes that the Syriac martyrdom narratives set during the reigns of Yazdgard and Bahram may have arisen not in Persia but out of "the Roman Christian discourse on active anti-pagan aggression," "a case of Romans pondering the subject through the example of Persia."[89] As such, it is possible that these sources are not "Persian" martyr acts but instead texts that represent how Syriac Christians in the eastern Roman Empire were using Persian Christians "to think with." As I discuss in the next chapter, there are other examples of this. The Syriac *History of the Holy Mar Ma'in*, perhaps more than any other text that is grouped among the *Acts of the Persian Martyrs*, demonstrates the extent to which Syriac Christians in the Roman Empire were writing their own histories of persecution and religious transformation. Invariably, these were influenced by goings-on in the West as much as by those in the East, but we cannot conclude with any certainty that they necessarily reflect the thought of the Christians of Persia.

CONCLUSIONS

What did the fifth-century Christians of Persia stand to gain by consistently emphasizing their Romanness and their social position as "captives" while spurning titles such as the one that the king gave Pusai? Indeed, as the *Martyrdom of Pusai* shows, although some Christians may have been captives in Sasanian Persia, there was no evident barrier that prevented them from achieving a relatively high social status in the empire.[90] Both of Simeon's martyr acts claim that he was at one point a friend to Shapur, even quite close to the king. Simeon tells Shapur that he would gladly remain friends so long as he was not forced to prove his friendship by worshiping the sun.[91] Even in the *Martyrdom of the Captives of Beth Zabdai*, in which no Sasanian authority comes across as particularly sympathetic, the Persians offer their prisoners

---

89. Herman, "Last Years of Yazdgird," 89–90. This conclusion stands in opposition to that of Michael Gaddis, who proposes that Syriac martyrdom narratives (such as those of Narsai and 'Abda) may demonstrate the movement of anti-pagan violence from Rome into a Sasanian context. See Gaddis, *There Is No Crime for Those Who Have Christ: Religious Violence in the Christian Roman Empire* (Berkeley: University of California Press, 2005), 196–98.

90. Payne, *State of Mixture* demonstrates the extent to which Christians in Sasanian Persia flourished under Zoroastrian rule.

91. *History of Simeon* 80; *Martyrdom of Simeon* 38, 40.

good land in abundance. These captives were brought to Persia not as slaves but as farmers and skilled laborers who could help bolster the economic growth of the empire. Yet the text also points out (as do the *Martyrdom of Pusai* and the *Martyrdom* and *History of Simeon*) how Christians rebelled against Sasanian authority. Rather than argue (as Simeon does in the *History of Simeon*) that Christians could be Christians while remaining loyal servants of Shapur, Dawsa of Beth Zabdai does not flinch when presented with the Romanness of his god. He tells his captors, "We hold steadfast to our faith and worship our true God—whom Caesar worships as well."[92]

This turn to the West among the Christians of Persia proved to be short lived. As Richard Payne details in his social history of Christian martyrological and legal texts from the late Sasanian period, the members of Christian communities in Persia had begun to shed their status as foreign captives by the sixth century, in order to appropriate more particularly Iranian modes of identity. According to Payne, the "ongoing description of Christians as captives" in the *Acts of the Persian Martyrs* "suggests the limitations placed on Christian belonging" prior to this time. This was, he indicates, partly a result of the Sasanian idea of "Ērānšahr," "a concept that subsumed the individual lands of the empire into a single entity." Additionally, he argues, "the places in which the [Roman] captives were settled were themselves often emblems of the religiously exclusive ideology of empire elaborated by kings and *mowbeds*."[93]

In the final chapter of this book, I consider the development of ideas about the "West" in later Syriac martyrdom narratives by looking at two texts: one, written in the Roman Empire, embraces Constantine and concocts a wholly counterfactual history of the fourth century; the other, written in the Persian Empire, rejects the emperor and the Christians of the West. Before the sixth century, because Christians had not yet begun to articulate a *Persian* Christian identity, they may have been able to imagine their identity only as Roman. Yet by the sixth century, once theological, ecclesiastical, and political divisions had further separated Christians in the East from their co-religionists in the West, the Christians of Persia could more readily ignore the Roman Empire and begin to create a religious identity that was tied to holy places in the land of Iran. In so doing, they could begin to categorize

---

92. *AMS* II, 321.
93. Payne, "Christianity and Iranian Society," 36. See also Payne, *State of Mixture*, 64–72.

Christianity not as a foreign cult of "Roman captives" but as a system of worship that was fully imbricated within a local Iranian milieu and Persian discourse of religiosity. Until this later period, however, an intermediate "captive" status prevailed, which Syriac texts such as the *History of Simeon bar Ṣabbaʿe*, the *Martyrdom of Pusai-Qarugbed*, and the *Martyrdom of the Captives of Beth Zabdai* acutely reflect.

SIX

*Memories of Constantine in
the* Acts of the Persian Martyrs

THE CONSTANTINE PRESENTED BY GREEK ecclesiastical historians is a pious and powerful king. He is portrayed as the protector of all Christians, as a second Moses who delivered the people of God from the tyranny of pagan emperors, as a letter writer and patron from afar who sought to end the oppression of Christians in Persia, and as a military leader who was so fearsome that he could cow foreign emissaries into suing for peace before war had even begun. The Constantine of Greek ecclesiastical history took on the role that Eusebius is said to have intended for him, becoming both an icon and a mirror for princes. In the later Byzantine Empire, Constantine was the ideal "bishop of those outside the Church."[1] He was the perfect emperor—or at least imagined as such—to whom Byzantine court panegyrists could turn by way of rhetorically bolstering the inevitably lesser virtues of their imperial patrons.[2]

---

1. Euseb. *VC* IV.24. Commenting on this idea of Constantine, Aaron Johnson explains that Eusebius "sought in effect to delimit and control the duties and character of a Christian emperor. The emperor was to do the work of God in the political, legal, and military spheres (as represented in his letter to Shapur, for instance), while the 'bishops of those within' the Church were to control ecclesiastical affairs." See Johnson, *Ethnicity and Argument in Eusebius' "Praeparatio Evangelica"* (Oxford: Oxford University Press, 2006), 195.

2. See Alexander Kazhdan's classic article "'Constantin imaginaire': Byzantine Legends of the Ninth Century about Constantine the Great," *Byz* 57 (1987): 196–250, which traces how Byzantine historians and chroniclers developed the constituent elements of the Constantine legend. To a certain extent, Theodosius the Great and Justinian the Great were also portrayed as embodiments of the imperial ideal. See the collected essays on this theme in P. Magdalino, ed., *New Constantines: The Rhythm of Imperial Renewal in Byzantium, 4th–13th Centuries* (London: Variorum, 1994), especially the contribution of J. Harries, "'Pius Princeps': Theodosius II and Fifth-Century Constantinople," 35–44, which argues that Socrates's and Sozomen's constructions of the kingly piety of Theodosius are emblematic of Eusebius's idea of Constantine.

Clearly, the Constantine of Greek history and legend had the presence of a lion, and he was celebrated as the savior of Christians everywhere. But how does the Syriac martyrological tradition remember him? In this chapter, I explain how the Syriac martyrdom narratives that are set during Shapur's persecution narrate and conceptualize the role and influence of the first Christian emperor. Perhaps surprisingly, Constantine does not appear often in Syriac martyrdom narratives set in the fourth century, and when he does there is no uniformity in his presentation or in the conceptualization of his reign. These texts are just as likely to ignore or even reject as to embrace and glorify the first Christian emperor.

CAESAR, CONSTANTINE, AND ROMAN CAPTIVES

As I discussed in chapter 5, Christian captives from the Roman Empire are present to a greater or lesser extent in a number of influential Syriac martyrdom narratives, most prominently the *Martyrdom of the Captives of Beth Zabdai*. An unnamed "Caesar" also shows up in the *Acts of the Persian Martyrs* but typically as an anonymous proxy for any generic yet presumably Christian king of Rome. Yet even "Caesar" is invoked less frequently than one might imagine given the common assumption that the Christians of Persia were persecuted because they were believed to have been allied with Caesar. In fact, besides the *Martyrdom of the Captives* and the *Martyrdom and History of Blessed Simeon bar Ṣabba'e*, just two other texts from the *Acts* discuss the Roman Caesar: the *Martyrdom of the Forty Holy Martyrs*, which, on the basis of internal evidence, could not have been composed until at least the second half of the fifth century; and the seventh-century *History of Saba Pirgushnasp*, which narrates the conversion of a Sasanian noble at Nisibis after Julian's death and Shapur's acquisition of the city.[3]

Specific references to Constantine (not just "Caesar") are rarer still. Just two of more than forty Syriac martyrdom narratives set during Shapur's reign name and discuss Constantine.[4] The most well known of these two

---

3. For the *Martyrdom of the Forty Holy Martyrs*, see *AMS* II, 325–47; for the *History of Saba Pirgushnasp*, see *AMS* IV, 222–49.

4. A third, the *History of Mar Behnam and Sarah* (*AMS* II, 397–441), mentions Constantine in its first few lines but says nothing substantial about him. The *History of Mar Behnam* is set decades after Constantine's death, during Julian's reign, and although Gernot Wiessner dates it to the late ancient period, more recent studies have proved that it must

is undoubtedly the *History of Simeon*. Although Simeon never utters Constantine's name, the narrator of the text praises the emperor at length. Still, he is keen to point out that "the triumphant Constantine" was dead before Shapur "began to harass the Christian people, to afflict and persecute the priests and the *qyama,* and to destroy the churches in all of his realm."[5] While the *History of Simeon* may consider Constantine "blessed" and "an angel of peace," it never claims that he did anything on behalf of the Christians of Persia or that he was even alive to have known about their persecution.[6]

CONSTANTINE AND THE LETTER TO SHAPUR IN THE *HISTORY OF THE HOLY MAR MAʿIN*

The only text besides the *History of Simeon* among the *Acts of the Persian Martyrs* that speaks about Constantine in the context of Shapur's persecution is the sixth-century *History of the Holy Mar Maʿin*. Although Sebastian Brock recently published a Syriac edition and English translation of the text, nothing else has been written about it besides an annotated summary in the nineteenth century and a brief article by Jean-Marie Fiey in the early 1970s.[7]

---

be a medieval composition, from perhaps as late as the twelfth century. See Wiessner, "Die Behnam-Legende," in *Synkretismusforschung: Theorie und Praxis,* ed. Wiessner (Wiesbaden: Otto Harrassowitz, 1978), 119–33; H. Younansardaroud, "Die Legende von Mar Behnam," in *Syriaca: Zur Geschichte, Theologie, Liturgie und Gegenwartslage der syrischen Kirchen, 2. Deutsches Syrologen-Symposium, Juli 2000, Wittenberg,* ed. M. Tamcke (Hamburg: Lit Verlag, 2002), 185–96; Younansardaroud and M. Novák, "Mar Behnam, Sohn des Sanherib von Nimrud: Tradition und Rezeption einer assyrischen Gestalt im iraqischen Christentum und die Frage nach den Fortleben der Assyrer," *AF* 29 (2002): 166–94; and J.-N.M. Saint-Laurent and K. Smith, *The History of Mar Behnam and Sarah,* Persian Martyr Acts in Syriac: Text and Translation, fasc. 5 (Piscataway, NJ: Gorgias, forthcoming).

5. *History of Simeon* 2. All citations of Simeon's acts refer to section numbers in K. Smith, *The Martyrdom and History of Blessed Simeon bar Ṣabbaʿe,* Persian Martyr Acts in Syriac: Text and Translation, fasc. 3 (Piscataway, NJ: Gorgias, 2014).

6. *History of Simeon* 3–4.

7. See S. P. Brock, *The History of the Holy Mar Maʿin with a Guide to the Persian Martyr Acts,* Persian Martyr Acts in Syriac: Text and Translation, fasc. 1 (Piscataway, NJ: Gorgias, 2009), 1, with reference (n. 1) to G. Hoffmann, *Auszüge aus syrischen Akten persischer Märtyrer,* Abhandlungen für die Kunde des Morgenlandes VII.3 (Leipzig, 1880), 28–33; and J.-M. Fiey, "Maʿin, général de Sapor II, confesseur et évêque," *Mus* 84 (1971): 437–53. Note that the confessor's name is Maʿin, while *mar* (my Lord) is a Syriac title of respect—one typically accorded to saints and bishops.

This dearth of scholarship is not uncommon. The case is similar for several other Syriac martyrdom narratives that are set during Shapur's persecution but were not composed until later centuries. Excluding these later texts from the discussion about fourth-century "events" is unfortunate. Without knowledge of them, our understanding is obscured: we cannot see how ideas about the role of Constantine and the Roman Empire during Shapur's persecution developed over time and in conversation with earlier narratives. Reintroducing these late texts into discussions about Shapur's persecution thus helps distinguish how Syriac-speaking Christians came to understand Constantine, which is often very different from how earlier eras understood him.

In at least one Syriac martyrdom narrative, the *History of Mar Ma'in*, Constantine is the patron of all Christians everywhere. That is, Syriac-speaking Christians came to understand him as Greek ecclesiastical historians had already long understood him. The influence of Greek ecclesiastical history on this sixth-century Syriac text cannot be underestimated. Indeed, the faith of the Romans is frequently on display in this narrative, which details the suffering of Mar Ma'in, a Christian convert who was formerly a general in Shapur's army. After abandoning his military duties and becoming a Christian, Mar Ma'in undergoes interrogation, imprisonment, and brutal torture. But he survives, thanks entirely to Constantine's direct intervention on his behalf, and then spends the rest of his life founding monasteries in and around the Sinjar Mountains in northern Mesopotamia.[8] Throughout, the text refers to Constantine as "the victorious king" and "the believing emperor." This in itself is unremarkable. The *History of Simeon* uses similar epithets for the Christian king. But there is a crucial difference between the *History of Simeon* and the *History of Mar Ma'in*: in the *History of Mar Ma'in*, Constantine is not recently deceased as Shapur's persecution begins but rather still alive and vociferously advocating on behalf of all the Christians in Persia.

From his capital in the Roman Empire, Constantine hopes to aid one far-distant Christian in particular—Mar Ma'in. The emperor sends an envoy to the Persian court, a man to whom the narrator refers as "the believing

---

8. *History of Mar Ma'in* 29–30 (on Mar Ma'in's conversion), 33–34 (on Shapur's search for his general), 70 (on Mar Ma'in's founding of many monasteries). All quotations of the *History of Mar Ma'in* are from Brock's edition and translation. Note that a number after "*History of Mar Ma'in*" refers to a section number in the text; after "Brock, *History of Mar Ma'in*," to a page number in Brock's introduction or appended annotations.

man" and more simply "the believer."⁹ At Constantine's order, this "believer" helps free Mar Ma'in from Shapur's afflictions. In so doing, he illustrates the continued zeal in the West to import both the relics and the stories of the martyrs and confessors in the East. After Mar Ma'in is released from prison, Constantine's envoy begs him for his clothes, which Shapur's torturers had bloodied. The believer takes the confessor's bloodstained garments back to the West as sanctified proof of the suffering of Christians in Persia.¹⁰

This strange fascination with a tactile reminder of Shapur's persecution is all the more curious considering the place and date of the text's composition. According to Sebastian Brock, a single, twelfth-century manuscript preserves the *History of Mar Ma'in,* a text dated, on philological grounds, to the sixth century. But this Syriac history about one of Shapur's former generals was not composed in Sasanian Persia; rather, it was written in the eastern Roman Empire.¹¹ "The author," Brock insists, "is clearly writing at a time when the Byzantine emperor controlled the area" west of the Sinjar Mountains, where many Syriac-speaking Christians lived. For Brock, this is not just a hypothesis: it is, he says, "self-evident" that the author of the *History of Mar Ma'in* "was writing within the Roman Empire."¹² According to the text, after Constantine threatens Shapur and the Persian king agrees to release Mar Ma'in, the confessor emigrates from the East to spend the twilight of his life in the West. Mar Ma'in explains his plans in advance to Constantine's envoy: "Once I have made converts here [Persia] and have built sanctuaries and monasteries for him [Christ], I will leave in them disciples of his, and I myself will

---

9. The Syriac term that Brock translates as "believing" or "believer" (*m-haymna*) can also be translated as "faithful."

10. *History of Mar Ma'in* 66.

11. The manuscript is British Library Add. 12,174, dated 1196, which contains many Syriac martyrdom narratives. Brock proposes a sixth-century composition based on a series of verbal constructions and other linguistic evidence that militate against dates both earlier and later. In the only previous study of the *History of Mar Ma'in,* Fiey also suggests a sixth-century date, albeit for reasons that Brock rejects. See Fiey, "Ma'in, général de Sapor II," 450; and Brock, *History of Mar Ma'in,* 4–6, 10.

Accurately dating anonymous martyrdom narratives from late antiquity is often very difficult. In his review of Gernot Wiessner's philological study of Simeon's acts, Brock points out that Wiessner studiously avoids any question of historical problems, dating, or when a particular martyrdom narrative may have reached the form in which it was finally preserved. See Brock, "Review of *Untersuchungen zur syrischen Literaturgeschichte I: Zur Märtyrerüberlieferung aus der Christenverfolgung Schapurs II.,* by Gernot Wiessner," *JTS* 19 (1968): 307.

12. See Brock, *History of Mar Ma'in,* 5–6, 69n55, 69n57, 70–71n73, 71n77.

come to your region [the Roman Empire] and make disciples there too; and there I shall complete my course."[13] Eventually he travels to a village near Dura Europos, whose ruins are west of the Sinjar Mountains in eastern Syria today. There he follows through on his promise to "make disciples" in the Roman Empire. He finds a village full of people who still worship idols but hold their "feasts and festivals for idols in secret" because they fear Christians and do not wish to be seen violating "the [anti-pagan] decree of Constantine, worthy of good memory."[14] To be sure, a number of other texts among the *Acts* may have been composed in Syriac-speaking cities of the Roman Empire—including several of those set during Yazdgard I's reign, as I discussed in chapter 5.[15] But the *History of Mar Ma'in* is unique as the only Syriac martyrdom narrative set during Shapur's persecution that presents such a clamorously pro-Western perspective in which Constantine emerges as a hero.[16]

Besides being the literary production of an author living under a Byzantine emperor centuries after Shapur's persecution, the *History of Mar Ma'in* holds another curious distinction: it is the only text among the *Acts of the Persian Martyrs* to mention a letter from Constantine to Shapur. Although this letter in the *History of Mar Ma'in* plays on themes in both Eusebius's *Life of Constantine* and the ecclesiastical historian's continuators, its tone and content here in its Syriac martyrological context are quite different. Still, it fits perfectly in the later Roman and Byzantine literary traditions that invert the chronology of Persian historiographical sources in order to reimagine Constantine's epistolary confrontation with Shapur on behalf of the Christians of Persia.

In both of Simeon's acts, the *Martyrdom* and the *History of Simeon*, it is "the Jews" who accuse Simeon of colluding with Caesar. A supposed exchange of letters between him and the Roman emperor is at the heart of their allegations against him. According to the narrator of the *History of Simeon*, the

---

13. *History of Mar Ma'in* 63.

14. *History of Mar Ma'in* 73. As Brock notes, the author of the *History of Mar Ma'in* apparently "retrojects Theodosius I's anti-pagan legislation to the time of Constantine." See Brock, *History of Mar Ma'in*, 70–71.

15. See also G. Herman, "The Last Years of Yazdgird I and the Christians," in *Jews, Christians and Zoroastrians: Religious Dynamics in a Sasanian Context*, ed. Herman (Piscataway, NJ: Gorgias, 2014), 67–90.

16. For a similarly fantastical Syriac narrative about the fourth century, see the *Julian Romance*, discussed in chapter 3. This text was also composed in the Roman Empire and also considers the plight of the Christians of Persia at length.

Jews levied this charge at Shapur's court, saying, "If you, the King of Kings, the lord of all the earth, were to send to Caesar great and learned letters of your royalty, along with glorious offerings and delicious gifts of your majesty, they would not be much revered in his eyes. But if Simeon were to send to him a single trivial and curt letter, (Caesar) would arise and bow and receive it with both his hands and diligently fulfill his command. In addition, there is no secret in your kingdom that (Simeon) does not write down and make known to Caesar."[17] The Roman emperor's interest in the Christians of the East—and, according to the allegations in the *History of Simeon*, Simeon's role in providing him with secret information—forms the basis for the decisive action that is taken against the Christians of Persia. Of course, these are only allegations. Simeon never mentions Constantine or "Caesar," nor does he respond to the allegations of the Jews nor mention either sending a letter to or receiving a letter from any Roman emperor, Constantine or Constantius.[18] By contrast, the *History of Mar Maʿin* is over the top in demonstrating the extent to which Constantine belligerently (and successfully) intervenes on behalf of the Christians of Persia. It shows how the incredible events that it narrates sustained, and further produced, a *Constantin imaginaire* and a Roman-influenced Syriac version of the history of Shapur's Persia.

Constantine, according to the narrator of the *History of Mar Maʿin,* was worried about the plight of Christians in Persia and chose to exercise no small role in securing their protection. The text says that Mar Maʿin's conversion to Christianity so angered Shapur that he himself interrogated his former general, to make him renounce his new faith.[19] If the Christian martyr is another Christ, then Shapur is another Pilate: he orders that Mar Maʿin be scourged and that salt and vinegar be rubbed into his wounds.[20]

---

17. *History of Simeon* 12. Cf. *Martyrdom of Simeon* 13, which repeats the accusation nearly verbatim but does not include the final sentence accusing Simeon of betraying the secrets of the Persian kingdom.

18. The *Martyrdom of the Forty Martyrs* also says that Persian Christians betrayed the secrets of Persia to "Caesar." Unlike Simeon's acts, however, which say that the Jews and, to a lesser extent, the magi accused Christians of such treachery, the *Martyrdom of the Forty Martyrs* says that it was the apostate nephew of a Christian bishop who claimed that his uncle (the bishop) was harboring Roman spies and using them to convey Persian secrets to the Romans. See *AMS* II, 333–34.

19. *History of Mar Maʿin* 37–44.

20. On the idea of martyrs as second Christs, see C. R. Moss, *The Other Christs: Imitating Jesus in Ancient Christian Ideologies of Martyrdom* (Oxford: Oxford University Press, 2010). This parallel is further emphasized in that the ascetic Benjamin, who catechized Mar Maʿin in the faith, had specifically told him how Jesus was scourged and given vinegar to drink

Fortunately for Mar Ma'in, at the time of his scourging an envoy of "the believing emperor Constantine" was at the Persian court "to make peace with Shapur and to receive tribute [*maddata*] from him." Shapur welcomed the Roman ambassador "with magnificence, giving him gifts and numerous tokens of honour; he even gave him a royal crown to take back to his master, the believing emperor."[21]

Brock suggests that Shapur sending Constantine tribute is "clearly wishful thinking." The reverse was more often the case: "It was," he explains, "normally the Romans who paid subsidies to the Persians . . . in order for them to guard the Caucasian Gates against incursions of the Huns."[22] It is possible, however, that the *maddata* from Shapur to Constantine, as the *History of Mar Ma'in* presents it, was not intended as an inversion of the system of tribute and imperial defense in the sixth century. Instead, it could be an allusion to Simeon's martyr acts and to Eusebius's *Life of Constantine*. In the *VC*, Eusebius explains that Constantine wrote his letter to Shapur when a Persian ambassador was visiting the Roman court. It was not a returning Roman envoy who paid Constantine tribute by bringing back "tokens of friendly compact" from Persia but rather a Persian ambassador who arrived before the emperor to present such gifts.[23] Likewise, the "numerous tokens of honour" and the "royal crown" that Shapur sends with the Roman envoy in the *History of Mar Ma'in* could be an allusion to the "glorious offerings and delicious gifts" that the *History of Simeon* mentions[24]—gifts that, according to the

---

on the cross. See *History of Mar Ma'in* 22, 45. Notably, the only texts among the *Acts of the Persian Martyrs* that mention Pilate are the *History of Mar Ma'in* (22) and the *Martyrdom of Simeon* (13).

21. *History of Mar Ma'in* 46.

22. Brock, *History of Mar Ma'in*, 67, with reference to R. C. Blockley, "Subsidies and Diplomacy: Rome and Persia in Late Antiquity," *Phoenix* 39 (1985): 62–74. A number of Byzantine emperors grudgingly agreed to make just these sorts of payments to the Persians (even though they occasionally broke the terms of the agreement) as a means of financing the shared defense of both empires by creating a bulwark across the northern gates that led south from the barbarian steppe into Armenia. See, for example, Z. Rubin, "Diplomacy and War in the Relations between Byzantium and the Sassanids in the Fifth Century AD," in *The Defence of the Roman and Byzantine East*, ed. P. Freeman and D. Kennedy (Oxford: BAR International Editions, 1986), 677–95. Payments often bypassed the Persians and went directly to the Huns as bribes so that they would not invade. Theodosius II's refusal to pay Attila what he was due is said to have resulted in a declaration of war in the fifth century. See E. A. Thompson, *The Huns* (Oxford: Oxford University Press, 1996), 281.

23. *VC* IV.8.

24. *History of Simeon* 12. Cf. *Martyrdom of Simeon* 13.

Persian Jews, Caesar would dismiss from the Persian king in favor of a "trivial and curt letter" from a Christian such as Simeon.

The *History of Mar Ma'in* transforms the allegations in Simeon's acts from hearsay into actuality, demonstrating that information about the Christians of Persia was, in fact, much more valuable to Constantine than any Persian tribute or tawdry token of honor. The Roman envoy in the *History of Mar Ma'in*, fulfilling his ascribed role as an emissary of a Christian king, reports back to Constantine with Shapur's gifts in tow. But once home he also conveys what he has discovered about the plight of Christians in Persia. He had witnessed Mar Ma'in's trial firsthand, and he details for Constantine the suffering that Christians beyond the eastern limes of the Roman Empire were forced to endure.[25] In contrast to the *VC*, in which Constantine declares his pleasure in learning from the Persian ambassador "that the most important parts of Persia" are "richly adorned" with Christians, the *History of Mar Ma'in* has him "greatly distressed" by the report that his returning ambassador delivers.[26] Constantine is so distraught to hear the bad news—and so uninterested in the lavish gifts and presents from the Persian king—that he weeps and refuses to eat. The *History of Mar Ma'in* joins him to the Christians of Persia in both body and spirit, claiming that the emperor spent a restless night "fasting in sympathetic mourning for the servants of God . . . [lying] on sackcloth and ashes, supplicating Christ for his fellow-believers, asking that they be not further afflicted."[27]

The following morning, imbued with the resolve of a prayerful and ascetic night, Constantine pens a letter to Shapur, whose vehement tone is in no way comparable to that of the formal imperial letter that Eusebius preserves. The emperor demands that Shapur issue an edict protecting all the Christians of Persia, specifically his former general Mar Ma'in. Constantine threatens Shapur with an ultimatum, saying,

> If you do not release all the Christians you have shut up in prison, and in particular your general, Ma'in, who is greatly oppressed, I will put to death the sons of your nobles who are here with me, and I will send you their heads. I will also annul the treaty which exists between you and me, and I will invade your whole country, causing destruction and devastation. I will pursue you and kill you; I will dismember you limb by limb, and not a hair

---

25. *History of Mar Ma'in* 46–47.
26. *VC* IV.13; *History of Mar Ma'in* 47.
27. *History of Mar Ma'in* 47.

from the head of anyone will escape, without my cutting off your limbs with the sword.²⁸

As if these threats were insufficient, the text further indicates that the sons of the Persian nobles kept hostage in the Roman Empire, who had been "confined and treated badly," were forced to write "letters to their families informing them of the hardships imposed on them by the emperor."²⁹ Constantine then collected these letters, bundled them together with his own, and dispatched the lot back to Persia via the same envoy. He instructed his ambassador, "Do not return from there before all the Christians who are incarcerated are released from prison, and (before Shapur) and his nobles put down in writing that anyone who oppresses or kills the Christians shall be required to pay three thousand pounds (*litra*) of gold. As for the blessed old man Ma'in, escort him out in honour, and if he wants to, let him come and live with me in honour. But if he is going to stay there, give him my royal seal, so that he may travel about without fear."³⁰

CONSTANTINE AS PROTECTOR OF PERSIAN CHRISTIANS IN ROMAN HISTORIOGRAPHY

The author of the *History of Mar Ma'in,* who asserts that Constantine challenged Shapur over the Christians of Persia, weaves his narrative around ambassadors, hostages, tributes, imperial letters, and war or threats of war. The ideas of Constantine as the chastiser of Shapur and as the patron of Christians beyond his own empire were widely prevalent in Roman historiography when the *History of Mar Ma'in* was written, and they continued to

---

28. *History of Mar Ma'in* 49. Earlier (48), the text refers to "the sons of your nobles" as "hostages" (*hmayre*). In a note, Brock mentions an article by A.D. Lee which suggests that hostages were taken as a customary way of formalizing a treaty but typically used only as "a short-term, localised guarantee preliminary to a formal peace settlement." Lee also cites the *History of Mar Ma'in* as the only "explicit statement" that "Romans held Persian hostages in the capital (and therefore presumably on a longer-term basis)," but he also acknowledges that such evidence in hagiographical texts is of a "highly dubious nature." See Brock, *History of Mar Ma'in,* 68n27, with reference to Lee, "The Role of Hostages in Roman Diplomacy with Sasanian Persia," *Historia* 40 (1991): 370, 372. Note that Ammianus Marcellinus mentions a short-term exchange of hostages during Jovian's negotiation of the treaty with Shapur. See Amm. Marc. XXV.7.13.

29. *History of Mar Ma'in* 48, 50.

30. *History of Mar Ma'in* 50.

circulate in subsequent centuries. While Constantine's letter in the *History of Mar Ma'in* is the only place in the *Acts of the Persian Martyrs* where there is any suggestion that Shapur bowed to Constantine, much less that the Roman emperor threatened (or engaged in) a full-scale invasion of Persia, neither idea was novel among historians writing in the Roman Empire. Various late ancient and medieval chroniclers writing in both Greek and Syriac attest to exactly these events, albeit with different conclusions about the success of Constantine's measures against the Persians.

The seventh-century *Chronicle* of the Egyptian bishop John of Nikiu, for example, claims that although the emperor Julian eventually goaded Shapur into war, the Persian king "was of a pacific disposition and had paid tribute to the God-loving Emperor Constantine."[31] Whereas the Constantine of the *History of Mar Ma'in* only threatens to invade, John claims that the emperor conquered "the cities of Persia." Having kindly received the Christians there, he "built beautiful churches in all the cities and villages," replacing Persian magistrates with Christian administrators.[32] John's assessment, as Garth Fowden points out, is probably an expansion of the sixth-century *Chronicle* of John Malalas, whose more muted remembrances of Constantine recall only that he initiated and won a campaign against Persia that resulted in a peace treaty with Shapur.[33]

The Byzantine historian Theophanes the Confessor—whose massive, ninth-century chronicle covers the years 284 to 813—wrote similarly about Constantine and the Christians of Persia. However, he pushes the time of Constantine's baptism and dealings with Shapur to an earlier period, well before the end of the Roman emperor's life. According to Theophanes, who was

---

31. Brock briefly mentions John of Nikiu. See Brock, *History of the Holy Mar Ma'in*, 68, with reference to the translation by R. H. Charles, *The Chronicle of John, Bishop of Nikiu* (London: Williams and Norgate, 1916), LXXX.3. It is not clear whether the *Chronicle* was originally written in Greek or Coptic, but the only known version is in Ethiopic (Ge'ez) and was probably translated via an Arabic intermediary. For the Ethiopic text with a French translation, see H. Zotenberg, *Chronique de Jean, évêque de Nikiou: Texte éthiopien publié et traduit* (Paris, 1883).

32. John of Nikiu, *Chron.* LXXVII.61–62.

33. G. Fowden, "The Last Days of Constantine: Oppositional Versions and Their Influence," *JRS* 84 (1994): 153; John Malalas, *Chron.* XIII.317. Fowden summons the *Chronicles* of Malalas and of John of Nikiu as evidence of the literary "devices by which many Christian writers, especially in the fifth century, avoided having to engage with the view ... that ultimate responsibility for the disastrous course of Romano-Iranian relations in the fourth century lay, not with Julian, but with Constantine." See also the discussion of this issue in chapter 2.

intent on portraying him as a staunch anti-Arian, Constantine was baptized not on his deathbed by the Arian bishop Eusebius of Nicomedia in 337 but in Rome by Bishop Sylvester, and prior to the Council of Nicaea in 325. It is only "the easterners," Theophanes writes, who say that Constantine was baptized late in his life: "They claim that he had deferred baptism in the hope of being baptized in the river Jordan."[34] Theophanes thus completely disconnects the emperor's baptism and death from his Persian campaign.[35] In so doing, Theophanes, who presents a distilled version of Sozomen's narrative about the Christians of Persia, also claims that in 324/25 (not in the late 330s, following Constantine's death) "the Jews and the Persians, seeing that Christianity was flourishing in Persia, brought an accusation before the Persian emperor Shapur against Simeon, archbishop of Ctesiphon, and against the bishop of Seleucia. They were charged with being friends of the Roman emperor and spies of Persian affairs. As a result a great persecution took place in Persia and a great many people were adorned with martyrdom for Christ's sake."[36] Theophanes does not quote Constantine's letter in response to this report of "a great persecution," but he does say that the emperor wrote a "brilliantly composed and most godlike" missive to the Persian king.[37] Unfortunately, it was unsuccessful in persuading Shapur to end his violence, and Theophanes does not mention the Christians of Persia again.

He does say, in a report about the end of Constantine's life, that because "many of the Assyrians in Persia were being sold in Mesopotamia by the Saracens" and because "the Persians declared war on the Romans[,] . . . pious

---

34. Theoph. *Chron.*, AM 5814 [AD 321/22]; translated by C. Mango and R. Scott in *The Chronicle of Theophanes Confessor: Byzantine and Near Eastern History, AD 284–813* (Oxford: Clarendon, 1997).

35. Roger Scott compares the sixth-century *Chronicle* of John Malalas to that of Theophanes to show how later visions of Constantine were nuanced and reimagined to fit particular rhetorical and theological agendas. For Malalas, Scott argues, Constantine was just a Christian, but for Theophanes he had to be an orthodox, anti-Arian, and anti-iconoclast emperor. See Scott, "The Image of Constantine in Malalas and Theophanes," in *New Constantines*, 57–71.

36. Theoph. *Chron.*, AM 5817 [AD 324/25]. The translation is that of Mango and Scott, but I have modified the spellings of the personal and place names.

37. Theoph. *Chron.*, AM 5817 [AD 324/25]. Mango and Scott comment that while Theophanes may have the correct date for the letter, the circumstances in which he places its composition are less certain. As I note in chapter 1, a 324/25 date for Constantine's letter is widely accepted, but the context to which Eusebius attributes the letter (*VC* IV.7–8)—a time when many nations were sending representatives to the Roman Empire to pay their respects to Constantine—clearly differs from that which Theophanes presents here.

Constantine went out to the city of Nicomedia on his way to fight the Persians, but became ill and died in peace."[38] Whether "Assyrians" should be read as "Christians" is not clear but, from the context, is probably unlikely. Theophanes presents the final conflict between Constantine and Shapur as turning on the Persian king's border raids and declaration of war. For the following year—AM 5829 [AD 336/37]—Theophanes explains that after Constantine died, "Shapur, the Persian emperor, invaded Mesopotamia, planning to destroy Nisibis, and besieged it for 63 days. But lacking the strength to capture it, he then withdrew. Jacob, bishop of Nisibis, remaining true to the proper worship of God, by his prayers easily achieved his purpose." Even if Constantine's preparations for war were not on behalf of the Christians of Persia, the defense of the Roman Empire—through the prayers of Jacob of Nisibis—was fundamentally Christian, at least according to Theophanes.

The twelfth-century Syriac *Chronicle* of the Syrian Orthodox patriarch of Antioch Michael I Rabo, better known as Michael the Syrian, seems to harmonize the accounts of several earlier historians.[39] Drawing on accusations similar to those leveled against Christians in Simeon's acts and repeated in subsequent texts, Michael indicates that "pagans" (not Jews) accused Christians of sending an envoy to "the Roman emperor." This accusation angered Shapur enough to inspire him to begin oppressing Christians in Persia, destroying churches throughout his realm.

Following the interpretation of Sozomen, which had become the consensus among ecclesiastical historians in the Roman Empire, Michael notes that Constantine wrote to the Persian king in response to this persecution. The snippet of Constantine's letter that he quotes is clearly a paraphrase of the first two lines of the emperor's letter as Eusebius preserves it. According to Michael, Constantine wrote to Shapur, saying, "Considering that I guard the divine faith, I dwell in the light of truth. Conducting myself

---

38. Theoph. *Chron.*, AM 5828 [AD 335/36].

39. Both Michael's *Chronicle* and that of Theophanes draw on the lost eighth-century work of Theophilos of Edessa. According to J.-B. Chabot, Michael gleaned some elements of Theophilos's narrative from a ninth-century intermediary, Dionysios of Tel Maḥre. See the introduction to Chabot, *Chronique de Michel le Syrien, patriarche jacobite d'Antioche*, vol. 1 (Paris: Leroux, 1899), xxxii–xxxiv. Theophanes seems to have had access to an abbreviated Greek translation of Theophilos's work. On the consequences of such historiographical exchange, see L. I. Conrad, "Theophanes and the Arabic Historical Tradition: Some Indications of Intercultural Transmission," *ByzF* 15 (1990): 1–44.

according to the light of the truth, I profess the true faith, and so forth."[40] Shapur was unmoved by the letter and immediately set out on a campaign against Nisibis. The prayers of "Mar Jacob and Mar Ephrem" turned back his assaults, but as he withdrew in defeat from the city, he pillaged the Mesopotamian countryside and took many captives back to Persia. The summary of these events in Michael's *Chronicle* concludes by noting that following this failed siege, Constantine prepared to meet the Persians on the battlefield. As in Eusebius's telling of the story in the *VC*, Michael explains that the Roman emperor fell ill on arriving at Nicomedia "and was baptized in this place because he had not yet been baptized since he had desired to be baptized in the Jordan."[41]

Commenting on these passages in Michael's *Chronicle,* Fowden says, "Clearly there was a view that Constantine's baptism and (intended) triumph over Iran constituted, together, one of the defining moments of his reign—a view he himself had encouraged by declaring at Nicomedia that his original intention was to be baptized in the River Jordan, presumably on his way to or return from an Eastern victory."[42] As I suggested in chapter 2, while there was clearly a temporal link between Constantine's (real? alleged? imagined?) Persian campaign and his deathbed baptism at Nicomedia—in that both happened at the end of his life, in the minds of some Roman and Byzantine historians—the further presumption that baptism in the Jordan was intended as a part of the Persian campaign is simply not borne out by any late antique witness—neither Eusebius nor any other chronicler. Indeed, that Michael explicitly pairs a planned campaign against Persia with Constantine's death and baptism at Nicomedia contradicts Fowden's claim that these events were purposefully dislodged from one another "as the polytheist and Christian narratives evolved."[43] Fowden's idea that certain Christian narratives about Constantine were invented to obfuscate the embarrassing failure of his campaign against Persia is compelling as a conspiracy theory. But for their own reasons, neither Michael the Syrian nor Theophanes found it

---

40. Michael the Syrian, *Chron.* VII.3, translated by S. Brock in M.H. Dodgeon and S.N.C. Lieu, eds., *The Roman Eastern Frontier and the Persian Wars, AD 226–363: A Documentary History* (New York: Routledge, 1991), 152. Compare this to Euseb. *VC* IV.9: "Guarding the divine faith I participate in the light of truth. Led by the light of truth I recognize the divine faith."

41. Michael the Syrian, *Chron.* VII.3; cf. Euseb. *VC* IV.62.

42. Fowden, "Last Days of Constantine," 168.

43. Fowden, "Last Days of Constantine," 168.

necessary to avoid talking about Constantine's death occurring just as his Persian campaign began.

As the histories of John of Nikiu, Theophanes, Michael the Syrian, and others attest, the accounts of Constantine's baptism, dealings with Persia, and last days all play on similar themes, but they are far from monolithic. John of Nikiu, who tells of Constantine's *successful* Persian campaign and the subsequent Christianization of Persia, is a definite outlier. But other Christian narratives, such as the *History of Mar Ma'in*, also avoid the "historical" questions that preoccupy certain chroniclers. Both John of Nikiu and the *History of Mar Ma'in* omit any discussion of Constantine's death or of Shapur's militant response to the Roman emperor's letter. The Constantine of the *History of Mar Ma'in*, as opposed to Michael the Syrian's Constantine, is an emperor to be feared and obeyed. Even his unnamed envoy merits dread. The *History of Mar Ma'in* describes this envoy as riding into the Persian court on horseback just as Mar Ma'in is being horrendously tortured before Shapur's approving gaze. After he dismounts, it is this visiting Roman (not Shapur or any of the Persian nobles) who orders the torturer to stop what he is doing, "whereupon he [the envoy] immediately gave the letter from the believing emperor to Shapur and to all the nobility of his kingdom."[44] Obviously, neither the envoy's order to the Persian torturers nor the seal of safe passage from Constantine that he was delivering to Mar Ma'in should have carried any authority in Persia. But the author of the *History of Mar Ma'in* is unambiguous: Constantine's jurisdiction spanned the world.

On reading Constantine's letter and the plaintive missives from the captive sons of the Sasanian nobles, "Shapur shook with fear, all the more so because the believer [the Roman envoy] had seen the blessed man under torture."[45] The Roman emperor's letter had the desired effect. The fear of Constantine that it inspired led Shapur to make a gaudy show of humility before the Roman envoy. After listening to the envoy repeat the threats outlined in the letter, Shapur ordered his heralds to go out to every town in the realm and announce that anyone who uttered so much as an unkind word against a Christian would be beheaded.[46] The Persian king then invited his nobles and the Roman envoy to a feast in his palace, at which Mar Ma'in, the freed Christian prisoner, was to be the guest of honor. Mar Ma'in initially refused

44. *History of Mar Ma'in* 57.
45. *History of Mar Ma'in* 57.
46. *History of Mar Ma'in* 58–59.

the king's conciliatory gesture but then agreed to accept the invitation after the Roman envoy gave him "bread and cheeses and dried fish that had come with him from the west."[47] Mar Ma'in, it seems, had become so Westernized by dint of his faith that he could no longer stomach Persian food.

In its visceral narration of Constantine's concern for Christians outside the Roman Empire, the *History of Mar Ma'in* is unique among the *Acts of the Persian Martyrs*. Once the Roman ambassador finally bids Mar Ma'in leave, he takes with him "the garment he [Mar Ma'in] was wearing that was full of blood from his wounds and lacerations." This must be an allusion to the *Martyrdom of Simeon*, whose narrator says that Simeon is rightly called bar Ṣabba'e, the "son of dyers," because "he dyed the garments of his soul with his own blood as a vestment for the holy kingdom."[48] Along with this relic from a Persian confessor, Mar Ma'in sends the Roman envoy back to the West with a blessing, asking him to "tell the believing emperor Constantine that 'Our Lord Jesus Christ in whom you have believed and have established his faith, shall preserve you and your crown, as with king David.'"[49]

"WESTERN" VERSUS "EASTERN" HISTORIES OF CONSTANTINE

There are effectively two stories that have been told about Constantine, Shapur, and the persecution of the Christians of Persia. The first, as a matter of shorthand, might be called the Western account. It is the historical narrative exemplified by the *History of Mar Ma'in* and outlined by historians and chroniclers writing in both Greek and Syriac, ranging from Sozomen in the fifth century to Michael the Syrian at the end of the twelfth. While the details of such histories vary—often dramatically—their common thread is that Constantine was alive when Shapur began oppressing Christians. Moreover, they give the sense that Constantine's role vis-à-vis the Christians of Persia was as a patron and protector. Therefore, he reacted to Shapur's persecution as a concerned shepherd, by either sending a letter, launching a military campaign, or otherwise intervening to exercise some combination of patronage and protection of the Christians of Persia. While it is true that these Western histories

---

47. *History of Mar Ma'in* 60–61.
48. *History of Mar Ma'in* 66; *Martyrdom of Simeon* 7.
49. *History of Mar Ma'in* 65.

report enormously differing results—from John of Nikiu's tale of the complete conquest and Christianization of Persia through Michael the Syrian's more sober, Eusebian-inflected story of Constantine's premature death at Nicomedia to Theophanes's account of Constantine's ineffectual letter to Shapur—they are united in insisting that the emperor was alive during the persecution and did something to stem Shapur's violence against Christians.

On the other hand, in what we might call the Eastern account of mid-fourth-century events (namely, the histories written in Persia or by representatives of the Church of the East), because Constantine was not alive to witness the persecution, he was obviously unable to defend the Christians of Persia against Shapur. Nevertheless, the Roman emperor is not dismissed as dead and gone and therefore irrelevant to the war and persecution that occurred after his death. Rather, the Eastern account establishes Constantine's death as a distinct turning point with extended repercussions. In the *History of Simeon,* it is less a temporal than a causal marker: "Immediately upon the death of the triumphant Constantine, Shapur, the king of the Persians, began to harass the Christian people, to afflict and persecute the priests and the *qyama,* and to destroy the churches in all of his realm," the narrator explains.[50] Constantine was the rampart that had held back Shapur's violence against the Christians of Persia. After his death, the floodgates of oppression opened.

It is crucial to see, however, that the *History of Simeon* speaks to the power and importance of Constantine in particular, not of Christian Roman emperors more generally. It was Constantine who deterred Shapur from mobilizing against Rome and the Christians of Persia. His son Constantius could exert no such power. The tenth-century *Chronicle of Seert,* a Christian Arabic text that knows the *History of Simeon,* also specifies that Constantine died prior to Simeon's arrest. Yet unlike the *History of Simeon* it speaks separately about Constantine, at quite some length. It emphasizes that while the emperor was alive, his mere presence on the throne thwarted any Persian aggression against Christians. While neither the *History of Simeon* nor the *Chronicle of Seert* mentions any letter or other formal statement of patronage from Constantine, both indicate that Shapur's oppression of Christians and assaults on the eastern Roman frontier began only after news of Constantine's death reached him.[51] In fact, virtually every later Syriac and Christian Arabic

---

50. *History of Simeon* 2.
51. See A. Scher, *Histoire nestorienne inédite (Chronique de Séert), première partie 1,* PO 4 (Paris: Firmin-Didot, 1908), 297 (in section XXVII), on Simeon's martyrdom.

chronicler from the Church of the East who discusses Simeon's life and death narrates it in this way. The details of these twelfth-, thirteenth-, and fourteenth-century summaries of Simeon's martyrdom go beyond the scope of this chapter, but none of them suggests that Constantine was alive when Shapur began persecuting Christians.[52]

This unwillingness among Persian Christian historians to attribute to Constantine a direct role as a patron of the Christians in the East is widespread. Many other East Syriac sources, some of which have nothing to do with Constantine or Shapur, also seek to establish some distance between Christians in Persia and the Roman Empire and its rulers. Frequently, this may be a result of the different theologies that developed in the two realms after the Council of Chalcedon (451). For example, the *Martyrdom of Gregory Pirangushnasp*, a text that is set in the mid-sixth century and thus wholly unconnected to Shapur's persecution, clearly acknowledges "Rome" as a Christian empire and "Caesar" as a Christian ruler but delineates a separation of Persian Christians from Roman Christians on theological grounds.[53] Adam Becker explains that Gregory, "a general responsible for the northern

---

52. In medieval Syriac, the thirteenth-century *Ecclesiastical Chronicle* of Barhebraeus briefly mentions Simeon; see J.-B. Abbeloos and T.J. Lamy, *Gregorii Barhebraei Chronicon ecclesiasticum*, vol. 3 (Leuven: Peeters, 1877), 33–35. In Christian Arabic, the East Syrian chronicles of Mari b. Sulaiman, 'Amr b. Matai, and Ṣaliba b. Joḥannan should be noted. For a brief overview of these sources and the *Chronicle of Seert*, see J.-M. Fiey, *Jalons pour une histoire de l'église en Iraq*, CSCO 310, Subsidia 36 (Leuven: Peeters, 1970), 19–23. For the accounts of the East Syrian patriarchs in the Arabic *Kitab al-majdal*, or "Book of the tower," see H. Gismondi, *Maris Amri et Slibae: De Patriarchis Nestorianorum*, 2 vols. (Rome: De Luigi, 1896–99). To my knowledge, the only comprehensive study of these texts is the early twentieth-century doctoral dissertation of Gustav Westphal, which deals briefly with the chroniclers' accounts of Simeon; see Westphal, "Untersuchungen über die Quellen und die Glaubwürdigkeit der Patriarchenchroniken des Mārī ibn Sulaimān, 'Amr ibn Matai und Ṣalība ibn Joḥannān" (PhD diss., Universität Strassburg, 1901), 81–94. Broader studies of the Christian martyrs of Beth Huzaye rehash much of Westphal's dissertation. See, for example, G. Wiessner, *Untersuchungen zur syrischen Literaturgeschichte I: Zur Märtyrerüberlieferung aus der Christenverfolgung Schapurs II.* (Göttingen: Vandenhoeck und Ruprecht, 1967), 80–94; and W. Schwaigert, "Das Christentum in Ḥūzistān im Rahmen der frühen Kirchengeschichte Persiens bis zur Synode von Seleukeia-Ktesiphon im Jahre 410" (PhD diss., Philipps-Universität Marburg, 1989), 76–101.

53. For Gregory's *Martyrdom*, see P. Bedjan, *Histoire de Mar-Jabalaha, de trois autres patriarches, d'un prêtre et de deux laïques, nestoriens* (Leipzig: Otto Harrassowitz, 1895; repr., *The History of Mar Jab-Alaha and Rabban Sauma* [Piscataway, NJ: Gorgias, 2007]), 347–94; and now F. Jullien, *Histoire de Mar Abba, catholicos de l'Orient: Martyres de Mar Grigor, général en chef du roi Khusro Ier et de Mar Yazd-panah, juge et gouverneur*, CSCO 658–59, Scriptores Syri 254–55 (Leuven: Peeters, 2015).

regions of Georgia (Iberia) and Caucasian Albania, comes from an elite Zoroastrian family. When he confesses Christ and openly blasphemes [King] Hormizd, the king strips him of his property and places him in a pit. Eventually his position and status are restored, but he then is taken prisoner by the Romans. 'Caesar' treats him as a guest, but Gregory decides to return [to Persia] because of the false Christology he finds in the west."[54]

Such ambivalence about Rome has often been read as an example of how Persian Christians of the post-Constantine era tried "to belie governmental suspicions of their loyalty by distancing themselves from the dominant orthodoxy of the eastern Roman Empire."[55] Mixed feelings about the West are evident not only in the sixth- and seventh-century *Acts of the Persian Martyrs* but in the *History of Simeon* too. This "distancing" of Persian Christians from Constantine demonstrates how the East was moderating or even rejecting the emperor's role as a central figure even as the West was affirming it. Perhaps more important, this shows that the idea of the Christian Roman emperor as a patron and protector of the Christians of Persia was largely a product of Roman reinterpretations of Constantine and events in the Persian Empire—not of any martyrdom narrative or historical chronicle that originated beyond a Roman or Byzantine sphere of influence.

THE ROMAN EMPIRE FROM SEVENTH-CENTURY PERSIA

As many Syriac and Arabic histories from Persia suggest, Constantine was remembered outside the Roman and Byzantine worlds for centuries, albeit in ways that were very different from how he was remembered within western Christendom. The *Summary History of the World* of John bar Penkaye, a late seventh-century world history by an East Syrian monk and eyewitness to the Arab conquest of the Sasanian Empire, is one of the few non-Byzantine sources to suggest that Constantine was alive when Shapur's persecution

---

54. A.H. Becker, "Martyrdom, Religious Difference, and 'Fear' as a Category of Piety in the Sasanian Empire: The Case of the *Martyrdom of Gregory* and the *Martyrdom of Yazdpaneh*," *JLA* 2 (2009): 305.

55. T.D. Barnes, "Constantine and the Christians of Persia," *JRS* 75 (1985): 136, with reference to S. Brock, "Christians in the Sasanian Empire: A Case of Divided Loyalties," in *Religion and National Identity*, ed. S. Mews (Oxford: Oxford University Press, 1982), 1–19.

began. But John is only a slight exception to the rule: because he believed that Shapur's persecution must have spanned the entire seventy years of the king's reign (309–79) and not just the last forty, he dates its beginning to the third year of Constantine's reign. Confusing the chronology again, he claims that the persecution did not end until Jovian surrendered Nisibis to Shapur.[56] Even so, John's Constantine never attempts to end the persecution—by means of either a letter, a war, or the threat of a war.

Among Syriac martyrdom narratives, the Christian Roman emperor is, by and large, a ghost, a rhetorical device, who is summoned by later commentators seeking to reenvision the bonds and allegiances of Christians and Christian communities in fourth-century Persia. Far from courting Constantine and other Christian emperors, the Christians of Persia kept them at a distance. As I have indicated, the list of *Acts of the Persian Martyrs* that narrate events during Shapur's persecution and invoke Rome and its rulers is short. And some of them have strange literary lineages. The *History of Mar Ma'in* is a sixth-century text that was composed in the Roman Empire, and it tells a unique story of earlier centuries. Likewise, the *History of Mar Qardagh* is a Syriac martyrdom narrative that, although set during Shapur's persecution, is unquestionably a seventh-century tale which addresses localized social and religiopolitical questions about Christian identity that were unique to northern Mesopotamia in the late Sasanian period. According to Joel Walker, whose study of the text includes both a translation and an analysis of its literary and historical context, the *History of Mar Qardagh* "preserves few, if any, reliable details about the fourth century" and instead presents a "window into the cultural world of seventh-century Iraq."[57]

---

56. John bar Penkaye, *Resh Melle* XIV. For the Syriac text, see A. Mingana, *Sources syriaques*, vol. 1 (Leipzig: Otto Harrassowitz, 1907), 115–31. Addai Scher provides a summary of the *Resh Melle*. For the sections relevant to Constantine, Simeon, Shapur II, and the persecution of the Christians of Persia, see Scher, "Notice sur la vie et les œuvres de Yoḥannan bar Penkayè," *JA* 10 (1907): 171–73. See also T. Jansma, "Projet d'édition du 'Kᵉtābā dᵉrēš mellē' de Jean bar Penkayé," *OrSyr* 8 (1963): 87–106. For an analysis of the *Resh Melle*'s textual tradition, see H. Kaufhold, "Anmerkungen zur Textüberlieferung der Chronik des Johannes bar Penkaye," *OC* 87 (2003): 65–79.

57. J. T. Walker, *The Legend of Mar Qardagh: Narrative and Christian Heroism in Late Antique Iraq* (Berkeley: University of California Press, 2006), 1. Walker surveys the previous scholarship on the *History of Mar Qardagh* in a brief section on pages 115–17, noting that much of it "has largely focused on issues of historicity and dating." This is the case for most of the *Acts of the Persian Martyrs*. For the Syriac text of the *History of Mar Qardagh*, see J. B. Abbeloos, *Acta Mar Ḳardaghi Assyriae praefecti* (Leipzig: Brockhaus, 1890).

Mar Qardagh, like Mar Ma'in, was a Christian convert and former Sasanian military leader. But unlike Mar Ma'in, he was a member of the Sasanian elite who did not become a partisan of the Roman Empire after his conversion. Quite the contrary. After becoming a Christian, Mar Qardagh shunned "battles, ceased from conflicts, and loved a life of peace." While the Romans and their Arab vassals prepared for war against Shapur and Persia, Mar Qardagh retreated in prayerful tranquility and went "up on the mountain to his teacher," a hermit called 'Abdisho'. In the subsequent "great pillaging raids" of the united Roman-Arab forces, Mar Qardagh's entire family was "led away into captivity" in the Roman Empire, and the lands under his authority were destroyed "up to the frontier city of Nisibis."[58] Living as a hermit, Mar Qardagh escaped his family's fate, but when he got word of what had happened, he returned from his mountain sanctuary and girded himself for battle once more. He wrote a letter to the Romans, saying, "From when I put on Christ, the peace of the world, I did not want of my own volition to clothe myself in the rage of battles. But send me my father, my mother, my wife, my brother, and my sister and all the men of my household and all the captives whom you led away from the lands beneath my rule. Take for yourselves the possessions, turn away, and depart from me. And do not force me to pursue you."[59]

In response to this letter from a Sasanian noble—one who clearly identifies himself as a peace-loving Christian who will allow the Roman soldiers to keep their spoils of war so long as they return his family unharmed—the Romans "cut off the head of his brother and sent it to him." Enraged by this act of brutality, Mar Qardagh ordered that the trumpet of war be sounded once more, and taking 234 of his soldiers with him into a church, "he extended his hands and prayed, saying, 'Judge, Lord, my case and fight against those who fight against me.... Unsheathe the sword and make it flash against my pursuers.'"[60] In the *Martyrdom of the Captives of Beth Zabdai*, it is Roman Christians who are taken by the Persians and beheaded. And in the *History of Mar Ma'in*, it is a Persian confessor who prays that the crown of David will be preserved on Constantine's head.[61] Yet here in the *History of Mar Qardagh*, it is Persian captives who are beheaded by the Romans, and there is no prayer that David's crown will continue to rest on the head of a

---

58. *History of Mar Qardagh* 41; all quotations follow Walker, *Legend of Mar Qardagh*.
59. *History of Mar Qardagh* 43.
60. *History of Mar Qardagh* 43, with reference to Psalms 35:1–3.
61. *History of Mar Ma'in* 65.

Roman king. Instead, David's psalm ("fight against those who fight against me") is on the lips of one who is about to "unsheathe the sword" against the armies of Rome.

News of Mar Qardagh's heroic victory against a far superior Roman-Arab force soon reached King Shapur. But so too did accusations that following his family's recovery, he "tore down the fire altars in which the fire was carried in procession by the impious *magi.*" In place of the blazing pagan altars, Mar Qardagh "set up shining altars to Christ."[62] That Mar Qardagh had become a Christian yet still wished to fight with the Sasanians against the Roman-Arab armies made no sense to Shapur. He was incredulous when he heard these accusations, that Mar Qardagh—his "*paṭaḥšā* [viceroy] of Assyria and *marzbān* [frontier commander] in the land of the West"—had become a Christian and overturned fire altars so as to set up altars to Christ. "How can you say these things?" he railed at the anonymous magus who informed against Mar Qardagh. "Have you not heard of that great victory Qardagh made, when with two hundred thirty-four men he destroyed thousands of Romans and tens of thousands of Arabs?"[63]

In many ways, the *History of Mar Maʿin* and the *History of Mar Qardagh,* and the Roman ecclesiastical-historical tradition more broadly, demonstrate just how ambivalent the relationship between the Christians of the East and the Christians of the West really was—or rather, how ambivalently this literature presents the relationship among Rome, Constantine, and the Christians of Persia and how that relationship was less a product of fourth-century realities than later rhetorical constructions that were retrojected into the fourth century. Unlike the *History of Mar Maʿin* and the *History of Mar Qardagh,* which have been almost universally read as legendary products of later eras, Simeon's acts have been used as evidence of real events during the fourth-century confrontation between Rome and Persia. The *Martyrdom* and *History of Simeon,* harmonized together, are turned to as a document from the fourth century rather than a text about it, while works such as the *History of Mar Maʿin* and the *History of Mar Qardagh* are dismissed as representative of much later social and political concerns. But the very oddity of the *History of Mar Maʿin* and the *History of Mar Qardagh* demonstrates how odd the *History of Simeon* is too. For the *History of Simeon,* the earliest text among the

---

62. *History of Mar Qardagh* 47.
63. *History of Mar Qardagh* 48. On the terms *paṭaḥšā* and *marzbān,* see Walker, *Legend of Mar Qardagh,* 22n13.

Acts to mention Constantine by name, was not composed until the late fifth century. And when it names Constantine, it stresses not only that the emperor was dead before Shapur began persecuting Christians but that his death—and Shapur's persecution—were providentially necessary for the Christians of Persia.

CONCLUSIONS

Constantine looms large in most studies of the fourth century. As he should. The fourth century was a major period of transformation throughout the late antique world, including both the Roman and the Persian Empires, and Constantine was at the center of a very literal and a more figurative shifting of religious and political frontiers.

Because it reevaluates how we understand the end of his reign and his legacy, this book might be called a revisionist history of the fourth century. The rereadings I have offered all seek to revise how we understand Constantine's last days and how we measure the impact of his religious transformations on the Christians of Sasanian Persia. I have argued that the generally accepted history of Constantine and the Christians of Persia is a reconstruction of a certain sequence of historical events—whose main outlines focus on Constantine's letter to Shapur, the war between Rome and Persia, and persecution of Christians under the Persian king. But the reconstructions of ancient historians are often in conflict. In the Roman Empire, Ammianus tells us one thing about the bishops of Mesopotamia, Ephrem another. In Persia, our sources tend to be limited to Syriac martyrdom narratives, but these too offer different reconstructions, and they were often written much later than is sometimes assumed. The earlier text about Simeon bar Ṣabbaʿe, for example, offers a profoundly different historical and theological narrative than does the later text about the same bishop of Seleucia-Ctesiphon. Indeed, these works tell us little, if anything, about events as they actually happened but quite a lot about the different trajectories of literary traditions as they manifested at various times in various places and among various Christian communities.

Although generally aware of the differences among our sources, modern scholarship, I have argued, tends to harmonize conflicting late antique texts in dubious ways, putting forth a particular perspective on the upheaval in fourth-century Mesopotamia (and a particular vision of Constantine) as the one that should be accepted as historically accurate. Raymond Van Dam has recently unraveled just how the many myths about Constantine's victory at the Milvian Bridge were constructed and memorialized.[64] In attempting a similar sort of revision of fourth-century history throughout this book, I have explicitly disavowed offering a *rewriting* of it. What I have tried to put forth is a revision, a re-seeing, of both the ancient sources and their scholarly reconstructions. In that sense, then, this book is not a revisionist history at all but rather a critique of positivist historiography. My aim has been to analyze the historical memory of a set of events—the letter, the war, the persecution—and the ways that late antique historians cite or recount these events for their own purposes. The essential error behind the accepted reconstruction of these events is that it interprets our various sources as evidence for the events themselves rather than as evidence for the diverse and conflicting historical memories of these events.

If there is one thing that needs rewriting, however, it is how we talk about religious persecution in late antique Persia. The many Syriac martyrdom narratives that are set during Shapur's reign must be read as ideological interventions. It is these texts that have created the idea of embattled religious minorities or clearly demarcated and bounded religious communities existing in a Zoroastrian "state."[65] Perhaps the most important difficulty with the traditional interpretations of persecution in the Sasanian Empire is the assumption that the Persian king understood that Constantine worshiped the Christian god and that this meant something—something profound—about the Roman Empire and the Christians of Persia. The scholarly presumption is that worshiping the Christian god would determine one's "political" allegiances and that all Christians could be identified as a collective whole on that basis.[66] In this view of history, Shapur grew suspicious of the Christians

---

64. See R. Van Dam, *Remembering Constantine at the Milvian Bridge* (Cambridge: Cambridge University Press, 2014).

65. The work of Adam Becker and Richard Payne has been helpful in offering just such a caution. See Becker, "The Ancient Near East in the Late Antique Near East: Syriac Christian Appropriation of the Biblical East," in *Antiquity in Antiquity*, ed. G. Gardner and K.L. Osterloh (Tübingen: Mohr Siebeck, 2008), 1–21; Becker, "Political Theology and Religious Diversity in the Sasanian Empire," in *Jews, Christians and Zoroastrians: Religious Dynamics in a Sasanian Context*, ed. G. Herman (Piscataway, NJ: Gorgias, 2014), 7–25; and Payne, *A State of Mixture: Christians, Zoroastrians, and Iranian Political Culture in Late Antiquity* (Berkeley: University of California Press, 2015).

66. The recent history of "religion" by Brent Nongbri throws into sharp relief the problem of using religion as if it were a category of thought in the ancient world. See Nongbri, *Before Religion: A History of a Modern Concept* (New Haven: Yale University Press, 2013).

of Persia immediately on Constantine's conversion, a conversion that entailed the financial, political, and architectural patronage of the Christian cult in the Roman Empire.

But Constantine's conversion did not, at a stroke, transform the Christians of Persia into a fifth column of the Roman Empire. Perhaps the research of the sociologist Rogers Brubaker may help explain why. His work focuses mainly on violence—or, more concretely, the rhetorical basis that reifies an underlying foundation for violence—among ethnic "groups" in contemporary Eastern Europe.[67] His critique of prevailing studies of ethnicity and ethnic identity is directed predominantly at what he calls "groupism"—an essentialist way of thinking about the world that tends to see ethnic, national, or religious groups "as substantial entities to which interests and agency can be attributed."[68]

The problem, Brubaker argues, is that even though it is common sense to "understand ethnic conflict ... as conflict between ethnic groups,"[69] when we do so we are adopting the language of the participants, who are embroiled in a conflict or retrospectively remembering a conflict in a certain way. These participants and often their heirs have a vested interest in construing and narrativizing the conflict as one between clearly bounded groups. It is, Brubaker continues, understandable that participants in violent struggle would "cast ethnic groups ... as the protagonists—the heroes and martyrs—of such struggles." Nevertheless, "this does not mean analysts should do the same. We must, of course, take vernacular categories and participants' understandings seriously, for they are partly constitutive of our objects of study. But we should not uncritically adopt *categories of ethnopolitical practice* as our *categories of social analysis.*"[70] Rather, we must adopt what Brubaker calls a "cognitive perspective" in order to better understand the narrative event schema of the texts we are studying—a one-step-removed view dedicated to interpreting "the social and mental processes that sustain the vision and divi-

---

67. See, for example, R. Brubaker, *Nationalist Politics and Everyday Ethnicity in a Transylvanian Town* (Princeton, NJ: Princeton University Press, 2006), which is a case study applying his more theoretical work toward the end of breaking down the grand, reifying ethnic narratives that are accepted as constitutive of "Hungarian" and "Romanian" ethnic identities.

68. R. Brubaker, *Ethnicity without Groups* (Cambridge, MA: Harvard University Press, 2004), 2.

69. Brubaker, *Ethnicity without Groups*, 11.

70. Brubaker, *Ethnicity without Groups*, 10; italics in the original.

sion of the social world" in religious, political, or ethnic terms and thereby frame the narration of a particular event history and group identity.[71]

As Brubaker readily concedes, however, even "identity" is problematic as a category of analysis. Imbricated as it is with the social constructivist operations that give it force, the idea of a socially and rhetorically constructed group identity is not wrong, Brubaker argues, but "too obviously right."[72] The term *identity*, he notes, has been so irredeemably softened by stances that discuss it as processual—an unstable, evanescent, "constructed, fluid, and multiple" product of fractured discourses—in order "to acquit it of the charge of 'essentialism'" that we have been left "without a rationale for talking about 'identities' at all and ill equipped to examine the 'hard' dynamics and essentialist claims" about identity. In other words, a "'soft' constructivism allows putative 'identities' to proliferate. But as they proliferate, the term loses its analytical purchase. If identity is everywhere, it is nowhere. If it is fluid, how can we understand the ways in which self-understandings may harden, congeal, and crystallize?"[73]

In this book I have assumed that Christian identity in late antiquity was—insofar as historians can access it—a textually constructed category.[74] What interests me, though, is not *that* particular Persian Christian identities were constructed in late antiquity but rather how they were constructed, when they were constructed, and why they were constructed. There were certainly multiple and repeated instances of crystallization among the Christians of Persia, and the assumption that fifth-, sixth-, and even seventh-century texts can tell us something about the perspective of fourth-century Christians, or fourth-century history, has wrongly colored our understanding of Persian Christianity during the time of Constantine. It may also have wrongly colored our understanding of Constantine himself. Indeed, one of the key problems that I have tried to highlight with the causal event narrative that is typically used to explain Shapur's persecution is that it assumes a nearly immediate crystallization of Christian identity on Constantine's

71. Brubaker, *Ethnicity without Groups*, 77, 79.
72. Brubaker, *Ethnicity without Groups*, 3.
73. Brubaker, *Ethnicity without Groups*, 28–29.
74. As studies on "identity" have been one of the major trends in recent scholarship on late antiquity, the bibliography on this topic is huge, but for a series of analyses of ethnicity and identity relevant to this book, see W. Pohl, C. Gantner, and R. Payne, eds., *Visions of Community in the Post-Roman World: The West, Byzantium and the Islamic World, 300–1100* (Burlington, VT: Ashgate, 2012).

conversion—an identity that would have spanned from Rome to Persia and included the contested Mesopotamian, Armenian, and Arabian borderlands between the two major empires. In this interpretation, Shapur compounded and, in fact, fostered a pan-Christian identity when he returned from the early years of his war against Rome and issued a tax edict against Christians.

A unification of peoples along religious lines is intelligible in a modern, post-Enlightenment context—that of Archbishop Rahho and the Christians of Mosul, for example—but in late antiquity, Christian identity (or "self-understanding," to use Brubaker's preferred term) was so fluid, multiple, and geographically, chronologically, and textually contingent that it is hard to discuss with any real meaning. Acknowledging the inherent difficulty in attempting to talk about religious groups in late antiquity may be unsettling, but by purposefully disharmonizing our sources, and thereby demonstrating their messiness, individuality, and mutual incompatibilities, I have tried to provide a richer, if more convoluted, historiographical picture of Christianity in Roman Mesopotamia and Sasanian Persia.

APPENDIX A

Constantine's Letter to Shapur

EUSEBIUS'S *LIFE OF CONSTANTINE* IV.8–14

8 When the Persian emperor also saw fit to seek recognition by Constantine through an embassy, and he too dispatched tokens of friendly compact, the Emperor negotiated treaties to this end, outdoing in lavish munificence the initiator of honorific gesture by what he did in return. Certainly, when he learnt that the churches of God were multiplying among the Persians and that many thousands of people were being gathered into the flocks of Christ, he rejoiced at the report, and, as one who had general responsibility for them everywhere, there too he again took prudent measures on behalf of them all. This also he shall explain for himself in his own words through the letter which he dispatched to the Persian emperor, commending these people to him with utmost tact and discretion. This document also is in circulation among us, written by the Emperor personally in Latin, which may be more readily understood by the reader when translated into Greek. It runs like this:

9 *Guarding the divine faith I participate in the light of truth. Led by the light of truth I recognize the divine faith. By these things therefore, as events confirm, I acknowledge the most holy religion. I confess that I hold this cult to be the teacher of the knowledge of the most holy God. Having the power of this God as ally, beginning from the shores of Ocean I have raised up the whole world step by step with sure hopes of salvation, so that all those things, which under the slavery of such great tyrants yielded to daily disasters and had come near to vanishing, have enjoyed the general restoration of right, and have revived like a patient after treatment. The God I represent is the one whose sign my army, dedicated to God, carries on its shoulders, and to whatever task the Word of Justice summons it goes directly; and from those men I get immediate and happy recompense in marks of signal victory. This is the God I profess to honour with*

undying remembrance, and him I clearly perceive with unsullied and pure mind to take highest place.

10 *Him I call upon with bended knee, shunning all abominable blood and foul hateful odours, and refusing all earthly splendour, since by all these things that lawless and unmentionable error is tainted, which has overthrown many of the nations and whole peoples, dropping them in the nethermost depths. Those things which the God of the Universe, out of concern for human welfare and because of his own love for mankind, has made available for use, should certainly not be diverted to suit the desire of individuals; he requires of men only a pure mind and soul unblemished, making these the measure of deeds of virtue and piety. He takes pleasure in works of kindness and gentleness, befriending the meek, hating the violent, loving faithfulness, punishing unfaithfulness, shattering all ostentatious power, taking vengeance on overweening arrogance; those who proudly exalt themselves he utterly destroys, while he gives what they deserve to the humble and forgiving. So because he also values highly righteous empire, he strengthens it with his own resources, and guards the imperial mind with the calm of peace.*

11 *I believe I am not mistaken, my brother, in confessing this one God the Author and Father of all, whom many of those who have reigned here, seduced by insane errors, have attempted to deny. But such punishment finally engulfed them that all mankind since has regarded their fate as superseding all other examples to warn those who strive for the same ends. Among them I reckon that one, who was driven from these parts by divine wrath as by a thunderbolt and was left in yours, where he caused the victory on your side to become very famous because of the shame he suffered.*

12 *Yet it would appear that it has turned out advantageous that even in our own day the punishment of such persons has become notorious. I have myself observed the end of those next to me, who with vicious decrees had harassed the people devoted to God. All thanks therefore are due to God, because by his perfect providence the entire humanity which reveres the divine Law, now that peace has been restored to them, exults triumphantly. Consequently I am convinced that for ourselves also everything is at its best and most secure when through their pure and excellent religion and as a result of their concord on matters divine he deigns to gather all men to himself.*

13 *With this class of persons—I mean of course the Christians, my whole concern being for them—how pleasing it is for me to hear that the most important parts of Persia too are richly adorned! May the very best come to you therefore, and at the same time the best for them, since they also are yours. For so you* *will keep the sovereign Lord of the Universe kind, merciful and benevolent. These therefore, since you are so great, I entrust to you, putting their very persons in your hands, because you too are renowned for piety. Love them in accordance with your own humanity. For you will give enormous satisfaction both to yourself and to us by keeping faith.*

14 Thus finally, all nations of the world being steered by a single pilot and welcoming government by the Servant of God, with none any longer obstructing Roman rule, all men passed their life in undisturbed tranquility.

Translation by A. Cameron and S. G. Hall, from *Life of Constantine*, by Eusebius (Oxford: Clarendon, 1999), 156–58.

APPENDIX B

Martyrdom of the Captives of Beth Zabdai

The *Martyrdom of the Captives of Beth Zabdai* is a Syriac history of the capture of Roman Bezabde (Beth Zabdai) on the upper Tigris.[1] Ammianus Marcellinus describes the siege of the city in his *Res Gestae,* and, as a military historian, he is concerned to explain the details of the battle and how the Persians overwhelmed the Roman defenses. But he also mentions a pernicious rumor about the city's bishop. According to Ammianus, the bishop of Bezabde met with Shapur II during a lull in the fighting and revealed to the king where the walls of the city were the weakest.[2] By contrast, the *Martyrdom of the Captives* says little about the siege or about Heliodorus, the city's bishop. Instead, it provides an account of what became of the "nine thousand people" whom Shapur captured and deported deep into Persia. The text claims that scores of Christians were then killed near a village on the mountain of Masabdan in the province of Beth Huzaye when they refused to exchange the "religion of Caesar" (*deḥlta d-qesar*) for the "religion of Shapur" (*deḥlta d-shabur*)—apparently a condition for beginning a new life in a "rich and fertile" land "planted with vines and olive trees and palms."[3]

---

1. See C. S. Lightfoot, "The Site of Roman Bezabde," in *Armies and Frontiers in Roman and Byzantine Anatolia,* ed. S. Mitchell (Oxford: BAR International Editions, 1983), 189–204. Guillermo Algaze contested Lightfoot's conclusions about Bezabde when he identified a major late Roman fortress that closely matches Ammianus's description. This site, which has not been fully excavated, is approximately ten kilometers upriver from the modern Turkish city of Cizre on the south bank of the Tigris. See Algaze, "A New Frontier: First Results of the Tigris-Euphrates Archaeological Reconnaissance Project, 1988," *JNES* 48 (1989): 241–81.
2. See Amm. Marc. XX.7 and the discussion in chapters 3 and 5.
3. *Deḥlta d-qesar* and *deḥlta d-shabur* are literally the "fear of Caesar" and the "fear of Shapur," respectively. On the importance of the Syriac term *deḥlta* (fear) in the *Acts of the Persian Martyrs,* see A. H. Becker, "Martyrdom, Religious Difference, and 'Fear' as a

As is frequently the case with Syriac martyrdom narratives, the date of the text's composition is difficult to establish with any certainty. That said, a Syriac account of the Christians of Beth Zabdai probably existed by the first quarter of the fifth century. We know from Ammianus that the siege was in 360. The *Martyrdom of the Captives* claims that it happened in "the fifty-third year of Shapur," or 362/63. We also know that Sozomen was aware of a tradition about the captives and martyrs of Beth Zabdai. He does not provide much information, but he says enough for us to surmise that some version of the *Martyrdom of the Captives* had made it to Constantinople by the early 440s, when he was writing his *Church History*. He says that the Persians captured and killed a bishop named "Dawsa" from "a place called Zabdaeus" along with his companion "Maryahb" (whom Sozomen describes as a "chorepiscopus") and 250 clergy.[4] Likewise, the author of the *History of Blessed Simeon bar Ṣabbaʿe* seems to have known about the deportation of captives from Beth Zabdai, although not necessarily the full story of their martyrdom. When discussing the bishops and priests who were killed with Simeon, the *History*'s narrator explains that Shapur "had recently built" the city of Karka d-Ledan in Beth Huzaye and that he "settled many captives" there, people he had taken from Beth Zabdai and other parts of Roman Mesopotamia.[5]

The end of the *Martyrdom of the Captives* indicates that the mountain on which the captives were killed had become a cult site complete with an annual memorial and a martyrium endowed by the abbot of a local monastery. As Richard Payne has demonstrated, "it was only from 410 onward, when the Sasanian king of kings began to patronize Christian institutions, that bishops, monks, and lay patrons established martyrs' cults openly and industriously in civic and rural contexts."[6] It is thus possible that the cult site was established in the early fifth century and that the accompanying martyrdom narrative had already made its way to Constantinople and

---

Category of Piety in the Sasanian Empire: The Case of the *Martyrdom of Gregory* and the *Martyrdom of Yazdpaneh*," *JLA* 2 (2009): 300–336.

4. Soz. *HE* II.13.

5. *History of Blessed Simeon bar Ṣabbaʿe* 25. Translation from K. Smith, *The Martyrdom and History of Blessed Simeon bar Ṣabbaʿe*, Persian Martyr Acts in Syriac: Text and Translation, fasc. 3. (Piscataway, NJ: Gorgias, 2014).

6. R.E. Payne, "The Emergence of Martyrs' Shrines in Late Antique Iran: Conflict, Consensus and Communal Institutions," in *An Age of Saints? Power, Conflict and Dissent in Early Medieval Christianity*, ed. P. Sarris, M. Dal Santo, and P. Booth (Leiden: Brill, 2011), 90.

Sozomen's scriptorium by the early 440s. It is more likely, however, that Sozomen knew some early story about the martyrs and that the Syriac text that has come down to us (and is translated here) is a late fifth- or even early sixth-century composition.

My translation is based on the Syriac text of Paul Bedjan; the numbers in curly brackets refer to page numbers in his edition.[7]

TRANSLATION

{316} In the fifty-third year of Shapur, the king of the Persians went up against the borders and the fortifications of the Romans. He besieged the fort [*qasṭra*] of Beth Zabdai and captured it. He demolished its walls and delivered many warriors to the blade of the sword. He captured about nine thousand people, men and women, including the bishop Heliodorus and the elderly priests Dawsa and Maryahb who were with him. Other priests, as well as {317} deacons and the *qyama* [covenant] of men and women, were captured with them. While they were being led to Beth Huzaye, the king and his army marched there on the road with them.

And it happened that at a certain way station called Dasqarta,[8] Bishop Heliodorus fell ill. He laid hands for the episcopacy upon Dawsa and made him the head of all. He also gave over to him the altar that he had brought with him so that he might honorably administer [the liturgy upon] it. And he fell asleep and was buried there in honor.

They left there, and, while they were walking on the road, they began to join together in one place and recite psalms in choirs. And as they were celebrating in this way every day the evil magi were pierced in their hearts, and their minds turned against them, and they accused them before Adarpar, the

---

7. See *AMS* II, 316–24. For a Greek version of the text's opening lines, see H. Delehaye, *Les versions grecques des Actes des martyrs persans sous Sapor II*, PO II.4 (Paris: Firmin-Didot, 1907), no. 7.

8. Or Dastaqarta. The location of this "way station" is uncertain, but it may have been near Ctesiphon. The Synod of Dadisho' in 424 referred to the excommunication of someone called "Sharbil of Dasqarta of the king." See K. Smith, "The Synod of Mar Dādišo'—424 CE," in *CCCOGD*, vol. 5, ed. A. Melloni and F. Lauritzen (Turnhout: Brepols, forthcoming). If this is the same city, then "of the king" might indicate that Dasqarta was a royal estate or a crown-owned agricultural area. It may also have been the residence of the Jewish exilarch, as the Babylonian Talmud mentions the city. See G. Herman, *A Prince without a Kingdom: The Exilarch in the Sasanian Era* (Tübingen: Mohr Siebeck, 2012), 137–38.

head of the mobeds,[9] at whose suggestion was shed much blood of the martyrs of God in the East.

This accursed one [Adarpar] went in before the king and said, "Good King, there is among these captives one who is the head of the Christians, and his name is Dawsa. He gathers together many of the captives, men and women who share his opinion, and they rise in unison and curse and revile your majesty. They do this every day, and {318} once or twice I sent for them and scolded them, but all the more did they vilify you with curses and slander the gods of the Persians."

The king was in the station of Dursak, in the land of Darraye,[10] and he ordered this mobed and a noble one who was with him, who was called Hazarpat, and he said to them, "Go, and bring with cunning the head of these Christians and all his followers, and say this to them: 'The king is well pleased to do you good, and he commanded that you settle here on this mountain, for the land is fertile, its villages are beautiful, the soil is rich in water, and [the villages] will continually provide for you all the days of your life.' Watch for when they are all together—those who have been gathering together every day to blaspheme our majesty and insult our gods—bring them up on to this mountain and interrogate them at some place. All those who do my will, who worship the sun and the moon and renounce the god whom Caesar worships, let them settle in these villages as they wish and desire. But whoever does not obey this command, let him be given to the sword and the blade."

Then these two nobles departed with a hundred cavalry and two hundred infantry, and they summoned before them Bishop Dawsa and Chorbishop Maryahb, the priests and deacons and *qyama*, and also the lay faithful {319} who were clinging to them. And they said to them all these words in deceit. Their crowd was about three hundred people, and they were taken to the mountain called Masabdan, to a village called Gpetta, and they were put outside the village.

Immediately, this cruel man and shedder of blood, Mobed Adarpar, revealed his treachery and demonstrated his craftiness, and he said to them, "You should know that because you dishonor the king every day and have reviled the gods of the Persians, the king has commanded that all of you are to be slain at this place. But now, if you listen to our advice, you will live and

9. A mobed is a Zoroastrian priest.
10. Beth Daraye? If so, this is about 150 kilometers east-southeast of modern-day Baghdad.

be saved. Therefore, do the will of the king and worship the sun and the moon. Abandon the religion of Caesar and embrace the religion of Shapur, the king of kings, because you are his servants and he has authority over you. If you are obedient in this, I have been granted authority by him to let you remain in these villages, which are rich and fertile, and in this land, which, as you can see with your eyes, is planted with vines and olive trees and palms. Moreover, he will give all of you presents and gifts, whatever you ask of me. But if you will not obey the command of the king, then know that today you will die by the sword {320} and not one of you will be allowed to live—according to the decree that we have received from him."

The courageous Dawsa responded with a loud voice and said, "O people drenched in the blood of their own land and, in addition, reveling in the blood of [other] lands: See your own people and foreigners being killed! Locals and immigrants are slain. And what did you gain, and which excuse will you use? For behold, your punishment is written down by [divine] justice, and the verdict has gone out against you and it will not fail, for you have greatly stained yourselves with the blood of the martyrs of the East, and lo, you will be sprinkled with the blood of the martyrs of the West, so that our innocent blood will seal your written contract along with the righteous blood of the holy martyrs that you have shed.[11]

"This secret treachery that you revealed to us is our hidden joy, and the iniquitous command that you have showed to us is our open exaltation. Thus, we have not been captured and removed from our country, nor have we died the death of an exile, nor will we die death in captivity. Who is our killer? Let him not stand still and hesitate! Who is our slayer? Let him not delay and linger! One is the god of us all, who, because of our sins, delivered us into your hands. And now he has mercy upon us and he is reconciled with us, for because of him we will die today by your hands.

"Far be it from us to worship the sun and the moon, the work of [God's] hands, and do the will of your king, that eater of human flesh. {321} For we hold steadfast to our faith and worship our true God—whom Caesar worships as well and in whom he has faith. But as for us, we journey in glory and goodness to the country that is prepared for our journey. But woe unto you, the unclean and impure, who led the East astray with your godless teaching. For

---

11. This is a complex passage. The implication seems to be that the Sasanian authorities, by killing Christians, have signed a contract in blood and will be punished by divine justice. Note that "the martyrs of the East" refers to Christians who have already been killed in Persia, while "the martyrs of the West" refers to Dawsa and the other captives of Beth Zabdai.

God will quickly destroy it in you and ruin you in it. He will bring your error to naught and blot out your falsehood from all the land of the East. So know that we all stand firm in this faithful state of mind, as I have made known to you! Therefore, do what you have been commanded and do not delay!"

Then [Mobed Adarpar] commanded the soldiers who were with him, and each time they began to take men and women by groups of fifty and to kill them together until they reached the number of 275. But twenty-five from among the men and women succumbed in the shame of themselves and worshiped the sun. And they allowed them to settle there until this day.

A certain deacon among them, who was called ʿAbdishoʿ, remained alive because the sword did not strike on its edge. After sunset he got up and went to the village. He met a poor man, who brought him into his house and washed and bandaged his wounds. When it was day, ʿAbdishoʿ led this man and his two sons with him, and they walked to the place of those who had been killed. He showed them the bodies of Dawsa, Maryahb, and the other elderly {322} priests. [The man and his sons] climbed a little farther up the mountain, found a small cave, and laid [the martyrs' bodies] in it and sealed it with large stones. Then they went back down to ʿAbdishoʿ, and they found him kneeling in prayer and crying at the place of those who had been killed.

There were some pagan, Carmanian shepherds who were grazing sheep, and for three nights they saw armies of angels praising God and ascending and descending over that place where the holy ones had been killed.[12] [The shepherds] were startled and afraid, and they announced this [event] throughout all the land. On account of this sight, they too converted to the faith.

ʿAbdishoʿ, who was killed by the sword and lived, began to lead to life the souls of those who had been killed by sin. Because of the bones of the righteous ones who had fallen there, he resolved to stay there all his days. And for thirty days he did not cease from teaching the fear of God through deeds and good works.

But when a wicked man, the lord of the village, saw that [ʿAbdishoʿ] converted people from error to knowledge of the truth, Satan entered him in envy and taught him the evil zeal of murder. He seized ʿAbdishoʿ and beat him, and he held him in chains for four days, and he said to him, "If you leave here {323} and never again teach this doctrine in this village, then I will free you and you may go where you please."

---

12. Ancient Carmania (which roughly accords with Kerman Province in contemporary Iran) was southeast of Beth Huzaye and north of the Strait of Hormuz.

The blessed 'Abdisho' said to him, "I have decided in my mind to remain here, and I will not desist from preaching this doctrine in everyone's ear so that it will hear, be persuaded, and turn to life."[13]

This unjust man was thereby enraged, and he led ['Abdisho'] outside the village to the place where his companions had been killed. He gave fifty silver coins to a Carmanian, and this Carmanian stabbed him with a sword, and he died.

That poor man went out again with his sons, and they lifted up the corpse of courageous 'Abdisho' and hid it. They erected a heap of many stones over it, and to this day it is called the Tomb of 'Abdisho'.

The wrath of heaven, however, reached the wicked murderer and his house. His four sons were delivered unto a demon, who quickly killed them. The man suffered from dropsy, and he sat on the dung heap in unspeakable agony for thirty days. When he died there, his dogs ate him. His fortune was lost all at once, his servants fled and scattered, his wife begged for bread, and, in her misery, she died as well. And, because it had been dug by hand, the Lord God let loose rats upon the village's water canal. The rats dug and filled in the water canal with soil. And when the inhabitants of the village gathered together and removed the soil, the rats dug {324} and filled it in again. This happened repeatedly. And since the village suffered from thirst and its plants withered, it became a desert for twenty-two years and was as a curse in the whole land.

After this time, a son of the man who had welcomed 'Abdisho' and buried him and had also hidden the martyrs of God came and prayed at the mouth of the opening of that cave. And he promised to come every year and to celebrate the memorial there. Then he dug out the village canal, built houses, and settled in peace. The Lord God blessed him in [the village], and he took possession of it and it was awarded to him. Every time he performed the memorial there, healing miracles occurred through those holy bones.

A certain abbot was inspired with beautiful zeal for God. He built a martyrium there on that place, took those bones from the cave, and put them in the building he had built. And lo, unto this day gatherings are being held there.

Completed is the *Martyrdom of the Captives of the Castra of Beth Zabdai*.

---

13. It sounds strange, but the "ear" must be the subject of the verbs that follow it.

APPENDIX C

Martyrdom of Abbot Barshebya, Ten Fellow Brothers, and One Magus

There are two heroes of this brief martyrdom narrative. The first is an abbot called Barshebya, literally "Son of the captivity." The second is an unnamed magus, a follower of Zoroaster, who is so astounded by the courage and endurance of Barshebya's monks and so dazzled by the fiery crosses that hover above them when they are killed that he makes a surreptitious roadside conversion. He too wishes to die a martyr's death—but secretly, without anyone knowing who he is.

According to the text, the mobed of the city of Istakhr arrested and brutally tortured Barshebya and his religious brothers. "Impious and evil men" accused the monks of "destroying the teachings of the magi" and corrupting people in the land of the Persians with their "sorcery." The equivalence of Christian catechesis with sorcery is a common charge in the *Acts of the Persian Martyrs*. Shapur II refers to Simeon bar Ṣabbaʿe as the "head of the sorcerers" on several occasions.[1] And at two points in Simeon's acts, when Shapur is attempting to persuade the old eunuch Gushtazad to reconsider his conversion to Christianity, the king comments that the "opinions of these sorcerers" led Gushtazad astray.[2]

While many of the acts set during Shapur's reign take place in Beth Huzaye, the events that the *Martyrdom of Abbot Barshebya* describes occur much farther to the southeast, in the Iranian province of Fars. Specifically, the text refers to the ancient Achaemenid city of Istakhr, just a few kilometers

---

1. *Martyrdom of Blessed Simeon bar Ṣabbaʿe* 12; *History of Blessed Simeon bar Ṣabbaʿe* 15, 18, 34. All translations of these texts are from K. Smith, *The Martyrdom and History of Blessed Simeon bar Ṣabbaʿe*, Persian Martyr Acts in Syriac: Text and Translation, fasc. 3. (Piscataway, NJ: Gorgias, 2014).
2. *Martyrdom of Simeon* 30; *History of Simeon* 54.

north of Persepolis and formerly near the monumental Sasanian relief sculptures and inscriptions at Naqsh-e-Rostam, where Valerian's submission to Shapur I is on display (see chapter 1). Somewhat oddly, the text mentions neither Shapur II nor the year of its events. Its last line says only that the martyrs "were crowned on the seventeenth day of the lunar month Ḥaziran." The first line, however, claims that Barshebya and his monks were arrested "at the time when blessed Miles was crowned." Miles, whose acts Sozomen summarizes, had been in the Persian army before becoming an apostolic vagrant. He purportedly wandered from Persia to Jerusalem and on to Egypt to visit the monks there, with nothing but the Gospels in his possession.[3] The *Martyrdom of Miles* claims that he was killed at the beginning of Shapur's persecution, in 340, but the events that the *Martyrdom of Abbot Barshebya* describes do not reflect a fourth-century context. It is more likely that this text dates to the sixth century.

The first thing to note is the abbot's status as a captive, which is even his name. As I discuss in chapter 5, a number of fifth- and sixth-century Syriac martyrdom narratives play up the captive status of Christians in Persia, but here all we are told is that the abbot happens to be called "Son of the captivity," as if this required no further explanation. In addition to Barshebya's name, there is the fact that he is an abbot of a monastery. The development of monastic institutions in Sasanian Persia, especially as far east as Istakhr, lagged well behind that of their Western counterparts. Only in 424, with the Synod of Dadishoʿ, do we hear about bishops from cities in Fars.[4] The two earlier synods, in 410 and 420, do not mention a bishop of Fars. And contrary to sources that invoke the legendary monastic evangelist Mar Awgin and thereby presume an early arrival of Egyptian-style cenobitic monasticism in Persia, such communal practices did not begin to flourish there until the

---

3. See Soz. *HE* II.14. Bedjan's edition of the *Martyrdom of Miles* precedes the *Martyrdom of Barshebya* by just a few pages. See *AMS* II, 260–75. On the theme of apostolic vagrancy, see D. Caner, *Wandering, Begging Monks: Spiritual Authority and the Promotion of Monasticism in Late Antiquity* (Berkeley: University of California Press, 2002).

4. The acts of the Synod of Dadishoʿ likely suffer from later interpolations and should be read with caution. See L. Abramowski, "Der Bischof von Seleukia-Ktesiphon als Katholikos und Patriarch der Kirche des Ostens," in *Syrien im 1.-7. Jahrhundert nach Christus: Akten der 1. Tübinger Tagung zum Christlichen Orient (15.-16. Juni 2007)*, ed. D. Bumazhnov and H.R. Seeliger (Tübingen: Mohr Siebeck, 2011), 1–55. A translation of the synod's records (with an introduction, notes, and analysis) is forthcoming: K. Smith, "The Synod of Mar Dādišoʿ—424 CE," in *CCCOGD*, vol. V, ed. A. Melloni and F. Lauritzen (Turnhout: Brepols).

sixth century.⁵ Finally, there is the conversion of the magus to Christianity. Although not unheard of in earlier Syriac martyrdom narratives, the conversion of magi and other high-ranking Sasanian officials becomes a prominent theme only in texts about fifth-century martyrs.⁶

My translation is based on the Syriac text of Paul Bedjan; the numbers in curly brackets refer to page numbers in his edition.⁷

TRANSLATION

{281} At the time when blessed Miles was crowned, there was an abbot in the land of the Persians whose name was Barshebya ["Son of the captivity"]. He dwelt in a monastery, and with him were ten disciples.

Impious and evil men accused them before the mobed of the city of Istakhr, saying, "He corrupts many people, and he teaches sorcery in our land, destroying the teachings of the magi with his instruction." [The mobed] ordered that [Barshebya] be arrested, he and the brothers with him, and they brought them to [the mobed] in shackles. He imposed cruel tortures and intense suffering upon them until even their knees were hacked down with a hammer. He destroyed their shins, arms, and sides with a spiked staff, and he mutilated their faces, ears, and eyes.⁸

{282} When the iniquitous judge saw—during all this destruction of their limbs and all the suffering they endured—that the true ones were not defeated and that the upright ones were not shaken nor turned from their

---

5. See F. Jullien, "Aux sources du monachisme oriental: Abraham de Kashkar et le développement de la légende de Mar Awgin," *RHR* 225 (2008): 37–52. For a survey of textual and, importantly, archaeological studies of cenobitic monasticism in the region of the Persian Gulf, including some discussion of Fars, see R. E. Payne, "Monks, Dinars and Date Palms: Hagiographical Production and the Expansion of Monastic Institutions in the Early Islamic Persian Gulf," *AAE* 22 (2011): 97–111.

6. For example, the *Martyrdom of Narsai* (*AMS* IV, 170–80). Studies that address this theme of conversion more broadly include J. P. Asmussen, "Das Christentum in Iran und sein Verhältnis zum Zoroastrismus," *ST* 16 (1962): 1–24; and, more recently, R. Kiperwasser and S. Ruzer, "To Convert a Persian and Teach Him the Holy Scriptures: A Zoroastrian Proselyte in Rabbinic and Syriac Christian Narratives," in *Jews, Christians and Zoroastrians: Religious Dynamics in a Sasanian Context*, ed. G. Herman (Piscataway, NJ: Gorgias, 2014), 101–38.

7. See *AMS* II, 281–84.

8. For a typological analysis of Sasanian methods of torture and execution as discussed in the *Acts of the Persian Martyrs*, see C. Jullien, "Peines et supplices dans les *Actes des martyrs persans* et droit sassanide: Nouvelles prospections," *Studia Iranica* 33 (2004): 243–69.

God nor lapsed in their faith, he ordered that they be taken to the outskirts of the city to be executed. While they were being led away they sang psalms and glorified God, and a great crowd surrounded them.

When they had begun to be executed, a certain magus came out from the city and passed by along the road. With him was his wife, who was sitting on a mule, and two of his sons and some of his servants. He raised up his eyes and saw the gathered multitude of people, and he said to those who were with him, "Come this way for a moment so I can find out the reason for this assembly." And he went ahead on his horse with one of his servants with him.

He went over and stood beside the martyrs while they were being killed, and he saw the courageous abbot holding the hands of each of the disciples whom he chose, one after the next, and whom he then gave over to be killed. [The abbot] comforted them with *madrashe* sung in sweet and dulcet tones.[9] Then the Lord opened the eyes of this magus, and he saw tongues of fire standing up in the form of the cross, and the fire blazed and flared and stood upon the corpses {283} of those who had been killed. [The magus] was terrified, and, trembling, he got down from his horse. He exchanged his clothes for those of his servant, and he drew near to the glorious one and whispered to him, "I have seen a strange vision, and your god has truly chosen me to die with you because he is God, he alone, and in him I put my faith with all my heart. So now let no one know that I have not come from among you, and hold me as [you held] each of your disciples and give me over to be killed. For I have a great longing to be killed with you, the holy and true and believing people."

And the blessed one believed him all the more because a wondrous vision was shown to him. After the nine others, [Barshebya] took [the magus] by the hands and gave him to be killed, and the killers did not know. And after him the eleventh was killed as well, with the abbot killed last of all as the seal of the twelve. In this the magus was perfected.[10]

9. *Madrashe* are Syriac catechetical hymns sung during the liturgy.

10. It is no accident that the addition of the magus to the group of eleven monks results in a number of obvious symbolism and importance for Christians. It is possible that the account here is intended as an allusion to the famous story the *Forty Martyrs of Sebaste*. According to this legend, forty Christians were stripped and left to die of exposure overnight on a frozen pond. One faltered and left his companions for the warm baths. Soon after, one of the guards who was watching the Christians saw a supernatural brilliance shining above them. He immediately stripped off his clothes, proclaimed himself a Christian, and joined the thirty-nine who remained on the pond. For Bedjan's edition of the Syriac version, see *AMS* III, 355–75.

Then they brought their heads into the city and hung them upon the temple of Anahid, the goddess of the Persians, to display them for the masses in order to deter them. Wild animals and birds of the heavens devoured their bodies.

Afterward, this thing became known about this magus himself, and there was great amazement throughout the land. Many converted to the truth because of him, and even his wife and sons and servants became {284} true believers because of him, and they lived all the days of their lives in the fear of God.

These holy ones were crowned on the seventeenth day of the lunar month Ḥaziran.

BIBLIOGRAPHY

PRIMARY SOURCES

Acts of the Persian Martyrs (Texts and Translations)

Abbeloos, J. B. *Acta Mar Ḳardaghi Assyriae praefecti*. Leipzig: Brockhaus, 1890.
Bedjan, P. *Acta Martyrum et Sanctorum*. 7 vols. Leipzig: Otto Harrassowitz, 1890–97.
———. *Histoire de Mar-Jabalaha, de trois autres patriarches, d'un prêtre et de deux laïques, nestoriens*. Leipzig: Otto Harrassowitz, 1895. Repr., *The History of Mar Jab-Alaha and Rabban Sauma*. Piscataway, NJ: Gorgias, 2007.
Braun, O. *Ausgewählte Akten persischer Märtyrer*. Munich: Kösel-Verlag, 1915.
Brock, S. P. *The History of the Holy Mar Maʿin with a Guide to the Persian Martyr Acts*. Persian Martyr Acts in Syriac: Text and Translation, fasc. 1. Piscataway, NJ: Gorgias, 2009.
———. *The Martyrs of Mount Berʾain*. With an introduction by P. C. Dilley. Persian Martyr Acts in Syriac: Text and Translation, fasc. 4. Piscataway, NJ: Gorgias, 2014.
Brock, S. P., and S. A. Harvey. *Holy Women of the Syrian Orient*. Berkeley: University of California Press, 1987.
Delehaye, H. *Les versions grecques des Actes des martyrs persans sous Sapor II*. PO II.4. Paris: Firmin-Didot, 1907.
Hoffmann, G. *Auszüge aus syrischen Akten persischer Märtyrer*. Abhandlungen für die Kunde des Morgenlandes VII.3. Leipzig, 1880.
Jullien, F. *Histoire de Mar Abba, catholicos de l'Orient: Martyres de Mar Grigor, général en chef du roi Khusro Ier et de Mar Yazd-panah, juge et gouverneur*. CSCO 658–59, Scriptores Syri 254–55. Leuven: Peeters, 2015.
Kmoskó, M. *S. Simeon Bar Ṣabbāʿē: Martyrium et Narratio*. PS I.2. Paris: Firmin-Didot, 1907.
McCollum, A. C. *The Story of Mar Pinḥas*. Persian Martyr Acts in Syriac: Text and Translation, fasc. 2. Piscataway, NJ: Gorgias, 2013.

Saint-Laurent, J.-N. M., and K. Smith. *The History of Mar Behnam and Sarah*. Persian Martyr Acts in Syriac: Text and Translation, fasc. 5. Piscataway, NJ: Gorgias, forthcoming.

Smith, K. *The Martyrdom and History of Blessed Simeon bar Ṣabbaʿe*. Persian Martyr Acts in Syriac: Text and Translation, fasc. 3. Piscataway, NJ: Gorgias, 2014.

Walker, J. T. *The Legend of Mar Qardagh: Narrative and Christian Heroism in Late Antique Iraq*. Berkeley: University of California Press, 2006.

Other Texts and Translations

Abbeloos, J.-B., and T. J. Lamy. *Gregorii Barhebraei Chronicon ecclesiasticum*. 3 vols. Leuven: Peeters, 1872–77.

Beck, E. *Des heiligen Ephraem des Syrers Carmina Nisibena*. CSCO 218–19, 240–41, Scriptores Syri 92–93, 102–3. Leuven: Peeters, 1961–63.

———. *Des heiligen Ephraem des Syrers Hymnen de Paradiso und Contra Iulianum*. CSCO 78–79. Leuven: Peeters, 1957.

Bekker, I. *Synopsis Historiarum*, by George Cedrenus. CSHB. Bonn, 1838.

Bickell, G. *Carmina Nisibena*, by Ephrem the Syrian. Leipzig, 1866.

Bidez, J. *L'Empereur Julien: Œuvres complètes*. Vol. 1.1. Paris: Les Belles Lettres, 1932.

Bidez, J., and G. C. Hansen. *Historia ecclesiastica*, by Sozomen. GCS 4, n.f. Berlin: Akademie Verlag, 1995.

Bleckmann, B., and H. Schneider. *Eusebius von Caesarea, De Vita Constantini, Über das Leben Konstantins*. Turnhout: Brepols, 2007.

Bosworth, C. E. *The History of al-Ṭabarī*, vol. 5, *The Sāsānids, the Byzantines, the Lakmids, and Yemen*. Albany: State University of New York Press, 1999.

Brandt, S. *De mortibus persecutorum*, by Lactantius. CSEL 27. Vienna, 1893.

Cameron, A., and S. G. Hall. *Life of Constantine*, by Eusebius. Oxford: Clarendon, 1999.

Chabot, J. B. *Chronique de Michel le Syrien, patriarche jacobite d'Antioche*. 4 vols. Paris: Leroux, 1899–1910.

———. *Synodicon orientale, ou recueil de synodes nestoriens*. Paris: Imprimerie nationale, 1902.

Charles, R. H. *The Chronicle of John, Bishop of Nikiu*. London: Williams and Norgate, 1916.

Defarrari, R. J. *Paulus Orosius: The Seven Books of History against the Pagans*. Washington DC: Catholic University of America Press, 2001.

Edwards, M. *Constantine and Christendom*. Liverpool: Liverpool University Press, 2003.

Gismondi, H. *Maris Amri et Slibae: De Patriarchis Nestorianorum*. 2 vols. Rome: De Luigi, 1896–99.

Gollancz, H. *Julian the Apostate*. London: Oxford University Press, 1928.

Helm, R. *Eusebius Werke*, vol. 7, *Die Chronik des Hieronymus*. GCS 47. Berlin: Akademie Verlag, 1956.

Hoffmann, J. G. E. *Iulianos der Abtruennige*. Leiden: Brill, 1880.
Lamy, T. J. *Historia Ephraemi*. In *Sancti Ephraem Syri: Hymni et Sermones*, vol. 2, cols. 3–89. Mechelen, 1886.
Lehto, A. *The Demonstrations of Aphrahat, the Persian Sage*. Gorgias Eastern Christian Studies 27. Piscataway, NJ: Gorgias, 2010.
Mango, C., and R. Scott. *The Chronicle of Theophanes Confessor: Byzantine and Near Eastern History, AD 284–813*. Oxford: Clarendon, 1997.
McVey, K. E. *Ephrem the Syrian: Hymns*. Mahwah, NJ: Paulist, 1989.
Mingana, A. *Sources syriaques*. Vol. 1. Leipzig: Otto Harrassowitz, 1907.
Parisot, J. *Aphraatis Sapientis Persae Demonstrationes I–XXII*. PS I.1. Paris: Firmin-Didot, 1894.
———. *Aphraatis Sapientis Persae Demonstrationes XXIII* (with lexicon). PS I.2, 1–489. Paris: Firmin-Didot, 1907.
Pierre, M.-J. *Aphraate le Sage persan: Les Exposés I–X*. SC 349. Paris: Éditions du Cerf, 1988.
Renoux, C. *Ephraem, Les discourses sur Nicomedie*. PO 37.2–3. Turnhout: Brepols, 1975.
Rolfe, J. C. *Ammianus Marcellinus*. 3 vols. London: Heinemann, 1935–40.
Schaff, P., and H. Wace. *A Select Library of Nicene and Post-Nicene Fathers of the Christian Church*. Vol. 2. New York: Christian Literature, 1890.
Scher, A. *Histoire nestorienne inédite (Chronique de Séert)*. PO 4, 5, 7, 13. Paris: Firmin-Didot, 1908, 1910, 1911, 1919.
Thurn, J. *Ioannis Malalae Chronographia*. CFHB 35. Berlin: Walter de Gruyter, 2000.
Wright, W. C. *The Works of the Emperor Julian*. Vol 1. London: William Heinemann, 1913.
Zotenberg, H. *Chronique de Jean, évêque de Nikiou: Texte éthiopien publié et traduit*. Paris, 1883.

SECONDARY SOURCES

Abramowski, L. "Der Bischof von Seleukia-Ktesiphon als Katholikos und Patriarch der Kirche des Ostens." In *Syrien im 1.-7. Jahrhundert nach Christus: Akten der 1. Tübinger Tagung zum Christlichen Orient (15.-16. Juni 2007)*, ed. D. Bumazhnov and H. R. Seeliger, 1–55. Tübingen: Mohr Siebeck, 2011.
Algaze, G. "A New Frontier: First Results of the Tigris-Euphrates Archaeological Reconnaissance Project, 1988." *JNES* 48 (1989): 241–81.
Altheim F., and R. Stiehl. *Ein asiatischer Staat: Feudalismus unter den Sasaniden und ihren Nachbarn*. Wiesbaden: Limes-Verlag, 1954.
Amar, J. P. "Byzantine Ascetic Monachism and Greek Bias in the *Vita* Tradition of Ephrem the Syrian." *OCP* 58 (1992): 123–56.
Andrade, N. J. *Syrian Identity in the Greco-Roman World*. Cambridge: Cambridge University Press, 2013.

Asmussen, J. P. "Das Christentum in Iran und sein Verhältnis zum Zoroastrismus." *ST* 16 (1962): 1–24.
Assemani, J. S. *Bibliotheca Orientalis Clementino-Vaticana*. Vol. 3. Rome, 1725.
Athanassiadi-Fowden, P. *Julian and Hellenism: An Intellectual Biography*. Oxford: Clarendon, 1981.
Back, M. *Die sasanidischen Staatsinschriften*. Acta Iranica 18. Leiden: Brill, 1978.
Balty, J. "Mosaïques romaines, mosaïques sassanides: Jeux d'influences réciproques." In *Ērān ud Anērān: Studien zu den Beziehungen zwischen dem Sasanidenreich und der Mittelmeerwelt—Beiträge des Internationalen Colloquiums in Eutin, 8–9 Juni 2000*, ed. J. Wiesehöfer and P. Huyse, 29–44. Stuttgart: Franz Steiner Verlag, 2006.
Barnes, T. D. *Ammianus Marcellinus and the Representation of Historical Reality*. Ithaca, NY: Cornell University Press, 1998.
———. *Constantine and Eusebius*. Cambridge, MA: Harvard University Press, 1981.
———. "Constantine and the Christians of Persia." *JRS* 75 (1985): 126–36.
———. "Constantine's Prohibition of Pagan Sacrifice." *AJP* 105 (1984): 69–72.
———. "Lactantius and Constantine." *JRS* 63 (1973): 29–46.
———. "Panegyric, History and Hagiography in Eusebius' *Life of Constantine*." In *The Making of Orthodoxy: Essays in Honour of Henry Chadwick*, ed. R. Williams, 94–123. Cambridge: Cambridge University Press, 1989.
Baynes, N. H. *Constantine the Great and the Christian Church*. London: Milford, 1931.
Becker, A. H. "The Ancient Near East in the Late Antique Near East: Syriac Christian Appropriation of the Biblical East." In *Antiquity in Antiquity*, ed. G. Gardner and K. L. Osterloh, 1–21. Tübingen: Mohr Siebeck, 2008.
———. "Beyond the Spatial and Temporal *Limes*: Questioning the 'Parting of the Ways' outside the Roman Empire." In *The Ways That Never Parted: Jews and Christians in Late Antiquity and the Early Middle Ages*, ed. Becker and A. Y. Reed, 373–92. Minneapolis: Fortress, 2007.
———. "The Comparative Study of 'Scholasticism' in Late Antique Mesopotamia: Rabbis and East Syrians." *AJSR* 34 (2010): 91–113.
———. *Fear of God and the Beginning of Wisdom: The School of Nisibis and Christian Scholastic Culture in Late Antique Mesopotamia*. Philadelphia: University of Pennsylvania Press, 2006.
———. "Martyrdom, Religious Difference, and 'Fear' as a Category of Piety in the Sasanian Empire: The Case of the *Martyrdom of Gregory* and the *Martyrdom of Yazdpaneh*." *JLA* 2 (2009): 300–336.
———. "Political Theology and Religious Diversity in the Sasanian Empire." In *Jews, Christians and Zoroastrians: Religious Dynamics in a Sasanian Context*, ed. G. Herman, 7–25. Piscataway, NJ: Gorgias, 2014.
Belcher, S. "Ammianus Marcellinus and the Nisibene Handover of A.D. 363." In *War and Warfare in Late Antiquity*, vol. 2, ed. A. Sarantis and N. Christie, 631–52. Leiden: Brill, 2013.

Blockley, R. C. *Ammianus Marcellinus: A Study of His Historiography and Political Thought.* Brussels: Collection Latomus, 1975.

———. "Constantius II and Persia." In *Studies in Latin Literature and Roman History* V (*Latomus: Revue d'études latines* 206), ed. C. Deroux, 465–90. Brussels: Latomus, 1989.

———. *East Roman Foreign Policy: Formation and Conduct from Diocletian to Anastasius.* Leeds: Francis Cairns, 1992.

———. "The Romano-Persian Peace Treaties of A.D. 299 and 363." *Florilegium* 6 (1984): 28–49.

———. "Subsidies and Diplomacy: Rome and Persia in Late Antiquity." *Phoenix* 39 (1985): 62–74.

Blum, G. G. "Zur religionspolitischen Situation der persischen Kirche im 3. und 4. Jahrhundert." *ZKG* 91 (1980): 11–32.

Bowersock, G. W. *Julian the Apostate.* Cambridge, MA: Harvard University Press, 1978.

Bowes, K. *Private Worship, Public Values and Religious Change in Late Antiquity.* Cambridge: Cambridge University Press, 2008.

Boyarin, D. *Dying for God: Martyrdom and the Making of Christianity and Judaism.* Stanford: Stanford University Press, 1999.

Bradbury, S. "Constantine and the Problem of Anti-Pagan Legislation in the Fourth Century." *CP* 89 (1994): 120–39.

Brock, S. P. "Christians in the Sasanian Empire: A Case of Divided Loyalties." In *Religion and National Identity,* ed. S. Mews, 1–19. Oxford: Oxford University Press, 1982.

———. "Eusebius and Syriac Christianity." In *Eusebius, Christianity, and Judaism,* ed. H. W. Attridge and G. Hata, 212–34. Detroit: Wayne State University Press, 1992.

———. "Review of *Untersuchungen zur syrischen Literaturgeschichte I: Zur Märtyrerüberlieferung aus der Christenverfolgung Schapurs II.,* by Gernot Wiessner." *JTS* 19 (1968): 300–309.

———. "Some Aspects of Greek Words in Syriac." In *Synkretismus im syrisch-persischen Kulturgebiet: Bericht über ein Symposion in Reinhausen bei Göttingen in der Zeit vom 4. bis 8. Oktober 1971,* ed. A. Dietrich, 80–108. Göttingen: Vandenhoeck und Ruprecht, 1975.

———. "St. Ephrem in the Eyes of Later Syriac Liturgical Tradition." *Hugoye* 2 (1999): 5–25.

Brock, S. P., A. M. Butts, G. A. Kiraz, and L. Van Rompay, eds. *Gorgias Encyclopedic Dictionary of the Syriac Heritage.* Piscataway, NJ: Gorgias, 2011.

Brody, R. "Judaism in the Sasanian Empire: A Case Study in Religious Coexistence." In *Irano-Judaica II: Studies Relating to Jewish Contacts with Persian Culture throughout the Ages,* ed. S. Shaked and A. Netzer, 52–62. Jerusalem: Ben-Zvi Institute, 1990.

Browning, R. *The Emperor Julian.* Berkeley: University of California Press, 1976.

Brubaker, R. *Ethnicity without Groups.* Cambridge, MA: Harvard University Press, 2004.

———. *Nationalist Politics and Everyday Ethnicity in a Transylvanian Town.* Princeton, NJ: Princeton University Press, 2006.
Buell, D. K. *Why This New Race: Ethnic Reasoning in Early Christianity.* New York: Columbia University Press, 2005.
Bundy, D. "Jacob of Nisibis as a Model for the Episcopacy." *Mus* 104 (1991): 235–49.
Burgess, R. W. "ΑΧΥΡΩΝ or ΠΡΟΑΣΤΕΙΟΝ: The Location and Circumstances of Constantine's Death." *JTS* 50 (1999): 153–61.
———. "The Dates of the First Siege of Nisibis and the Death of James of Nisibis." *Byz* 69 (1999): 7–17.
———. "The Dates of the Martyrdom of Simeon Bar Ṣabbāʿē and the 'Great Massacre.'" *AB* 117 (1999): 9–66.
———. "The Summer of Blood: The 'Great Massacre' of 337 and the Promotion of the Sons of Constantine." *DOP* 62 (2008): 5–51.
Butts, A. M. *"Julian Romance."* In *Gorgias Encyclopedic Dictionary of the Syriac Heritage,* ed. S. P. Brock, A. M. Butts, G. A. Kiraz, and L. Van Rompay (Piscataway, NJ: Gorgias, 2011), 208–9.
———. "The Use of Syriac Derivational Suffixes with Greek Loanwords." *Orientalia* 83 (2014): 207–37.
Cameron, A. "Eusebius of Caesarea and the Rethinking of History." In *Tria Corda: Scritti in onore di Arnaldo Momigliano,* ed. E. Gabba, 71–88. Como: New Press, 1983.
———. "Eusebius' *Vita Constantini* and the Construction of Constantine." In *Portraits: Biographical Representations in the Greek and Latin Literature of the Roman Empire,* ed. M. J. Edwards and S. Swain, 145–74. Oxford: Clarendon, 1997.
Canepa, M. "Topographies of Power: Theorizing the Visual, Spatial and Ritual Contexts of Rock Reliefs in Ancient Iran." In *Of Rocks and Water: Towards an Archaeology of Place,* ed. Ö. Harmanşah, 55–92. Oxford: Oxbow Books, 2014.
———. *The Two Eyes of the Earth: Art and Ritual of Kingship between Rome and Sasanian Iran.* Berkeley: University of California Press, 2009.
Caner, D. *Wandering, Begging Monks: Spiritual Authority and the Promotion of Monasticism in Late Antiquity.* Berkeley: University of California Press, 2002.
Castelli, E. A. *Martyrdom and Memory: Early Christian Culture Making.* New York: Columbia University Press, 2004.
———. "Religious Identity through the Prism of Spectacle in Early Christianity." Paper presented at the Center for Late Ancient Studies symposium "Constructing and Contesting Late Ancient Identities," Duke University, Durham, NC, February 20, 2009.
Chaumont, M.-L. *La christianisation de l'empire iranien: Des origines aux grandes persécutions du IVe siècle.* CSCO 499, Subsidia 80. Leuven: Peeters, 1988.
———. "L'Inscription de Kartir à la 'Ka'bah de Zoroastre' (texte, traduction, commentaire)." *JA* 248 (1960): 339–80.
Chauvot, A. "Parthes et Perses dans les sources du IVe siècle." In *Institutions, société et vie politique dans l'empire romain au IVe siècle ap. J.-C.,* ed. M. Christol,

S. Demougin, and Y. Duval, 115–25. Rome: École française de Rome / Palais Farnèse, 1992.

Christensen, A. *L'Iran sous les Sassanides*. 2nd ed. Copenhagen: Ejnar Munksgaard, 1944.

Conrad, L. I. "Theophanes and the Arabic Historical Tradition: Some Indications of Intercultural Transmission." *ByzF* 15 (1990): 1–44.

Corcoran, S. "Emperor and Citizen in the Era of Constantine." In *Constantine the Great: York's Roman Emperor*, ed. E. Hartley, J. Hawkes, and M. Henig, 41–51. York: Lund Humphries, 2006.

Daryaee, T. "Ethnic and Territorial Boundaries in Late Antique and Early Medieval Persia (Third to Tenth Century)." In *Borders, Barriers, and Ethnogenesis: Frontiers in Late Antiquity and the Middle Ages*, ed. F. Curta, 123–37. Turnhout: Brepols, 2005.

Debié, M. "Devenir chrétien dans l'Iran sassanide: La conversion à la lumière des récits hagiographiques." In *Le problème de la christianisation du monde antique*, ed. H. Inglebert, S. Destephen, and B. Dumézil, 329–58. Nanterre: Picard, 2010.

———. "L'Héritage de la chronique d'Eusèbe dans l'historiographie syriaque." *JCSSS* 6 (2006): 18–26.

———. "L'Héritage de l'historiographie grecque." In *L'Historiographie syriaque*, Études syriaques 6, ed. Debié, 11–31. Paris: Geuthner, 2009.

———. "Writing History as 'Histoires': The Biographical Dimension of East Syriac Historiography." In *Writing 'True Stories': Historians and Hagiographers in the Late Antique and Medieval Near East*, ed. A. Papaconstantinou, 43–75. Turnhout: Brepols, 2010.

de Blois, F. "*Naṣrānī* (Ναζωραῖος) and *ḥanīf* (ἐθνικός): Studies on the Religious Vocabulary of Christianity and of Islam." *BSOAS* 65 (2002): 1–30.

Decret, F. "Les conséquences sur le christianisme en Perse de l'affrontement des empires romain et sassanide: De Shâpûr Ier à Yazdgard Ier." *RecAug* 14 (1979): 91–152.

De Decker, D. "Sur le destinataire de la lettre au Roi des Perses (Eusèbe de Césarée, *Vit. Const.*, IV, 9–13) et la conversion de l'Arménie à la religion chrétienne." *Persica* 8 (1979): 99–116.

Dennett, D. C. *Conversion and the Poll Tax in Early Islam*. Cambridge, MA: Harvard University Press, 1950.

Devos, P. "Les martyrs persans à travers leurs actes syriaques." In *Atti del Convegno sul tema: La Persia e il mondo greco-romano*, 213–25. Rome: Accademia Nazionale dei Lincei, 1966.

———. "Sozomène et les actes syriaques de S. Syméon bar Ṣabbāʿē." *AB* 84 (1966): 443–56.

Digeser, E. D. *The Making of a Christian Empire: Lactantius and Rome*. Ithaca, NY: Cornell University Press, 2000.

Dignas, B., and E. Winter. *Rome and Persia in Late Antiquity: Neighbours and Rivals*. Cambridge: Cambridge University Press, 2007.

Dimaio, M. "The Transfer of the Remains of the Emperor Julian from Tarsus to Constantinople." *Byz* 48 (1978): 43–50.

Dodgeon, M. H., and S. N. C. Lieu, eds. *The Roman Eastern Frontier and the Persian Wars, AD 226–363: A Documentary History.* London: Routledge, 1991.

Drake, H. A. *Constantine and the Bishops: The Politics of Intolerance.* Baltimore: Johns Hopkins University Press, 2000.

———. "What Eusebius Knew: The Genesis of the *Vita Constantini*." *CP* 83 (1988): 20–38.

Drijvers, H. J. W. "The Syriac Romance of Julian: Its Function, Place of Origin and Original Language." In *VI Symposium Syriacum 1992*, OCA 247, ed. R. Lavenant, 201–14. Rome: Pontificio Istituto Orientale, 1994.

Drijvers, J. W. "Ammianus, Jovian, and the Syriac *Julian Romance*." *JLA* 4 (2011): 280–97.

———. "Ammianus Marcellinus' Image of Sasanian Society." In *Ērān ud Anērān: Studien zu den Beziehungen zwischen dem Sasanidenreich und der Mittelmeerwelt—Beiträge des Internationalen Colloquiums in Eutin, 8–9 Juni 2000,* ed. J. Wiesehöfer and P. Huyse, 45–69. Stuttgart: Franz Steiner Verlag, 2006.

———. "Ammianus Marcellinus 23.1.2–3: The Rebuilding of the Temple in Jerusalem." In *Cognitio Gestorum: The Historiographic Art of Ammianus Marcellinus,* ed. J. den Boeft, D. den Hengst, and H. C. Teitler, 19–26. Amsterdam: Royal Netherlands Academy of Arts and Sciences, 1992.

———. "The Emperor Jovian as New Constantine in the Syriac *Julian Romance*." *SP* 45 (2010): 229–33.

———. "Julian the Apostate and the City of Rome: Pagan-Christian Polemics in the Syriac *Julian Romance*." In *Syriac Polemics: Studies in Honour of Gerrit Jan Reinink,* OLA 170, ed. W. J. van Bekkum, Drijvers, and A. C. Klugkist, 1–20. Leuven: Peeters, 2007.

———. "The Syriac Julian Romance: Aspects of the Jewish-Christian Controversy in Late Antiquity." In *All Those Nations . . . Cultural Encounters within and with the Near East,* ed. H. L. J. Vanstiphout, 31–42. Groningen: Styx, 1999.

Duchesne-Guillemin, J. "Zoroastrian Religion." In *The Cambridge History of Iran,* vol. 3, pt. 2, *The Seleucid, Parthian and Sasanian Periods,* ed. E. Yarshater, 866–906. Cambridge: Cambridge University Press, 1983.

Elton, H. *Frontiers of the Roman Empire.* Bloomington: Indiana University Press, 1996.

Fiey, J.-M. "Les évêques de Nisibe au temps de Saint Éphrem." *PdO* 4 (1973): 123–35.

———. *Jalons pour une histoire de l'église en Iraq.* CSCO 310, Subsidia 36. Leuven: Peeters, 1970.

———. "Ma'in, général de Sapor II, confesseur et évêque." *Mus* 84 (1971): 437–53.

———. "Martyropolis syriaque." *Mus* 89 (1976): 5–38.

———. "Maruta de Martyropolis d'après Ibn al-Azraq (†1181)." *AB* 94 (1976): 35–45.

———. *Nisibe, métropole syriaque orientale et ses suffragants des origines à nos jours.* CSCO 388. Leuven: Peeters, 1977.

Fowden, E. K. *The Barbarian Plain: Saint Sergius between Rome and Iran.* Berkeley: University of California Press, 1999.
Fowden, G. "The Last Days of Constantine: Oppositional Versions and Their Influence." *JRS* 84 (1994): 146–70.
Frendo, D. "Constantine's Letter to Shapur II: Its Authenticity, Occasion, and Attendant Circumstances." *BAI* 15 (2001): 57–69.
———. "Sasanian Irredentism and the Foundation of Constantinople: Historical Truth and Historical Reality." *BAI* 6 (1992): 59–66.
Frye, R. N. "Minorities in the History of the Near East." In *A Green Leaf: Papers in Honour of Professor Jes P. Asmussen,* Acta Iranica 12, ed. W. Sundermann, J. Duchesne-Guillemin, and F. Vahman, 461–71. Leiden: Brill, 1988.
Gaddis, M. *There Is No Crime for Those Who Have Christ: Religious Violence in the Christian Roman Empire.* Berkeley: University of California Press, 2005.
Garsoïan, N. G. "Le rôle de l'hiérarchie chrétienne dans les rapports diplomatiques entre Byzance et les Sassanides." *RÉArm* 10 (1973): 119–38.
Gerö, S. "The See of Peter in Babylon: Western Influences on the Ecclesiology of Early Persian Christianity." In *East of Byzantium: Syria and Armenia in the Formative Period,* ed. N. G. Garsoïan, T. F. Mathews, and R. W. Thomson, 45–51. Washington DC: Dumbarton Oaks, 1982.
Ghirshman, R. *Bīchāpour II: Les mosaïques sassanides.* Paris: Geuthner, 1956.
Gignoux, P. "Church-State Relations in the Sasanian Period." In *Monarchies and Socio-religious Traditions in the Ancient Near East (Papers Read at the 31st International Congress of Human Sciences in Asia and North Africa),* ed. T. Mikasa, 72–80. Wiesbaden: Otto Harrassowitz, 1984.
———. "Problèmes de distinction et de priorité des sources." In *Prolegomena to the Sources on the History of Pre-Islamic Central Asia,* ed. J. Harmatta, 137–41. Budapest: Akadémiai Kiadó, 1979.
———. *Les quatre inscriptions du mage Kirdīr.* Leuven: Peeters, 1991.
Goodblatt, D. M. "The Poll Tax in Sasanian Babylonia: The Talmudic Evidence." *JESHO* 22 (1979): 233–95.
Gnoli, G. *The Idea of Iran: An Essay on Its Origin.* Rome: Istituto Italiano per il Medio ed Estremo Oriente, 1989.
Greatrex, G. "The Two Fifth-Century Wars between Rome and Persia." *Florilegium* 12 (1993): 1–14.
Grégoire, H. "Eusèbe n'est pas l'auteur de la *Vita Constantini* dans sa forme actuelle et Constantin ne s'est pas 'converti' en 312." *Byz* 13 (1938): 561–83.
Griffith, S. H. "Asceticism in the Church of Syria: The Hermeneutics of Early Syrian Monasticism." In *Asceticism,* ed. V. L. Wimbush and R. Valantasis, 220–45. New York: Oxford University Press, 1995.
———. "Ephraem, the Deacon of Edessa, and the Church of the Empire." In *Diakonia: Studies in Honor of Robert T. Meyer,* ed. T. Halton and J. P. Williman, 22–52. Washington DC: Catholic University of America Press, 1986.
———. "Ephraem the Syrian's Hymns 'Against Julian': Meditations on History and Imperial Power." *VChr* 41 (1987): 238–66.

———. "Images of Ephraem: The Syrian Holy Man and His Church." *Traditio* 45 (1989): 7–33.
Hage, W. "Die oströmische Staatskirche und die Christenheit des Perserreiches." *ZKG* 84 (1973): 173–87.
Harrak, A. "Trade Routes and the Christianization of the Near East." *JCSSS* 2 (2002): 46–61.
Harries, J. "'Pius Princeps': Theodosius II and Fifth-Century Constantinople." In *New Constantines: The Rhythm of Imperial Renewal in Byzantium, 4th–13th Centuries,* ed. P. Magdalino, 35–44. London: Variorum, 1994.
Heim, F. "Les figures du prince idéal au IVᵉ siècle: Du type au modèle." In *Figures de l'Ancien Testament chez les Pères,* Cahiers de Biblia Patristica 2, 277–301. Strasbourg: Centre d'analyse et de documentation patristiques, 1989.
Herman, G. "'Bury My Coffin Deep!' Zoroastrian Exhumation in Jewish and Christian Sources." In *Tiferet Leyisrael: Jubilee Volume in Honor of Israel Francus,* ed. J. Roth, M. Schmelzer, and Y. Francus, 31–59. New York: Jewish Theological Seminary of America, 2010.
———. "The Last Years of Yazdgird I and the Christians." In *Jews, Christians and Zoroastrians: Religious Dynamics in a Sasanian Context,* ed. Herman, 67–90. Piscataway, NJ: Gorgias, 2014.
———. *A Prince without a Kingdom: The Exilarch in the Sasanian Era*. Tübingen: Mohr Siebeck, 2012.
Herrmann, G. "The Rock Reliefs of Sasanian Iran." In *Mesopotamia and Iran in the Parthian and Sasanian Periods: Rejection and Revival c. 238 BC–AD 642,* ed. J. E. Curtis, 35–45. London: British Museum Press, 2000.
Herrmann, G., D. N. Mackenzie, and R. Howell. *The Sasanian Reliefs at Naqsh-i Rustam: Naqsh-i Rustam 6, The Triumph of Shapur I*. Iranische Denkmaler 13. Berlin: Dietrich Reimer Verlag, 1989.
Higgins, M. J. "Aphraates' Dates for Persian Persecution." *ByzZ* 44 (1951): 265–71.
Hollerich, M. J. "The Comparison of Moses and Constantine in Eusebius of Caesarea's *Life of Constantine*." *SP* 19 (1989): 80–85.
———. "Religion and Politics in the Writings of Eusebius: Reassessing the First 'Court Theologian.'" *CH* 59 (1990): 309–25.
Holum, K. "Pulcheria's Crusade A.D. 421–22 and the Ideology of Imperial Victory." *GRBS* 18 (1977): 153–72.
Hopkins, K. "Christian Number and Its Implications." *JECS* 6 (1998): 185–226.
Howard-Johnston, J. "The Two Great Powers in Late Antiquity: A Comparison." In *The Byzantine and Early Islamic Near East,* vol. 3, *States, Resources and Armies,* ed. A. Cameron, 157–226. Princeton, NJ: Darwin, 1995.
Hunt, E. D. "Christians and Christianity in Ammianus Marcellinus." *CQ* 35 (1985): 186–200.
Huyse, P. "Kerdir and the First Sasanians." In *Proceedings of the Third European Conference of Iranian Studies,* vol. 1, ed. N. Sims-Williams, 109–20. Wiesbaden: Otto Harrassowitz, 1998.

---. "La revendication de territoires achéménides par les Sassanides: Une réalité historique?" In *Iran, questions et connaissances: Actes du IVe congrès européen des études iraniennes, organisé par la Societas Iranologica Europaea, Paris, 6–10 septembre 1999*, vol. 1, *La période ancienne*, ed. Huyse, 297–311. Leuven: Peeters, 2002.

Isaac, B. "The Army in the Late Roman East: The Persian Wars and the Defence of the Byzantine Provinces." In *The Near East under Roman Rule: Selected Papers*, 437–69. Leiden: Brill, 1998.

Jansma, T. "Projet d'édition du 'Kᵉtābā dᵉrēš mellē' de Jean bar Penkayé." *OrSyr* 8 (1963): 87–106.

Johnson, A. P. *Ethnicity and Argumentation in Eusebius' "Praeparatio Evangelica."* Oxford: Oxford University Press, 2006.

Jones, A. H. M. *Constantine and the Conversion of Europe*. London: English Universities Press, 1948.

Jones, A. H. M., and T. C. Skeat. "Notes on the Genuineness of the Constantinian Documents in Eusebius' *Life of Constantine*." *JEH* 5 (1954): 196–200.

Jullien, C. "Contributions des *Actes des martyrs perses* à la géographie historique et à l'administration de l'empire sassanide I." In *Contributions à l'histoire et la géographie historique de l'empire sassanide*, Res Orientales 16, ed. R. Gyselen, 141–69. Bures-sur-Yvette: Groupe pour l'étude de la civilisation du Moyen-Orient, 2004.

---. "Contributions des *Actes des martyrs perses* à la géographie historique et à l'administration de l'empire sassanide II." In *Des Indo-Grecs aux Sassanides: Données pour l'histoire et la géographie historique*, Res Orientales 17, ed. R. Gyselen, 81–102. Bures-sur-Yvette: Groupe pour l'étude de la civilisation du Moyen-Orient, 2007.

---. "La minorité chrétienne 'grecque' en terre d'Iran à l'époque sassanide." In *Chrétiens en terre d'Iran I: Implantation et acculturation*, StIran 33, ed. R. Gyselen, 105–42. Leuven: Peeters, 2006.

---. "Peines et supplices dans les *Actes des martyrs persans* et droit sassanide: Nouvelles prospections." *Studia Iranica* 33 (2004): 243–69.

Jullien, C., and F. Jullien. *Apôtres des confins: Processus missionnaires chrétiens dans l'empire iranien*. Res Orientales XV. Bures-sur-Yvette: Groupe pour l'étude de la civilisation du Moyen-Orient, 2002.

---. "Aux frontières de l'iranité: 'Nāṣrāyē' et 'krīstyonē' des inscriptions du mobad Kirdīr: Enquête littéraire et historique." *Numen* 49 (2002): 282–335.

---. "Porteurs de salut: Apôtre et marchand dans l'empire iranien." *PdO* 26 (2001): 127–43.

Jullien, F. "Aux sources du monachisme oriental: Abraham de Kashkar et le développement de la légende de Mar Awgin." *RHR* 225 (2008): 37–52.

Kalmin, R. *Jewish Babylonia between Persia and Roman Palestine*. Oxford: Oxford University Press, 2006.

Kaufhold, H. "Anmerkungen zur Textüberlieferung der *Chronik* des Johannes bar Penkaye." *OC* 87 (2003): 65–79.

Kazhdan, A. "'Constantin imaginaire': Byzantine Legends of the Ninth Century about Constantine the Great." *Byz* 57 (1987): 196–250.

Kelly, G. A. J. "Adrien de Valois and the Chapter Headings in Ammianus Marcellinus." *CP* 104 (2009): 233–42.

———. *Ammianus Marcellinus: The Allusive Historian*. Cambridge: Cambridge University Press, 2008.

Kettenhofen, E. "Deportations." In *Encyclopedia Iranica* VII.3, ed. E. Yarshater, 297–312. Costa Mesa, CA: Mazda, 1994.

———. *Die römisch-persischen Kriege des 3. Jahrhunderts. n. Chr. nach der Inschrift Šāhpuhrs I. an der Ka'be-ye Zartošt (ŠKZ)*. Wiesbaden: Reichert Verlag, 1982.

Kiperwasser, R., and S. Ruzer. "To Convert a Persian and Teach Him the Holy Scriptures: A Zoroastrian Proselyte in Rabbinic and Syriac Christian Narratives." In *Jews, Christians and Zoroastrians: Religious Dynamics in a Sasanian Context,* ed. G. Herman, 101–38. Piscataway, NJ: Gorgias, 2014.

Koltun-Fromm, N. *Hermeneutics of Holiness: Ancient Jewish and Christian Notions of Sexuality and Religious Community*. Oxford: Oxford University Press, 2010.

———. "A Jewish-Christian Conversation in Fourth-Century Persian Mesopotamia." *JJS* 47 (1996): 45–63.

Kruger, P. "Jacob von Nisibis in syrischer und armenischer Überlieferung." *Mus* 81 (1968): 161–79.

Labourt, J. *Le christianisme dans l'empire perse sous la dynastie sassanide (224–632)*. Paris: Librairie Victor Lecoffre, 1904.

Lane, D. J. "Of Wars and Rumours of Peace: Apocalyptic Material in Aphrahaṭ and Šubḥalmaran." In *New Heaven and New Earth: Prophecy and the Millennium—Essays in Honour of Anthony Gelston,* ed. P. J. Harland and C. T. R. Hayward, 229–45. Leiden: Brill, 1999.

Lee, A. D. "Embassies as Evidence for the Movement of Military Intelligence between the Roman and Sasanian Empires." In *The Defence of the Roman and Byzantine East,* ed. P. Freeman and D. Kennedy, 455–61. Oxford: BAR International Editions, 1986.

———. "The Role of Hostages in Roman Diplomacy with Sasanian Persia." *Historia* 40 (1991): 366–74.

Lerouge, C. *L'Image des Parthes dans le monde gréco-romain: Du début du Ier siècle av. J.-C. jusqu'à la fin du Haut-Empire romain*. Wiesbaden: Franz Steiner Verlag, 2007.

Levenson, D. B. "The Ancient and Medieval Sources for the Emperor Julian's Attempt to Rebuild the Jerusalem Temple." *JSJ* 35 (2004): 409–60.

Lieu, J. "Accusations of Jewish Persecution in Early Christian Sources, with Particular Reference to Justin Martyr and the *Martyrdom of Polycarp*." In *Tolerance and Intolerance in Early Judaism and Christianity,* ed. G. N. Stanton and G. G. Stroumsa, 279–95. Cambridge: Cambridge University Press, 1998.

———. *Neither Jew nor Greek? Constructing Early Christianity*. London: T&T Clark, 2002.

Lieu, S. N. C. "Captives, Refugees and Exiles: A Study of Cross-Frontier Civilian Movements and Contacts between Rome and Persia from Valerian to Jovian." In *The Defence of the Roman and Byzantine East,* vol. 2, ed. P. Freeman and D. Kennedy, 475–505. Oxford: BAR International Editions, 1986.

Lightfoot, C. S. "Facts and Fiction: The Third Siege of Nisibis (A.D. 350)." *Historia* 37 (1988): 105–25.

———. "The Site of Roman Bezabde." In *Armies and Frontiers in Roman and Byzantine Anatolia,* ed. S. Mitchell, 189–204. Oxford: BAR International Editions, 1983.

Lincoln, B. *Religion, Empire, and Torture: The Case of Achaemenian Persia, with a Postscript on Abu Ghraib.* Chicago: University of Chicago Press, 2007.

———. "The Role of Religion in Achaemenian Imperialism." In *Religion and Power: Divine Kingship in the Ancient World and Beyond,* ed. N. Brisch, 221–41. Chicago: University of Chicago Press, 2008.

MacMullen, R. "Roman Bureaucratese." *Traditio* 18 (1962): 364–78.

Macomber, W. F. "The Authority of the Catholicos Patriarch of Seleucia-Ctesiphon." In *I Patriarcati orientali nel primo millennio,* OCA 181, ed. I. Žužek, 179–200. Rome: Pontificium Institutum Studiorum Orientalium, 1968.

Magdalino, P., ed. *New Constantines: The Rhythm of Imperial Renewal in Byzantium, 4th–13th Centuries.* London: Variorum, 1994.

Marcus, R. "The Armenian *Life* of Marutha of Maipherkat." *HTR* 25 (1932): 47–71.

Marôth, M. "Le siège de Nisibe en 350 après J.-Ch. d'après des sources syriennes." *AAntHung* 27 (1979): 239–45.

Matthews, J. F. "Ammianus and the Eastern Frontier in the Fourth Century: A Participant's View." In *The Defence of the Roman and Byzantine East,* ed. P. Freeman and D. Kennedy, 549–64. Oxford: BAR International Editions, 1986.

———. "Hostages, Philosophers, Pilgrims, and the Diffusion of Ideas in the Late Roman Mediterranean and Near East." In *Tradition and Innovation in Late Antiquity,* ed. F. M. Clover and R. S. Humphreys, 29–49. Madison: University of Wisconsin Press, 1989.

———. *The Roman Empire of Ammianus.* Baltimore: Johns Hopkins University Press, 1989.

McDonough, S. J. "Bishops or Bureaucrats? Christian Clergy and the State in the Middle Sasanian Period." In *Current Research in Sasanian Archaeology, Art and History: Proceedings of a Conference Held at Durham University, November 3rd and 4th, 2001,* ed. D. Kennet and P. Luft, 87–92. Oxford: BAR International Editions, 2008.

———. "Power by Negotiation: Institutional Reform in the Fifth Century Sasanian Empire." PhD diss., University of California at Los Angeles, 2005.

———. "A Second Constantine? The Sasanian King Yazdgard in Christian History and Historiography." *JLA* 1 (2008): 127–41.

Millar, F. "Emperors, Frontiers and Foreign Relations, 31 B.C. to A.D. 378." *Britannia* 13 (1982): 1–25.

———. "Ethnic Identity in the Roman Near East, AD 325–450: Language, Religion and Culture." *MedArch* 11 (1998): 159–76.

Mitchell, S. "Maximinus and the Christians in A.D. 312: A New Latin Inscription." *JRS* 78 (1988): 105–24.

Momigliano, A. "Christianity and the Decline of the Roman Empire." In *The Conflict between Paganism and Christianity in the Fourth Century*, ed. Momigliano, 1–16. Oxford: Clarendon, 1963.

Morony, M. *Iraq after the Muslim Conquest.* Princeton, NJ: Princeton University Press, 1984. Repr., Piscataway, NJ: Gorgias, 2005.

———. "Population Transfers between Sasanian Iran and the Byzantine Empire." In *La Persia e Bisanzio: Atti del Convegno internazionale (Roma, 14–18 Ottobre 2002)*, ed. G. Gnoli and A. Panaino, 161–79. Rome: Accademia Nazionale dei Lincei, 2004.

———. "Religious Communities in Late Sasanian and Early Muslim Iraq." *JESHO* 17 (1974): 113–35.

Morrison, C. E. "The Reception of the Book of Daniel in Aphrahaṭ's Fifth Demonstration, 'On Wars.'" *Hugoye* 7 (2004): 55–82.

Mosig-Walburg, K. "Die Christenverfolgung Shāpūrs II. vor dem Hintergrund des persisch-römischen Krieges." In *Inkulturation des Christentums im Sasanidenreich*, ed. A. Mustafa and J. Tubach, 171–86. Wiesbaden: Reichert Verlag, 2007.

———. "Christenverfolgung und Römerkrieg: Zu Ursachen, Ausmaß und Zielrichtung der Christenverfolgung unter Šāpūr II." *Iranistik* 7 (2005): 5–84.

———. *Römer und Perser: Vom 3. Jahrhundert bis zum Jahr 363 n. Chr.* Gutenberg: Computus Druck Satz, 2009.

———. "Zur Westpolitik Shāpūrs II." In *Iran, questions et connaissances: Actes du IVe congrès européen des études iraniennes, organisé par la Societas Iranologica Europaea, Paris, 6–10 septembre 1999*, vol. 1, *La période ancienne*, ed. P. Huyse, 329–47. Leuven: Peeters, 2002.

Moss, C. R. *The Other Christs: Imitating Jesus in Ancient Christian Ideologies of Martyrdom.* Oxford: Oxford University Press, 2010.

Munt, H. "Ibn al-Azraq, Saint Marūthā, and the Foundation of Mayyāfāriqīn (Martyropolis)." In *Writing 'True Stories': Historians and Hagiographers in the Late Antique and Medieval Near East*, ed. A. Papaconstantinou, 149–74. Turnhout: Brepols, 2010.

Neri, V. "Ammianus' Definition of Christianity as *absoluta et simplex religio*." In *Cognitio Gestorum: The Historiographic Art of Ammianus Marcellinus*, ed. J. den Boeft, D. den Hengst, and H. C. Teitler, 59–65. Amsterdam: Royal Netherlands Academy of Arts and Sciences, 1992.

Neusner, J. *Aphrahaṭ and Judaism: The Christian-Jewish Argument in Fourth-Century Iran.* Leiden: Brill, 1971.

———. "Babylonian Jewry and Shapur II's Persecution of Christianity from 339 to 379 A.D." *HUCA* 43 (1975): 77–102.

Nongbri, B. *Before Religion: A History of a Modern Concept.* New Haven: Yale University Press, 2013.

Noret, J. "La vie grecque ancienne de S. Maruta de Mayferqat." *AB* 91 (1973): 77–103.

Odahl, C. M. *Constantine and the Christian Empire.* London: Routledge, 2004.

Panaino, A. "Astral Characters of Kingship in the Sasanian and Byzantine Worlds." In *La Persia e Bisanzio: Atti del Convegno internazionale (Roma, 14–18 Ottobre 2002)*, ed. G. Gnoli and Panaino, 555–94. Rome: Accademia Nazionale dei Lincei, 2004.

Payne, R. E. "Christianity and Iranian Society in Late Antiquity, ca. 500–700 C.E." PhD diss., Princeton University, 2010.

———. "The Emergence of Martyrs' Shrines in Late Antique Iran: Conflict, Consensus and Communal Institutions." In *An Age of Saints? Power, Conflict and Dissent in Early Medieval Christianity*, ed. P. Sarris, M. Dal Santo, and P. Booth, 89–113. Leiden: Brill, 2011.

———. "Monks, Dinars and Date Palms: Hagiographical Production and the Expansion of Monastic Institutions in the Early Islamic Persian Gulf." *AAE* 22 (2011): 97–111.

———. *A State of Mixture: Christians, Zoroastrians, and Iranian Political Culture in Late Antiquity*. Berkeley: University of California Press, 2015.

Peeters, P. "La légende de Saint Jacques de Nisibe." *AB* 38 (1920): 285–373.

Penn, M. P. "Monks, Manuscripts, and Muslims: Syriac Textual Changes in Reaction to the Rise of Islam." *Hugoye* 12 (2009): 235–57.

Pierre, M.-J. "Thèmes de la controverse d'Aphraate avec les tendances judaïsantes de son église." In *Chrétiens en terre d'Iran II: Controverses des chrétiens dans l'Iran sassanide*, StIran 36, ed. C. Jullien, 115–28. Leuven: Peeters, 2008.

Pigulevskaja, N. *Les villes de l'état iranien aux époques parthe et sassanide: Contribution à l'histoire sociale de la basse antiquité*. Paris: Mouton, 1963.

Poggi, V. "Costantino e la chiesa di Persia." In *Costantino il Grande nell'età bizantina: Atti del Convegno internazionale di studio, Ravenna, 5–8 aprile 2001* (Bizantinistica V), ed. G. Bonamente and A. Carile, 61–95. Spoleto: Fondazione Centro italiano di studi sull'alto medioevo, 2003.

Pohl, W., C. Gantner, and R. Payne, eds. *Visions of Community in the Post-Roman World: The West, Byzantium and the Islamic World, 300–1100*. Burlington, VT: Ashgate, 2012.

Pourshariati, P. *Decline and Fall of the Sasanian Empire: The Sasanian-Parthian Confederacy and the Arab Conquest of Iran*. New York: I. B. Tauris, 2008.

Rapp, C. "Comparison, Paradigm and the Case of Moses in Panegyric and Hagiography." In *The Propaganda of Power: The Role of Panegyric in Late Antiquity*, ed. M. Whitby, 277–98. Leiden: Brill, 1998.

———. "Imperial Ideology in the Making: Eusebius of Caesarea on Constantine as 'Bishop.'" *JTS* 49 (1998): 685–95.

Reiner, E. "The Reddling of Valerian." *CQ* 56 (2006): 325–29.

Rist, J. "Die Verfolgung der Christen im spätantiken Sasanidenreich: Ursachen, Verlauf und Folgen." *OC* 80 (1996): 17–42.

Rives, J. B. "The Decree of Decius and the Religion of Empire." *JRS* 89 (1999): 135–54.

Robinson, C. *Empire and Elites after the Muslim Conquest: The Transformation of Northern Mesopotamia*. Cambridge: Cambridge University Press, 2000.

———. "Ibn al-Azraq, His *Ta'rīkh Mayyāfāriqīn*, and Early Islam." *JRAS* 6 (1996): 7–27.

Rubin, Z. "Diplomacy and War in the Relations between Byzantium and the Sassanids in the Fifth Century AD." In *The Defence of the Roman and Byzantine East*, ed. P. Freeman and D. Kennedy, 677–95. Oxford: BAR International Editions, 1986.

———. "The Reforms of Khusro Anushirwan." In *The Byzantine and Early Islamic Near East*, vol. 3, *States, Resources and Armies*, ed. A. Cameron, 227–97. Princeton, NJ: Darwin, 1995.

Russell, P. S. "Nisibis as the Background to the Life of Ephrem the Syrian." *Hugoye* 8 (2005): 179–235.

Saint-Laurent, J.-N. M. *Missionary Stories and the Formation of the Syriac Churches*. Berkeley: University of California Press, 2015.

Sako, L. *Le rôle de la hiérarchie syriaque orientale dans les rapports diplomatiques entre la Perse et Byzance aux Ve–VIIe siècles*. Paris: Lille–Atelier national de reproduction des thèses, 1986.

Sansterre, J.-M. "Eusèbe de Césarée et la naissance de la théorie 'césaropapiste.'" *Byz* 42 (1972): 131–95, 532–94.

Scher, A. "Notice sur la vie et les œuvres de Yoḥannan bar Penkayè." *JA* 10 (1907): 161–78.

Schneider, R. M. "Orientalism in Late Antiquity: The Oriental in Imperialism and Christian Imagery." In *Ērān ud Anērān: Studien zu den Beziehungen zwischen dem Sasanidenreich und der Mittelmeerwelt—Beiträge des Internationalen Colloquiums in Eutin, 8–9 Juni 2000*, ed. J. Wiesehöfer and P. Huyse, 241–78. Stuttgart: Franz Steiner Verlag, 2006.

Schott, J. M. *Christianity, Empire, and the Making of Religion in Late Antiquity*. Philadelphia: University of Pennsylvania Press, 2008.

Schrier, O. J. "Syriac Evidence for the Roman-Persian War of 421–422." *GRBS* 33 (1992): 75–86.

Schwaigert, W. "Das Christentum in Ḥūzistān im Rahmen der frühen Kirchengeschichte Persiens bis zur Synode von Seleukeia-Ktesiphon im Jahre 410." PhD diss., Philipps-Universität Marburg, 1989.

Schwartz, D. L. "Religious Violence and Eschatology in the *Syriac Julian Romance*." *JECS* 19 (2011): 565–87.

Scott, R. "The Image of Constantine in Malalas and Theophanes." In *New Constantines: The Rhythm of Imperial Renewal in Byzantium, 4th–13th Centuries*, ed. P. Magdalino, 57–71. London: Variorum, 1994.

Seager, R. "Perceptions of Eastern Frontier Policy in Ammianus, Libanius, and Julian (337–363)." *CQ* 47 (1997): 253–68.

Segal, J. B. *Edessa: The Blessed City*. Oxford: Clarendon, 1970.

Seston, W. "Constantine as a 'Bishop.'" *JRS* 37 (1947): 127–31.

Shahbazi, A. S. "Early Sasanians' Claim to Achaemenid Heritage." *IJAIS* 1 (2001): 61–73.

———. "The Horse that Killed Yazdagerd 'the Sinner.'" In *Paitimāna: Essays in Iranian, Indo-European, and Indian Studies in Honor of Hans-Peter Schmidt*, ed. S. Adhami, 355–62. Costa Mesa, CA: Mazda, 2003.

Shaked, S. "Zoroastrian Polemics against Jews in the Sasanian and Early Islamic Period." In *Irano-Judaica II: Studies Relating to Jewish Contacts with Persian Culture throughout the Ages*, ed. Shaked and A. Netzer, 85–104. Jerusalem: Ben-Zvi Institute, 1990.

Shayegan, M. R. "Approaches to the Study of Sasanian History." In *Paitimāna: Essays in Iranian, Indo-European, and Indian Studies in Honor of Hans-Peter Schmidt*, ed. S. Adhami, 363–84. Costa Mesa, CA: Mazda, 2003.

———. "On the Rationale behind the Roman Wars of Šābuhr II the Great." *BAI* 18 (2004): 111–33.

Smith, K. "Constantine and Judah the Maccabee: History and Memory in the *Acts of the Persian Martyrs*." *JCSSS* 12 (2012): 16–33.

———. "The Synod of Mar Dādišoʻ—424 CE." In *CCCOGD*, vol. 5, ed. A. Melloni and F. Lauritzen. Turnhout: Brepols, forthcoming.

Sprengling, M. "Kartir, Founder of Sasanian Zoroastrianism." *AJSL* 57 (1940): 197–228.

Stark, R. *The Rise of Christianity: A Sociologist Reconsiders History*. Princeton, NJ: Princeton University Press, 1996.

Strong, J. D. "Candida: An Ante-Nicene Martyr in Persia." *JECS* 23 (2015): 389–412.

Teitler, H. C. "Ammianus and Constantius: Image and Reality." In *Cognitio Gestorum: The Historiographic Art of Ammianus Marcellinus*, ed. J. den Boeft, D. den Hengst, and Teitler, 117–22. Amsterdam: Royal Netherlands Academy of Arts and Sciences, 1992.

Teixidor, J. "Conséquences politiques et culturelles de la victoire sassanide à Nisibe." In *Les relations internationales: Actes du Colloque de Strasbourg*, ed. E. Frézouls and A. Jacquemin, 499–510. Paris: De Boccard, 1995.

Ter-Petrossian, L. "L'Attribution du receuil des passions perses à Maroutha de Maypherqat." *AB* 97 (1979): 129–30.

Thompson, E. A. *The Huns*. Oxford: Oxford University Press, 1996.

Turcan, R. "L'Abandon de Nisibe et l'opinion publique (363 ap. J.-C.)." In *Mélanges d'archéologie et d'histoire offerts à André Piganiol*, ed. R. Chevallier, 875–90. Paris: Service d'edition et de vente des publications de l'Education nationale, 1966.

Utas, B. "Byzantium Seen from Sasanian Iran." In *Aspects of Late Antiquity and Early Byzantium*, ed. L. Rydén and J. O. Rosenqvist, 21–30. Uppsala: Swedish Research Institute in Istanbul, 1993.

Van Dam, R. *Remembering Constantine at the Milvian Bridge*. Cambridge: Cambridge University Press, 2014.

———. *The Roman Revolution of Constantine*. Cambridge: Cambridge University Press, 2007.

Van Rompay, L. "Impetuous Martyrs? The Situation of the Persian Christians in the Last Years of Yazdgard I (419–420)." In *Martyrium in Multidisciplinary*

Perspective: Memorial Louis Reekmans, ed. M. Lamberigts and P. Van Deun, 363–75. Leuven: Peeters, 1995.

Vivian, M. R. "Eusebius and Constantine's Letter to Shapur: Its Place in the *Vita Constantini.*" *SP* 29 (1997): 164–69.

———. "A Letter to Shapur: The Effect of Constantine's Conversion on Roman-Persian Relations." PhD diss., University of California at Santa Barbara, 1987.

Walker, J. T. *The Legend of Mar Qardagh: Narrative and Christian Heroism in Late Antique Iraq.* Berkeley: University of California Press, 2006.

———. "A Saint and His Biographer in Late Antique Iraq: The *History of St. George of Izla* (†614) by Babai the Great." In *Writing 'True Stories': Historians and Hagiographers in the Late Antique and Medieval Near East,* ed. A. Papaconstantinou, 31–41. Turnhout: Brepols, 2010.

Warmington, B. H. "Ammianus Marcellinus and the Lies of Metrodorus." *CQ* 31 (1981): 464–68.

———. "The Sources of Some Constantinian Documents in Eusebius' *Ecclesiastical History* and *Life of Constantine.*" *SP* 18 (1986): 93–98.

Watts, E. J. *The Final Pagan Generation.* Berkeley: University of California Press, 2015.

Weisweiler, J. "Christianity in War: Ammianus on Power and Religion in Constantius' Persian War." In *The Power of Religion in Late Antiquity,* ed. A. Cain and N. Lenski, 383–96. Burlington, VT: Ashgate, 2009.

Westphal, G. "Untersuchungen über die Quellen und die Glaubwürdigkeit der Patriarchenchroniken des Mārī ibn Sulaimān, ʿAmr ibn Matai und Ṣalība ibn Joḥannān." PhD diss., Universität Strassburg, 1901.

Whitby, M. *Rome at War: AD 293–696.* Oxford: Osprey, 2002.

Wiesehöfer, J. "'Geteilte Loyalitäten': Religiöse Minderheiten des 3. und 4. Jahrhunderts n. Chr. im Spannungsfeld zwischen Rom und dem sasanidischen Iran." *Klio* 75 (1993): 362–82.

———. *Iraniens, grecs et romains.* StIran 32. Leuven: Peeters, 2005.

Wiessner, G. "Die Behnam-Legende." In *Synkretismusforschung: Theorie und Praxis,* ed. Wiessner, 119–33. Wiesbaden: Otto Harrassowitz, 1978.

———. *Untersuchungen zur syrischen Literaturgeschichte I: Zur Märtyrerüberlieferung aus der Christenverfolgung Schapurs II.* Göttingen: Vandenhoeck und Ruprecht, 1967.

———. "Zum Problem der zeitlichen und örtlichen Festlegung der erhaltenen syropersischen Märtyrerakten: Das Pusai-Martyrium." In *Paul de Lagarde und die syrische Kirchengeschichte,* 231–51. Göttingen: Lagarde Haus, 1968.

Wigram, W. *An Introduction to the History of the Assyrian Church, or The Church of the Sassanid Persian Empire, 100–640 A.D.* London: Society for Promoting Christian Knowledge, 1910.

Wood, P. *The Chronicle of Seert: Christian Historical Imagination in Late Antique Iraq.* Oxford: Oxford University Press, 2013.

Wright, W. *Catalogue of Syriac Manuscripts in the British Museum, Acquired since the Year 1838.* 3 vols. London, 1870–72.

Wright, W., and N. McLean. *The Ecclesiastical History of Eusebius in Syriac.* Cambridge: Cambridge University Press, 1898.

Yohannan, A. *The Death of a Nation, or The Ever Persecuted Nestorians or Assyrian Christians.* New York: Knickerbocker, 1916.

Younansardaroud, H. "Die Legende von Mar Behnam." In *Syriaca: Zur Geschichte, Theologie, Liturgie und Gegenwartslage der syrischen Kirchen, 2. Deutsches Syrologen-Symposium, Juli 2000, Wittenberg,* ed. M. Tamcke, 185–96. Hamburg: LIT Verlag, 2002.

Younansardaroud, H., and M. Novák. "Mar Behnam, Sohn des Sanherib von Nimrud: Tradition und Rezeption einer assyrischen Gestalt im iraqischen Christentum und die Frage nach den Fortleben der Assyrer." *AF* 29 (2002): 166–94.

INDEX

Aba, Mar: *Life* of, 133
'Abda (bishop of Hormizd-Ardashir), martyrdom of, 148–49. See also *Martyrdom of 'Abda*
'Abdishoʻ (deacon): martyrdom of, 138, 190; ministry of, 189–90; survival of slaughter, 137–38, 189; Tomb of, 138–39, 190
'Abdishoʻ (hermit), 174
'Abdishoʻ bar Brikha, 147n75
Abgar legend, 89n94
Acacius (bishop of Amida), at Synod of Yahbalaha, 128
Achaemenids: ethnography of, 75, 76; Greco-Roman literary tropes concerning, 75; homage paid to, 18n8; Sasanian emulation of, 46n3, 71
Acts of the Persian Martyrs, 7; Aphrahaṭ's *Demonstrations* and, 104n16; authorship of, 147; "Caesar" in, 155; Constantine in, 12–13, 154–80; fear in, 126n6, 184n3; historiographical richness of, 100; languages of, 99n1; origins of, 126n5; places of composition, 159; Roman captives in, 126, 142, 152; Sasanian geography in, 142n58; scholarship on, 99–100; Shapur in, 87, 102, 173; sorcerers in, 191; torture in, 193n8; views of West in, 172; Zoroastrianism in, 140n48. See also specific martyrdom narratives
Adarpar (mobed), 187–89; Dawsa's defiance of, 188–89

Algaze, Guillermo, 184n1
al-Qaeda, anti-Christian violence by, 3
Amida, fall to Shapur, 135
Ammianus Marcellinus, 10; knowledge of Ephrem, 80; negativity toward Constantius, 50n15
—*Res Gestae*: barbarization of enemies, 86n80; Christianity in, 72, 75n34, 76–77, 80, 81; Constantine's Letter in, 19; Constantius in, 50n15, 65n1, 76; Eustathius in, 74; on evacuees from Nisibis, 85n77; fall of Amida in, 135; and *History of Blessed Simeon bar Ṣabbaʻe*, 142; on Julian's death, 50n16; on Maiozamalcha, 70n15; on Mesopotamian bishops, 176; Metrodorus in, 51–52; military history in, 76; on Nisibis, 68, 69, 77, 86n77; Persian culture in, 75; Persian hostages in, 163n28; Roman-Persian war in, 51, 73–81; Shapur in, 23, 46; siege of Bezabde in, 78–80, 127, 184, 185; on Temple of Solomon, 70n15; territorial losses in, 142; Theodosian audience of, 76n38; use of Cassius Dio, 76n37
Anahid (temple of the goddess of the Persians), martyrs' heads at, 195
Antioch, Christian population of, 131
antiquity, late: Christian identity in, 180; periodization of, 7–9; religious groups of, 180; religious thought in, 177n66; state religion in, 46n3
Antoninus (merchant), betrayal of Romans, 77n44

Aphrahaṭ: baptismal name of, 104n17; identity of, 104
—*Demonstrations*, 103–9; *Acts of the Persian Martyrs* and, 104n16; apocalyptic aspects of, 107–8; biblical exegesis of, 11, 105–9, 123; Book of Daniel in, 107–8; date of composition, 104; as historical testimony, 104–5; Jewish-Christian relations in, 105–6, 108; manuscript witnesses to, 104; "On the Grape Cluster," 106; "On Persecution," 104–5, 107; "On Wars," 104, 107, 108; Persian Christians in, 123; place of composition, 104; purpose of, 105; on Roman Empire, 108; Shapur's persecutions in, 104–7, 109n34
Arimhar (Zoroastrian priest), 91–92
Armenia, role in Roman-Persian relations, 29n40
Assyrian Empire, divine punishment of, 42
Athanassiadi-Fowden, Polymnia, 72
Aurelia Ammounis, certification of sacrifice, 122
Awgin, Mar, 192

Bahram V (Sasanian king), persecutions of, 69n14, 149, 150
Barhebraeus, *Ecclesiastical Chronicle* of, 171n52
Barnes, Timothy D., 6; on Ammianus, 80; on barbarian conquests, 26n30; on Constantine's Persian campaign, 10n29; on Constantine's writings, 41; on Letter to Shapur, 25–26, 28n39, 52; on Nisibis, 66n4
Barshebya, Abbot: martyrdom of, 191–2, 194–95; sorcery accusations against, 193
Becker, Adam, 26n33, 46n3, 116, 177n65; on Gregory Pirangushnasp, 171–72
Benjamin (ascetic), 160n20
Beth Huzaye, Roman captives at, 135–37, 171n52. *See also* Masabdan
Beth Lapaṭ, clerics of, 140, 142
Beth Zabdai (Mesopotamian fortress): bishop of, 79–80, 135–36, 184; fall to Shapur, 78–80, 127, 135–36, 184–6; Roman captives of, 127, 135–39, 145, 186–90; site of, 184n1

Bezabde. *See* Beth Zabdai; *Martyrdom of the Captives of Beth Zabdai*; Zabdaeus
Bineses (Persian noble), 88–89
Bishapur (Fars): deportees from, 144; mosaics of, 131; Roman construction of, 130–31
bishops: and Constantine's Persian campaign, 10n29, 47–49, 60; embassy to Yazdgard, 128; as envoys, 146n71; spiritual authority of, 116–17
bishops, Eastern, 106; of Bezabde, 79–80, 135–36, 184; defense of Nisibis, 72, 84, 86; of Fars, 192; hierarchy of, 141–42; martyred, 140; of Mesopotamia, 80; sources for, 176; and tax collection, 116, 118
Blockley, Roger, 10n29, 80; on Letter to Shapur, 25
Blum, Georg, 29
Bowersock, Glen, 72
Boyarin, Daniel, 133
British Library: Add. MS **12,174**, 158n11; Add. MS **12,150**, 27, 126n5
Brock, Sebastian, 26–27, 53n24, 134; on Aphrahaṭ, 108; edition of *History of the Holy Mar Ma'in*, 156, 158, 159n14, 161; on Ephrem, 81n61; on John of Nikiu, 164n31; on Persian hostages, 163n28; on Simeon's acts, 158n11
Browning, Robert: on Julian, 71
Brubaker, Rogers, 178, 180
Burgess, Richard, 48n11; on Nisibis, 66n4
Busan (Mesopotamian fortress): Christian virgins of, 78; fall of, 77–78

Cameron, Averil, 22, 31, 34; on Eusebius, 48n11, 63
Canepa, Matthew, 131
captives, Roman: in *Acts of the Persian Martyrs*, 126, 142, 152; at Beth Huzaye, 135–37, 171n52; of Bezabde, 127, 135–39, 185–90; construction of Bishapur, 130–31; cult of, 153; descendants of, 152; ethnicities of, 134; in *History of Blessed Simeon bar Ṣabba'e*, 139–42, 153, 185; intermarriage with Persians, 144; martyrdom at Karka d-Ledan, 139–40; martyrdom at Masabdan, 105, 109–10,

135–39, 142, 151–53, 155, 174, 184, 189; in martyrdom narratives, 127–28, 145, 155, 192; in *Martyrdom of Pusai-Qarugbed*, 143–45; in *Martyrdom of the Captives of Beth Zabdai*, 105, 109–10, 135–39, 142, 151–53, 155, 174, 184; from Mesopotamia, 126, 135–39, 167, 185, 186–90; from Nisibis, 84–85, 93n205, 95; Persian Christians as, 12, 124, 127–29; relics of, 138; in Sasanian Empire, 126–29; Shapur's, 12, 124; skills of, 152; social status of, 151; soldiers, 130

Cassius Dio, Ammianus's use of, 76n37

Castelli, Elizabeth, 39n78; on historicity, 3; on Lactanius, 40–41

catholicos (title), 5, 116, 118, 128n13, 141

Chabot, J.-B., 166n39

Chauvot, Alain, 71n19

Christianity, late ancient: in Ammianus, 72, 75n34, 76–77, 80–81; Constantine's use of, 62n60; effect on Roman foreign relations, 19n12, 25–26; imperial, 25–27, 34n57; interweaving with Roman Empire, 26; Jewish criticism of, 106; political allegiances of, 177; populations of, 131n23; as Roman, 4, 11, 33–34, 129, 152; and Roman-Persian war, 72, 76; social ascent of, 8; Syriac sources for, 7; universal mission of, 25; value for Sasanian Empire, 35; Zoroastrian confusion over, 133

Christianization, Roman: effect on foreign policy, 25–26; effect on Persian Christians, 26; triumphalist narratives of, 8. *See also* Constantine: Christian emperorship

Christianization, Sasanian, 32

Christians: Constantine's protection of, 21–27, 33, 154, 157–59; Constantine's reassurance of, 43; effect of sacrifice decree on, 121–22; of India, 132n25; Marcionites and, 110, 133

Christians, Eastern: Assyrian, 4; effect of Constantine's conversion on, 4–6, 9–13; persecution of, 125–26; relationship with Western Christians, 125, 128, 137, 175

Christians, Iraqi: Chaldean, 4n15; Islamic extremist violence against, 3–4; protection payments for, 1, 2

Christians, Mesopotamian, 10, 72, 135; abandonment of God, 86–87, 94; captives, 126, 135–39, 167, 186–90; deportation from Nisibis, 84–85, 93n205, 95; during Roman-Persian war, 69, 78–81; Shapur's treatment of, 78–79, 87, 93n105

Christians, Persian: allegiance to Western Christians, 112–13, 116; ambivalence about Rome, 172; bilingual, 134n29; as clients of Rome, 25, 34, 155; Constantine's knowledge of, 32; Constantine's Letter to Shapur and, 19–22, 24–25, 34–36, 38, 53–54; Constantine's protection of, 125, 160, 162–69, 172; effect of Constantine's conversion on, 9–10; effect of Roman Christianization on, 26; effect of Valerian's death on, 38; as enemies of state, 6, 53, 111–13, 178; ethnicities of, 134n29; Eusebius's writings and, 27; flight from Persia, 149; hagiography of, 12; historical memory of, 177; histories by, 111; in *History of Blessed Simeon bar Ṣabbaʿe*, 111; in imperial histories, 70; Islamic taxation of, 119; Judaism and, 105–6; in *Julian Romance*, 69; loyalty to Persian state, 117; Maccabees and, 123; in *Martyrdom of Pusai-Qarugbed*, 153; martyrs, 44, 54–55; occupations of, 12, 124; Persian identity among, 152–53; refugees from persecution, 38–39; return to Roman Empire, 12; as Roman captives, 12, 124, 127–29; *Romanitas* of, 11, 33–34, 129, 151–52; and Roman-Persian war, 49, 63; scholarship on, 6n23; separate judicial system for, 119; Shapur's authority over, 25, 116; of sixth century, 152; soldiers, 113n49; sorcery charges against, 191; sources for, 123, 176–77; taxation of, 112–13, 116–23, 180; terminology for, 132–35; treachery accusations against, 160n18; understanding of Constantine, 157–59; use of Roman martyrdom narratives, 12; view of Shapur, 106–7; under Yazdgard, 69n14, 146–47, 150;

Christians, Persian *(continued)*
    under Zoroastrian rule, 26, 151n90. *See also* martyrdom; persecution
Christians, Western: East Syriac sources on, 171; persecution of, 121–22, 125–26; relationship with Eastern Christians, 125, 128, 137, 175; in Syriac martyrdom narratives, 49, 112–13, 116
Chronicle of Seert, 171n52; Constantine's death in, 170; deportations in, 131; Valerian in, 38
Chronicle of Zuqnin, taxation in, 120
Church of the East: episcopal hierarchy in, 141; founding of, 74n32, 128, 146; Roman bishops at, 146. *See also* bishops, Eastern; Christians, Eastern
church-state relations: Constantine's, 63; of fourth century, 29n42
conflict, ethnic rhetoric of, 178
Constantine (emperor of Rome), 4
—adjudication of disputes, 17
—Byzantine panegyrists on, 154
—Christian emperorship: anti-Arianism of, 165; awareness of martyrs, 22n15; as bishop, 34, 62, 154; as "caesaropapist," 34n57; church and empire under, 63; conversion of barbarians, 61n56; divine kingship of, 20–21; ecclesiastical building program, 8; piety of, 59; political use of, 62n60; protection of all Christians, 21–27, 33, 154, 157–59; protection of Persian Christians, 125, 160, 162–69, 172; religious mission of, 8, 34; as second Moses, 49, 59–64
—connection with Shapur II, 7–8, 35, 177–78; praise for, 24; presents to, 35
—conversion: baptism following, 49n11, 55, 57–59, 90, 164–65; changes following, 33; effect on Christian identity, 179–80; effect on Eastern Christians, 4–6, 9–13; effect on Sasanian Empire, 8; Persian unease over, 112n44; providence of God in, 43; Shapur and, 177–78
—court of, 18, 29
—decree to Eastern provincials, 31, 32
—financial reforms of, 17
—foreign homage to, 18–19
—foreign policy of, 28
—as ideal emperor, 154–55
—in *Acts of the Persian Martyrs*, 12–13, 154–80
—in *History of the Holy Mar Ma'in*, 156–60, 164, 168, 174
—John Malalas on, 164
—last years and death: aftermath of, 65; comet foretelling, 59; death of, 45, 58, 64; Michael I Rabo on, 167–68; at Nicomedia, 57–58, 166–67; persecution following, 125, 170–71; sources for, 10; successors, 65n1; Theophanes on, 167–68; tomb, 47; understanding of, 176
—legacy of, 176
—Letter to Shapur, 145, 176; as apology for oppression, 38; authenticity of, 20, 26–32; circulation of, 31; completeness of, 22; composition of, 30n45; confession of faith in, 22; contents of, 22–25; courteousness of, 28n39; date of, 19n9, 28–30; divine justice in, 34–37; divine kingship in, 21, 35–36; divine rhetoric in, 23–25; divine victories in, 23–24; effect on Shapur, 30; English translation of, 181–83; Greek translation of, 9n28, 32; healing tropes in, 23; in *History of the Holy Mar Ma'in*, 159, 162–64, 168; influence of, 27; laudatory tone of, 30; in Michael's *Chronicle*, 166–67; military victories in, 35; persecution and, 20–21, 34–36, 45, 54, 56–57; Persian Christians and, 19–22, 24–25, 34–36, 38, 53–54; pragmatism in, 23; praise for Shapur, 24; purpose of, 20; reassessment of, 32–44; reception history of, 9; recipient of, 28–30; as reconceptualization of Roman history, 45; recontextualization of, 20; religiosity of, 28; repudiation of paganism, 45; restoration of order in, 43; rewriting of pagan past, 34; rhetorical force of, 55; role in Roman-Persian relations, 28, 52; as source, 30–32; sources for, 19, 27; Sozomen on, 36n63, 53–56, 145; as text, 30–32; Theophanes the Confessor on, 165; translations of, 9n28, 19, 32, 181–83; transmission history of, 20; tyrannical emperors in, 23; Valerian in, 20, 35–37, 40

—military campaigns: barbarian conquests, 18, 61n56; with Diocletian, 46; in Letter to Shapur, 35; against Licinius, 60; Milvian Bridge, 60, 177; against Persians (planned), 10, 30, 45–48, 51–53, 57–61, 66n4, 164–68; traveling church tent for, 48–49, 59–62; victories, 56
—treaty with Goths, 61n56
—use of Latin, 21n13, 32
—"Western" versus "Eastern" accounts of, 169–70, 172
—modern interpretations of, 176–77
—opinions: on Christian Rome, 43; on deaths of persecutors, 39–43; on providence of God, 43; on Shapur I, 88
—*Oration to the Assembly of the Saints*, 41–42, 45; authenticity of, 41n86; borrowing from Lactantius, 42; divine punishment in, 42; Moses in, 62; persecution in, 42
—Persian embassy to, 19, 48, 55, 59
—philanthropy of, 17
—residence in Antioch, 58
—and Roman-Sasanian conflict, 9
—Sasanian tribute to, 18n5, 162
—self-conception of, 62
—Syriac-speakers' understanding of, 157–59
—as transformative figure, 176
Constantius II (emperor of Rome): Arianism of, 76n38; Christianity of, 76; Christian writers on, 65n1; correspondence with Shapur, 19, 23, 29n39, 46, 75, 101; death of, 50; embassy to Shapur, 74, 157–59, 163, 168–69; fortification of Amida, 135; hold on frontier, 73; Julian's praise of, 70–73, 76–77; Persian campaign of, 45; relations with Julian, 49–50, 71; Shapur's vision of, 81, 83–84
Corcoran, Simon, 17n2
Council of Chalcedon (451), East-West theologies following, 171
Craugasius of Nisibis, 77–78
Ctesiphon, Julian's siege of, 50. *See also* Seleucia-Ctesiphon

Dadisho' (archbishop of Seleucia-Ctesiphon), 128n13

Darius, homage paid to, 18n8
Dasqarta, in *Martyrdom of the Captives of Beth Zabdai*, 186
Dawsa (bishop of Bezabde), 136–38, 186; Adarpar's accusation of, 187; defiance of Adarpar, 188–89; martyrdom of, 137, 185, 189; Romanness of, 152
Debié, Muriel, 27n35, 100; on *naṣraye*, 135n32
Decius (emperor of Rome): edict on sacrifices, 121–22; Jews under, 121n72
De Decker, Daniel, 28n39
deportation: from Bishapur, 144; economic purpose of, 145; from Nisibis, 84–85, 93n205, 95; by Sasanians, 130–31; spread of Christianity through, 130. *See also* captives, Roman
Devos, Paul, 101
Digeser, Elizabeth, 42n87
Dignas, Beate, 5
Diocletian (emperor of Rome): divine punishment of, 42; persecution of Christians, 38, 53n24; Persian campaign of, 46
Drake, Harold, 29n43, 41; on Constantine's *Oration*, 41n86; on Eusebius, 62n60; on imperial legitimacy, 62
Drijvers, Han J. W., 90–92; on Eusebius of Rome, 89n94; on occupation of Nisibis, 93n104
Drijvers, Jan Willem, 52, 75; on *Julian Romance*, 90n95
Duchesne-Guillemin, Jacques, 6

elephants, Persian, 68, 84, 86, 94
emperors, Roman: association with divinity, 62; Christian, 75n34; correspondence of, 19; persecution of Christians, 35–36; tyrannical, 23
emperorship, Christian, 63n62; ideal, 154–55
empires, procession of, 108
enemies, unnamed: in rhetoric, 35n61
Ephrem the Syrian, 123; on Christian martyrs, 80–81; eschatology of, 77; exile of, 85; on fall of Nisibis, 67–69, 77, 85–89; on Julian, 10, 69; on Mesopotamian bishops, 80, 176; on Roman-

Ephrem the Syrian *(continued)*
   Persian war, 77; at sieges of Nisibis, 82; sources for Nisibis, 81n59; Syriac hymns, 10; Syriac *Lives* of, 81–82
—*Hymns against Julian*, 67, 87–88; composition of, 69, 85; divine defense of Nisibis in, 86, 88; John bar Penkaye's use of, 93n105; on Julian's corpse, 89; Roman Mesopotamia in, 85; Shapur in, 85–86, 94
—*Hymns on Nisibis*, 67, 85; composition of, 69
Ērānšahr, Sasanian concept of, 152
Eunapius, *Lives of the Sophists*, 74
Eusebius of Caesarea: and beginning of imperial Christianity, 25–27; on Christian emperors, 154n1; on Christian Rome, 43; on Constantine as Moses, 49; on Constantine's baptism, 58; on Constantine's *Oration*, 41; on Constantine's Persian campaign, 45–47, 58; on Constantine's piety, 59; continuators of, 57; on Decian persecution, 122; effect on history of Christianity, 26n33, 27; effect on Persian Christians, 27; influence on Syriac historiography, 27; on providence of God, 43; Syriac audience of, 27, 100, 126n25; Theodoret's use of, 56
—*Church History*, 26; Milvian Bridge victory in, 60; in Syriac, 27, 126n25
—*Life of Constantine*, 9, 17–19, 26; authorship of, 31n46; barbarian conquests in, 18; Christian kingship in, 62–63; Christian providence in, 63; Constantine as Moses in, 60–61; Constantine's baptism in, 59; Constantine's court in, 18; Constantine's philanthropy in, 17; Constantinian documents in, 29–31; foreign embassies in, 18–19; as hagiography, 32; and *History of the Holy Mar Ma'in*, 161; lacunae in, 47–49, 58–60; Letter to Shapur in, 19–25, 27–32, 34–37, 159, 165n37, 167n40, 181–83; pagan sacrifice in, 24n27; sources of, 22, 31
—*On the Martyrs of Palestine*, 27, 126n5
—*On Theophany*, 27

Eusebius of Nicomedia: baptism of Constantine, 49n11, 55, 58n41, 90, 165; education of Julian, 90; exile of, 55
Eusebius of Rome, 90; in *Julian Romance*, 91
Eustathius, in embassy to Shapur, 74
execution methods, Sasanian, 193n8
exilarchs, Persian: collection of taxes, 118

Festus, on Constantine's Persian preparations, 59
Fiey, Jean-Marie, 156
fire cult, Persian, 87, 148–49, 175
Forty Martyrs of Sebaste, 194n10
Fowden, Garth: on Constantine's Persian campaign, 48, 51, 167; on Eusebius's *Life of Constantine*, 47; on John Malalas, 164; on Rufinus, 57n40; on Socrates (historian), 61n54
Frendo, David, 31n46, 43–44; on Aphrahaṭ, 108–9

Gaddis, Michael, 151n89
Galerius (emperor of Rome), Persian campaign of, 46
Gallienus (emperor of Rome), repeal of anti-Christian edicts, 39n78
Gelasius of Caesarea, *Church History*, 61n54
Gelasius of Cyzicus, 61n54
Gerö, Stephen, 141n53
Gignoux, Philippe, 101
Goodblatt, David, 117–18
Greek language: interchange with Syriac, 7n24; Sasanian knowledge of, 21; in Syriac martyrdom narratives, 150
Grégoire, Henri, 28
Gregory Pirangushnasp, martyrdom of, 171–72
Griffith, Sidney, 82n61, 89
Gushtazad (Christian martyr), 140

Hall, Stuart, 22, 34, 48n11
Ḥananya (martyr), 143
Harrak, Amir, 129
Harries, Jill, 150n86
Hazarpat (Persian noble), 187
Heliodorus (bishop of Bezabde), 136, 184, 186

Heliodorus of Emesa, *Aethiopica*, 83
Herman, Geoffrey, 118, 150–51
Herodian, on Persia, 76n37
historians, ecclesiastical: on Constantine, 157, 169–70; on Constantine's patronage, 171; East/West Christians in, 175; historiographical exchange among, 166n39; idealization of Constantine in, 154; on Persian martyrs, 44; versus Roman historians, 169–70. *See also* martyrdom narratives; persecution narratives
historians, Roman: Christian, 81–93; on Christian emperors, 75n34; classicizing, 70–73, 75; on Constantine's patronage of Christians, 163; on Constantine's Persian campaign, 164; versus Eastern historians, 169–70; on fall of Nisibis, 66–70; non-Christian, 51, 58, 68; on the "Orient," 75n36; on Roman-Persian war, 70; on Shapur, 68, 86n80
historiography: positivist, 177; Syriac, 27, 99–102
history, Sasanian: literary archetypes of, 100n5; literary sources for, 101; non-Christian authors of, 101; post-Constantinian, 102; as stories, 100–101; in Syriac martyrdom narratives, 99–102
History of Blessed Simeon bar Ṣabbaʿe, 11, 54; bishops' authority in, 116; *bnay shebya* (captives) in, 140; "Caesar" in, 155; Christian-Jewish relations in, 102; Christian loyalty in, 117; Christian Persians in, 12, 102, 111–13, 123; Christian rebellion in, 152; Christian soldiers in, 113n49; Christian unity in, 125; composition of, 139, 141; Constantine in, 111, 125–26, 157, 176; Constantine's power in, 170; date of, 102, 175–76; Eastern/Western Christians in, 125; ecclesiastical hierarchy in, 141; episcopal authority in, 102; execution of Simeon in, 109–10; fear in, 113n48; Jews in, 159–60; Julian in, 69; martyrs in, 140–42; *naṣraye* in, 112n45, 132–33; parallels with Ammianus, 142; relationship to *Martyrdom of Blessed Simeon bar Ṣabbaʿe*, 102–3, 110–11; Roman captives in, 124, 127, 139–42, 153, 185; Roman emperor in, 156; Roman-Persian war in, 111, 123–24, 139; Shapur in, 66, 70n15, 116, 132–33, 161; Shapur's persecution in, 111–13, 115, 125–26, 140–41, 156, 170; Shapur's raids in, 65; Simeon's interrogation in, 110; Simeon's parents in, 169; sources for, 110; spin-offs from, 144n65; sun worship in, 110; synodal list in, 141; taxation of Christians in, 112–13, 116–23; theological debate in, 110, 133; use of Theodoret, 70n15; views of West, 172
History of Mar Behnam and Sarah, 155n4
History of Mar Qardagh, 173–75; East/West Christians in, 175; fire cult in, 175; Roman aggressors in, 174–75; scholarship on, 173n57; seventh-century Iraq in, 173
History of Saba Pirgushnasp, 85n79; "Caesar" in, 155
History of Sultan Mahdukt, Christian Persians in, 22n15
History of the Holy Mar Maʿin: composition of, 158, 173; Constantine in, 156–60, 164, 168, 174; East/West Christians in, 175; Letter to Shapur in, 159, 162–64, 168; persecution in, 151, 157–58; Persian Christians in, 157–63; Persian hostages in, 158; Roman envoy in, 161–62; Shapur in, 161–62, 168; tribute in, 18n5; Western character of, 169
Holum, Kenneth, 150
Hormizd, Prince: at Constantine's court, 29
Huns, bribes to, 161n22
Hunt, E. D., 75n34, 78n46
Huyse, Philip, 76n37

Ibn al-Azraq, on Marutha, 146
identity, Christian: effect of Constantine's conversion on, 179–80; in late antiquity, 180; Persian, 152–53, 179; Roman, 149; Shapur's effect on, 180
Iran, Christianity in, 32n52, 152–53
Iraq, religious communities of, 119–20
Islamic Conquest: dhimmi communities of, 119–20; taxation of Christians following, 119

Istakhr (Fars): martyrs of, 191–92; mobed of, 191

Jacob (bishop of Nisibis), 166; and Aphrahaṭ, 104; death of, 66n4; hagiography of, 81n59; miracles of, 81, 83–84
Jerome: on Nisibis, 66n3; on Valerian, 37
Jerusalem Temple: Ammianus on, 70n15; Julian and, 69n15
Jesus: scourging of, 160n20; synchrony with Augustus, 108n32
Jews: converts to Christianity, 133; under Decius, 121n72; in martyrdom narratives, 159–60; relations with Christians, 102, 105–6, 108; of Sasanian empire, 118
jizya (protection tax), 119–20
John bar Penkaye, *Summary History of the World* (*Resh Melle*), 93n105, 172–73
John Malalas, *Chronicle* of, 164, 165n35
John of Nikiu: *Chronicle*, 164; on Constantine's Persian campaign, 168; Western character of, 170
Johnson, Aaron, 154n1
Jovian (emperor of Rome): and Christians of Edessa, 92n101; in *Julian Romance*, 90n95, 91–95; as new Constantine, 90n95, 95; proclamation as emperor, 50–51; service under Julian, 91; treaty with Shapur, 45–46, 51, 68, 84–85, 163n28, 173
Judah the Maccabee: in *Martyrdom of Blessed Simeon bar Ṣabbaʿe*, 11, 114; and Simeon bar Ṣabbaʿe, 11n31
Julian (the Apostate, emperor of Rome): on Alexander, 72; altar at Nisibis, 87; death of, 9, 37, 50, 88–89; defeat (363); 67; history of Mesopotamia, 71; and Jerusalem Temple, 69n15; as Parthicus, 71n19; persecutions by, 89; proclamation as emperor, 50; relations with Constantius II, 49–50, 71; in Roman-Persian war, 50; and Shapur, 10, 71, 83; siege of Ctesiphon, 50
—*The Caesars*, 72
—*Orations*: classicizing in, 71–72; Nisibis in, 69, 83, 85, 94; in praise of Constantius, 70–73, 76–77

Julian Romance, 10, 89–93; Christian Roman Empire in, 94; Christians of Persia in, 69; composition of, 69, 89n94, 159n16; fall of Nisibis in, 91; Greek novel tradition in, 94; Jovian in, 90n95, 91–95; manuscript witnesses to, 90n94; origins of, 89n94; paganism in, 91; polemics of, 90n95; Roman evacuees in, 93n104; Roman-Persian plotting in, 91–93; sacrifice of Nisibis in, 93; settings of, 90n95; Shapur in, 69, 90–93
Jullien, Christelle and Florence, 32n52; on merchant-missionaries, 129; on *naṣraye*, 134–35
Justinian I (emperor of Rome), 154n2

Karka d-Ledan (Beth Huzaye), Roman captives of, 139–40, 144, 185–86
Kazhdan, Alexander, 154n2
Khusro I Anoshirvan (Sasanian king), tax reforms of, 117–18
kingship, divine: Constantine's, 20–21; in Letter to Shapur, 21, 35–36; in Sasanian Empire, 133n26
Kirdir (mobed), inscription of, 132
Kmoskó, Michael, 102
Koltun-Fromm, Naomi, 105, 117n59
Kramer, A. E., 2n7
kresṭanye (Persian Christians), 132–33; ethnolinguistic connotations of, 134. *See also* Christians, Persian

Labourt, Jérôme, 5, 150
Lactantius: on Christian Rome, 43; Constantine's borrowing from, 42; *On the Deaths of the Persecutors*, 39–43, 45; on Decian persecution, 122; on divine punishment, 40–41; renarration of Roman history, 40–41; on Shapur I, 88; on Valerian, 39
Lane, David, 107
Lee, A. D., 33, 163n28
Levenson, D. B., 70n15
Libanius, on Julian's death, 50n16, 72–73
Licinius, Constantine's war with, 60
Lieu, Samuel, 130–31

Lightfoot, Christopher, 71–72, 184n1; on Nisibis, 81n59, 83n68
Lincoln, Bruce, 18n8

Maccabees, Persain Christians and, 123. *See also* Judah the Maccabee
madrashe (Syriac hymns), 69, 194n9
magi: conversion of, 191, 194; Roman depictions of, 75n36; in Syriac martyrdom narratives, 193
Maḥoza (Seleucia-Ctesiphon), Jewish population of, 70n15
Ma'in, Mar: Constantine's aid to, 157–59; at Dura Europos, 159; emigration to West, 158–59; persecution of, 160–61; sacred garment of, 158, 169; trial of, 162; Westernization of, 169
al-Maliki, Nouri: on death of Paulos Rahho, 3; support for Iraqi Christians, 4
Mango, C., 165n37
Marcionites, 110, 133
Marianus (imperial official), 22n17
Martha (daughter of Pusai), 144n65
martyr cults: of Masabdan, 138–39, 185, 190; Persian, 113n49
martyrdom narratives, 4; Christian Arabic, 171n52; East-West ambivalence in, 175; fear in, 126n6; final form of, 158n11; Greek Christian, 126n5, 143n63; as historical documents, 176; literary traditions of, 176; Roman captives in, 127–28, 145, 155, 192; set in Shapur's reign, 21n15. *See also* persecution narratives; specific titles
martyrdom narratives, Roman: Persian Christian use of, 12; during Decius's reign, 121–22; in Greek and Latin, 143n63
martyrdom narratives, Syriac, 6–7; antipagan violence in, 151n89; B-Zyklus cycle of, 144; Christian allegiances in, 173; on Constantine, 49, 155–56, 173; contents of, 100; dates of, 6–7, 128; Greek loan words in, 150; as ideological interventions, 177; magi in, 191, 193–95; number of, 99; place of composition, 6–7; Roman captives in, 127–28, 192;

Roman Christian discourse in, 151; Roman decrees in, 121; Roman titles in, 150; Sasanian history in, 99–102; scholarship on, 102, 157; Sozomen's use of, 56, 145; Theodoret's use of, 150; transmission of texts, 111n41; on Western Christians, 49, 112–13, 116; witnessing in, 144; Yazdgard in, 147–49; of Yazdgard's time, 159
Martyrdom of Abbot Barshebya, 191–95; date of, 192; English translation of, 193–95; location of, 191; magus of, 191, 193–95; monks of, 191–92, 193–95; Roman captives in, 127–28; witnessing in, 144
Martyrdom of 'Abda: naṣraye in, 149; Yazdgard in, 148–50
Martyrdom of Blessed Simeon bar Ṣabba'e, 65n2; Christian-Jewish relations in, 102; Christian rebellion in, 152; Christians of Persia in, 11, 102, 123; composition of, 102; economic theology of, 114–15; episcopal authority in, 102; Jews in, 159; Judah the Maccabee in, 11, 114; Pusai in, 143–44; refusal of apostasy in, 110, 114–15; relationship to *History of Blessed Simeon bar Ṣabba'e*, 102–3, 110–11; royal authority in, 115; Shapur's persecution in, 113–15, 143; Simeon's martyrdom in, 109–10; Simeon's power in, 117; sources for, 110; Sozomen's use of, 54; sun worship in, 110, 114–15; taxation in, 113–15, 119, 121
Martyrdom of Gregory Pirangushnasp, 171–72; "Caesar" in, 172
Martyrdom of Jacob the Notary, Yazdgard in, 148
Martyrdom of Miles, 140n50, 192
Martyrdom of Narsai the Ascetic, 148, 193n6
Martyrdom of Peroz, Yazdgard in, 148
Martyrdom of Pusai-Qarugbed: Persian Christians in, 12, 151; Christian rebellion in, 152; date of, 144; *naṣraye* in, 132; Roman captives in, 127, 143–45, 153; Shapur in, 144–45

Martyrdom of the Captives of Beth Zabdai, 78n47, 184–90; Persian Christians in, 12; date of, 185; English translation of, 186–90; Roman captives in, 105, 109–10, 135–39, 142, 151–53, 155, 174, 184–90; Shapur in, 136–37; Simeon's parents in, 127; Sozomen's use of, 185–86; Western Christianity in, 127; Zoroastrianism in, 140n48. *See also* Bezabde

Martyrdom of the Forty Holy Martyrs: "Caesar" in, 155; Christian betrayal in, 160n18

Martyrdom of Zebina and His Companions, 53n24

martyrs, Christian: bishops, 140; Eastern/Western, 188; Ephrem on, 80–81; at Karka d-Ledan, 139–40; relics of, 138, 147, 158; as second Christs, 160n20. *See also* persecution

Marutha (bishop of Maypherqaṭ): in embassy to Persia, 146–47; in establishment of Church of the East, 74n32; Greek sources for, 147n74; healing by, 12, 74, 146; at Sasanian court, 12, 74, 146; Socrates on, 147n74; at Synod of Isaac, 128, 146–47; translation of martyrdom narratives, 147; writings of, 147n75

Maryahb (Christian martyr), 138, 185–87, 189

Masabdan (Beth Huzaye): Carmanian shepherds of, 189; martyr cult at, 138–39, 185, 190; martyrdom of Christians at, 105, 109–10, 135–39, 142, 151–53, 155, 174, 184, 189

Matthews, John, 80

Maypherqaṭ, martyr relics at, 147

McDonough, Scott, 146

merchant-missionaries, in Sasanian Empire, 129. *See also* missionaries, Christian

Mesopotamia: bishops of, 176; Christian identity in, 174; political allegiances of, 10n29; sources for fourth century, 8–9; spread of Christianity in, 129

Mesopotamia, Roman: bishops of, 80; Christians of, 10, 69, 72, 78–79; divine defense of, 81–83, 86–88; loss to Shapur, 46, 49–50, 135, 167; role of Nisibis in, 66–67; Roman captives from, 126, 135–39, 167, 185–90; Roman historians on, 70

Mesopotamians, Roman: Shapur's treatment of, 78–79

Metrodorus (philosopher), and Roman-Persian war, 51–52

Michael I Rabo (patriarch of Antioch): *Chronicle*, 166–68; on Constantine, 167–68; Letter to Shapur in, 166–67; sources of, 166n39; Western character of, 169–70

Mikhail, Fr. Najeeb, 2n7

Miles (bishop of Susa), 140n50, 192

Millar, Fergus, 19; on Roman Near East, 67n9

Milvian Bridge, Constantine's victory at, 60, 177

missionaries, Christian: hagiography of, 129n15; merchants, 129; and Roman-Persian war, 149n85; in Sasanian Empire, 129

Momigliano, Arnaldo, 8

monasticism: of Nisibis, 66n5, 67n6; of Sasanian Empire, 192–93

Morony, Michael: *Iraq after the Muslim Conquest*, 119–20; on Roman deportations, 130–31

Moses: Constantine as, 59–64; as model of authority, 63; tabernacle of, 59, 61

Mosig-Walburg, Karin, 28, 29n40

mshiḥaya (Persian Christians), 134. *See also* Christians, Persian

Mygdonius (river), Shapur's channeling of, 82–84, 86

Naqsh-e-Rostam, relief sculptures of, 36, 192

narrative, cognitive perspectives on, 178–79

Narsai, martyrdom of, 148

Narseh (Sasanian king), defeat by Romans, 46

naṣraye (Persian Christians), 132–35; ethno-linguistic connotations of, 132n25, 134. *See also* Christians, Persian

Nebuchadnezzar, 42

Neri, V., 76n38

Neusner, Jacob, 107

Nicomedia: Constantine at, 57–58, 166; strategic location of, 58n43
Nile, military channeling of, 83
Nisibis: Alexander the Great at, 66n6; apostate Christians of, 86–87, 94; in Christian history, 81–93; Christian inhabitants of, 68, 77, 94; commercial importance of, 67; diversity in, 67; Julian on, 69, 83, 85; Julian's altar at, 87; metropolitan of, 142; monasteries of, 66n5; monastic "school movement" of, 67n6; Persian Christian sources on, 69–70; Persian flag over, 89; role in Roman Mesopotamia, 66–67; Roman army at, 79, 82; as sacrifice for Christianity, 93–95; scholarship on, 66n6; as Shield of Empire, 68; sources for, 68–70; strategic importance of, 66–67; and writing of imperial history, 66–70
—sieges and fall of, 51nn17–18, 81–84, 173; bishops' defense during, 72, 84, 86; Christian memory of, 84; Christian/non-Christian authors on, 94; Craugasius of Nisibis in, 77–78; defeat of paganism in, 89; divine defense in, 81–93, 86, 88; Ephrem on, 67–69, 77, 85–89; first siege, 66n4, 81; in *Julian Romance*, 91, 93; pagan soldiers defending, 82; Roman deportees from, 84–85, 93n205, 95; second siege, 81n59; Shapur at, 10, 66–70, 82–84, 166; third siege, 68n10, 71–72, 81, 86n81; use of flooding in, 81–84, 86; vision of Constantius at, 83–84
Nongbri, Brent, 177n66

order, divine restoration of, 42–43
Orosius, on Valerian, 37
Ottoman empire, millet system of, 119

paganism: defeat in Roman Empire, 89; in *Julian Romance*, 91; Letter to Shapur on, 45. *See also* sacrifice, pagan
papyrus, Egyptian: Decian edict in, 122
Papyrus Lond. **878**, 31–32
Payne, Richard, 119–20, 152, 177n65; on martyrs' cults, 185
Penn, Michael, 111n41

persecution: Bahram V's, 69n14, 149–50; cessation of, 89n94; Christian refugees from, 38–39; conflicting sources on, 7; and Constantine's Letter to Shapur, 20–21, 34–36, 45, 54, 56–57; during Constantine's lifetime, 169–73; Diocletian's, 38, 53n24; divine punishment for, 39, 42; evidence for, 22n15; following Constantine's death, 125, 170–71; historical memory of, 177; Julian's, 89; pre-Decian, 42n87; reasons for, 54; role of Roman-Persian war in, 53n24; in Roman Empire, 35–36, 105, 121–22; as stain on Romans, 38; theological explanation for, 126; traditional interpretations of, 177; Valerian's, 35–37. *See also* martyrdom narratives
persecution, Shapur's, 176; in Aphrahaṭ's *Demonstrations*, 104–7, 109n34; causal narratives of, 179; in *History of Blessed Simeon bar Ṣabbaʿe*, 111–13, 115, 125–26, 140–41, 156, 170; in *Julian Romance*, 91; in *Martyrdom of Blessed Simeon bar Ṣabbaʿe*, 113–15, 143; motives for, 46n3; narratives of, 4, 6, 22n15, 29, 34–36, 45, 49, 52, 69n14, 78n46, 86, 109; providential necessity of, 176; in Sozomen's *Church History*, 53–54; Theophanes the Confessor on, 165; of 339/40, 86, 109
persecution narratives, 4; concerning Sasanian kings, 6; concerning Shapur II, 4, 6, 22n15, 29, 34–36, 45, 49, 52, 69n14, 78n46, 86, 109; Sozomen's use of, 53–55, 145; Western influences on, 151. *See also* martyrdom narratives
Persian Gulf, monasticism in, 193n5
Petesouchos (Egyptian god), sacrifice to, 122
Philip the Arab, 71n19
Pigulevskaja, N., 66n6
plague, following the martyrdom of ʿAbdishoʿ, 138, 190
Poggi, Vincenzo, 38
Pourshariati, Parvaneh, 130n17
Prat d-Maishan, metropolitan of, 142
providence, Christian, 43, 63
punishment: divine, 37, 39–42; pedagogical, 40–41; in Roman history, 40–41

Pusai-Qarugbed (*bar shebya*): daughter of, 140, 144n65; father of, 144; love of martyrdom, 144; martyrdom of, 127, 140, 143–45; in *Martyrdom of Blessed Simeon bar Ṣabbaʿe*, 143–44; title of, 151; trial before Shapur, 143

Qardagh, Mar: conflict with Romans, 174–75; conversion of, 174–75
qyama (ascetic group), 111, 156, 170; of Bezabde, 186–87

Rahho, Ghazi, 2n7
Rahho, Paulos (archbishop of Mosul), 180; death of, 1–3; payment of protection money, 1–2; on persecution, 4
Rapp, Claudia, 34n57; on Constantine as Moses, 60n52, 63
Reman (Mesopotamian fortress): Christian virgins of, 78; fall of, 77–78
Rives, James, 121
Roman Empire: advantages over Sasanian Empire, 130n17; contact with Persia, 32–33; defeat of paganism in, 89; definition of religion in, 121n71; divine kingship in, 20–21; frontier integrity of, 49; interweaving of Christianity in, 26; in *Julian Romance*, 94; merchant-missionaries of, 32, 129; persecution in, 105, 121–22; Persian hostages in, 163; Persian officials in, 29; power struggles in, 33; tribute to Persians, 161; universalizing cults of, 121
Roman Empire, Eastern: battle for, 10; Christian narratives of, 80; ethnolinguistic religious identity of, 67n9
Romanitas, identification with *Christianitas*, 11, 33–34, 129, 151–52
Roman-Persian relations, 5, 8; Constantine and, 9, 164n33; negotiations in, 33n54; role of Armenia in, 29n40; role of Constantine's Letter in, 28; Theophanes the Confessor on, 166; trade in, 67. *See also* Sasanian Empire
Roman-Persian war, 6, 7, 9–10, 176; Ammianus on, 51, 73–81; ancient commentaries on, 66n3; beginning of, 45; causes of, 52; Christianity and, 72, 76; Christian Persians and, 49, 63; Christian taxation and, 112n46; classicizing histories of, 70–73; Constantine's Letter to Shapur and, 51–53; Constantine's plans for, 10, 30, 45–48, 57–61, 66n4, 164–68; historical memory of, 177; historiographical legacy of, 99; in *History of Blessed Simeon bar Ṣabbaʿe*, 111; imperial historians on, 70; Julian in, 50; Mesopotamian Christians during, 69, 78–81; non-Christian historians on, 51, 58; persecution during, 53n24; religious concerns in, 47n6, 51, 52n23, 147; Roman-Christian identity in, 149; Roman defeat in, 45–47; Roman missionaries and, 149n85; Roman view of, 11. *See also* captives, Roman
Rubin, Zeev, 118, 149n85
Rufinus, Theodoret's use of, 56
Russell, Paul, 68

sacrifice, pagan: abolition of, 33; certification of, 122; Christian compliance with, 121–22; Decius's edict on, 121–22; in *Life of Constantine*, 24n27. *See also* paganism
Sako, Louis (archbishop of Kirkuk), 1–2; on *Nasrani*, 132n25
Sasanian Empire: advantages of Roman Empire over, 130n17; Christianization in, 32, 129; chronology of, 159; collapse of, 130n17; decentralization of, 130n17; deportation of Romans, 130–31; divine kingship in, 133n26; effect of Constantine's conversion on, 8; emulation of Achaemenids, 46n3, 71; execution methods of, 193n8; geography of, 142n58; knowledge of Greek in, 21; labor shortage in, 130; martyr cults of, 185; material culture of, 102; monastic institutions of, 192–93; political realities of, 71n19; relief sculptures of, 36, 192; religious communities of, 177; religious segmentation of, 120n66; Roman captives in, 126–29; Roman contact with, 32–33; Roman styles in, 131; Roman tribute to, 161; taxation policies of, 117–20; territorial ambitions of, 76n37; torture in, 193n8;

value of Christianity for, 35; Zoroastrian monarchs of, 26. *See also* Roman-Persian relations; Roman-Persian war

Sasanian studies, 99–100; debates in, 102

Schneider, Horst, 31n46

Schott, Jeremy, 42

Schwartz, Daniel, 90n95

Scott, Roger, 165nn35,37

Seleucia-Ctesiphon: episcopal preeminence of, 141; synods of, 128

Shahbazi, Alireza, 46n3

Shapur I (Sasanian king): defeat of Valerian, 36, 88, 192; depiction as Pilate, 160; deportations under, 131; God's use of, 88; humiliation of Valerian, 39–42; sack of Antioch, 131

Shapur II (Sasanian king): in *Acts of the Persian Martyrs*, 87, 102, 173; anger at Christians, 106; in Aphrahaṭ's *Demonstrations*, 104–7, 109n34; authority over Christians, 25, 116; behavior toward Christian virgins, 78; and bishop of Bezabde, 135–36, 184; capture of Amida, 135; capture of Singara, 79, 84–85, 135; challenge to Constantine's sons, 65; Christian Persians' view of, 106–7; and Constantine's conversion, 177–78; Constantius's embassy to, 74, 157–59, 163, 168–69; correspondence with Constantius II, 19, 23, 29n39, 46, 75, 101; defeats at Nisibis, 66; effect of Constantine's letter on, 30; effect on Christian identity, 180; Ephrem on, 85–86, 94; Great Persecution (339/40), 86, 109; homage to Christian churches, 87, 93n205; and Julian, 10; in *Julian Romance*, 69, 90–93; on *naṣraye*, 132–33; persecution narratives concerning, 4, 6, 22n15, 29, 34–36, 45, 49, 52, 69n14, 78n46, 86, 109; raid on Roman frontier, 65–66; regnal dates of, 19n9; relations with Simeon bar Ṣabbaʿe, 105, 109–10, 151; reputation among Romans, 86n80; in Roman historiography, 75–76; siege of Bezabde, 78–80, 127, 135–36, 184–86; sieges of Nisibis, 10, 66–70, 82–84, 166; state religion of, 46n3; sun worship of, 110, 114–15; territorial aims of, 46n3, 73; Theophanes the Confessor on, 165; and Tiridates's conversion, 29; treatment of Mesopotamian Christians, 78–79, 87, 93n105; treaty with Jovian, 45–46, 51, 68, 84–85, 163n28, 173; vision of Constantius, 81, 83–84. *See also* Constantine (emperor of Rome), Letter to Shapur; persecution, Shapur's; Roman-Persian war

Simeon bar Ṣabbaʿe (bishop of Seleucia-Ctesiphon): accusers of, 165–66; authority of, 119; death date of, 103n13, 109n34; Eastern narratives of, 171; ecclesiastical preeminence of, 141; execution of, 5, 106, 109–10, 139–40; and Judah the Maccabee, 11n31, 114; letter to Shapur, 114; martyrdom narratives of, 11–12, 30, 102; mocking of Persian gods, 109–10; parents of, 127, 169; Shapur's relations with, 105, 109–10, 151; sorcery charges against, 191; Sozomen on, 54; tax resistance by, 109, 112–13, 116; as traitor, 160, 162; trial of, 112. *See also History of Blessed Simeon bar Ṣabbaʿe*; *Martyrdom of Blessed Simeon bar Ṣabbaʿe*

Singara (Mesopotamian garrison), Shapur's capture of, 79, 84–85, 135

Skeat, T. C., 31

Socrates, *Church History*, 53; on Bahram, 149–50; Constantine's Persian campaign in, 61; Marutha in, 147n74; Roman-Persian war in, 149; sources of, 61n54

Sozomen: knowledge of Beth Zabdai, 185; legal training of, 53

—*Church History*, 29; chronology of, 54; composition of, 53; Constantine in, 57, 125; Constantine's church tent in, 61; on Ephrem, 81n61; on Julian's death, 50n16; Letter to Shapur in, 36n63, 53–56, 145; martyred bishops in, 140n50; on martyrs of Persia, 53–55, 145; Nicene Fathers' edition of, 55; Shapur's persecution in, 53–54; on Simeon bar Ṣabbaʿe, 54, 165; use of Eusebius, 53, 55; use of martyrdom narratives, 56, 145; use of *Martyrdom of the Captives of Beth Zabdai*, 185–86; use of Marutha, 147; Valerian in, 37; Western character of, 169

Strong, J. D., 22n15
sun worship, in martyrdom narratives, 110, 114–15, 137
Sylvester, Bishop, 58n41,165
Synodicon orientale, Petrine language of, 141n53
Synod of Dadisho' (424), 128n13, 186n8, 192
Synod of Isaac (410), 128; on ecclesiastical hierarchy, 141–42; Marutha at, 146–47
Synod of Yahbalaha (420), 128, 147
Syriac language: Eusebius's translation into, 27, 100, 126n25; interchange with Greek, 7n24; transliteration of, 13

al-Ṭabari: on Persians of Nisibis, 85; on Yazdgard's death, 147
Talmud, Babylonian, 118; Dasqarta in, 186n8
taxation, Islamic, 119–20
taxation, Sasanian: exilarchs' collection of, 118; extortion in, 113; of Jews, 118; Khusro's reform of, 117–18; of Persian Christians, 112–13, 116–23, 180; poll taxes, 120; of religious groups, 118–19; types of, 113
temples, Persian: destruction of, 148–49; human trophies in, 40n80, 195
Themistius (eulogist), 72
Theodoret of Cyrrhus, *Church History*: on 'Abda, 149; *History of Simeon*'s use of, 70n15; idealization of Constantine, 57; Letter to Shapur in, 56–57; Nisibis in, 69, 81–84; on persecution, 69n14; sources of, 56, 81n61, 150; use of *Life of Ephrem*, 81; use of martyrdom narratives, 150; vision of Constantius in, 83–84
Theodosius I (emperor of Rome): antipagan legislation of, 159n14; as ideal emperor, 154n2
Theodosius II (emperor of Rome): envoy to Yazdgard, 128, 146; and Persian Christians, 149; piety of, 150n86; refusal to pay tribute, 161n22
Theophanes the Confessor: on Constantine's baptism, 58n41, 164–65; on Constantine's death, 167–68; on Persian Christians, 164–65; Roman-Persian relations in, 166; on Shapur, 165–66; on Simeon's accusers, 165; sources of, 166n39
Theophilus of Edessa, 166n39
Thomas (the Apostle), evangelization of Persia, 129
thrēskeia (religion), Constantine on, 22
Timothy I, Patriarch, 141n53
Tiridates (king of Armenia), 28; conversion to Christianity, 29
torture, Sasanian, 193n8
Turcan, R., 51n18

Ursicinus (*magister militum*), 67
Utas, Bo, 101

Valerian (emperor of Rome): as bad model, 21; captive soldiers of, 130–31; capture and death of, 20, 36–40, 55n33, 88, 192; in *Chronicle of Seert*, 38; Constantine on, 20, 35–37, 40–42; divine punishment of, 37, 40–41; humiliation of, 39–42; in Letter to Shapur, 20, 35–37, 40; paganism of, 37; persecution of Christians, 35–37; Sozomen on, 37
Valois, Adrien de, 85n77
Van Dam, Raymond, 176–77
Van Rompay, Lucas, 148
violence, rhetorical basis for, 178. *See also* martyrdom; persecution
Vivian, Miriam, 27–28, 29n43

Walker, Joel, 100, 173
Walters, James, 104n15
Warmington, B. H., 22n17
Weisweiler, John, 80
Westphal, Gustav, 171n52
Whitby, Michael, 65n1
White, Andrew, 2n7
Wieshöfer, Josef, 112n44
Wiessner, Gernot, 102, 110, 155n4; on Marutha, 147n75; on Simeon's acts, 158n11
Wigram, William, 5
Winter, Engelbert, 5

Yazdgard I (Sasanian king), 145–51; death of, 128, 150; and establishment of Church of the East, 146; martyrdom narratives from time of, 159; Marutha's healing of, 12, 74; patronage of bishops, 148; Persian Christians under, 69n14, 146–47, 150; rebuilding of churches, 128; in Syriac martyrdom narratives, 147–49; Theododius's envoy to, 128

Yazdgard II (Sasanian king), martyrdom narratives from time of, 148

Yohannan, Abraham: *The Death of a Nation*, 4–5

Zabdaeus (Beth Zabdai/Bezabde), captives from, 145

Zoroastrianism, 132; Christian Persians under, 151n90; Christian threat to, 46n3; communal judges of, 119; confusion over Christianity, 133; death customs of, 140n48; fire cult of, 87, 148–49, 175; mobeds of, 132, 187–89, 191; texts of, 101

Zosimus, *New History*, 85

www.ingramcontent.com/pod-product-compliance
Lightning Source LLC
Chambersburg PA
CBHW030538230426
43665CB00010B/947